TERRORISM:
PROTECTION OF
WITNESSES
AND COLLABORATORS
OF JUSTICE

The views expressed in the analytical report are those of the author and do not necessarily reflect the position of individual states, the Committee of Experts on the Protection of Witnesses and Pentiti in relation to Acts of Terrorism (PC-PW) or the Council of Europe as a whole with regard to the interpretation of the legislation and situations referred to.

The national contributions are those originally submitted by delegations, subject to editorial revision. The contributions originally submitted in French have been translated for the purposes of this publication.

Design: Council of Europe Graphic Design Workshop

Council of Europe Publishing
F-67075 Strasbourg Cedex

ISBN-10: 92-871-5811-8
ISBN-13: 978-92-871-5811-6
© Council of Europe, March 2006
Printed at the Council of Europe

TABLE OF CONTENTS

Foreword 5

Analytical report 7

Situation in member and observer states of the Council of Europe 67

Questionnaire on protection of witnesses and *"pentiti"* in relation to acts of terrorism 69

States's replies to the questionnaire:

Armenia 73
Austria 81
Azerbaijan 95
Belgium 107
Bosnia and Herzegovina 131
Czech Republic 137
Finland 151
France 161
Georgia 173
Germany 175
Greece 189
Hungary 193
Italy 205
Latvia 221
Lithuania 233
Luxembourg 247
Moldova 257
The Netherlands 267
Norway 279
Poland 291
Portugal 301
Russian Federation 311
Spain 319
Sweden 327
Switzerland 333
"The former Yugoslav Republic of Macedonia" 349
Turkey 365
United States of America 369
Japan 383

Recommendation Rec(2005)9 of the Committee of Ministers of the Council of Europe to member states on the protection of witnesses and collaborators of justice 391

FOREWORD

Terrorism is one of the most blatant forms of assault on human rights, democracy and the rule of law. Yet the Council of Europe was set up to stand for these values and it has dedicated the last 56 years to upholding them. Consequently, its determination to combat terrorism is absolute and its response to date has been based on three cornerstones: strengthening legal action against terrorism, safeguarding fundamental values and addressing the causes of terrorism.

Since the terrorist attacks of 11 September 2001, the Council of Europe has put together a significant legal framework and its task today is to put it into action, to make sure the various guidelines, declarations and provisions of the conventions related to the fight against terrorism are applied in practice. In this connection, the protection of witnesses and collaborators of justice, and other persons participating in proceedings involving persons accused of terrorist crimes, is currently at the forefront of its legal action against terrorism.

This is due to the growing recognition of the special role of witnesses in criminal proceedings. Their evidence is often crucial to securing the conviction of offenders, especially in respect of serious crime. However, in some areas of criminality, such as organised crime and terrorism, there is an increasing risk that witnesses will be subjected to intimidation. This is particularly true for those who are closely connected to terrorist groups and who are often even more vulnerable than others to the use of intimidation against them or against people close to them.

It is against this backcloth that the Council of Europe undertook to study the means of strengthening the protection of witnesses and collaborators of justice in relation to acts of terrorism, including those at international level, with a view to preparing an appropriate legal instrument, bearing in mind the links with related criminal activities. This work resulted in the adoption in 2005 of Recommendation Rec(2005)9 of the Committee of Ministers to member states on the protection of witnesses and collaborators of justice.

In this Recommendation, governments of the 46 Council of Europe member states are encouraged, when formulating their internal legislation and reviewing their criminal policy and practice, to be guided by the principles and measures it contains. Emphasis is placed on international co-operation, which is all-important, not only because a number of terrorist organisations have branches all over the world, but also because international co-operation can help increase the level of protection of those persons whose protection would prove difficult on a merely national basis, given the conditions in the country where they are located.

This publication contains a survey of national laws and practice in 27 Council of Europe member states and two observer states together with an analytical report which examines the protection of witnesses and collaborators of justice, its regulations and use, and international co-operation in this field. It constitutes a further Council of Europe contribution to the international community's efforts to combat terrorism.

Guy DE VEL
Director General of Legal Affairs of the
Council of Europe

ANALYTICAL REPORT

by Mr Nicola PIACENTE

Nicola Piacente is currently a member of the Anti-Terrorism Unit at the Prosecution Office in Milan, Italy. He has acquired extensive experience in investigations and cases versus transnational criminal organisations and as a former Trial Attorney at the International Criminal Tribunal for the former Yugoslavia, in investigations and cases on war crimes and crimes against humanity. He recently acted as a scientific expert for the Council of Europe's Committee of Experts on the Protection of Witnesses and *Pentiti* in relation to Acts of Terrorism (PC-PW), which elaborated Recommendation Rec(2005)9 of the Committee of Ministers to member states of the Council of Europe on the protection of witnesses and collaborators of justice.

INTRODUCTION

All serious crimes differ from each other with reference to their nature and their complexity. What they have in common is that there is a precise strategy behind almost any serious crime.

Every instance of a misconduct perpetrated within national borders is often a segment of a more widespread (often transnational) and systematic criminal activity and is perpetrated in execution of a precise criminal design. The investigation of a single instance of misconduct should therefore be an opportunity to try to identify the criminal network to which it is related.

Currently, many criminal organisations such as the Italian mafia, Russian and Eastern European organisations are involved in a wide range of criminal activities (drug, weapons and human beings trafficking, illegal gambling, extortion) on a transnational level.

Terrorist organisations are also currently operational at a transnational level.

Wider opportunities to engage in transborder illicit conduct are emerging in several parts of the world (such as in the area of the European Union) as a consequence of the enhanced mobility and the decreasing significance of national frontiers brought about by economic and politic integration movements and other similar factors.

The fight against serious and organised crime has so far suffered several limitations. Victims and witnesses (including insiders) are not usually available to co-operate with justice since they are fully aware that their testimony makes them subject to retaliation.

Investigations have been run within the national borders; the exchange of information and co-operation among states has been unsatisfactory for a long time.

This approach cannot be successful. Detecting and prosecuting serious and organised crime can no more be considered as a domestic issue for any country.

In stark contrast with the past decades when issues of criminal justice were thought of in almost exclusively national terms, the need for enhanced international co-operation and co-ordination now occupies an important position on the agenda of national and international institutions.

The testimony of victims, witnesses and collaborators of justice must still be considered vital in order to set up a successful case. They are available to testify, however, only if they are ensured concrete and effective protection.

Witness protection is especially important in the fight against organised crime and terrorism because the closed nature of criminal and terrorist groups makes it very difficult to use traditional investigative methods successfully. Testimony obtained in this way can provide useful information about a whole criminal group, which is capable, by intimidating, harming or bribing witnesses, of obstructing investigations and justice.

Significant efforts have been made by national and international legislation in order to ensure effective protection and any other measure encouraging witnesses to co-operate with justice.

Important steps on co-operation among states in the fight against serious and organised crime have been made. Many countries have set up specific rules on the protection of witnesses and collaborators of justice. In the last decade, specific rules for the protection of witnesses and on international co-operation on this issue have been set up in several international instruments. A major role in this field has been played by the Council of Europe.

This analytical report is a short overview of the existing national and international instruments ensuring protection to witnesses and collaborators of justice and contemplating co-operation among states on this very important issue.

PART I

NATIONAL LEGISLATION

I - GENERAL INFORMATION

The relevant information on national legislation has been collected through the responses that many member and observer states gave to questionnaires that were disseminated in 2003 (pursuant to the conclusions reached at the first meeting of the Committee of Experts on the Protection of Witnesses and *Pentiti* in relation to Acts of Terrorism (PC-PW)), and in 2005.

A preliminary comment must be made. The institutions of most member and observer states are fully aware that:

- criminal and terrorist organisations are operational almost all over Europe and that fighting these organisations has become a priority;
- a great contribution to this fight can be made by witnesses and *pentiti*[1] (hereinafter collaborators of justice) who decide to co-operate with justice;
- co-operation can be solicited and encouraged only if persons who can provide useful information and testify in court enjoy adequate protection and support that allows them to deal with the cross examinations and the questions addressed.

According to the information collected in most of the countries, rules on the protection of witnesses and of those (including suspects and defendants) who participate in criminal proceedings have been established recently (Austria, Belgium, Bosnia and Herzegovina, Czech Republic, France, Hungary, Luxembourg, "the former Yugoslav Republic of Macedonia",[2] the Netherlands,[3] Portugal, Slovak Republic) or recently amended (Germany, Italy).

Countries that pioneered specific legislation on the protection of witnesses and collaborators of justice established these measures long before, in 1921

---

[1] The word *pentito* does not correspond to any legal definition existing in Italy, where the word originated.

[2] The Law on Witness Protection, adopted by the Parliament on 5 May 2005, entered into force on 1 January 2006.

[3] A bill for the suspected and criminal witness (i.e. a witness who is a suspect or who has already been convicted, the so-called collaborator of justice) has been adopted by the Dutch Parliament and will come into force in 2006 (Cf. the Law of 12 May 2005 on changes to the Code of Criminal Law and the Code of Criminal Procedure, and its addition, published in the official publications journal for laws in The Netherlands: Staatsblad 254 and 255).

(Belgium, concerning drugs), and in the 1970s (Italy, United States of America).

In Italy, laws aiming at encouraging members of terrorist organisations to co-operate with justice were approved from 1979 to 1987 and special mitigating circumstances were set up for members of terrorist organisations who co-operate with police forces and prosecutors to prevent these criminal groups from committing further crimes.

The amendments to the previous legislation in Italy have set up stricter criteria of admissibility to the so-called special protection programme. Collaborators of justice must make their statements within six months of having communicated their decision to co-operate with justice. Collaborators of justice must also give relevant information on their assets and proceeds derived from the perpetration of the crimes that can be seized and on the assets and proceeds of the other members of the criminal group they belonged to. Another prerequisite for admission to the special protection programme is their ability to provide accurate and up-to-date information about the criminal organisations and the crimes perpetrated by their members.

Pursuant to a very recent law that was approved in July 2005, foreigners who co-operate with police forces and prosecutors to prevent terrorist organisations from committing crimes and/or give relevant information to identify and prosecute persons responsible for terrorist acts are eligible for a special residential status.

In most systems, there is the same legal framework for the protection of witnesses and collaborators of justice.

Belgium has established specific rules for the protection of threatened witnesses, but not for collaborators of justice. The same framework can be found in the Russian Federation.

In most countries except Greece and Italy, pursuant to the aforementioned law, no legislation provides specific rules aimed at encouraging witnesses and collaborators of justice to co-operate with justice. The protective measures set up in each system are *per se* deemed as an incentive to co-operate.

According to the information provided, in most of the member states there is no specific rule established for those who co-operate in relation to acts of terrorism.

In most national systems, the adoption of protective measures for those who co-operate in relation to particularly serious crimes (such as drug and human trafficking, and, in Italy, kidnapping) and/or to the activities of criminal and terrorist organisations is contemplated in legislative acts.

In 1989 Germany passed a law providing for the reduction of punishments for participants in crimes concerning terrorist organisations who provided information on such crimes. The law was abolished in 1999, due to its low practical relevance.

In this respect, it should be mentioned that also the International Criminal Tribunal for the former Yugoslavia (hereinafter ICTY) set up specific rules on the protection of witnesses called to testify in the cases falling within the jurisdiction of the Tribunal (serious breaches of the Geneva Conventions of 1949 and the laws and customs of war, genocide, crimes against humanity).

II - PROTECTIVE MEASURES

As stated above, the legislation of almost all states contemplates the adoption of protective measures for victims, witnesses and collaborators of justice.

With reference to suspects and defendants, co-operation is encouraged and compensated with significant reduction of prison sentences. In some countries, the reduction may be below the minimum term established by the law when the defendant has made a significant contribution to the clarification of the criminal offences that were committed or attempted by the criminal organisation (Austria, Belgium - in specific cases related to drugs and the illegal use of hormonal and/or anti-hormonal substances, Bosnia and Herzegovina, Slovak Republic, Portugal, Germany - in specific cases such as drug offences, Italy - in specific cases such as drug and terrorist offences, crimes related to mafia and terrorist organisations, kidnappings, Switzerland). In some countries, such as the Netherlands and Poland, the systems contemplate a special category of collaborators and witnesses, the so-called crown witnesses. In the Polish system, they are perpetrators who act as witnesses in cases of organised crime or in cases of conspiracy aimed at committing certain crimes, specified in the legislation. The legislation provides for the possibility to include such witnesses in a special protection programme.

The category of crown witnesses is being contemplated by a bill being discussed by the Czech Parliament, which regulates measures to encourage witnesses to co-operate with bodies involved in criminal proceedings in greater detail (measures such as mitigation of sentence or granting of immunity).

In other countries, such as the United States of America, prosecutors can recommend to the sentencing judge a lower sentence after the co-operator has pled guilty and after he/she has rendered his/her co-operation and testified completely and truthfully.

In France, the judge can reduce the penalty of an accused if he/she helps police authorities to detect a crime or to prevent a crime from being committed.

In the Netherlands, current rules provide for negotiations between the suspect/witness, assisted by his/her lawyer, and the public prosecutor on the possible reduction of his/her sentence in exchange for an incriminating statement against another suspect. The agreement is subject to the approval of a judge. A new instruction on pledges given to witnesses in criminal cases will be sent to public prosecutors.

In the United States of America, if collaboration takes place after the conviction, the prosecutor may file a post-verdict motion to the judge in order to reduce the sentence of an already convicted person after the co-operator's testimony has been rendered at trial.

In some cases, the enforcement of sentences can be suspended (Portugal and Poland - if the offender, acting together with other people, discloses information to a body of justice administration on the persons who took part in the crime and important circumstances of its perpetration). The Italian system contemplates several cases where mitigating circumstances or even immunity (in the case of an attempt to commit serious crimes related to terrorism, if the perpetrator prevents the crime from being committed) can be applied. Similar provisions related to immunity are applied in France (pursuant to the law which was approved in March 2004, that, under very strict circumstances, provides immunity if a co-perpetrator of a serious crime prevents that crime from being committed), "the former Yugoslav Republic of Macedonia" and Luxembourg.

An offender's co-operation with the authority in clarifying his/her offence is a mitigating circumstance that must be taken into account in sentencing (Austria, Czech Republic, Finland, France, Germany, Italy). The German Federal Courts have set up a number of rules concerning plea bargaining. If already finally convicted, co-perpetrators who co-operated can ask for a reduction of the sentence or a suspension of the enforcement of the sentence for a probation period.

In other states (such as Germany, Hungary, Greece, Moldova, Belgium, Latvia - but in the same framework as mentioned above and under extremely strict conditions, if the defendant has not committed a serious offence and co-operates before the beginning of the prosecution), in the case of a significant contribution to the investigations given by the accused, the prosecutor (in Germany, with the consent of the court) can dismiss the charges against him/her or decide that the enquiry or the proceedings against him/her should be discontinued.

In the United States of America, the decision of the prosecutor not to prosecute the co-operator for one or several crimes he/she has committed is an option more rarely offered. In this country's view, complete exoneration for truthful and complete testimony, which is what is expected of every witness, would depreciate the seriousness of the crime. It would also ignore the public's right to have admitted participants in serious crime accept responsibility for their crimes and then be held accountable and sentenced, even if to a lesser degree, for these crimes. The expenditure of public funds on the collaborator is also far less to protect him/her in prison than out of custody. In the rare cases where immunity on some important charges may be justified and offered, immunity is almost never granted prior to the rendering of the co-operation because once granted it cannot be revoked, and then the co-operator may lose all motivation to co-operate.

Moreover, in most countries the relatives of collaborators of justice can be provided with protective measures (such as relocation, concealing of their personal data, economic assistance).

In most countries, urgent protective measures, for a restricted period of time, can be arranged, after proposals made by police forces or prosecution offices, if an immediate danger threatening the witness, the collaborator of justice and his/her relatives (such as immediate relocation to a secret place, disguising the real identity of the protected person, relocation, economic subsidies and, for those in custody and/or serving a sentence in jail, immediate relocation to special detention facilities) can be established before permanent protective measures are set up by the relevant Institutions (the Witness Protection Service in Hungary, Commission for Special Protection Programmes in Portugal, the Special Unit of Police Forces in the Slovak Republic, the Central Commission for the Adoption of Protective Measures in Italy, the Witness Protection Commission in Belgium and France, the Investigative and Prosecution Offices in the United States of America). In some systems (Moldova, the Russian Federation) the prerequisites for the adoption of urgent protective measures include threats to the witness's property and the protective measures can include patrolling the protected person's property.

III - INSTITUTIONS INVOLVED

In almost all countries, the institutions involved in the protection of witnesses and collaborators of justice are police and other Ministry of the Interior forces, prosecutors' offices, courts and penitentiary institutions. Usually, prosecution offices and police forces (that can better appreciate the relevance of the contribution and the seriousness of the danger to which the witnesses might be exposed) are entitled to recommend the adoption of these measures. The Ministry of the Interior (Bosnia and Herzegovina, Czech Republic), or special commissions and/or agencies (whose members are officers from the Ministry of the Interior, from other police forces, prosecutors and judges) that have been set up are competent to issue decisions on the adoption, modification or revocation of the protective measures.

In the Netherlands, it is the Board of Procurators General that takes the decision on whether or not to take witness protection measures.

In Latvia, the relevant decision is taken by the general prosecutor or a prosecutor who is specially authorised by the general prosecutor.

In Luxembourg, the relevant decision, under the terms of the Victims and Witnesses Bill, is taken by the State Prosecutor or the investigating judge.

In "the former Yugoslav Republic of Macedonia", the State Public Prosecutor submits a proposal to the competent state body (the Witness Protection Council) which makes a decision on inclusion in the Programme. The Department for Witness Protection, within the Ministry of Justice, is responsible for the implementation of protection measures.

In Belgium, every decision of the Witness Protection Commission is anticipated by the so-called *service de protection des témoins* (Witness Protection Service), a special unit of the Directorate General of the Criminal Investigation Division of the federal police that deals with the arrangement and the co-ordination of the witness protection. The Directorate General of Prisons is responsible for implementing the protection for witnesses detained in prison.

In Germany, the law enforcement agency investigating the case assesses the danger of the situation and informs the protection agency which is organised as an administratively separate part of the law enforcement agency and, in order to avoid the charge of undue influence on the witness, the protection measures are never implemented by officers immediately related to the case.

In Moldova, judges rule on the adoption of protective measures. The Ministry of Internal Affairs, the Security and Information Service and the Centre for Corruption and Economic Crime Control and other state institutions are responsible for the implementation of protective measures.

NGOs and other public institutions are involved in some countries (such as Hungary).

In some countries, such as the United States of America, the institutions involved may vary depending on the duration of the protective measures. If protective measures are needed for a short period of time, investigative agencies and prosecuting offices have funds to secure temporary protection measures. If the danger is at its greatest before trial and is not likely to continue after trial, the Emergency Witness Assistance Programme and other bodies become involved. Several institutions are entitled to initiate a request that a federal prosecutor file an application for the implementation of the Federal Witness Security Programme. A request for the adoption of a programme of special protective measures or the relocation of a witness is submitted to the Office of Enforcement Operations (OEO) by the US Attorney's Office.

IV - PROCEDURAL MEASURES

Procedural protective measures can be defined, in a broad sense, as all the measures which operate within the scope of criminal procedure and which affect its rules.

Protection for witnesses can be provided at any stage of criminal proceedings. It is decided pursuant to the decision of the judge which can be issued *ex officio*, or at the request of the prosecutor and/or investigating police forces (in Belgium, the investigating judge is also entitled to propose the adoption of protective measures).

With reference to legal assistance, most of the systems ensure legal representation for victims and collaborators of justice. In some systems, the expenses related to legal assistance are covered by the State (Czech Republic, Finland, Germany, Italy).

According to a recent amendment of the Austrian Code of Criminal Procedure, persons who allegedly were exposed to force or dangerous threat by an intentionally committed offence, and certain close relatives to such persons are – under specified conditions, especially if this is necessary for ensuring their rights – entitled to psycho-social and legal accompaniment during the proceedings. This encompasses, *inter alia*, legal consultation and representation by a lawyer during the proceedings (in both pre-trial and main trial phases).

Pursuant to the Latvian legislation, an attorney, who has the right to represent the interests of the protected person, can participate (both) in pre-trial examination actions, in the hearings, in Courts of Appeal and Courts of Cassation and may declare rejections, submit petitions and plaints.

Pursuant to the French legislation, only the accused who co-operates with justice is entitled to legal assistance.

In Norway, according to Section 130a, paragraph 6, of the Criminal Procedure Act, the court may decide to admit the evidence of an anonymous witness made during the preparatory proceedings. This statement can be used as evidence during the main hearing. The decision shall be taken by three professional judges, or by the president of the court if the case is prosecuted by the District Court. In Norway, the court may on application appoint a lawyer for the aggrieved person if there is reason to believe that as a result of the criminal act the said person will suffer considerable harm to body or health and there is deemed to be a need for a lawyer.

The legislation in almost all member states provides that courts can allow witnesses to testify behind a curtain, with voice and/or face distortion, in closed session, by video-conference and, in Belgium, "the former Yugoslav Republic of Macedonia" and Luxembourg, by telephone conference. In some systems (such as Norway), courts can exclude the accused and/or the public from the courtroom. In Japan, the judge may take measures to ensure that the defendant, or the witness, or both, is unable to establish the state of the other.

In "the former Yugoslav Republic of Macedonia", when witnesses and collaborators of justice during testimony are intimidated, threatened or when there is a need for them to be protected, they are only questioned in the presence of the public prosecutor and the investigative judge or the President of the Council, in a place where the protection of their identity can be guaranteed. In some cases, with the consent of the witness, the Council decides to hold the hearing in a different way through the court or to use technical equipment and other appropriate means of communication. A transcript of the minutes with the witness's statement, without the witness's signature, shall be delivered to the accused and his/her lawyer, who may put questions to the witness through the court.

Some systems provide for full and/or partial anonymity, such as concealment of the witness's appearance and the withholding of some (partial anonymity) or all (full anonymity) of his/her personal data (Austria, Belgium, Czech Republic, Germany, Latvia, Luxembourg, the Netherlands, Poland, that allows witnesses to testify under a pseudonym pursuant to a court order, although this does not occur frequently) at a very early stage of the criminal proceedings.

Pursuant to the Czech legislation, if the personal data of the witness is concealed, his/her name and surname and other personal data are not included in the record of his/her examination or of other activities, but are recorded separately from the criminal records in a special record to which only subjects involved in criminal proceedings have access. This record must be labelled with the relevant degree of concealment and must be handled in accordance with the regulations concerning the manipulation of concealed records. No entity, other than bodies involved in criminal proceedings, may consult a record containing the personal data of a witness whose identity is concealed.

In Norway, if there is a risk that the witness or any person to whom the witness has such a relationship as specified in Section 122, may be exposed to a felony impairing life, health or liberty, or to considerable material loss of another kind, the president may decide that information concerning the place of residence or workplace of a potentially endangered witness shall only be given in writing to the court.

In Japan, the presiding judge may control the examination and cross-examination of a witness if he/she deems that the disclosure of the whereabouts and of any information related to the workplace of the witness may be harmful for the witness, his/her relatives, or his/her property. The judge may admit a third person to accompany the witness when he/she testify who is deemed likely to reduce the anxiety of the witness.

This protective measure is usually adopted pursuant to a decision taken by a judge *ex officio* or at the request of the prosecutor or of the witness (in Finland also on a request by the defence), if the witness's testimony contains relevant information related to a very serious crime and if the disclosure of the witness's identity would expose him/her or his/her relatives to serious threats.

In Belgium, the anonymous witness is always interrogated by the investigating judge, during the preliminary enquiry or at the later stages of the proceedings. The investigating judge is instructed to assess the credibility of the witness.

In France, the right to testify anonymously is granted by the *juge des libertés et de la détention* (judge for civil liberties and detention), at the request of the prosecutor or the investigating judge. The *juge des libertés et de la détention* is entitled to examine the anonymous witness, whose name and whereabouts are registered in a separate record.

Special rules on anonymity have been established in Finland, the Netherlands and Germany, with reference to the so-called undercover agents who infiltrate criminal organisations.

In Norway, the court may on the application of the public prosecutor's order decide to hear the evidence of an anonymous witness, according to Section 130a of the Criminal Procedure Act, if knowledge of the witness's identity may entail a risk that a witness playing an undercover part in the investigation of other cases of the kind specified by law will encounter considerable difficulty.

In the Czech Republic and Latvia, full anonymity is not guaranteed if the accused already knows the name of the witness. In this case other personal data (such as the new address in the case of relocation) must be concealed.

Full anonymity is not granted in Italy or Finland. In Finland, the protection of the witness during the trial is granted with video-conference or the exclusion of the accused when the protected person is giving evidence.

Anonymity is never granted to a trial witness in the United States of America, so as to allow the judge or jury to assess the witness's credibility in order to place the greatest possible weight on the testimony of the witness.

Anonymity can be granted to co-operators who do not agree to testify at trial but offer only untraceable information or leads that, at their discretion, criminal law enforcement investigators decide to use in the pre-trial investigation of the case as the basis for search warrants or other special investigative techniques, but these persons do not receive witness protection.

Several countries provide video-conferences for the testimony of witnesses and collaborators of justice and provide that the accused and/or public may be excluded from the courtroom while the witness is giving evidence, where there are grounds to believe that the presence of the accused and of the public would prevent the witness from giving evidence. In France, the Czech Republic and the Slovak Republic, the accused who has been excluded from the courtroom has the right to know what the witness stated and may ask questions through the judges.

In the Russian Federation, in cases where there is a need to protect the witness and his/her close relatives, the court, without disclosing the witness's real personal data, is entitled to interrogate him/her in the conditions excluding the possibility of visual observation of the witness by other parties in criminal proceedings, to which effect the court makes a determination or a decision.

V - THE RESPECT OF HUMAN RIGHTS

In most systems, the adoption of protective measures is not deemed to jeopardise the rights of the defence. Even when the identity and appearance of the protected person is concealed, the defence always has the right to be present during investigative activities (Czech Republic) and to put questions to the protected witnesses (Czech Republic, the Netherlands, Portugal). Protected persons can always be cross-examined by the defence (Italy).

In Norway, a decision to hear the evidence of an anonymous witness may only be made if it is strictly necessary and does not entail considerable misgivings in regard to the defence of the person charged.

In France, the right to testify anonymously cannot be granted if disclosure of the identity of the witness is the only way to safeguard the rights of the defence. The defence can also challenge the decision to grant anonymous testimony taken by the *juge des libertés et de la détention*.

Special protective measures during a public hearing when the protected person has to appear in the courtroom (such as video-conferences, face concealment) can be imposed by the court (Italy). When a change is made to the personal data of the witness, the real name of the protected person is always known to all parties that can always cross-examine the witness or collaborator of justice.

Pursuant to the Italian Constitution and rules of procedural code, no-one can be convicted if the person who made allegations against him/her refuses to be interviewed or cross-examined by the defendant or his/her defence counsel. In Italy and France, allegations made by collaborators of justice must be corroborated by other evidence. In Luxembourg, allegations made by witnesses testifying through video-conference need corroboration.

The same rule can be found in Germany and Belgium with reference to anonymous witnesses, in the Netherlands (where no conviction is based either solely or to a decisive extent on evidence provided by anonymous witnesses (Article 342-2 Dutch Code of Civil Procedure) and the conviction cannot be based on the testimony of just one witness (Article 342-3 Sv, *unus testis nullus testis*)), in Portugal and Luxembourg with reference to the testimony given by protected witnesses, and in France (where no conviction can be based on anonymous testimony).

In other countries (such as Finland, Germany, Latvia - with reference to non-anonymous witnesses), the credibility of protected persons is assessed normally.

In Hungary, specially protected witnesses who enjoy anonymity cannot be summoned for hearings. During investigations, before the suspect has been arraigned, specially protected witnesses are interrogated by the investigative judge in the presence of the public prosecutor. The defence has the right to have access to the minutes of the interview. The particulars related to the identity of the witness cannot be disclosed to the defence. On the basis of these minutes, further questions can be addressed to the specially protected witness or his/her anonymity can be challenged.

In Belgium, the identity of the protected witness is known at every stage of the proceedings and the defendant may exercise his/her own rights. When a change of the personal data of the witness is provided, the real name of the protected person is always known to all the parties, which can always examine and interview the witness.

If testimony is given by telephone conference and not by video-conference, it cannot be deemed to be evidence unless it is corroborated. In such cases, the witness cannot be observed by the accused and the defence during the testimony and the rights of the defence are therefore jeopardised.

In the United States of America, the credibility of witnesses who are not willing to testify and are granted anonymity during the pre-trial investigative stage of the case is assured by having a named law enforcement officer, who is familiar with the anonymous witness, list under oath several circumstances where the information provided by the witness has been confirmed to be reliable. These witnesses can only be used to gather other evidence. They are not used at trial to prove guilt.

In Poland, once a judge issues a decision on the admissibility of the testimony of a crown witness, the crown witness must give answers. The credibility of a crown witness is checked by admitting other evidence during preparatory proceedings.

In Norway, according to Section 130a, paragraph 6, of the Criminal Procedure Act, the court may decide to admit that the evidence of an anonymous witness shall be made during the preparatory proceedings. This statement can be used as evidence during the main hearing. The decision shall be taken by three professional judges, or by the president of the court if the case is prosecuted for the District Court.

If protected persons mendaciously make allegations against another person, a special aggravating circumstance is contemplated by the law (Italy).

The establishment of protective measures does not affect the traditional guarantees of the defence (Hungary).

In Bosnia and Herzegovina, the possibility for the accused and the defence to challenge the credibility of the protected witness is limited to the minimum.

In Latvia, the defendant has the right to consider all the materials of the case from the moment of the completion of the pre-trial examination, as well as with the identification data of persons who are testifying in that case, except where the person testifying has acquired a pseudonym. In this case, the rights of the defendant are restricted to protect the persons who are the subject of Special Procedural Protection against possible endangerment.

Pre-trial statements given by witnesses and collaborators of justice and the testimonies of anonymous witnesses (where allowed) are, in most systems, regarded as valid evidence if the parties have the chance to participate in the examination and interrogate and/or cross-examine the witnesses.

In the Slovak Republic, pre-trial statements can be read in court and be deemed to be valid evidence if the court does not consider it necessary to examine the witness in court, if the prosecutor and the defendant give consent to it and if the witness has died or cannot be reached.

Pre-trial statements can be used as valid evidence in court if facts stated during examination or cross-examination in court differ from the statements during the pre-trial stage (Finland) and evidence is shown that the witness was intimidated or bribed (Italy).

In some countries, such as Bosnia and Herzegovina, pre-trial statements are regarded as valid evidence when there is a chance that the witness will not be available at the main trial.

In Turkey, pre-trial statements are regarded as valid evidence as far as they are declared before the court.

In Hungary, pre-trial statements can always be admitted as valid evidence. The collaborator of justice is given credibility, pursuant to the most recent case-law, if he/she admits his/her guilt. In the case of anonymous witnesses, the investigating judge conducting the interview shall explore the trustworthiness of the witness for the trial court.

In some systems, witnesses can be examined at the pre-trial stage if they are going to move abroad (Portugal) or each time that there is due reason to believe, on the basis of specific, tangible evidence, that the witness is seriously sick and thus will not be able to be examined in court or that he/she will be bribed or intimidated (Italy).

In Moldova, testimonies of anonymous witnesses are not regarded as valid evidence if they are not corroborated by other evidence. The protected witness is, however, allowed not to give his/her own name and whereabouts when examined. The examining magistrate will register the real name of the witness in a separate record. The accused can examine the protected witness at any stage of the criminal proceedings.

Some systems, such as the Portuguese, contemplate a specific hypothesis of conflict of interest. The judge who rules on the establishment of protective measures cannot issue any decision against the accused at the investigation stage. Nobody can be convicted on the basis of the sole testimony of a protected witness.

All protective measures in Finland guarantee respect for human rights and fundamental freedoms as described in the European Convention on Human Rights (hereinafter ECHR) and in the national constitution. Compliance with these requirements is monitored at different stages. In Finland, protective measures can be taken for witnesses of both parties: prosecution and defence.

In Germany, the defence of the accused can challenge the protected witness but cannot examine the witness on the protective measures (e.g. about his/her new location).

VI - NON-PROCEDURAL MEASURES

Non-procedural protective measures can be defined as all the measures which do not affect the rules of criminal procedure and have no influence on the rights of the defence (bodyguards, change of identity intended to operate outside the trial, subsequent change of address and profession, economic and psychological assistance, etc.).

Among the non-procedural measures, the Latvian law contemplates:

- to secure the conversations of the person to be protected against unsanctioned wiretapping and his/her correspondence against unsanctioned monitoring;
- to issue special technical devices and weapons to the protected person; and train him/her in their use.

Norway contemplates:

- to remove or restrict the access to the name and address of the protected person in all official registers.

They are usually set up by the Ministry of the Interior (in Bosnia and Herzegovina, Czech Republic), or special commissions and/or agencies (whose members are usually officers from the Ministry of the Interior, from other police forces, prosecutors and judges).

In Poland, protective measures for crown witnesses are adopted on the basis of a decision by the prosecutor when the court issues its decision on the court witness.

The legislation of many countries contemplates so-called protection programmes, which include protective measures adopted for the witnesses/collaborators of justice and their relatives that might change according to the seriousness of the danger and of the threats to which the person to be protected is exposed.

Belgian law contemplates the adoption of ordinary measures of protection (such as psychological assistance, the concealment of personal data, patrol services by the police and wire taps) and special measures, in cases where their co-operation relates to particularly serious crimes, such as crimes against humanity or crimes perpetrated by the members of a criminal organisation.

The protective measures for witnesses and collaborators of justice can be set up at the very beginning of the investigation. Usually, the duration of the protection programme depends on the relevance of the contribution given (which is evaluated by prosecution offices and investigative authorities), on the seriousness of the danger the protected person is subject to, on the number of cases in which he/she gives testimony, and on his/her behaviour.

Before the adoption of the protective measures, the persons concerned must commit themselves to respecting a number of rules, for their own safety and that of other protected persons. They must also undertake not to commit further crimes. The duration itself is periodically evaluated, in co-operation with the investigation authorities.

The decisions taken by the relevant authorities on the adoption, revocation or termination of the protective measures can be appealed in some countries (Czech Republic, Germany, Portugal). In other systems, protected persons are entitled to be notified of any change, suspension or revocation of the protective measures and can make representations.

Despite a great number of criminal organisations operating in several countries which have to be perceived as transnational, there are very few countries that have entered into international (bilateral or multilateral) agreements on the protection of witnesses and collaborators of justice.

VII - INTERNATIONAL CO-OPERATION

Most of the member states that replied to the questionnaire have signed no specific international agreements on the protection of witnesses and collaborators of justice.

Latvia has entered international agreements on the protection of witnesses and collaborators of justice, for example, bilateral agreements with Lithuania, Estonia and Slovenia. Agreements with the Czech Republic and Austria are in the stage of elaboration. These agreements regulate the relocation of protected persons to another country for an appropriate period of time. Moreover such persons may be relocated to other countries, subject to mutual arrangements with the appropriate justice authorities.

Bilateral agreements have been concluded in the field of police co-operation by some countries, such as the Czech Republic, which allow for the carrying out of specific procedures within police co-operation and which may be also used for the protection of witnesses and collaborators of justice within the limits of legal regulation.

In most cases, thanks to the international instruments already available (such as the European Union Treaty on Mutual Assistance in Criminal Matters between member states and the European Union), if a person is in one member state's territory and is to be heard as a witness or expert by the judicial authorities of another member state, the latter may request that the hearing take place by video-conference.

The efforts made by the Slovak Republic to draft new legislation on witnesses and collaborators of justice compatible with all international provisions concerning the protection of witnesses must be highlighted.

VIII - STATISTICS

According to the figures provided by states, Italy and Germany have set up protective measures for a great number of witnesses/collaborators of justice and their relatives. Despite its relatively new legislation, the figures provided by Poland indicate that a considerable number of crown witnesses have been admitted to protective measures.

In the United States of America, thousands of witnesses have been authorised to receive Witness Protection Programme services since the programme's inception in 1970. While many witnesses enter the programme alone it is also common for them to enter with their immediate family members or other persons close to them. Occasionally it has been necessary to place large family groups in the programme with a witness.

Many other countries, due also to their relatively small population and to the fact that specific legislation has been passed recently, have adopted protective measures for a small number of persons.

It should be highlighted that in some countries (Austria, Belgium, the Netherlands and the United States of America) a considerable number of protected witnesses and collaborators come from abroad. A smaller number of foreign protected persons (compared to global figures) has been recorded in Italy.

This implies that criminal organisations expand from their native countries to other states and that the co-operation of witnesses and collaborators of justice with reference to these organisations must be encouraged. It would be interesting if all the countries affected by criminal and terrorist organisations provided statistics on the number of protected persons coming from foreign countries. This might allow the evaluation of the impact that the legislation on the protection of witnesses and collaborators of justice has on foreign criminal groups.

PART II

EXISTING INTERNATIONAL INSTRUMENTS ON THE PROTECTION OF WITNESSES AND COLLABORATORS OF JUSTICE [4]

Specific rules for the protection of witnesses have been set up in several international instruments:

- Council Resolution of 20 December 1996 on individuals who co-operate with judicial process in the fight against international organised crime;
- Recommendation No. Rec(97)13 of the Committee of Ministers to member states of the Council of Europe concerning intimidation of witnesses and the rights of the defence, of 10 September 1997;
- Council of Europe Criminal Law Convention on Corruption of 27 January 1999 (ETS No. 173) – Article 22;
- Resolution No. 59/26-P – Convention of the Organization of the Islamic Conference on Combating International Terrorism, of 1 July 1999 (ensuring, among the measures to combat terrorism, effective protection of persons working in the field of criminal justice, as well as of witnesses and investigators, and effective protection of information sources and witnesses of terrorist crimes).

International co-operation on the protection of witnesses is established by several international instruments:

- Council Resolution of 23 November 1995 on the protection of witnesses in the fight against international crime (urging states to facilitate judicial assistance in the field of the protection of witnesses in the fight against international organised crime,[5] even in the absence of a specific provision in the legislation of the state to which the request of protection is addressed);
- Recommendation No. Rec(97)13 of the Committee of Ministers to member states of the Council of Europe concerning intimidation of witnesses and the rights of the defence, of 10 September 1997 – Article 30;
- Council Act of 29 May 2000 establishing, in accordance with Article 34 of the Treaty on European Union, the Convention on Mutual Assistance in Criminal Matters between the member states of the European Union;
- United Nations Convention against Transnational Organized Crime of 15 November 2000 – Article 24 (establishing that each State Party shall

---

[4] For instruments elaborated by:
  - Council of Europe: see http://conventions.coe.int.
  - European Union: see http://europa.eu.int.
  - United Nations: see http://untreaty.un.org.

[5] Witness means any person who possesses intelligence or information regarded by competent authorities as being material in criminal proceedings and liable to endanger that person if divulged.

take appropriate measures within its means to provide effective protection from potential retaliation or intimidation for witnesses in criminal proceedings who give testimony concerning offences covered by the convention and, as appropriate, for their relatives and persons close to them, and that States Parties shall consider entering into agreements or arrangements with other states for the relocation of witnesses in criminal proceedings who give testimony concerning offences covered by the convention);

- Recommendation No. Rec(2001)11 of the Committee of Ministers to member states of the Council of Europe concerning guiding principles on the fight against organised crime, of 19 September 2001;
- Recommendation No. Rec(2005)9 of the Committee of Ministers to member states of the Council of Europe on the protection of witnesses and collaborators of justice, of 20 April 2005, calling on states to achieve the following objectives:
    - adopt appropriate measures to protect witnesses and collaborators of justice against intimidation when designing a framework of measures to combat serious offences, including those related to organised crime and terrorism, and violations of international humanitarian law;
    - provide assistance in relocating abroad protected witnesses, collaborators of justice and persons close to them and ensuring their protection, in particular in those cases where no other solution can be found for their protection;
    - facilitate and improve the use of modern means of telecommunication, such as video-links, and the security thereof, while safeguarding the rights of the parties;
    - co-operate and exchange best practices through the use of already existing networks of national experts;
    - contribute to the protection of witnesses and collaborators of justice within the context of co-operation with international criminal courts.
- Second Additional Protocol to the European Convention on Mutual Assistance in Criminal Matters of the Council of Europe, of 8 November 2001 (ETS No. 182) – Articles 9, 10 (on hearings by video-conference and by telephone conference) and 23 (on the protection of witnesses);
- Resolution No. 59/26-P – Convention of the Organization of the Islamic Conference on Combating International Terrorism, of 1 July 1999 – Article 37;[6]

---

[6] Pursuant to Article 37, related to Part III:
Mechanism for Implementing Co-operation, in case of rogatory commission.
1. The requesting State shall undertake all necessary measures to ensure the protection of a witness or expert from publicity that could endanger him, his family or his property as a result of his testimony and in particular:
a. To ensure confidentiality of the date and place of his arrival as well as the means involved.

- Bilateral agreements reached by the ICTY with states willing to relocate the ICTY endangered witnesses within their territory;[7]
- Statute of the International Criminal Court – Article 93 providing that the Court may request States Parties' co-operation on the protection of victims and witnesses.

With reference to procedural protective measures, Articles 9 and 10 of the Second Additional Protocol to the European Convention on Mutual Assistance in Criminal Matters of the Council of Europe, which was adopted in November 2001, contemplate the possibility for witnesses to be examined by video or telephone conference if a person in one party's territory must be heard as a witness or expert by the judicial authority of another party. These rules can be deemed as procedural protective measures, pursuant to the definition given in the Final Report of the PC-PW.[8]

The Second Additional Protocol to the European Convention on Mutual Assistance in Criminal Matters (as well as any of the other instruments taken into consideration) does not mention any other procedural protective measures (to be adopted and implemented in addition or as an alternative to hearings by video or telephone conference), such as:

- voice and/or face distortion;
- evidence given in closed session;
- testimony given under a pseudonym;
- full and/or partial anonymity, such as concealment of the witness's appearance and the withholding of some (partial anonymity) or all (full anonymity) of his/her personal data.

This instrument does not specifically mention, among persons to be protected, collaborators of justice and persons close to them.

With reference to non-procedural protective measures, Article 23 of the Second Additional Protocol to the European Convention on Mutual Assistance in Criminal Matters establishes that where a party requests assistance under the convention or one of its protocols in respect of a witness at risk of intimidation or in need of protection, the competent authorities of the requesting and requested state shall endeavour to agree

---

b. To ensure confidentiality of his accommodation, movements and locations where he may be found.
c. To ensure confidentiality of the testimony and information given to the competent judicial authorities.
2. The requesting State shall provide necessary security required by the condition of the witness or expert and of his family, and circumstances of the case and types of expected risks.

[7] States hosting ICTY witnesses often provide them with residential status, welfare, health care and housing. These benefits are followed, after a period of time, by citizenship.

[8] See document PC-PW(2003)17.

on measures for the protection of the person concerned, in accordance with their national law.

Article 24 of the United Nations Convention against Transnational Organized Crime provides that states shall consider setting up international agreements and arrangements on the relocation of persons.[9]

Pursuant to its Explanatory Report,[10] Article 23 of the Second Additional Protocol to the European Convention on Mutual Assistance in Criminal Matters is to apply only where a request for assistance has been made under the Convention or one of its Protocols in respect of a witness at risk of intimidation or in need of protection. The requesting party is responsible for evaluating whether or not the witness is at risk of intimidation or in need of protection.

Article 23 of the above-mentioned Second Additional Protocol clearly subordinates any practical effects deriving from its application to any agreement between the parties involved. The obligation deriving from the Article is not to act with practical effects, but rather to endeavour to agree.

The Second Additional Protocol to the European Convention on Mutual Assistance in Criminal Matters and the United Nations Convention against Transnational Organized Crime do not explicitly provide for co-operation on the protection of collaborators of justice and of persons close to witnesses and collaborators of justice at risk.

The above-mentioned instruments do not contemplate mutual assistance between states with reference to other non-procedural protective measures such as:

- bodyguards;
- change of the personal data of the protected person and of people related to the protected person.

Article 23 of the above-mentioned Second Additional Protocol and Article 24 of the above-mentioned United Nations Convention do not cover other situations, that is, when requests for co-operation relate to persons

---

[9] States Parties shall consider entering into agreements or arrangements with other states for the relocation of witnesses in criminal proceedings who give testimony concerning offences covered by the convention and, as appropriate, of their relatives and persons close to them.

[10] Following the practice instituted by the Committee of Ministers of the Council of Europe in 1965, explanatory reports have been published on some of the treaties. These reports, prepared by the committee of experts instructed to elaborate the European convention or agreement in question and published with the authorisation of the Committee of Ministers, might facilitate the application of the provisions of the respective treaties, although they do not constitute instruments providing an authoritative interpretation of them.

(including witnesses, collaborators of justice and persons close to them) who co-operate with justice with reference to any serious crime and who are already subject to protective measures in one country and need relocation and/or any other procedural or non-procedural protective measures in another state.

In fact two cases might arise in the event of co-operation between different countries:

-   the country requesting relocation has already adopted other protective measures (such as change of personal identification data) and asks that they be implemented in the other country;[11]
-   the country requesting relocation asks the requested country to adopt other protective measures.[12]

In both cases, the requesting and the requested countries must recognize the authority of the relevant institutions of the counterpart involved in the protection of the witness, their assessments, requests, the information they provide and the decisions they issue.

It can be concluded that there is no binding instrument that expressly establishes mutual assistance on the following issues:

-   adoption and implementation of procedural protective measures, other than hearings by video or telephone conference in another country;
-   adoption and implementation of non-procedural protective measures, other than relocation to another country;
-   adoption and implementation of any procedural or non-procedural protective measures for collaborators of justice giving testimony and co-operating in cases related to serious crimes[13] and for persons close to witnesses and collaborators of justice;
-   costs related to the implementation of procedural and non-procedural protective measures (other than hearings by video or telephone

---

[11] Pursuant to the Final Report of the PC-PW (PC-PW(2003)17), in this case the person to be relocated must already be included in a witness protection programme in the requesting country in accordance with the provisions in place in that country. Once the criteria for acceptance in the host nation's witness protection programme have been fulfilled, it should not be necessary for the receiving authority to re-examine the original reasons for inclusion. However, this should not preclude the receiving authority from further medical, psychological or sociological assessment in accordance with the provisions in place.

[12] Pursuant to the Final Report of the PC-PW (PC-PW(2003)17), in the second case, any decision related to the adoption, modification, revocation or termination of the protective measures, unless agreed otherwise, should be taken by the requested country, pursuant to its own legislation, on the basis also of the recommendations and information provided by the requesting state.

[13] Definitions of serious crime have been set up by the United Nations Convention against Transnational Organized Crime (Article 2).

conference and relocation to another country) to be adopted and/or executed in another country.

With reference to this issue, the Final Report of the PC-PW[14] proposed that an international instrument, if adopted, might also provide for the establishment of a fund aimed at covering all the expenses related to relocation and to other protective measures, as well as to the training of personnel. The fund, which might partially be financed by the proceeds and assets seized from the perpetration of crimes, would help less wealthy countries afford the expenses related to relocation and protection of witnesses/collaborators of justice and their family members in another country.

---

[14] Op. cit.

PART III

PATHS TO BE CLEARED FOR MORE EFFECTIVE NATIONAL AND INTERNATIONAL LEGISLATION

I - GENERAL CONSIDERATIONS

A - Nature of the instrument

A legal framework should be created for facilitating the establishment of domestic systems and international co-operation in matters related to the protection of witnesses and collaborators of justice (*pentiti*), including (a) mutual recognition, by countries involved in the (cross-border) execution of protection measures, of decisions taken with regard to persons (for example, witnesses, but also relatives) to be protected; (b) the procedures to be followed when mutual assistance is sought; (c) exchanges of information regarding witness protection; (d) the use of advanced technical (tele)communication means to facilitate the transmission of witness testimony in cases where, for reasons of protection, the witness cannot appear in court; and (e) mutual assistance in relocating witnesses in need of protection and in other practical matters concerning the effective protection of those witnesses.

The reasons for protecting witnesses can vary widely. Apart from the fact that a collaborator of justice acts as a witness on behalf of the prosecution in the proceedings against his/her former co-authors of crimes, there will always be a certain concrete assessment of the concrete threats and dangers. Once the status of protected witnesses has been granted, this should be recognized by other countries, if they – as a requested state – become involved in the follow-up. This follows from the principle of confidence in mutual assistance. Nevertheless, it does not affect the right of the requested state to refuse to comply with a request for particular reasons. The question of whether or not "the instrument" should include a list of reasons for refusal should be discussed.

In so far as possible, the procedures to be followed should be uniform and consistent with existing procedures in the field of mutual assistance in accordance with the various European conventions concerning this field.

Taking into consideration the requirement of maximum confidentiality in concrete cases, it is important to regulate the exchange of information between countries. To this end, it is recommended to have one national authority per country dealing with mutual assistance concerning witness protection. This authority could (for example) be a special unit of the agency responsible for witness protection or an already existing national authority in charge of matters concerning international co-operation in criminal cases.

When shelter has been found for a threatened witness in another country, technical means of communication should be available in case an examination of the witness is needed, if the protection measures prevent the witness from giving testimony in open court.

Specific measures/programmes/mechanisms for protection of threatened witnesses and collaborators of justice (and people related to them) whose testimony would be of particular relevance for the investigation and/or prosecution and/or judgment of a particular case should be provided.

Pursuant to the legislation of various member states, there is a system (which often contemplates "protection programmes") dealing with protective measures. They are divided into ordinary and special measures.

Ordinary measures can be defined as measures which provide protection for witnesses and collaborators of justice that do not imply the relocation or a change of the personal data of the persons to be protected, are usually implemented in their place of residence, and last for the duration of the investigation or trial and for a short period of time thereafter.

These measures can be:

- protection of the personal data of the witness/collaborator of justice and the people related to him/her;
- change of the telephone numbers and car plates of the witness/collaborator of justice and of the people related to him/her;
- police patrols in the area around their houses;
- bodyguards and other physical protection;
- electronic control of telephone calls to and from the telephone numbers of the protected person;
- psychological and financial support.

Special measures are measures implying more dramatic changes in the life/privacy of the protected person (such as relocation and change of personal data) and being part of a programme or a scheme that must be applied to witnesses and collaborators of justice who need protection beyond the duration of the criminal trials where they give testimony and may last for a limited period or for life.

B - Discussion and possible definition of criteria justifying the admissibility of an individual to special protection measures (for example, evaluation of danger and relevance of the contribution)

The following can be identified as criteria entitling a witness/collaborator of justice to enjoy special protective measures:

- involvement of the person to be protected (as a victim, witness, co-perpetrator, accomplice or aider and abetter) in the investigation and/or in the case;
- relevance of the contribution;
- seriousness of the danger;
- willingness and suitability to be subject to protective measures.

(i) Relevance of the contribution

For a testimony in relation to a serious offence to be particularly relevant, it should be:

- credible (genuine and spontaneous);
- the crucial evidence available in order to prosecute a specific serious offence;
- necessary to corroborate other evidence in order to successfully prosecute a specific serious offence;
- necessary to challenge other evidence favourable to the accused (if the latter is considered mendacious);
- crucial in order to dismantle a terrorist organisation and detect the proceeds derived from the perpetration of crimes;
- likely, despite other evidence available, to cause the person testifying to be subject to bribery or intimidation;
- necessary (for example, if it is the only source of evidence) to start an investigation or to prevent a crime from being committed.

The evidence to be given by the witness must therefore be crucial, decisive and critical to the case. In other words, the law enforcement agencies could not reasonably take the matter before the courts without the evidence of the witness believed to be at risk.

(ii) Seriousness of the danger

The special protective measures must only be adopted where there are concrete, objective indications (different from personal and subjective concerns) that the testimony will subject the witness/collaborator of justice or their immediate family or associates to serious and sustained retaliation and harm and where any ordinary measure would be inadequate, given the relevance of the testimony and the seriousness of the offence about which he/she can testify or give information.

The more the information is relevant according to the afore-mentioned criteria, the more these measures should make sure that the witness/collaborator of justice and the people related to them are not subject to any threat, intimidation, retaliation, harm or bribery aimed at preventing him/her from giving testimony.

The aim of these measures is to make sure that evidence is given in court by a fully protected witness/collaborator of justice and to ensure that this person is not thereafter harmed on account of his/her testimony.

(iii) Willingness

This principle implies that the witness/collaborator of justice should voluntarily accept to be protected by ordinary or special protective measures. The principle implies also that the protective measures can also be revoked at the specific request of the witness/collaborator of justice.

The voluntary entry of witnesses implies the informed consent of the witness/collaborator of justice to the rules of security he/she has to respect and the extent of the limitations for him/her that follow from the adoption of protection measures.

Willingness is important because the witness/collaborator of justice must not only comply with but also voluntarily support all means taken to ensure his/her safety and prevent danger to his/her life and limb, as well as to the overall programme, which also has the responsibility to safely protect other witnesses, past and future. These means will include voluntary restrictions on his/her right to publish witness-protection related matters or speak about them with other persons or the media.

(iv) Suitability

This refers to the psychological, social and medical condition of the person to be protected.

The criteria of the seriousness of the danger and the willingness and suitability of the person to be protected should also be applied to people related to the witness/collaborator of justice to make them eligible for protective measures.

C - Provision of adequate measures against the risk of the collaborators of justice committing further crimes

In the case of a witness who has been involved as the perpetrator of a crime (and more specifically, with reference to collaborators of justice), protection should also be aimed at preserving his/her credibility and public security.

Both are jeopardised if the collaborator of justice commits further crimes while under protection. In most systems, the intentional perpetration of an offence by the collaborator of justice while under protection implies the immediate revocation of protective measures. Moreover, the perpetration of a crime by a protected person would cause the real name and current whereabouts of the protected person to be revealed and undermine his/her security.

Specific measures, aiming at preventing collaborators of justice from committing crimes while under protection and therefore, even involuntarily, jeopardising the case in court, must be considered, such as:

- relocation to areas not affected by criminal organisations that might recruit the collaborator of justice (if in prison, relocation to special detention facilities where other collaborators of justice are held);
- adoption of temporary financial support measures for the collaborator of justice and his/her immediate family members and associates;
- assistance with job searches;
- change of personal data;
- special attention to the grievances of the collaborator of justice and his/her family. They should be periodically visited by an officer designated by the manager of the witness protection unit to ensure that the witness/family has no grievances with regard to their treatment by the body responsible for their protection and that no medical or psychological problems have gone undetected;
- strict surveillance and control of the collaborator of justice and his/her immediate family members and associates.

The last solution surely implies limitations to the freedom and privacy of the protected persons.

The criteria for identifying the boundaries of these limitations are presented further in the text.

It should not be forgotten that the protective measures (and the rules and limitations related to them) are adopted with the informed consent of the person to be protected.

D - Ensuring that no terrorism-related crimes are excluded from the offences for which specific witness protection measures / programmes / mechanisms are envisaged

In Resolution No. 1 on Combating International Terrorism adopted at the 24th Conference of European Ministers of Justice, the Committee of Ministers was invited "urgently to adopt all normative measures considered necessary for assisting States to prevent, detect, prosecute and punish acts of terrorism, such as [...] the improvement of the protection of witnesses and other persons participating in proceedings involving persons accused of terrorist crimes".[15]

---

[15] Resolution No. 1 on Combating International Terrorism, 24th Conference of European Ministers of Justice, Moscow (Russian Federation), 4-5 October 2001.

This implies that the protection of witnesses and collaborators of justice giving evidence in terrorism-related cases is crucial in order to achieve successful results in the fight against terrorist organisations.

The Reflection Group on developments in international co-operation in criminal matters (PC-S-NS) of the Council of Europe took the view that terrorism is a form of crime and that co-operation against terrorism must be part of the co-operation against all forms of crime; as much as responses to other forms of crime, it must live up to existing standards.[16]

In some systems (e.g. in the Russian Federation), security measures apply to witnesses in the course of investigating criminal cases concerning all grades of offences (including, therefore, terrorism-related crimes). It might not, therefore, be necessary for those systems to recommend that no terrorism-related crimes be excluded from the offences for which specific witness protection measures/programmes/mechanisms are envisaged.

Having previously stated that testimony related to a serious offence can be particularly relevant, there is no doubt that terrorism-related offences can be deemed as serious offences. [17]

---

[16] See the summary report of the 3rd meeting of the PC-S-NS (Strasbourg, 15-16 October 2001): document PC-S-NS(2001)05.

[17] States might also find some (not exhaustive) indications for the identification of terrorism-related crimes in the offences listed in Article 1.1 of the European Convention on the Suppression of Terrorism of the Council of Europe (27 January 1977), as revised by the Protocol of Amendment (15 May 2003):
a. an offence within the scope of the Convention for the Suppression of Unlawful Seizure of Aircraft, signed at The Hague on 16 December 1970;
b. an offence within the scope of the Convention for the Suppression of Unlawful Acts against the Safety of Civil Aviation, signed in Montreal on 23 September 1971;
c. an offence within the scope of the Convention on the Prevention and Punishment of Crimes Against Internationally Protected Persons, Including Diplomatic Agents, adopted in New York on 14 December 1973;
d. an offence within the scope of the International Convention Against the Taking of Hostages, adopted in New York on 17 December 1979;
e. an offence within the scope of the Convention on the Physical Protection of Nuclear Material, adopted in Vienna on 3 March 1980;
f. an offence within the scope of the Protocol for the Suppression of Unlawful Acts of Violence at Airports Serving International Civil Aviation, done in Montreal on 24 February 1988;
g. an offence within the scope of the Convention for the Suppression of Unlawful Acts Against the Safety of Maritime Navigation, done in Rome on 10 March 1988;
h. an offence within the scope of the Protocol for the Suppression of Unlawful Acts Against the Safety of Fixed Platforms Located on the Continental Shelf, done in Rome on 10 March 1988;
i. an offence within the scope of the International Convention for the Suppression of Terrorist Bombings, adopted in New York on 15 December 1997;
j. an offence within the scope of the International Convention for the Suppression of the Financing of Terrorism, adopted in New York on 9 December 1999.

Pursuant to Articles 17 and 18 of Recommendation No. Rec(2001)11 of the Committee of Ministers to member states of the Council of Europe concerning guiding principles on the fight against organised crime, adopted on 19 September 2001:

"Member states should provide effective, physical and other, protection for witnesses and collaborators of justice who require such protection because they have given or agreed to provide information and/or give testimony or other evidence in relation to organised crime. Similarly, such protection measures should be available for those who participate in or have agreed to participate in the investigation or the prosecution of organised crime as well as for the immediate family members and associates of the individuals who require protection. Member states should adopt appropriate measures to ensure, both within and outside the country of trial, the protection of witnesses prior to, during or after criminal proceedings."

The Report on Witness Protection (1st Best Practice Survey)[18] properly highlighted witness protection as especially important in the fight against organised crime and terrorism. According to that report, it could be explained by the closed character of criminal and terrorist groups, which makes it very difficult to use traditional investigative methods successfully.

This is a clear sign that member states also intend to extend a system of protective and encouraging measures for terrorism-related crimes.

In most systems, crimes of "terrorist association" or crimes related to terrorist organisations receive heavy sentences, as they are perceived as serious crimes (see the United Nations Convention on the Suppression of Financing Terrorism). Moreover, despite most systems' decree that only individuals can be prosecuted, perpetrators of terrorism-related crimes are generally members of a wider group. Giving testimony against such individuals is like speaking against a whole criminal group. Threats and retaliation can therefore come from the whole group and a larger number of people than the accused against whom the witness/collaborator of justice will give evidence. There is no difference between organised crime and terrorist organisations in this respect. Both are capable, by intimidating, harming or bribing witnesses, of obstructing justice.

The financing of terrorism, terrorist acts and terrorist organisations, pursuant to Resolution 1373 of the Security Council of the United Nations, can also be considered a terrorism-related crime.

[18] Report adopted by the Committee of Experts on Police Ethics and Problems of Policing (PC-CO) at its 3rd plenary meeting, (15-17 February 1999).
See document PC-CO(1999)8 rev posted at:
http://www.coe.int/t/e/legal_affairs/legal_co-operation/
Combating_economic_crime/8_Organised_crime/Documents/
2Best_Practices_Survey.asp#TopOfPage.

E - Reflection on the relationship between measures protecting collaborators of justice and other measures aiming at encouraging individuals to co-operate with justice; consequently, reflection on the potential relationship between measures aiming at encouraging individuals to co-operate with justice and the balance of the different interests, including pursuing the investigation of serious crimes, ensuring punishment, protecting the rights of the victims

Despite the fact that most systems do not contemplate a clear distinction between measures protecting witnesses and collaborators of justice and other measures aiming at encouraging individuals to co-operate with justice, protective measures can be defined as measures aiming at preventing any intimidation[19] and/or any dangerous effects deriving from intimidation of from the decision to co-operate with justice.[20] However, measures encouraging co-operation are measures that do not directly protect witnesses and collaborators of justice from intimidation, but provide recognition for the effort they are making in taking the risk of co-operating with justice and any other direct or indirect consequence of that risk.

Non-procedural[21] encouraging measures (such as financial support, help in the search for a new job) and procedural[22] encouraging measures (such as dismissal of charges, significant reduction of prison sentence, the temporary suspension of the enforcement of a sentence, special penitentiary privileges) can be distinguished among these measures.

---

[19] Recommendation No. Rec(97)13 of the Committee of Ministers to member states of the Council of Europe defines intimidation as "any direct, indirect or potential threat to a witness, which may lead to interference with his duty to give testimony free from influence of any kind whatsoever. This includes intimidation resulting either (i) from the mere existence of a criminal organisation having a strong reputation of violence and reprisal, or (ii) from the mere fact that the witness belongs to a closed social group and is in a position of weakness therein."

[20] Pursuant to Article 26 of the United Nations Convention against Organized Transnational Crime:
"Each State Party shall take appropriate measures to encourage persons who participate or have participated in organised crime groups to supply information useful to competent authorities for investigative and evidentiary purposes on specific matters. For this purpose, each State Party shall consider providing for the possibility, in appropriate cases, of mitigating punishment of an accused person who provides substantial co-operation in the investigation or prosecution of an offence covered by the Convention and providing for the possibility, in accordance with fundamental principles of its domestic law, of granting immunity from prosecution to a person who provides substantial co-operation in the investigation or prosecution of an offence covered by the Convention."

[21] That is, measures which do not affect the rules of criminal procedure and have no influence on the rights of the defence or of the victims.

[22] That is, measures which operate within the scope of criminal procedure and do affect its rules.

These measures may have an impact on the right to pursue the crimes committed by the collaborators of justice and on the right of the victims to get compensation for the crimes committed by criminals who decide to co-operate with justice.

Pursuant to Article 25 of the United Nations Convention against Organized Transnational Crime:

"Each State Party shall take appropriate measures within its means to provide assistance and protection to victims of offences covered by the Convention, in particular in cases of threat of retaliation or intimidation and shall establish appropriate procedures to provide access to compensation and restitution for victims of offences covered by the Convention."

Encouraging measures for collaborators of justice and protective measures, such as relocation or change of personal identification data, must necessarily co-exist with the principles of safeguarding the rights and expectations of victims and a balance between these two principles should be struck.

It should be ensured that victims can claim compensation for injuries or damages suffered as the result of a criminal offence perpetrated by criminals who then co-operate with justice.[23]

II - ADOPTION OF (PROCEDURAL AND NON-PROCEDURAL) PROTECTION MEASURES AND PROGRAMMES

A - Indicative overview of different procedural and non-procedural protection measures

Bearing in mind the difference between procedural and non-procedural measures, and according to analysis of the responses given by the member and participating states, it can be assumed that in most of the systems:

- Urgent non-procedural measures include immediate relocation to a different place or detention facility, economic subsidies, physical protection, protecting the identity of the protected person, and, for those in custody and/or serving a sentence in jail, immediate relocation to special detention facilities with special security measures. These

---

[23] Article 2 of the European Convention on the compensation of victims of violent crimes already contemplated a duty for states to compensate victims of violent crimes (and terrorism-related crimes can be included in this category), when compensation is not fully available from other sources and even if the offender cannot be prosecuted or punished. (Council of Europe European Convention on the compensation of victims of violent crimes, of 24 November 1983, ETS No. 116, see: http://conventions.coe.int).

measures are often temporary, before a protection programme is adopted;

- Procedural measures include voice and/or face distortion, evidence given in closed session and/or by video or telephone conference, exclusion of the accused and/or the public from the courtroom, full and/or partial anonymity, such as concealment of the witness's appearance and the withholding of some (partial anonymity) or all (full anonymity) of his/her personal data;
- Non-procedural measures include: relocation of the protected person and his/her family members, bodyguards, change of the personal data of the protected person and people related to the protected person.

B - Ensuring an adequate legal basis and review (at different stages)

The adoption of special protective measures needs an adequate legal basis.

In accordance with this principle, ordinary and special measures and the relevant procedure to adopt them should be provided for by law.

The systems of most of the member states that replied to the questionnaire contemplate the possibility of adopting protective measures through a procedure regulated by law.

The legal basis allows exact knowledge of:

- which protective measures (either ordinary or special) can be adopted;
- the necessary prerequisites for the adoption of these measures;
- the procedure that must be followed for their adoption;
- the duration of the protective measures;
- the possibility for their renewal or revocation and/or suspension;
- the rights and obligations of the persons eligible for or subject to protection, including the right to be assisted during the above-mentioned procedure and to challenge the decisions taken in this regard.

It also better protects the principle of non-discrimination and regulates the use of discretionary power by the relevant authorities.

Moreover, the necessity of a legal basis for the adoption of protective measures has been stressed by countries that do not have rules specifically established by law in this regard.

In fact, according to the Report on Witness Protection (1st Best Practice Survey),[24] in two member states where the protection programmes for witnesses do not have a formal basis in law, the respective protection agencies hold the opinion that the existing laws are not adequate to the requirements of effective witness protection measures.

---

[24] Op. cit.

A legal basis for witness protection would imply that the law provides for the adoption and the implementation of specific protection measures, such as the change of personal data and the use of covert documents, and of those measures that might constitute an interference in the privacy of the witness/collaborator of justice and the people related to him/her.

A legal basis is also a necessary prerequisite to making legal assistance for witnesses and collaborators of justice, particularly in the event of acceptance of a protection programme/measure, really effective, as it provides the framework for the effective implementation of legal assistance.

C - Applicability of the principles of subsidiarity, proportionality and equality

The adoption and implementation of special protective measures implies a considerable amount of human and economic resources. The decision to adopt protective measures is subsequently subject to the respect of the principles of subsidiarity and proportionality.

According to the principle of subsidiarity, protective measures can only be adopted when the testimony meets the standards listed under Point IV (A) of the Final Report of the PC-PW (document PC-PW(2003)17, paragraph 118 regarding the relevance of the testimony) and there is no other evidence available that can be deemed sufficient to establish a successful case related to a serious offence.

The principle of proportionality is the evaluation and the comparison of the relevance of the testimony of the witness/collaborator of justice together with:
- the seriousness of the threats and dangers (to be considered as different from the personal and subjective concerns) to the witness/collaborator of justice;
- the protective measures that must consequently be taken; and
- the aim of the protection to be adopted.

There must therefore be a rational connection between the measures adopted and the objective of these measures.

The number and the type of protective measures to be taken is the product of the aforementioned evaluation and comparison. Special protective measures shall be adopted only if any other measures are not deemed sufficient to protect the witness/collaborator of justice and his/her immediate family members and associates. As the adoption of special protective measures implies a restriction of the freedom and the privacy of the protected person, the principles of subsidiarity and proportionality might help identify the boundaries of these restrictions. In fact, the underlying objectives of the measures that would limit rights should be pressing and substantial.

The following should also be required:
- a rational connection between the measures adopted and the objective of these measures;
- a minimal impairment of the rights and freedoms in question;
- proportionality between the effects of the measures and the objective that has been identified.

The principle of equality should also inspire the adoption of the special protective measures.

Witnesses/collaborators of justice giving testimony of equivalent relevance in equivalent cases on serious crimes and being subject to equivalent threats and dangers should be entitled to equivalent protective measures and therefore to comparable treatment.

The unjustified adoption of different measures (for example, in the case of two collaborators of justice giving evidence against the same terrorist organisation) might make some witnesses and collaborators of justice and people related to them more vulnerable than others facing the same threats.

This principle might be better implemented if the type of protective measures and the procedures for their adoption, modification or revocation were provided for by a legal basis.

With reference to special protective measures, the principle of equality would be more easily implemented if they were provided by a sole agency operating at the national level.

D - Balance between witness (and, where appropriate, collaborator of justice) protection and human rights and fundamental freedoms, in different categories of protection measures

In as far as the protection of witnesses and collaborators of justice only concerns their physical protection by means that only affect their own freedoms (for example, free movement, free choice of profession, etc.), it seems to be only a matter of informed consent: the witness must be well informed about the extent of the limitations to him/her resulting from the protection measures.

Informed consent implies a certain intake procedure, in which the witness should also be entitled to legal assistance should he/she so wish (the reasoning behind this opinion is that the situation affects the civil rights and duties of the person involved, which makes paragraph 1 of Article 6 of the European Convention on Human Rights (hereinafter ECHR) applicable).

In most legal systems, it is a legal duty to give testimony, if the person is known as a potential witness. Nevertheless, the criminal justice system should not put the witness in an unnecessarily dangerous position. That is exactly the reason for protection measures. One step further is to make measures available that encourage the witness to give testimony. What has just been said about informed consent and legal assistance applies here too.

If the measures to encourage are related to a collaborator of justice, the situation becomes even more complicated, since there will also be a plurality of procedures, including the one in which the collaborator of justice is the suspect/accused/defendant. It is slightly more complex to assess the situation from a human rights perspective, in as far as not only paragraph 1 of Article 6 of the ECHR is applicable, but also paragraphs 2 and 3. The implications here are not so clear as beforehand, since in practice the situation will be similar to the process of plea bargaining.

So far, the rights of the defendant against whom the protected witness will testify have not been discussed. This is different as soon as the protection measures affect his/her procedural rights. Then it really becomes a matter of balancing the interests and rights of the witness against those of the defence. Extensive case-law from the European Court of Human Rights relates to the handicaps for the defence when the witness is kept away from the trial, especially when anonymity becomes part of the protection.[25]

The point of departure is that all evidence in criminal cases must normally be produced at a public hearing, in the presence of the accused and with a view to adversarial argument. However, there are exceptions to this principle.

These exceptions find their limitations when they infringe on the rights of the defence. As a general rule, paragraphs 1 and 3(d) of Article 6 of the ECHR require that the defendant be given an adequate and proper opportunity to challenge and question a witness against him/her, either when this witness gives testimony or at a later stage.

---

[25] See the case-law of the European Court of Human Rights: *Kostovski v. The Netherlands* (Application No. 11454/85, judgment of 20 November 1989, A166); *Windisch v. Austria* (Application No. 12489/56, judgment of 27 September 1990, A186), *Lüdi v. Switzerland* (Application No. 12433/86, judgment of 15 June 1992, A238); *Doorson v. The Netherlands* (Application No. 20524/92, judgment of 26 March 1996, Reports 1996-II); *Solakov v. "the former Yugoslav Republic of Macedonia"* (Application No. 47023/99, judgment of 31 October 2001, Reports of Judgments and Decisions 2001-X); *P.S. v. Germany* (Application No. 33900/96, judgment of 20 December 2001); *Visser v. The Netherlands* (Application No. 26668/95, judgment of 14 February 2002); *Birutis and others v. Lithuania* (Applications No. 47698/99 and 48115/99, judgment of 28 March 2002). See: http://www.echr.coe.int.

The use of statements made by anonymous witnesses is not in all circumstances incompatible with the ECHR, according to the European Court of Human Rights. However, if the anonymity of a witness is maintained, the defence will be faced with difficulties which criminal proceedings should not normally involve. Accordingly, the European Court of Human Rights has recognized that in such cases paragraphs 1 and 3(d) of Article 6 require that the handicaps under which the defence labours be sufficiently counterbalanced by the procedure followed by the judicial authorities.

Therefore the defendant should not be prevented from testing the reliability of the witness and his/her statement. Moreover, no conviction should be based either solely or to a decisive extent on anonymous statements. The consequence might be that in a case in which the authorities are fully justified in keeping the witnesses anonymous, there is not sufficient evidence for a criminal conviction.[26]

E - Characteristics of the mechanism responsible for implementing protection programmes/measures (including budgetary aspects)

These characteristics should be:

(i) Co-operation with law enforcement agencies (prosecution offices, investigative units)

The success of the adoption and implementation of protective measures can be ensured if there is co-operation among the relevant institutions.

Co-operation is necessary in the case of a request for special protective measures, in order to assess the relevance of the contribution the witness/collaborator of justice can give, the seriousness of the threats and dangers to which they are subject, and the kind of measures that can be deemed adequate.

This mainly implies a frequent and complete communication, redacted as appropriate, from the law enforcement agencies related to:

-    personal details and curriculum vitae of the persons to be protected (such as criminal records when authorised by judicial authorities, school education, vocational training, professional skills, state of health);
-    the threats to the witness/collaborator of justice (such as personal details of the persons/criminal organisations posing a threat to the witness and details of their relationship to organised crime);

---

[26] The reasoning follows the argumentation of the ECHR in the *Birutis* judgment.

- current whereabouts of the persons/criminal organisations posing a threat, previous whereabouts and previous convictions of the persons/criminal organisations posing a threat (radius of action);
- potential aggressiveness of the persons/criminal organisations posing a threat, also in geographical terms;
- the current status and progress of the investigation or of the case in court;
- the importance of the contribution given by the witness in the investigation or in the trial;
- the legal status of the witness (for example, victim, principal/accomplice, incidental witness) and the extent of his/her co-operation in the investigation;
- the possible measures issued against the witness/collaborator of justice, where he/she is liable to prosecution (for example, enforcement/withdrawal of an arrest warrant);
- information which might be reinforced by the specific liaison officers within the investigation teams. They might provide a clear link to protection officers and be accessible to other investigators for advice and guidance.

Law enforcement agencies dealing with the investigation of cases in which protected persons are involved should be entitled to make representations, suggestions and recommendations before any decision is taken with reference to the adoption, modification or revocation of the protection measures. These decisions (with the exception of the details, such as the indication of the place to which the witness will be relocated or his/her new identity) should also be communicated to the law enforcement agencies.

Law enforcement agencies should also be entitled, in the framework of co-operation, to set up recommendations for admission to special protective measures and for the adoption, modification or revocation of specific measures.

Agencies dealing with the protection of witnesses/collaborators of justice should also inform the law enforcement agencies of all the threats and pressures suffered by the protected persons during the implementation of the protective measures and of any misconduct perpetrated by the protected person, any change in their decision to co-operate with justice and comply with the duties related to the protective measures to which they are subject. Any change in attitude of the protected witness or collaborator of justice during the investigation or the trial that might undermine the result of the investigation or of the trial would be more easily predicted or detected.

In the case of relocation, agencies dealing with the protection of witnesses should have contact points convenient to the areas to which witnesses and collaborators of justice have been relocated.

They must co-operate with local police forces and law enforcement agencies and give them the information, redacted as appropriate, necessary to prevent, detect and suppress any threat to or illegal pressure on the protected persons.

In particular, local police forces and law enforcement agencies should be entitled to receive information, redacted as appropriate, about the threats to which the witness/collaborator of justice is subject (such as personal details of the persons/criminal organisations posing a threat to the witness and details of their relationship to organised crime, current whereabouts of the persons/criminal organisations posing a threat, previous whereabouts and previous convictions of the persons/criminal organisations posing a threat (radius of action), and potential aggressiveness of the persons/criminal organisations posing a threat, also in geographical terms).

(ii) Confidentiality

All the stages of the procedure related to the adoption, implementation, modification and revocation of ordinary or special (temporary or final) protective measures must be kept confidential from everybody except the members of the agency responsible for protecting the witnesses.

The part of the organisation of law enforcement agencies responsible for witness protection should operate independently of the other elements of the organisation.

The implementation of a task whose primary aim is to protect witnesses and collaborators of justice requires confidentiality. Any effort made by the defendant and/or terrorist organisations to trace witnesses and collaborators of justice must be thwarted with secure covert means of operation.

The mechanism must therefore have direct control over all the financial and administrative matters related to the protection.

(iii) Separation from the law enforcement agencies involved in the investigation or in the preparation of the case

The contributions made by, among the various states, Italy and Germany, raise the question of whether it is appropriate for witnesses and collaborators of justice to be protected and assisted by agencies which are not involved in the investigation.

Staff dealing with the implementation of protective measures should not be involved either in the investigation or in the preparation of the case where the witness/collaborator of justice is to give evidence.

This will preserve the confidentiality of all operations related to the protection of witnesses, effectively stop any criminal effort to trace the protected persons, avoid any interference with or influence on the statements and testimony the collaborator of justice and the witness are to give before the investigators, the prosecutor or the judges.

Moreover, as law enforcement agencies often deal with suspects or defendants, this will prevent any information about the protected persons being involuntarily disseminated to the latter.

F - Entitlement to legal assistance, particularly in the event of acceptance of a protection programme/measure

In the case of the adoption of special protective measures, their implementation can be ruled by a contract or Memorandum of Understanding.

In many member states the witness protection agencies usually make use of a Memorandum of Understanding or (less frequently) of a contract when they implement protective measures.

The difference is that no right for the protected person derives from the Memorandum of Understanding, which can be deemed a sort of code of conduct describing what the protected person should or should not do in order to continue to enjoy protective measures.

The content of this code of conduct is usually discussed with the person to be protected. At this stage, the witness/collaborator of justice and the other persons eligible for protection should be entitled to make representations and it would be advisable that they be assisted by a lawyer, if they so wish (also in order to achieve better informed consent to the duties and limitations contemplated by the Memorandum). The same considerations may apply in case of revocation and modification of the protective measures.

The Report on Witness Protection (1st Best Practice Survey)[27] emphasised that the systems of three countries provided that the persons to be protected can be assisted during the discussion of the Memorandum of Understanding.

If a contract is signed, the person concerned should be entitled to question, make representations and go before a judge or another relevant authority if he/she thinks his/her own rights have been jeopardised.

Legal assistance would be extremely useful in case of grievances by the witnesses/collaborators of justice and their families with regard to their

---

[27] Op. cit.

treatment by the body responsible for their protection or security, or to economic, medical or psychological problems that have gone undetected.

III – INTERNATIONAL CO-OPERATION

Recommendation No. Rec(2005)9 of the Committee of Ministers to member states on the protection of witnesses and collaborators of justice was adopted on 20 April 2005 and took into account most of the considerations set out above.

The necessity of harmonisation and mutual recognition of national protection systems and evaluation of the need for and the importance of promoting a network of national contact points should be considered as a step further.

International social mobility, communication opportunities, trade and traffic have contributed greatly to the globalisation of many sectors of society. During the last two decades, the volume of transborder crimes as well as of transborder criminal investigations has grown dramatically.

International co-operation between the police, prosecutors and the judiciary has increased, as has the work of the bar and of forensic experts. In all these professional sectors of the criminal justice system, not only has the number of international aspects in concrete cases grown, but so also has the degree to which their core work has become subject to insights, norms and standards that are no longer purely national.[28]

Arguments to enhance the internationalisation of the criminal justice system by harmonising, or at least making compatible, procedures, rules and standards can be found not only in the facilitation of international co-operation in investigation, prosecution, and adjudication, but also in the growing awareness of the requirements of a European – or even Western – legal space, in which the legal position of all inhabitants is equally guaranteed.

In this perspective, of course, the role of the ECHR in setting European minimum standards for procedures from a human rights perspective is very important. But, in general, the activities within the framework of the Council of Europe that aim at greater unity within the larger area of the 46 member states, should be promoted.[29] This is especially appropriate where countries face the same problems and seek similar remedies, as in the case of terrorism and the protection of witnesses and collaborators of justice.

---

[28] From J.F. Nijboer & W.J.J.M. Sprangers, *Harmonisation in forensic expertise – an inquiry into the desirability and opportunities for international standards*, Thela Thesis, Amsterdam, 2000.

[29] See the preamble of Recommendation No. Rec(97)13 of the Committee of Ministers to member states of the Council of Europe.

An additional argument for co-operation in the field of witness protection is the fact that, as soon as protection measures include temporary or permanent relocation, most of the European countries are far too small in terms of population and/or surface to effectively apply those measures. To do so requires comparable treatment of protected witnesses throughout Europe, which implies again the harmonisation of procedures and standards.

Above all, the confidentiality which is inherent in these matters requires that not too many entities and people become involved in concrete cases and it is wise to have a single agency dealing with protection programmes. If it is necessary to involve another country in a concrete case, this should be done within a framework of central national authorities given competence for these matters. Another important requirement, which follows from the principle of mutual confidence in legal co-operation and from the civil rights of the protected witnesses, is the mutual recognition of decisions made in relation to witness protection and the application of measures.

However, this consideration should not imply that countries that are not willing to accept the testimonies of anonymous witnesses or comprehensive witness protection programmes (including change of identity) would be forced to do so.

A - The feasibility, the nature and the contents of a binding instrument focused on international co-operation

The Explanatory Memorandum to Recommendation No. Rec(2001)11 of the Committee of Ministers to member states of the Council of Europe concerning guiding principles on the fight against organised crime, which was adopted in September 2001, took into account the implementation of witness protection programmes across borders, which requires close co-operation, considerable trust and burden-sharing between the requested (receiving) and the requesting (sending) countries. The Explanatory Memorandum observed: so far, this kind of co-operation is not explicitly covered by any treaty on mutual assistance, but the need to create at the level of the Council of Europe such an instrument (which might be indispensable for small countries, where it is virtually impossible to hide witnesses and collaborators of justice from organised crime) has been recognized by Recommendation No. Rec(97)13 (Item 30) and the Report on Witness Protection (1st Best Practice Survey).[30]

The Recommendation makes a clear reference to the relocation of witnesses (in custody or not) to another country, which is a non-procedural protective measure.

---

[30] Op. cit.

Two questions arise with regard to the problematic question of a binding instrument focused on international co-operation:

- Is an international binding instrument which provides for full co-operation and (if necessary) mutual recognition of decisions taken on the protection of witnesses, collaborators of justice and persons close to them necessary or recommendable?
- Is co-operation on relocation of witnesses and collaborators of justice in custody already provided for by existing international instruments?

As for the necessity of such an instrument, an international binding instrument establishing full co-operation on the adoption and implementation of any procedural and non-procedural protective measures for witnesses and collaborators of justice in cases related to serious crimes and persons close to them would cover the lacunae in the existing international binding instruments and be consistent with the aims of Recommendation No. Rec(2001)11.

It must be stressed that in most systems, the adoption of protective measures is not deemed to jeopardise the rights of the defence. Even when the identity and appearance of the protected person is concealed, the defence always has the right to be present during investigative activities and/or to put questions to or cross-examine the protected witness or test his/her credibility.

With reference to victims of crimes committed by persons who then co-operate with justice, protective measures, such as relocation or change of personal identification data, must necessarily co-exist with the principles of safeguarding the rights and expectations of victims and a balance between these two principles should be struck.

It should be ensured that victims can claim compensation for injuries or damages suffered as the result of a criminal offence perpetrated by criminals who then co-operate with justice.[31]

The grounds for the refusal of a request should in any case be contemplated in the international binding instrument, where, for instance, compliance with a request for assistance would be contrary to the general principles of the state's law, but these aspects should generally be dealt with prior to the

---

[31] Article 2 of the European Convention on the compensation of victims of violent crimes already contemplates a duty for states to compensate victims of violent crimes (and terrorism-related crimes can be included in this category), when compensation is not fully available from other sources, even if the offender cannot be prosecuted or punished. (Council of Europe European Convention on the compensation of victims of violent crimes, of 24 November 1983, ETS No. 116, see: http://conventions.coe.int).

request. In these cases, special agreements could be made in order to avoid this kind of problem.

A new international instrument should also require states to set up common criteria for the applicability of the principles of subsidiarity and proportionality while co-operating in the adoption of protective measures.[32] Moreover, such an instrument should set up common criteria aiming at preserving an acceptable balance between the protection measures and the human rights and fundamental freedoms of all the parties involved (witnesses, collaborators of justice, defendants, victims).

---

[32] With reference to these principles, see paragraphs 163 ff of the Final Report of the PC-PW (PC-PW(2003)17):

163) The adoption and implementation of special protective measures implies a considerable amount of human and economic resources. The decision to adopt protective measures is subsequently subject to the respect of the principles of subsidiarity and proportionality.

164) According to the principle of subsidiarity, protective measures can only be adopted when the testimony meets the standards listed under Point IV (A) (Paragraph 118 regarding the relevance of the testimony) and there is no other evidence available that can be deemed sufficient to establish a successful case related to a serious offence.

165) The principle of proportionality is the evaluation and the comparison of the relevance of the testimony of the witness/collaborator of justice together with:
- the seriousness of the threats and dangers (to be considered as different from the personal and subjective concerns) to the witness/collaborator of justice;
- the protective measures that must consequently be taken; and
- the aim of the protection to be adopted.

166) There must therefore be a rational connection between the measures adopted and the objective of these measures.

167) The number and the type of protective measures to be taken is the product of the aforementioned evaluation and comparison. Special protective measures shall be adopted only if any other measures are not deemed sufficient to protect the witness/collaborator of justice and his/her immediate family members and associates.

168) As the adoption of special protective measures implies a restriction of the freedom and the privacy of the protected person, the principles of subsidiarity and proportionality might help identify the boundaries of these restrictions.

169) In fact, the underlying objectives of the measures that would limit rights should be pressing and substantial.

170) The following should also be required:
- a rational connection between the measures adopted and the objective of these measures;
- a minimal impairment of the rights and freedoms in question;
- proportionality between the effects of the measures and the objective that has been identified.

As stated previously, in the case of a request for assistance, two cases might arise with regard to mutual recognition:

- the country requesting relocation has already adopted other protective measures (such as change of personal identification data) and asks that they be implemented in the other country;[33]
- the country requesting relocation asks the requested country to adopt other protective measures.[34]

In both cases, the recognition of the authority of the relevant institutions of the counterpart involved in the protection of the witness, their assessments, requests, the information they provide and decisions they issue would facilitate and expedite the proceedings for the implementation of the protective measure requested.

This implies that the principle of mutual recognition of the decisions issued by the relevant institutions of the requesting and requested countries should also be taken into account in an international binding instrument. The purpose of mutual recognition is to make decisions issued by the judicial or governmental institutions of one state on the protection of witnesses and collaborators of justice directly applicable and enforceable in other states. Grounds for mandatory or optional refusal of a request should be provided in any case, where compliance with a request for assistance would be contrary to the general principles of the state's law and fundamental human rights.

Relocation to another country, which is one of the non-procedural protective measures most related to international co-operation, includes the displacement of witnesses and the transfer of collaborators of justice in custody to the detention facilities of another state.

The transfer of detainees to the detention facilities of another state is provided for by the Council of Europe Convention on the Transfer of Sentenced Persons of 1983, by the Convention on Mutual Assistance in Criminal Matters between the member states of the European Union of 2000 and by the United Nations International Convention for the Suppression of the Financing of Terrorism of 1999.[35]

None of these instruments establishes relocation as a (non-procedural) protective measure for persons in custody. In fact, the Council of Europe Convention does not aim at protecting detainees who collaborate with justice but deals with the problems posed by prisoners of foreign nationality,

---

[33] Op. cit.
[34] Op. cit.
[35] See also:
 - Council of Europe: http://conventions.coe.int.
 - European Union: http://europa.eu.int.
 - United Nations: http://untreaty.un.org.

including the question of providing provisions for their transfer, so that they may serve their sentence in their home country. In this respect, the Select Committee of Experts on Foreign Nationals in Prison was set up in order to, *inter alia*, study the problems relating to the treatment of foreigners in prison and to consider the possibility of drawing up a model agreement providing for a simple procedure for the transfer of foreign prisoners.[36]

As for the European Union Convention, its Article 9 stipulates that a person held in custody in the territory of a member state may be temporarily transferred to the territory of another member state which has requested an investigation in its territory for which the presence of the detainee is required.

Concerning the United Nations Convention, its Article 16 establishes that "a person who is being detained or is serving a sentence in the territory of one State Party whose presence in another State Party is requested for purposes of identification, testimony or otherwise providing assistance in obtaining evidence for the investigation or prosecution of offences set forth in Article 2 [of the Convention], may be transferred [...]."

It can be concluded that no binding instrument expressly establishes that states shall co-operate on the relocation (as a protective measure) and protection of collaborators of justice (in custody or not) and persons close to them in another country.

The preparation of a binding instrument would therefore be consistent with the tendency of states to co-operate in the field of protection of witnesses and collaborators of justice.

A new binding instrument should cover the cases not contemplated by Article 23 of the Second Additional Protocol to the European Convention on Mutual Assistance in Criminal Matters (2001), by Article 24 of the United Nations Convention on Transnational Organized Crime or by any of the other international binding instruments taken into consideration in this analytical report.

B - Possible implications of a new binding international instrument

The Explanatory Memorandum to Recommendation No. Rec(2001)11 explicitly states that the implementation of witness protection programmes across borders requires mutual trust between the requested and the requesting countries.

Mutual trust is the basis of the mutual recognition of judicial decisions, with reference to the Council Framework Decision on the European arrest warrant and the surrender procedures between Member States (hereinafter

---

[36] See Introduction of the Explanatory Report, paragraphs 1 ff.

Decision on the European arrest warrant), and the Council Framework Decision on the execution in the European Union of orders freezing property or evidence (hereinafter Decision on orders freezing property or evidence).[37]
The Tampere European Council defined the principle of mutual recognition as a cornerstone of judicial co-operation in civil and criminal matters. Point 36 of its conclusions stated that the same principle should apply "to pre-trial orders, in particular to those which would enable competent authorities quickly to secure evidence and to seize assets which are easily movable".

The "evidence to be secured" taken into consideration by the Tampere European Council is perhaps other than the testimony given by a witness or a collaborator of justice. Nevertheless, decisions on the adoption and implementation of procedural and non-procedural protective measures for these categories of persons can be deemed as solutions that enable competent authorities to secure the evidence that witnesses and collaborators of justice are expected to give and to prevent witnesses, collaborators of justice and persons close to them from being intimidated or subject to retaliation.

The objective of the aforementioned Decisions is to facilitate the arrest of persons accused of serious crimes with a view to preventing their escape and to freeze property or evidence within the framework of criminal proceedings with a view to preventing their destruction, transformation and transfer.

In November 2000, the European Council adopted a programme of measures to implement the principle of mutual recognition in criminal matters, giving priority (measures 6 and 7) to the adoption of an instrument applying the principle of mutual recognition to the freezing of property or evidence and to the implementation of the arrest warrant issued by national judges without the normal extradition procedure.

The purpose of this initiative was to make arrest warrant and orders freezing property or evidence issued in a given member state directly enforceable in other member states without it being necessary for further orders and arrest warrants to be issued, or without activating the extradition procedures.

The Decision on the European arrest warrant specifically establishes that the mechanism of the European arrest warrant is based on a high level of confidence between Member States.

---

[37] Council Framework Decision 2002/584/JHA of 13 June 2002 on the European arrest warrant and the surrender procedures between Member States, in Official Journal L 190 of 18 July 2002, p. 1; Council Framework Decision 2003/577/JHA of 22 July 2003 on the execution in the European Union of orders freezing property or evidence, in Official Journal L 196 of 2 August 2003, p. 45;See http://europa.eu.int.

There is no doubt that the principle of mutual recognition has so far referred to judicial decisions and that this principle has been implemented in a restricted number of states whose systems resemble each other.

It should not be forgotten that at the first meeting of PC-PW, held in October 2004, some delegations expressed concern at the possible adoption of binding provisions establishing the automatic "mutual recognition" – in the meaning attributed to this term in European Union law - of decisions taken for the protection of witnesses and collaborators of justice in other member states, without the prior harmonisation of substantive criminal law, and/or without the introduction of specific safeguard clauses, such as specific additional grounds for refusal. Another potential problem raised related to the nationality of persons to be relocated in other countries (see the meeting report, PC-PW(2004)05).

This concern focused especially on non-procedural protective measures, as they are set up and implemented pursuant to governmental (and therefore) non-judicial decisions. For procedural protective measures (which are usually issued by judges) the acceptance principle of mutual recognition should raise fewer problems.

Procedural protective measures are in fact set up mainly by judicial decisions. These decisions may be subject to recognition and execution, if the requesting and the requested country have procedural systems resembling each other.

Despite these concerns, it must be stressed that mutual recognition represented only one of the issues on which the former PC-PW had concluded on the advisability of a binding instrument, and that effective international co-operation would not be sufficiently secured in the absence of such a binding instrument.

Moreover, notwithstanding the terminological problems raised by the expression "mutual recognition", the objective of this particular form of co-operation would be to facilitate the acceptance of persons to be relocated for reasons related to their protection.

Mutual assistance in the implementation of any kind of protective measure does not necessarily always imply mutual recognition and direct automatic execution in the requested state of the (judicial or non-judicial) decisions taken in the requesting state.

An international binding instrument should not be focused only on the principle of mutual recognition of the decisions taken on the adoption and implementation of protective measures, but mainly on the principle of mutual assistance in the decisions (judicial and non-judicial) on the adoption and implementation of any protective measure.

With reference to mutual recognition, the Council Framework Decision on the European arrest warrant and the surrender procedures between Member States specifically states that decisions on the execution of a European arrest warrant must be subject to sufficient controls, which means that the judicial authority of the member state where the requested person has been arrested will have to take the decision on his/her surrender. The Framework Decisions on the European arrest warrant and orders freezing property or evidence also provide grounds for the non-execution of European arrest warrant and orders freezing property or evidence.[38]

Mutatis mutandis, in the case of a request for assistance in the implementation in one country of decisions on the protection of witnesses, collaborators of justice and persons close to them issued in another country, the requested country will have to take a decision on their execution. Grounds for non-execution of a European arrest warrant or orders freezing property or evidence should be provided.

The Report on Witness Protection (1st Best Practice Survey)[39] pointed out that the existing witness protection agencies in Europe already work together on an informal basis.

Because the number of national protection agencies is rather small, the heads of the agencies know each other personally and meet more than once a year. The existing national protection agencies help each other when a witness needs to be transferred out of his/her own country.

According to paragraph 20 of the aforementioned report, "the fact that the co-operation between the existing national protection services is good can be partly explained by the fact that all schemes resemble one another [...]".

It can be assumed that:

- *de facto* mutual recognition by national agencies of decisions on non-procedural protective measures taken by foreign institutions already exists since 1999;
- mutual recognition exists and is viable when systems (judicial or not) resemble or are harmonised with one another.

Non-procedural protective measures are usually issued by governmental or administrative authorities. International co-operation on the adoption and implementation of these measures implies mutual assistance in administrative matters.

---

[38] See Articles 3 and 4 of the Council Framework Decision on the European arrest warrant and the surrender procedures between Member States, Op. cit.
[39] Op. cit.

Mutual assistance in administrative matters, including administrative/criminal matters, is presently covered by a number of conventions, such as the European Convention on the Service Abroad of Documents relating to Administrative Matters of 24 November 1977 and the European Convention on the Obtaining Abroad of Information and Evidence in Administrative Matters of 15 March 1978.

Recognition of administrative decisions is contemplated in the Additional Protocol to the Convention on the Transfer of Sentenced Persons of 18 December 1997. With reference to Article 3 of this instrument, the Explanatory Report says that "the situation described in this Article is one where the person is subject to deportation or expulsion as a consequence of the sentence. The verbs "to expel" and "to deport" are both used in order to accommodate the varying terminology of member states. The meaning given to both in this Protocol is such as to include any measure as a result of which the person is subject to removal from the territory of the sentencing State at some point in time. It includes expulsion orders by administrative authorities".

Co-operation on administrative measures is provided by Article 18 paragraph 3, of the United Nations International Convention on the Suppression of the Financing of Terrorism, stating that "States Parties shall further co-operate in the prevention of offences set forth in Article 2 by exchanging accurate and verified information [...] and co-ordinating administrative and other measures taken, as appropriate, to prevent the commission of offences set forth in Article 2 [of the Convention]".

Article 29, paragraph 2, of the United Nations Convention against Transnational Organized Crime already implies mutual assistance in non-judicial matters when it establishes that "States Parties shall assist one another in planning and implementing research and training programmes designed to share expertise in the areas referred to in paragraph 1 of this Article [including also methods used in the protection of victims and witnesses – author's note] and to that end shall also, where appropriate, use regional and international conferences and seminars to promote co-operation and to stimulate discussion on problems of mutual concern, including the special problems and needs of transit States".

Article 24, paragraph 3, of the United Nations Convention against Transnational Organized Crime establishes that States Parties shall consider entering into agreements or arrangements with other states for the relocation of witnesses who give testimony concerning offences covered by this convention and, as appropriate, for their relatives and other persons close to them.

This implies that a requested country might, in accepting the relocation of a protected person in its territory, recognize the non-judicial decision of the requesting country giving a witness the status of a protected person and providing the relocation of that witness and the persons close to him/her. As stated above, relocation is to be deemed a non-procedural protective measure, which is usually set up by non-judicial institutions.

Co-operation between judicial and administrative authorities of States Parties is also provided for by Article 4 of the Second Additional Protocol to the European Convention on Mutual Assistance in Criminal Matters which establishes that requests for mutual assistance may also be forwarded directly by the administrative or judicial authorities of the requesting party to the administrative or judicial authorities of the requested party.

The Explanatory Report to the Second Additional Protocol to the European Convention on Mutual Assistance in Criminal Matters states that it is not excluded that a judicial authority may forward requests concerning "administrative/criminal offences" to an administrative authority.

It cannot be ignored that the systems existing in the member states of the Council of Europe differ from each other.

A new convention might extend its scope and include international co-operation in its provisions, not only in the case of a testimony by video or telephone conference or relocation but also in the overall implementation of (procedural and non-procedural) protective measures in favour of witnesses, collaborators of justice and persons close to them.

In accordance with Article 23 of the Second Additional Protocol to the European Convention on Mutual Assistance in Criminal Matters, any practical effect of a new binding instrument should be subordinated to an agreement between the parties involved (including third transit countries, in case of relocation) and the obligation deriving from a new binding instrument should be to endeavour to agree.

The purpose of a new binding instrument is to reinforce the ability of member states, as well as partner states, to respond to crimes through adequate international co-operation in the protection of witnesses, collaborators of justice and persons close to them.

This need is mostly perceived by small countries that cannot adequately protect witnesses and collaborators of justice within their own borders. The purpose of protection can be achieved only by modernising the existing binding provisions governing mutual assistance and the protection of witnesses, extending the categories of persons to be protected (collaborators of justice and persons close to witnesses and collaborators of justice) and the range of circumstances in which mutual assistance may be requested, accomplished and implemented in the field of protection of witnesses, collaborators of justice and persons close to them.

Only the relevant member states can evaluate the resemblance of their own systems with the systems of other countries.

The international binding instrument might call on states to co-operate at various levels.

An international binding instrument might provide that:

-   States having systems and programmes of protection resembling each other shall consider entering into bilateral or multilateral agreements on mutual assistance in the protection of witnesses, collaborators of justice and persons close to them and shall consider that mutual assistance is based on mutual recognition of the decisions taken on the protection of those persons;
-   States not having harmonised systems and programmes of protection shall consider entering into bilateral or multilateral agreements with no implication of mutual recognition of decisions taken by the States Parties.

In any case, a binding instrument should provide specific safeguard clauses, such as specific additional grounds for refusal to co-operate on the protection of witnesses and collaborators of justice and persons close to them. It might therefore call on states to enter into bilateral or multilateral agreements providing various levels of co-operation, depending on the resemblance of the systems of the States Parties.

It should also provide that the co-operation requested may be refused where compliance with the request for assistance would be contrary to the general principles of the requested state's law.

A binding instrument might also provide that when entering into bilateral and multilateral agreements, States Parties should also consider the role of third transit states (in case they are requested to provide temporary protection and/or other facilities to the protected person bound for the country where he/she is to be relocated and protected, or obliged to enforce arrest warrants against the protected person) and entering into agreements with third transit states.

The purpose of such a new binding instrument would be to further reinforce the ability of States Parties to respond adequately to crime. This purpose would be achieved by modernising the existing provisions governing mutual assistance, extending the range of circumstances in which assistance may be requested and including in this range co-operation in the adoption, execution and implementation of protective measures.

Considering the current provisions set out in the European Convention on Mutual Assistance in Criminal Matters (1959, which refers to any crime) and in the First and Second Additional Protocols to the European Convention on

Mutual Assistance in Criminal Matters (1979 and 2001), it would be consistent to elaborate a Third Additional Protocol to the European Convention on Mutual Assistance in Criminal Matters.

Such a protocol might provide that member states should consider setting up bilateral or multilateral agreements on mutual assistance in the field of the relocation and/or any other kind of protection (with procedural and non-procedural measures) of witnesses, collaborators of justice and persons close to them.

Bilateral and multilateral agreements on mutual assistance, and if necessary on mutual recognition, should be set up according to the decisions taken by the member states and the degree of harmonisation or resemblance of relevant domestic legislation.

It must be considered that mutual recognition and the mechanism of the European arrest warrant are based on a high level of confidence between member states and the resemblance of their own systems and that this principle has been implemented in countries belonging to a common area of freedom, security and justice.

The same principles will soon be applied by the same countries to "pre-trial orders, in particular to those which would enable competent authorities quickly to secure evidence and to seize assets which are easily movable" and to collect in one country the evidence needed by the judicial authority of another country.

Decisions on the adoption and implementation of procedural and non-procedural protective measures for witnesses and collaborators of justice can be deemed as solutions that enable competent authorities to secure the evidence that these persons are expected to give and prevent witnesses and collaborators of justice and persons close to them from being intimidated or subject to bribery or retaliation.

The principle or mutual recognition can therefore be applied also to these decisions, especially if these decisions involve countries belonging to a common area of freedom, security and justice.

These countries might therefore be bound by an international instrument providing that member states shall consider entering into agreements or arrangements on mutual assistance and mutual recognition on the issues suggested by the scientific expert and some member and observer states in the PC-PW meeting held on 8-10 December 2004.[40]

---

[40] See report of the 2nd meeting of the PC-PW held on 8-10 December 2004 (document PC-PW(2004)12).

C - Significant existing regional agreements

International binding instruments can be either bilateral or multilateral. In the field of judicial co-operation, where a bilateral or regional instrument exists, provisions are usually very comprehensive and detailed, because when negotiating the relevant instrument the parties involved are in a position to compare the own legal systems and therefore to set the most appropriate provisions. In the case of multilateral conventions, provisions may be of a more general nature as the difference in the various legal systems has to be taken into account.

Among regional agreements, the Agreement between the Governments of Lithuania, Estonia and Latvia on Co-operation in Protection of Witnesses and Victims contains quite specific provisions. It should be underlined that the provisions of this agreement partly mirror the proposals made by the Lithuanian delegation at the PC-PW meeting of December 2004.[41]

Pursuant to this agreement:
- The parties, through their central competent institutions, shall co-operate and render mutual assistance in preventing and combating crime, and implementing complex measures to ensure protection and transportation of persons under protection.
- The parties shall provide adequate and effective protection of persons under protection during the investigation of the criminal case, during and after the legal proceedings, in cases where it has been acknowledged as necessary in the manner defined in the legislation.
- The applicable laws and other legal regulations of the receiving party shall define the rights and duties of the person who is temporarily moved to the territory of the receiving party.
- Each of the parties, via diplomatic channels in due course, informs the other parties about the central competent institutions for the aims of this agreement.
- Each of the parties in due course informs the other parties about changes in the list of their central competent institutions.
- The central competent institutions seeking to implement this agreement directly contact each other.

The above-mentioned instrument also regulates the following forms of co-operation among State Parties:

- under Article 2:
- exchange of operative, search, inquiry and other information at the disposal of law enforcement authorities and duly respecting the necessary confidence, about any crimes expected or committed and

---

[41] Op. cit.

related to threats to persons under protection when international assistance is required to prevent such threats;

- implementation of operative and investigative measures deemed necessary to ensure protection of the relevant persons, determination of the validity of the requesting party's decision on the protection of a person of the requesting party in the territory of the receiving party;[42]
- reduction of criminal punishment for persons who have rendered assistance to the law enforcement authorities of the other party;
- temporary or permanent relocation of the persons under protection to the territory of the receiving party without disclosing the identity of the endangered persons and, if necessary, by guarding or supervising over the place of their stay;
- creation of joint groups of experts for solving more complicated issues of protection of persons under protection and developing procedural norms, taking into account the legislation of the parties; training and preparation of personnel.

- under Article 3: the instrument regulates the form and the content of the request for protection;
- under Article 4: the obligations of the receiving party;
- under Article 5: the termination of protection;
- under Article 6: the maintaining and forwarding of information;
- under Article 7: the costs.

The Agreement between the Governments of Lithuania, Estonia and Latvia on Co-operation in Protection of Witnesses and Victims is undoubtedly the most detailed among the international binding instruments to date taken into account within a perspective of tighter co-operation among states.

---

[42] The provision on the determination of the validity in the requested party of decisions taken in the requesting party on the protection of persons might lead to similar effects of the principle of mutual recognition of judicial decisions.

CONCLUSIONS

Criminal organisations, including terrorist organisations, are operational almost all over the world and fighting these organisations has become a priority. A great contribution to this fight can be made by witnesses and collaborators of justice who decide to co-operate with the judiciary. Such a contribution can be ensured only if persons who can provide useful information and evidence enjoy adequate protection and support that allows them to deal with all the risks and implications related to the decision to co-operate with justice.

A serious need to develop a coherent common international framework for the effective protection of witnesses and collaborators of justice is perceived. Given the essentially transnational nature of serious crimes – such as organised crime and terrorism – and violations of international humanitarian law, improved and effective international co-operation seems to be particularly important. It is necessary to define a comprehensive set of measures to increase the protection of witnesses and collaborators of justice, especially with respect to the fight against terrorism, and in particular to the need to strengthen international co-operation.

The existing lacunae in current national and international legislation must soon be filled following a serious reflection on the instruments necessary to achieve effective co-operation among states on the protection of witnesses and collaborators of justice.

Apart from any current reluctance by states, these instruments can be identified in a convention urging states to co-operate with each other and to consider setting up bilateral or multilateral agreements providing mutual recognition of judicial and governmental decisions on the protection of witnesses and collaborators of justice. Instead of jeopardising the sovereignty of states, these instruments would give further credibility to the fight against any serious crime.

SITUATION IN MEMBER AND OBSERVER STATES
OF THE COUNCIL OF EUROPE

Questionnaire on protection of witnesses and *"pentiti"* in relation to acts of terrorism

Foreword

The aim of this questionnaire is to gather information about the situation in member and observer States concerning the protection of witnesses and *pentiti*, its regulation and use.

The information gathered through this questionnaire is intended to serve the purpose of implementing the terms of reference of the PC-PW which are "to study the means for strengthening the protection of witnesses and *pentiti* in relation to acts of terrorism, including those at international level, and to make proposals as to the feasibility of preparing an appropriate instrument, bearing in mind the links with other related criminal activities".[1]

For the purposes of this activity, witnesses are tentatively defined as persons, irrespective of their status under national criminal procedural law, who possess information relevant to criminal proceedings. *"Pentiti"* are taken to mean "collaborators of justice", and are tentatively defined as persons who face criminal charges, or were convicted, of having taken part in an association of criminals or other criminal organisation of any kind, or in organised crime offences, but agree to co-operate with criminal justice authorities, particularly by giving information about the criminal association or organisation or any criminal offence connected with organised crime.[2]

---

[1] See document PC-PW (2003)1.

[2] As defined in Recommendation No. R(97)13 of the Committee of Ministers concerning intimidation of witnesses and the rights of the defence. In the Explanatory Memorandum to this Recommendation, it is explained that the term "Collaborators of justice" is used in the Recommendation in a narrow sense: these persons have knowledge of the structures and activities of criminal organisations, their links with other local or foreign criminal groups, and they are accused or convicted of having taken part in criminal offences (cf. European Union Resolution 95/C 327/04). The testimony of such persons is crucial in most organised crime cases for obtaining evidence concerning the offences committed by the organisation. The collaborating person may become eligible for certain protection measures in view of the collaboration. These measures may take different forms, such as a special penitentiary regime, admission to a witness protection programme, material compensation, and so on. Recommendation Rec(2001)11 of the Committee of Ministers concerning guiding principles on the fight against organised crime indicates that "member States should provide effective, physical and other, protection for witnesses and collaborators of justice who require such protection because they have given or agreed to provide information and/or give testimony or other evidence in relation to organised crime. Similarly, such protection measures should be available for those who participate in or have agreed to participate in the investigation or the prosecution of organised crime as well as for the relatives and associates of the individuals who require protection."

Questions

a. *General information*

1. Please describe the framework (legal provisions and established practice) governing the use of measures protecting witnesses and *pentiti*.
2. Please describe the framework (legal provisions and established practice) governing the use of measures encouraging witnesses and *pentiti* to co-operate with justice.
3. Can measures/benefits encouraging the co-operation of witnesses and *pentiti* be used in combination with protection measures (arrangements concerning trial proceedings, sentencing conditions, special penitentiary regimes, etc.)? If so, please specify and indicate under which conditions they are applied.
4. For which kind of crime and under which circumstances can witness and *pentiti* protection be applied? Can the measures be extended to the relatives or other persons close to the witness/*pentito*?
5. What urgent measures (e.g. immediate relocation to a secret place) can be taken in order to protect witnesses and *pentiti*?
6. Which institutions are involved in the protection of witnesses and *pentiti* and what is their role (e.g. law enforcement agencies, special independent agencies, prosecutor's offices, judicial authorities, etc.)? How does co-operation between the relevant institutions work in practice?
7. Are there any specific provisions governing the protection of witnesses and *pentiti* in relation to acts of terrorism? If so, please specify. Are there any specialised counter-terrorism institutions? If so, what is their role in the protection of witnesses and *pentiti* in relation to acts of terrorism?
8. How does the framework governing the use of measures protecting witnesses and *pentiti* and encouraging them to co-operate with justice guarantee respect for human rights and individual freedoms?[3] Please indicate the procedures in place, if any, to monitor compliance with human rights standards.

"Member states should adopt appropriate measures to ensure, both within and outside the country of trial, the protection of witnesses prior to, during or after criminal proceedings." See document PC-PW(2003)4.

[3] For example, the principle of equality of arms, the principle of proportionality, the rights of the defence, the rights of witnesses and victims, etc.

b. Procedural measures

9.   At which stage(s), and in which context, is it possible for witnesses and *pentiti* to benefit from procedural measures of protection?

10.   Is there the possibility for witnesses and *pentiti* to obtain legal assistance at this(these) stage(s)?

11.   Are there alternative methods of giving evidence which allow the protection of witnesses and *pentiti* from intimidation resulting from face to face confrontation with the accused? If yes, please specify (e.g. full or partial anonymity, video-conference, disguise, exclusion of the defendant from the courtroom when the witness is giving evidence, exclusion of the media or the public from the trial, etc.) and indicate under which conditions these methods are used.

12.   On which grounds and on the basis of which criteria can anonymity be granted? Is there the possibility to obtain legal assistance at this stage?

13.   Are pre-trial statements of witnesses and *pentiti* and testimonies of anonymous witnesses and *pentiti* regarded as valid evidence? If yes, under which conditions?

14.   Is it possible, and if so, under which conditions, to use information provided by "*pentiti*"? How is their credibility assessed?

15.   Which are the opportunities for the defence to exercise its rights, including the right of the accused to challenge the witness'/*pentito*'s credibility in criminal proceedings (including at the pre-trial stage) and the respect of the "equality of arms" principle?

c. Non-procedural measures

16.   At which stage(s), and in which context, is it possible for witnesses and *pentiti* to benefit from a protection programme?

17.   Is there the possibility for witnesses and *pentiti* to obtain legal assistance at this(these) stage(s)?

18.   What is the procedure for admittance to a protection programme? Please specify, in particular, who takes the initiative, the criteria for admittance, the assessment of the relevance of a testimony and how admittance to the programme is formalised.

19.   Please indicate the measures that can be adopted for the protection of witnesses and *pentiti* (e.g. surveillance of the residence, physical protection, protection of personal records, relocation, change of identity, subsidies, assistance in job search, relocation of a detainee to another prison or to special units).

20.   What can the duration of a protection programme be? Which are the procedures for assessing the degree of danger for the witnesses/*pentiti* and their compliance with the obligations of the programme? Is it possible to challenge a decision of suspension, revocation or termination of a protection programme?

d. International co-operation

21. Which measures (e.g. use of modern telecommunications means, assistance in relocating protected witnesses, exchange of information between witness protection authorities) have been adopted in the context of mutual legal assistance in order to facilitate international co-operation? How are the financial implications of international co-operation activities dealt with?

22. Has your country entered international (bilateral or multilateral) agreements on the protection of witnesses and *pentiti*? If so, please indicate what kind of provisions they include.

23. How can international co-operation in the field of the protection of witnesses and *pentiti* be improved?

e. Statistics

24. How many people currently benefit from witness or *pentiti* protection measures/programmes, and for how long? How many of them are foreign people? If the measures/programmes can be extended to relatives and other close persons, please indicate (and, if possible, specify the relationship with the witness/*pentito*) how many people are included in this category. Please also provide figures on the different kinds of measures (procedural and non-procedural) adopted, and on the number of cases involving international co-operation.

f. Proposals and comments

25. Please provide any comments/proposals concerning the implementation of the terms of reference of the PC-PW and, in particular, instruments to be adopted to strengthen the protection of witnesses and *pentiti*.

Armenia

1.   The legal protection of witnesses and *pentiti* is regulated by the criminal procedure legislation of the Republic of Armenia.

According to Article 98 of the Criminal Procedure Code of the Republic of Armenia (hereinafter CPC) protection is provided not only to witnesses, but also to victims, defendants, defenders and other persons participating in criminal proceedings.

In accordance with that Article, if the authority implementing criminal proceedings establishes that the above-mentioned persons need to be protected from the encroachments prohibited by criminal law, that authority, at the request of such persons or on its own initiative, shall take the necessary protection measures for those persons by issuing the relevant order.

Moreover, if the persons participating in criminal proceedings or their close relatives have been threatened with physical violence or with the destruction of their property or with violent actions against them due to their participation in the criminal proceedings, the application of protective measures by the authority implementing criminal proceedings is mandatory. If the latter refuses to apply protective measures, then the witness, the accused, the injured party or any other person participating in the criminal proceedings may obtain a judicial order for protective measures.

Article 99 of the CPC prescribes, *inter alia*, the following protection measures:
a)   Official warning of the possible imposition of criminal liability from the court or prosecutor to any person threatening the use of violence or of another action prohibited by criminal law;
b)   Restriction of access to information regarding the person under protection;
c)   Provision of security to the person under protection.

The provision of security to the protected person may consist in the application of one or more of the following measures:
a)   Provision of a personal escort to the protected person or his/her relative(s);
b)   Guarding of the protected person's residence or of property owned or used by him/her;
c)   Temporary relocation of the protected person to a place where his/her security can be ensured;
d)   Transfer of a detained person to a facility where his/her security can be ensured.

The above-mentioned protective measures can be applied as they become necessary, by a decision of the authority implementing criminal proceedings as long as such a necessity exists. The protective measures are terminated by a motivated decision of the authority implementing criminal proceedings.

This means that protective measures can be applied at any stage of the criminal proceedings. It should be noted that even if a decision is taken to remove the protective measures, these measures can be re-implemented if, after their removal, the person is again subjected to a threat or assault or if there are other circumstances requiring the application of protective measures which did not previously exist.

The enforcement of protective measures can be combined with judicial actions or be accompanied by them without detriment to the efficiency of the protective measures.

Protective measures can be implemented in respect of any crime (the circumstances are mentioned above) and, as mentioned above, also with respect to the close relatives of witnesses and *pentiti*. In accordance with Article 6, paragraph 40, of the CPC, close relatives are considered to be: parents, children, adoptive parents, adopted children, siblings or step-siblings, grandparents and grandchildren, and the spouse and his/her parents.

An official warning is given to any person threatening the use of violence or other actions prohibited under criminal law: he/she is summoned to the prosecutor, the investigator or an inquest officer, who gives him/her an official warning. A record of the official warning must be drawn up, and the record must be signed by the person who has been warned.

When the protection measure applied is a restriction on access to information about the protected person, all the information on this person is removed from the criminal case materials and kept separately from the main file.

The materials separated from the main file are accessible only to the court and the criminal prosecution authorities; the other participants in the trial may view them only with the permission of the authority implementing criminal proceedings, if this is necessary to find any material circumstances necessary for the protection of the suspect or the accused.

At the request of the authority who has made the decision to implement protection measures in respect of the protected person, the competent state authorities (such as internal affairs, national security or penal institutions) may be involved in applying the protection measures required for the security of the protected person.

In the Republic of Armenia there are no special laws which regulate the protection of witnesses and *pentiti* in relation to acts of terrorism. A structural division of the National Security Service is a specialised counter-terrorism structure whose activities are implemented in accordance with the legislation of the Republic of Armenia and with the Charter of its National Security Service.

2. The legislation of the Republic of Armenia does not consider the witness as a participant in a criminal proceeding requiring legal assistance. Such assistance is provided only to the suspect or the accused, while the witness does not fall into the category of persons who require legal assistance from the state as he/she is not subject to criminal prosecution. The witness is personally responsible for testifying on the circumstances and facts that are known to him/her (Article 86 of the CPC).

If the witness has not yet reached the age of 14, then his/her legal representative has the right to know about his/her principal being summoned to the authority implementing criminal proceedings and to accompany him/her during the investigation or judicial action.

The legal representative has the right to take part in the investigation and in any other judicial actions and:
a)   to file motions;
b)   to object to the actions of the authorities implementing the criminal proceedings;
c)   to object to the actions of the person presiding over the trial;
d)   to review the records of the investigation and other judicial actions in which he/she has taken part during the pre-trial proceedings and make comments on the accuracy and completeness of such records.

With the permission of the authority implementing the criminal proceedings, the legal representative of a minor above 14 years of age may enjoy the above-mentioned rights.

In addition, the witness (or his/her legal representative) may, at his/her own initiative and at any time, receive legal aid from a lawyer or any other person in relation to his/her testimony, but prior to any procedural action in which he/she participates. This means that the witness must personally give the authorities implementing the criminal proceedings any evidence or information on the circumstances that he/she knows about that criminal case.

A pentito has the right to a counsel at any time (from the moment he/she is arrested, detained, or arraigned, according to Article 40 of the Constitution of the Republic of Armenia and Articles 63 and 65 of the CPC): a *pentito* has the right to a lawyer at his/her own discretion. Moreover, Article 69 of the

Code prescribes the instances in which the presence of a defence attorney is obligatory. These include instances where the *pentito* expresses such a wish; it is difficult for him/her to exercise the right to counsel, or he/she is insane or has a temporary mental disorder, he/she has no command or insufficient knowledge of the language of the criminal proceedings, or he/she was a minor at the time of the crime, as well as in a number of other instances.

The mandatory involvement of a defence counsel is ensured by the authority implementing criminal proceedings.

The examination of the witness is carried out by the authority implementing criminal proceedings separately from the other witnesses, in the place where the preliminary investigation is conducted or where the witness is located (Article 206 of the CPC). A witness can be confronted with another witness if their statements contain essential contradictions. Such confrontation may also be conducted if there are essential discrepancies between the testimonies of the accused and another person (Article 216 of the CPC). Furthermore, the witness is warned that he/she will be subject to liability for refusal to testify, evasion of testimony or perjury, as well as about the right to refuse to testify against his/her spouse or a close relative (perjury and refusal to give evidence by the witness or injured party during the preliminary investigation or the trial are deemed offences against justice which are punishable by a fine, corrective labour or detention under the Criminal Code of the Republic of Armenia (Articles 338-339 of the new Criminal Code).

The *pentito* has the right to refuse to testify (point 6 of Part 2 of Article 65 of the CPC). Prior to the interrogation, the investigator informs the *pentito* of his/her right to refuse to testify (Article 212 of the CPC).

A witness under 14 years of age or, at the discretion of the investigator, under 16 years of age, is interrogated in the presence of his/her legal representative (Article 207 of the CPC). The interrogation of a deaf, mute or blind witness or *pentito* is conducted in the presence of a translator who understands his/her signs or sign language. If the witness has a mental illness or any other severe illness, the interrogation is conducted with the permission of a physician and in his/her presence (Articles 208 and 212 of the CPC).

The accused is interrogated separately from the other persons involved in the case. The investigator takes measures to prevent the accused from communicating with the other persons involved in the case. He/she is entitled to be interrogated in the presence of counsel.

In accordance with point 9 of Article 62 of the Criminal Code, the *pentito* shall be subject to a lesser penalty for his/her offence than a person who has not expressed regret for his/her offence. This Article also considers as a *pentito* any person who, after the commission of a crime, has given him/herself up to the criminal investigative bodies or has contributed to the detection of the committed crime, the identification of his/her accomplices or has assisted in a search of the property acquired by the crime.

Furthermore, point 4 of Article 217 of the Criminal Code determines that a person who has participated in the preparation of a terrorist act is released from criminal liability if he/she contributes to the prevention of the terrorist act by informing the authorities or by other means and his/her actions do not contain other *corpus delicti*.

The *pentito* has the right to write his/her testimonies him/herself (Article 214 of the CPC).

A person who implements proceedings with respect to a witness or *pentito* may issue a subpoena if he/she, having been duly summoned by the authority implementing criminal proceedings, fails to come to the investigator or prosecutor without reasonable grounds. The person who has issued the subpoena must make a motivated decision to be executed by the preliminary investigation body (Article 153 of the CPC).

The security of witnesses and *pentiti* is provided for by the law on human rights and freedoms. It is clear from the above that a person conducting a criminal case is obliged to take protective measures, which must be based on the circumstances expressly stated by law. This means that without legal grounds the person who conducts the proceedings cannot decide to take protective measures against a person who has not threatened the witness or *pentito* or has not otherwise intimidated the witness or *pentito* into evading assisting with the investigation or trial.

3. The presence of the *pentito* at trial is obligatory. His/her absence adjourns the trial (Articles 302-303 of the CPC).

Once the presence of the summoned persons has been verified, the witnesses are separated to the rooms allocated to them (Articles 318-319 of the CPC).

Once the trial has begun and the plea of the defendant and the views of the parties to the trial have been heard, the person presiding over the case firstly invites the defendant to testify on the accusation and the other circumstances of the case, notifying the defendant that his/her testimony is not obligatory and his/her refusal to testify cannot be used against him.

After the testimony of the defendant, he/she is examined first by his/her counsel, by the other defendants and their counsels, by the civil defendant and his/her representative, and then by the prosecution, the injured party, the civil plaintiff and his/her representative (Article 333-336 of the CPC).

During the investigation, before the examination, the defendant is informed of his/her right to refuse to testify against him/herself, his/her spouse or close relatives. He/she is also informed that the defendant will be subject to liability for refusing to testify, for evading testimony or for perjury.

A witness under 16 years of age need not be notified about liability for refusal to testify or for evading testimony or perjury because he/she is not subject to such liability.

Witnesses are examined separately from each other and in the absence of any witnesses who have not yet been examined.

The summoned witness is examined first by the prosecution, then by the defence and thereafter by the court.

A witness that is called at the request of one of the parties is examined first by that party, then by other persons in that party and thereafter by the representatives of the other party and the court.

The examination of a minor may take place without the presence of the defendant, if this is necessary to obtain a full picture of the case and to allow an objective and comprehensive analysis.

After his/her return to the court room, the testimonies of witnesses who are minors are published for the defendant and he/she is given an opportunity to ask questions and give evidence regarding the facts told by witness (Articles 339-341 of the CPC).

The Code does not envisage the opportunity for witnesses and *pentiti* to testify anonymously.

4. The Republic of Armenia has signed international agreements on mutual assistance in legal matters with Bulgaria, Georgia, Greece and Romania, as well as with the Commonwealth of Independent States (CIS) (CIS Convention on Legal Assistance and Legal Relations in Civil, Family and Criminal Matters of 1993).

These agreements set out the possibilities for criminal extradition. Extradition is undertaken by authorised bodies which are responsible for convicts' security and transfer from one country to another. The expenses for transfer are covered by the party that has requested extradition.

The extradited person cannot be called to account for crimes committed before he/she crossed the border of one party if his/her extradition is not a result of such actions.

Some of the above-mentioned agreements (Bulgaria, Greece, CIS Convention) envisage that the authorised bodies of the parties can call witnesses situated in the territory of the other parties.

The witness him/herself decides whether to travel to the territory of another country in response to a judicial call; if he/she does not wish to travel to the territory of the other country to participate in the criminal proceedings, then he/she cannot be compelled to do so.

If the witness does decide to participate, the party who has requested the call covers all the expenses of the witness. The witness travels independently, and the above-mentioned agreements do not envisage that the authorised bodies of the party requesting the call shall undertake appropriate measures to provide necessary security for him/her. These issues are regulated by the national legislation of the parties to these agreements, and we have already described above how these issues are regulated by the legislation of the Republic of Armenia.

The Republic of Armenia also is a Party to the European Convention on Extradition.

In order to improve international co-operation in the field of the protection of witnesses and *pentiti*, it would be necessary to develop and draft an appropriate multilateral agreement and present it for ratification by the Council of Europe member states. It would be reasonable to determine defence measures in this agreement and require that these measures be laid down in the national legislations of the member states.

Austria

a. *General information*

1. Please describe the framework (legal provisions and established practice) governing the use of measures protecting witnesses and *pentiti*.

In Austria there exists no distinction between *pentiti* and witnesses. First of all, protective measures in this area are incumbent on the police authorities. The legal basis for the protection of witnesses has been adopted according to the Council Resolutions of 23 November 1995 on the Protection of Witnesses in the fight against international organised crime and of 20 December 1996 on individuals who co-operate with the judicial process in the fight against international organised crime. Witness protection is seen as a security police task, which is regulated in the Austrian Security Police Law (Sicherheitspolizeigesetz – SPG). To avoid possible misunderstandings, it has to be pointed out in this context, that according to the Austrian legal system the notion of Security Police only refers to the maintenance of quiescence, order and security and to the common duty to render first assistance (see Section 3 of the Austrian Security Police Law).

If there are good reasons for the assumption that a witness might be a target for a punishable offence directed against his/her life, health or against his/her personal liberty, the police is obliged to inform the endangered witness and to take the protective measures required by the situation (Section 22, paragraph 4, of the Austrian Security Police Law). Furthermore, the security authorities are entrusted with the protection of any person who might be able to disclose information about a dangerous attack or a criminal association and will therefore be particularly at risk and – if necessary – with the protection of the relatives of such people (see Section 22, paragraph 1, No. 5 of the Austrian Security Police Law especially in connection with Section 54a of the Austrian Security Police Law).

As a matter of principle, measures to protect endangered witnesses within the scope of criminal procedure include provisions to hear witnesses whose identity is not disclosed, to allow the pre-trial records of the cross-examination of witnesses and to hear the cases *in camera*. These measures pursue protective interests whilst respecting the requirement for the trial to be held in public.

Apart from combating terrorism, Austria has always been a pioneer in the field of the protection of children as victims and witnesses. Since 1993, the Austrian Code of Criminal Procedure has provided the possibility for videotaped testimonies, usually conducted by an expert, to be used in court. These new instruments have proved to be very worthwhile in that they allow the examination of vulnerable witnesses to be carried out in a particularly careful, respectful and thorough manner. A child witness is questioned only once, if the prosecutor and the accused (with his/her defendant) participated in the interrogation before the trial.

Section 162a, paragraph 1, of the Austrian Code of Criminal Procedure provides for the pre-trial examination of witnesses if there is a risk that the examination of a witness at the trial will be impossible for reasons of fact or of law. In this case the investigating judge has to give the prosecutor, the defendant and the defence counsel the opportunity to take part in the examination and to interrogate the witness.

In order to avoid the repeated examination of victims of sexual offences, the Penal Code Amending Act of 1998, Federal Law Gazette I No. 153, introduced the obligation to conduct such examinations at an early stage of the proceedings (pre-trial stage). Section 162a, paragraph 2, of the Austrian Code of Criminal Procedure takes into consideration the protection of the witness's interests in view of his/her age, psychological condition or health. The investigating judge, in protecting those interests, may restrict the opportunity to participate in the examination in such a way that the prosecutor, the defendant and the defence counsel follow the examination and interrogate the witness in a separate room using audio-visual equipment.

A psychological expert can conduct such a "restricted examination". It is very beneficial for a child to be interrogated by such an expert without being present in the courtroom. In order to ensure that the child will not be traumatised the psychologist can modify the questions of the judge into a child's language. All courts are equipped with technical equipment so that videotaped testimonies are commonly used now. The fact that a record of the examination can be read out or shown during the trial guarantees that the examination need not be repeated (after such an examination the witness has the right to refuse to testify again; see Sections 152, paragraph 1, sub-paragraphs 2a and 3, and 162a, paragraph 3, of the Austrian Code of Criminal Procedure).

Taking into account the need to strike a fair balance between the protection of the rights of the defence and the protection of the life and safety of witnesses and their relatives, the graduated protection of witnesses is provided by Sections 166, paragraph 1, and 166a of the Austrian Code of Criminal Procedure.

Pursuant to Section 166, paragraph 1, of the Austrian Code of Criminal Procedure the personal data of witnesses, with the exception of the statement of their name and an eventual relationship to the accused or others involved, are to be recorded in the minutes in such a way that such personal data are not disclosed in the presence of third persons. This protection of the personal sphere of witnesses is to be observed in particular in the trial on indictment (Section 248, paragraph 1, of the Austrian Code of Criminal Procedure).

Furthermore, during the first interrogation on his/her personal data, a witness is allowed to declare another address, suitable for the serving of a summons, instead of his/her permanent residence. These provisions are designed to provide for the reasonable risk of witnesses' exposing themselves or their relatives to danger by declaring their personal data and location in public.

If there is a risk that, because of certain facts, the witness would expose him/herself or another person to a grave danger to his/her life, health or personal liberty, Section 166a of the Austrian Code of Criminal Procedure entitles the judge to exempt the witness from any depositions on his/her personal identity or from answering any other questions allowing the witness's identity to be discovered. This provision also allows a witness to remain anonymous at the court conducting the proceedings.

According to the Austrian Constitution (principle of fair trial subject to Article 6, paragraph 3d, of the ECHR), Section 166a of the Austrian Code of Criminal Procedure, as well as a ministerial order of the Federal Ministry of Justice, it is common practice, on the above-mentioned conditions, for witnesses to be allowed to disguise themselves, by wearing wigs, sunglasses, etc.

Any witness, independent of his/her age, may testify in the absence of the accused. Section 250, paragraph 1, of the Austrian Code of Criminal Procedure entitles the judge to banish the accused from the courtroom exceptionally while a witness is testifying.

The witness's protection can be reinforced during the trial by testifying anonymously in a separate room using a video-recorder (Section 250, paragraph 3, of the Austrian Code of Criminal Procedure). In such a case, the witness is examined by the other members of the court, the prosecutor and the defence counsel with the help of a monitor.

Moreover, there is the possibility to conduct the questioning by means of video-conferencing if such a witness is unable to appear in court (to attend the trial) without exposing him/herself to a grave danger (Section 247a, paragraph 1, of the Austrian Code of Criminal Procedure).

According to Article 90, paragraph 1, of the Austrian Constitution and Article 6, paragraph 1, of the European Convention on Human Rights, all court proceedings are public, unless otherwise provided by statute. Thus, all criminal trials are, within technical limits, generally open to all unarmed adults. Audio and video-recorders and cameras are not permitted. Section 229, paragraph 2, of the Austrian Code of Criminal Procedure provides for the possibility of excluding the public from the court during the examination of endangered witnesses.

Taking into account the possibility that the probative value of an anonymous witness's statement may be reduced, the court is obliged to consider carefully how the secrecy of the personal data of the witness examined affects the probative value of such a witness (Section 258, paragraph 3, and Section 323, paragraph 2, of the Austrian Code of Criminal Procedure).

2. **Please describe the framework (legal provisions and established practice) governing the use of measures encouraging witnesses and *pentiti* to co-operate with justice.**

In connection with the fight against organised crime, the necessity has emerged in Austria, as it has everywhere, to protect endangered witnesses as well as *pentiti* against intimidation. Although there are several measures for protecting vulnerable witnesses in Austria and encouraging them to give evidence, there is no possibility for granting such witnesses full or limited immunity before the Austrian jurisdiction. The facility of granting a witness exemption from punishment in return for his/her co-operating with justice is unknown in the Austrian Code of Criminal Procedure.

It is only possible to reduce the penalties of an accused person who co-operates with the law enforcement and justice authorities in the investigation or prosecution of an offence in the field of organised crime. This possibility is laid down in Section 41a of the Austrian Penal Code (the so-called quasi crown witness provision):

"Section 41a

(1) If the perpetrator of a criminal offence punishable under Sections 277, 278, 278a or 278b or of a criminal offence connected with a conspiracy, association or organisation informs a prosecution authority about facts which contribute essentially:

1. to removing or reducing considerably the dangers arising from the conspiracy, association or organisation;

2. to promoting the clearing up of such an offence in addition to his/her own complicity; or

3. to finding a person who participated in such a conspiracy in a leading position or had a leading position in such an association or organisation;

his/her sentence may be reduced to under the legal minimum penalty under Section 41 if this is adequate given the significance of the disclosed facts compared with the guilt of the perpetrator. Section 41, paragraph 3, is applicable *mutatis mutandis*.

(2) Paragraph 1 applies *mutatis mutandis* to the participant in a conspiracy, association or organisation punishable under the prohibition law or to the perpetrator of a criminal offence connected with such a conspiracy, association or organisation.

(3) In the case where the knowledge of the perpetrator relates to criminal offences to which the Austrian penal laws are not applicable, paragraph 1 shall apply nevertheless so far as legal assistance would be admissible."

(As amended by Federal Law Gazette I No. 105/1997 and most recently by Federal Law Gazette I No. 134/2002).

"Section 278 – Criminal association

(1) A person who founds a criminal association or participates in such an association as a member is to be sentenced to imprisonment of up to three years.

(2) A criminal association is a union planned for a long period of time of more than two persons aimed at the commission of one or more crimes by one or more members of the association, other considerable acts of violence against life and limb and not only minor damage to property, theft, fraud or misdemeanours under Sections 104a, 165, 177b, 223 to 239, 241a to 241c, 241e, 241f, 304 or 307 or under Sections 104 or 105 of the Aliens Act.

(3) A member of a criminal association who commits a criminal offence within the scope of its criminal orientation or participates in its activities by providing information or assets or in another way with the awareness that he/she thereby promotes the association or its criminal acts.

(4) If the association does not commit to a planned criminal offence, no member shall be punished if the association dissolves itself voluntarily or if it is clear from its conduct that it has given up its plan voluntarily. Furthermore a person who withdraws voluntarily from the association before a planned offence is committed or attempted shall not be punished for criminal association. A person who participates in the association in a leading position shall not be punished for criminal association only if he/she ensures that the danger presented by the association is removed by informing the authorities (Section 151, paragraph 3) or in another way."

(As amended by Federal Law Gazette I No. 134/2002 and most recently by Federal Law Gazette I No. 15/2004)

"Section 278a – Criminal organisation

Whoever establishes an association of a considerable number of persons, intended to last for a long period of time and similar to an enterprise, or who participates in such an association as a member (Section 278, paragraph 3), shall be liable to imprisonment for a term of six months to five years if the association:

1. is oriented, even if not exclusively, towards the repeated and planned commission of grave offences against life and limb, freedom, or property, or of grave offences relating to the sexual exploitation of human beings, smuggling of aliens, illegal trafficking in military weapons, nuclear and radioactive material, dangerous waste, counterfeit money or drugs, and

2. aims at profits on a high scale or at considerable influence on politics or economy, and

3. undertakes to corrupt, or intimidate, others, or to particularly protect itself against prosecution measures.

Section 278, paragraph 4, shall apply *mutatis mutandis*.

Section 278b – Terrorist association

(1) A person who leads a terrorist association (paragraph 3) is to be sentenced to imprisonment from five to fifteen years. A person who leads a terrorist association that confines itself to threatening terrorist offences (Section 278c, paragraph 1) is to be sentenced to imprisonment from one year to ten years.

(2) A person who participates in a terrorist association as a member (Section 278, paragraph 3) is to be sentenced to imprisonment from one year to ten years.

(3) A terrorist association is a union planned for a long period of time of more than two persons aimed at the commission of one or more terrorist criminal offences (Section 278c) by one or more members of the association."

(As amended by Federal Law Gazette I No. 134/2002)

<u>For the sake of completeness:</u>

According to Section 34, paragraph 1, No. 16 and 17 of the Austrian Penal Code, it would constitute a special mitigating ground in the sentencing, if the perpetrator surrendered to the police when it would have been easy for him/her to escape or if he/she made a confession or if he/she contributed considerably to the establishment of the truth.

3. **Can measures/benefits encouraging the co-operation of witnesses and *pentiti* be used in combination with protection measures (arrangements concerning trial proceedings, sentencing conditions, special penitentiary regimes, etc.)? If so, please specify and indicate under which conditions they are applied.**

These measures can be implemented in connection with judicial authorities and law enforcement. However, as mentioned above (question 2), there is no possibility in Austria to grant a witness exemption from punishment in the case of co-operation with justice. Apart from the possibility laid down in Section 41a of the Austrian Penal Code, which assumes a certain kind of perpetrator (perpetrator of a criminal offence punishable under Sections 277, 278, 278a or 278b or of a criminal offence connected with such a conspiracy, association or organisation), no special sentencing conditions or special penitentiary regimes for witnesses and *pentiti* are foreseen in the Austrian Penal Law.

4. **For which kind of crime and under which circumstances can witness and *pentito* protection be applied? Can the measures be extended to the relatives or other persons close to the witness/*pentito*?**

Witness protection is only foreseen in cases involving serious crime (organised crime and terrorism). If the admission criteria are fulfilled, besides the protected person, his/her close relatives can also be admitted to the programme.

Apart from terrorism, there is no restriction on the type of case. Witnesses are given protection if they need it (in most cases children and victims of sexual offences). Please see the reply to question 1.

5. **What urgent measures (e.g. immediate relocation to a secret place) can be taken in order to protect witnesses and *pentiti*?**

In the first instance, the main measure is to relocate the protected person, although it is also possible to provide him/her with personal protection at his/her place of residence.

6. **Which institutions are involved in the protection of witnesses and** *pentiti* **and what is their role (e.g. law enforcement agencies, special independent agencies, prosecutor's offices, judicial authorities, etc.)? How does co-operation between the relevant institutions work in practice?**

Regarding protection measures, the security authorities have exclusive competence. In the scope of the whole witness protection programme, competence is given both to the judicial and the law enforcement authorities. The law enforcement authorities decide whether a person will be admitted to the programme.

Combating terrorism in general lies within the competence of the Ministry of the Interior, more precisely the Federal Agency for State Protection and Counterterrorism, whereas protection of source, even in relation to terrorist activities, is provided by the competent special branch of the Federal Criminal Office. The Ministry of the Interior informs the Ministry of Justice about relocated *pentiti* in Austria, but otherwise the Ministry of Justice is not the competent authority for questions relating to the relocation of protected witnesses.

7. **Are there any specific provisions governing the protection of witnesses and** *pentiti* **in relation to acts of terrorism? If so, please specify. Are there any specialised counter-terrorism institutions? If so, what is their role in the protection of witnesses and** *pentiti* **in relation to acts of terrorism?**

There are no special legal provisions for the protection of source in connection with terrorist activities and there exists no special terrorism witness protection service. However, pursuant to Section 22, paragraph 1, No. 5 in connection with Section 54a of the Austrian Security Police Law, the security authorities have been entrusted with providing particular protection to any person who might be able to disclose information about a dangerous attack or a criminal association and who will, therefore, be especially endangered.

8. **How does the framework governing the use of measures protecting witnesses and** *pentiti* **and encouraging them to co-operate with justice guarantee respect for human rights and individual freedoms? Please indicate the procedures in place, if any, to monitor compliance with human rights standards.**

The witness protection programme is based on the willingness of the protected person and may be terminated without further declared reasons at any time.

b. Procedural measures

9. At which stage(s), and in which context, is it possible for witnesses and *pentiti* to benefit from procedural measures of protection?

In principle it is possible for witnesses and *pentiti* to benefit from measures of protection at any stage of the proceedings. For example, as already mentioned under question 1, "restricted examinations" of victims of sexual offences take place at a pre-trial stage in order to avoid repeated examinations.

10. Is there the possibility for witnesses and *pentiti* to obtain legal assistance at this (these) stage(s)?

As a matter of principle, all authorities active in criminal proceedings (including the police) are obliged to inform witnesses and *pentiti* about their rights and to take into account their interests, especially with regard to the protection of privacy.

The legal situation of witnesses who are crime victims was improved to a considerable extent by a governmental bill, which was introduced into Parliament recently and entered into force on 1 January 2006 (thus anticipating the improvement of the situation of crime victims by the "Strafprozessreformgesetz", Federal Law Gazette I No. 19/2004, which will enter into force on 1 January 2008 and represents a complete reorganisation of the pre-trial phase of criminal proceedings as regulated in the Austrian Code of Criminal Procedure).

However, besides this amendment, multi-disciplinary support is available for certain witnesses. Besides information and legal advice, several institutions provide temporary shelter as well as psychological, social and financial assistance. For instance, a psychologist supports children when they are examined. A non-profit association called "Weißer Ring" which supports crime victims financially or with legal advice and information about therapy, should be mentioned in this context.

Furthermore, according to the Crime Victims Act (Verbrechensopfergesetz – VOG), which has been recently amended by Federal Law Gazette I No. 48/2005, victims of intentionally committed offences are entitled to economic compensation and social benefits (like psychological care) under certain conditions.

Witnesses, who are crime victims, can find important information on the homepage of the Austrian Federal Ministry of Justice (www.bmj.gv.at or www.justiz.gv.at): http://www.justiz.gv.at/_cms_upload/_docs/opferschutz.pdf.

Please also see the reply to question 18.

11. **Are there alternative methods of giving evidence which allow the protection of witnesses and** *pentiti* **from intimidation resulting from face to face confrontation with the accused? If yes, please specify (e.g. full or partial anonymity, video-conference, disguise, exclusion of the defendant from the courtroom when the witness is giving evidence, exclusion of the media or the public from the trial, etc.) and indicate under which conditions these methods are used.**

and

12. **On which grounds and on the basis of which criteria can anonymity be granted? Is there the possibility to obtain legal assistance at this stage?**

Please see the reply to question 1.

13. **Are pre-trial statements of witnesses and** *pentiti* **and testimonies of anonymous witnesses and** *pentiti* **regarded as valid evidence? If yes, under which conditions?**

Yes, pre-trial statements of witnesses and *pentiti* and testimonies of anonymous witnesses and *pentiti* are regarded as valid evidence, if the parties have had the opportunity to be part of the examination and to examine the witness. Otherwise the witness must be re-examined in the trial (principle of immediacy – Section 252, paragraph 1, of the Austrian Code of Criminal Procedure). Additionally, according to Section 258, paragraph 3, and Section 323, paragraph 2, of the Austrian Code of Criminal Procedure, the court is obliged to consider carefully if the secrecy of the personal data of the witness examined affects the probative value of such a witness. That is, the judges have to take into account the possibility that the probative value of an anonymous witness's statement may be reduced.

Please also see the reply to question 15.

14. **Is it possible, and if so, under which conditions, to use information provided by** *"pentiti"***? How is their credibility assessed?**

Yes, in Austria it is possible to use information provided by *"pentiti"*, if they are able to testify in the trial or if the parties of the proceedings examined them in the pre-trial stage.

Please see the reply to question 15.

15. Which are the opportunities for the defence to exercise its rights, including the right of the accused to challenge the witness'/*pentito*'s credibility in criminal proceedings (including at the pre-trial stage) and the respect of the "equality of arms" principle?

Please see the reply to question 1 (Section 162a, paragraph 1, of the Austrian Code of Criminal Procedure: pre-trial examination of witnesses; the investigating judge has to give the prosecutor, the defendant and the defence counsel the opportunity to take part in the examination and to interrogate the witness; Section 250, paragraph 3, of the Austrian Code of Criminal Procedure: the defence counsel is allowed to examine the witness with the help of a monitor; Section 258, paragraph 3 and Section 323, paragraph 2, of the Austrian Code of Criminal Procedure).

According to the Austrian Constitution (principle of fair trial subject to Article 6, paragraph 3d, of the European Convention on Human Rights), Section 166a of the Austrian Code of Criminal Procedure as well as a decree of the Federal Ministry of Justice, it is common practice for witnesses to be able to change their looks, for example by wearing wigs, etc. However, the rights of the defence must be ensured by providing an adequate personal impression of the witness and his/her visual expressions. Therefore further measures to provide anonymity, such as the distortion of his/her voice, cannot be based upon Section 166a of the Austrian Criminal Procedure Code. His/her figure, voice, body language and gestures must be sufficiently apparent ("non verbal communication") for an evaluation of his/her credibility to be possible in the context of assessment of evidence. Witnesses are not allowed to give evidence totally disguised or masked (for instance while wearing a boiler suit, gloves and a helmet so that no impression of his/her non-verbal communication is possible).

In order to give the above-mentioned common practice a legal basis, Section 162 of the Draft Act amending the Code of Criminal Procedure provides that an endangered witness can change his/her appearance (using wigs, etc.), but may not cover his/her face in such a way as to prevent a sufficient impression of his/her body language.

Concerning the framework (legal provisions and established practice) governing the use of measures encouraging witnesses and *pentiti* to co-operate with justice, see the reply to question 2.

c. Non-procedural measures

16. At which stage(s), and in which context, is it possible for witnesses and *pentiti* to benefit from a protection programme?

The witness protection measures can be applied from the beginning of the investigation and end when the reason for the danger no longer exists. This is also possible after the conclusion of a non-appealable procedure.

17. Is there the possibility for witnesses and *pentiti* to obtain legal assistance at this (these) stage(s)?

Access to the assistance of a lawyer is still possible at this stage of the procedure.

Please see the reply to question 10.

18. What is the procedure for admittance to a protection programme? Please specify, in particular, who takes the initiative, the criteria for admittance, the assessment of the relevance of a testimony and how admittance to the programme is formalised.

Initiative:
Judicial Authority or law enforcement.

Admission criteria:
relevant case of organised crime or terrorism, importance of the testimony, relevant danger, willingness and capability of the protected person.

Evaluation of the testimony:
1. done by the prosecutor.
2. done by the investigation authorities.

Admission procedure:
1. Conversation with the investigation authorities (law enforcement, collection of relevant information, contact with judicial authorities);

2. First contact with the witness (willingness), examination of the criteria and capacity evaluation;

3. Analysis (evaluation of the admission criteria);

4. Witness instruction/advice (admission of or objection to a witness by the law enforcement).

19. Please indicate the measures that can be adopted for the protection of witnesses and *pentiti* (e.g. surveillance of the residence, physical protection, protection of personal records, relocation, change of identity, subsidies, assistance in job search, relocation of a detainee to another prison or to special units).

The implemented measures are so complex that reference is only made to the most important ones, such as those mentioned in the questionnaire.

20. What can the duration of a protection programme be? Which are the procedures for assessing the degree of danger for the witnesses/*pentiti* and their compliance with the obligations of the programme? Is it possible to challenge a decision of suspension, revocation or termination of a protection programme?

The duration of the protection depends on the degree of danger of the protected person. If the threat to the witness is removed or reduced, he/she must be taken out of the protection programme. The level of danger is evaluated periodically in close co-operation with the investigation authorities.

Observance of the admission conditions is guaranteed by the permanent monitoring of the protected person by the witness protection service. The Austrian legal provisions foresee no right of appeal against a decision to remove a person from the witness protection programme.

d. *International co-operation*

21. Which measures (e.g. use of modern telecommunications means, assistance in relocating protected witnesses, exchange of information between witness protection authorities) have been adopted in the context of mutual legal assistance in order to facilitate international co-operation? How are the financial implications of international co-operation activities dealt with?

The measures are restricted primarily to resettlement, exchanges of information, protection at the place of residence, maintenance of recourse to public authorities (courts), etc. The sending state must cover the costs of the protected person. The personal costs for the witness protection service are covered by the state that admits the protected person to the programme.

22. Has your country entered international (bilateral or multilateral) agreements on the protection of witnesses and *pentiti*? If so, please indicate what kind of provisions they include.

So far, no bilateral or multilateral witness protection agreements have been concluded (except one with Hungary, which is under elaboration). Co-operation in the field of witness protection is on the basis of police secondment.

23. How can international co-operation in the field of the protection of witnesses and *pentiti* be improved?

One goal for the future, which should be envisaged, could be the harmonising of witness protection provisions in this area, in order to guarantee an efficient compliance procedure.

e. *Statistics*

24. How many people currently benefit from witness or *pentito* protection measures/programmes, and for how long? How many of them are foreign people? If the measures/programmes can be extended to relatives and other close persons, please indicate (and, if possible, specify the relationship with the witness/*pentito*) how many people are included in this category. Please also provide figures on the different kinds of measures (procedural and non-procedural) adopted, and on the number of cases involving international co-operation.

At present fifteen protected persons are in a witness protection programme, ten of these persons coming from abroad. Seven persons are close relatives in the sense of the questionnaire.

Eight witness protection cases are involved in criminal law proceedings. Out of these eight cases, seven refer to international proceedings.

f. *Proposals and comments*

25. Please provide any comments/proposals concerning the implementation of the terms of reference of the PC-PW and, in particular, instruments to be adopted to strengthen the protection of witnesses and *pentiti*.

Please refer to the concepts of Europol, which have been elaborated in the scope of expert meetings.

Azerbaijan

a. General information

1. Please describe the framework (legal provisions and established practice) governing the use of measures protecting witnesses and *pentiti*.

The fundamental legal provisions for the protection of witnesses and collaborators of justice are introduced in the Constitution of the Republic of Azerbaijan (1995) by Articles 12 (the highest priority objective of the state), 26 (protection of rights and freedoms of each person and citizen), and 31 (right to live in safety). Article 71 (guarantees of rights and freedoms of each person and citizen) imposes an absolute obligation on legislative, executive and judicial branches of power to protect the rights and freedoms of each person and citizen set out in the Constitution.

There are a number of legal provisions in various legal acts of the Republic of Azerbaijan describing and determining the categories of persons protected by the state. The most important instruments in this sphere are the Law on State Protection of Persons Involved in Criminal Procedures (11 December 1998), the Law on Operative Investigation Activity (28 October 1999) and the Code of Criminal Procedure (1 September 2000).

According to Article 17 of the Law of the Republic of Azerbaijan on Operative Investigation Activity, Article 3 of the Law on State Protection of Persons Involved in Criminal Procedures and Article 123 of the Criminal Procedure Code, the persons protected by the state are the victims in criminal cases, their lawyers and witnesses, including other persons involved in criminal procedures.

However, other legislative acts such as the Law on Combating Terrorism (18 June 1999), the Law on National Security (29 June 2004) and the Law on Combating Trafficking in Persons (28 June 2005) dealing with specific threats and crimes (e.g. terrorism, trafficking in persons, etc.) also contain provisions guaranteeing the appropriate protection of the persons in question.

Under Article 95 of the Criminal Procedure Code, each person who is aware of any facts of a criminal case may be invited to report as a witness on those facts during preliminary investigations and trials. The legislation of the Republic of Azerbaijan does not contain the concept of *pentiti*. However, there is a provision on collaborators of justice in Article 3 of the Law on State Protection of Persons Involved in Criminal Procedures. Sub-paragraph 1 of paragraph 2 of the given Article describes a collaborator of justice as a person who reports on a crime to the law enforcement agencies, or takes an active part in detecting, preventing and/or revealing this or that crime.

In Azerbaijan, witnesses are summoned and interrogated under the procedure provided for by Articles 226-230 of the Code of Criminal Procedure. Under Article 95.6, a witness has the following rights:

- to be informed about the criminal case for which he/she is summoned to testify;
- to turn down the interpreter participating in the interrogation;
- to make requests;
- to refuse to testify against him/herself, his/her close relatives, and to submit materials and information;
- to use necessary materials (documents, maps, etc.) while testifying on facts, circumstances and places which are difficult to memorise;
- to be interrogated in the presence of his/her lawyer;
- to be compensated for expenses and material damages deriving from the criminal proceedings, etc.

2. **Please describe the framework (legal provisions and established practice) governing the use of measures encouraging witnesses and *pentiti* to co-operate with justice.**

In Azerbaijan there are legal provisions governing the use of measures encouraging witnesses and *pentiti* to co-operate with justice agencies. These provisions could be split into two categories:

- provisions concerning *collaborators of justice*, which allow them to reduce their own sentence;
- provisions encouraging witnesses and *pentiti* by fixing rules in relation to the guarantees for their security and material maintenance.

Thus, it is possible to find articles in legislative acts of the Republic of Azerbaijan, which take the collaboration of a criminal sufficiently into account. Article 30 (voluntary refusal from the commission of a crime) of the Criminal Code of the Republic of Azerbaijan (1 September 2000) states that "any person, who voluntarily and definitely refuses to complete the commission of a crime is released from responsibility". In accordance with Article 59 (mitigating circumstances) the following types of behaviour by any person involved in a crime are considered as the mitigating circumstances (Article 59.1.9 and 59.1.10):

- to confess voluntarily to having committed a crime;
- to actively support the state bodies in revealing a crime and holding the other perpetrators of that prime responsible;
- to take an active part in searching and finding the property obtained as the result of criminal activity;
- to provide medical and any other necessary assistance to the victim of a crime;
- to compensate material losses and/or moral damages emerging from the commission of a crime, etc.

In addition, under Article 72, any person who commits a crime for the first time, which did not result in grave social dangers, may be released from criminal responsibility if he/she voluntarily confesses to his/her guilt, takes an active part in revealing the crime, recovers suffered losses, or eliminates the consequences of suffered damages by other means. Moreover, part VII of Article 17 of the Law on Operative Investigation Activity stipulates that when a member of the criminal group co-operating with law enforcement agencies and actively providing assistance to them in revealing the crime, commits offences not resulting in grave consequences, he/she may be released from criminal responsibility if he/she voluntarily confesses to his/her guilt and recovers losses. Legal provisions directed at guaranteeing the anonymity of witness and *pentito*, as the encouraging measures, are included in Article 14 of the Law on Operative Investigation Activity, Article 11 of the Law on State Protection of Persons Involved in Criminal Procedures, and Article 17.4 of the Law on Combating Trafficking in Persons.

Article 22 of the Law on State Protection of Persons Involved in Criminal Procedures, Article 17 of the Law on Operative Investigation Activity, Article 14 of the Law on Combating Terrorism, and Article 12-20 of the Law on Combating Trafficking in Persons provide the following rights and measures for witnesses and *pentiti* to encourage them to co-operate with justice agencies:

- right to salaries, awards, and other social guarantees;
- right to security (if necessary, their close relatives are also allowed to use this right);
- right to compensation for suffered losses and damages;
- if necessary, the duration of co-operation with law enforcement agencies is included in their term of professional service (with regard to collaborators of justice);
- financial maintenance provided for a collaborator of justice may be three times more than usual, when he/she operates within a criminal group as an undercover agent.

3. **Can measures/benefits encouraging the co-operation of witnesses and *pentiti* be used in combination with protection measures (arrangements concerning trial proceedings, sentencing conditions, special penitentiary regimes, etc.)? If so, please specify and indicate under which conditions they are applied.**

Yes, the use of some incentive measures/benefits in combination with protection measures is possible in practice. However, the use of some encouraging measures (reducing sentences, defining the type of punishment, etc.) in relation to witnesses and *pentiti* falls under the law courts' competence, and it is up to them for taking a decision on this matter.

4. For which kind of crime and under which circumstances can witness and *pentito* protection be applied? Can the measures be extended to the relatives or other persons close to the witness/*pentito*?

According to Article 17, paragraph 1, of the Law of the Republic of Azerbaijan on State Protection of Persons Involved in Criminal Procedures, and Article 17, paragraph 4, of the Law of the Republic of Azerbaijan on Operative Investigation Activity, valid information obtained by security services on the existence of threats of murder, use of violence against protected persons and their immediate relatives, and destruction or damage of their property due to their input to the investigation of criminal cases or legal proceedings, gives grounds for taking security measures.

Article 15 of the Criminal Code establishes categories of crime, including crimes of non-grave danger to society, less grave crimes, grave crimes, and seriously grave crimes. However, there are no separate provisions in the legislative acts of the Republic of Azerbaijan specifying a list of crimes for which witness and *pentito* protection is to be applied. Nevertheless, according to the practice of law enforcement agencies of the Republic of Azerbaijan witness and *pentito* protection measures should preferably be applied for the following categories of crimes:

1.   crimes against peace and humanity;
2.   war crimes;
3.   terrorism and terrorism related crimes;
4.   a wide range of transnational crimes (trafficking in persons, illegal migration, illegal circulation of drugs, etc.).

In accordance with paragraph 3 of Article 3 of the Law on State Protection of Persons Involved in Criminal Procedures, security measures may be extended to the close relatives of protected persons, if there is threat that such persons will be put under pressure in order to influence protected persons. Under Article 6 of the Law on Operative Investigation Activity and Article 14 of the Law on Combating Terrorism, protection measures concern close relatives of protected persons as well.

5. What urgent measures (e.g. immediate relocation to a secret place) can be taken in order to protect witnesses and *pentiti*?

According to Article 7 of the Law of the Republic of Azerbaijan on State Protection of Persons Involved in Criminal Procedures, the urgent security measures taken in respect of protected persons include providing defendants with special security facilities, notifying them of the existing threat, providing their temporary accommodation in safe places, safeguarding their apartments and property, and securing the confidentiality of information concerning them.

6. Which institutions are involved in the protection of witnesses and *pentiti* and what is their role (e.g. law enforcement agencies, special independent agencies, prosecutor's offices, judicial authorities, etc.)? How does co-operation between the relevant institutions work in practice?

According to Article 6 of the Law of the Republic of Azerbaijan on State Protection of Persons Involved in Criminal Procedures, security services include authorities that adopt decisions on taking security measures and authorities taking security measures based on those decisions. According to the aforementioned Article, decisions on taking security measures in respect of protected persons are adopted by courts (judges), prosecutors and, upon prosecutor's approval, by investigators and investigation agencies, which conduct the investigation of criminal cases or have information concerning criminal cases. A relevant executive authority is assigned to carry out security measures in respect of persons protected by those decisions. According to the Decree of the President of the Republic of Azerbaijan on the Enactment of the Law of the Republic of Azerbaijan on State Protection of Persons Involved in Criminal Procedures, the Ministry of Internal Affairs and the Ministry of National Security of the Republic of Azerbaijan are empowered to carry out, within their respective authorities, the functions of "relevant executive authorities" provided for in paragraph 2 of the aforementioned Article 6.

7. Are there any specific provisions governing the protection of witnesses and *pentiti* in relation to acts of terrorism? If so, please specify. Are there any specialised counter-terrorism institutions? If so, what is their role in the protection of witnesses and *pentiti* in relation to acts of terrorism?

In general, all provisions related to the protection of witnesses and victims of crimes are also applied in cases of terrorist acts. Furthermore, according to Article 14 of the Law of the Republic of Azerbaijan on Combating Terrorism, besides the officials of relevant executive authorities directly participating in combating terrorism, persons combating terrorism and who are protected by the state include persons permanently or temporarily assisting public authorities in preventing and detecting terrorist activities and in minimising the possible damage occurring as a result, and their immediate relatives if they have suffered damage to their health and property.

According to the Decree of the President of the Republic of Azerbaijan on the Enactment of the Law of the Republic of Azerbaijan on Combating Terrorism, the President of the Republic of Azerbaijan is empowered to carry out, within his/her authority, the functions (providing anti-terrorist activities with necessary forces and facilities as well as directing the fight against terrorism) of the "relevant executive authority" provided for in Article 5, paragraph 1, while the Ministry of Internal Affairs, the Ministry of National

Security, the Ministry of Defence of the Republic of Azerbaijan as well as the Central Security Departments of the State Superior Bodies and Executive Authorities of the Republic of Azerbaijan (at present Special State Security Department) are empowered to carry out, within their respective authorities, the functions of "relevant executive authorities" provided for in Article 5, paragraph 2, of the aforementioned Law.

8. **How does the framework governing the use of measures protecting witnesses and *pentiti* and encouraging them to co-operate with justice guarantee respect for human rights and individual freedoms? Please indicate the procedures in place, if any, to monitor compliance with human rights standards.**

According to Article 12, paragraph 2, of the Constitution of the Republic of Azerbaijan "rights and liberties of persons and citizens listed in the present Constitution are guaranteed in accordance with international treaties, to which the Republic of Azerbaijan is a party". Article 148, paragraph 2, of the Constitution stipulates that international agreements, to which the Republic of Azerbaijan is a party, constitute an integral part of the legislative system of the Republic of Azerbaijan. In relation to this legal fact, it is necessary to mention the European Convention for the Protection of Human Rights and Fundamental Freedoms.

According to Article 12.1 of the Criminal Procedure Code of the Republic of Azerbaijan, authorities carrying out criminal procedures shall ensure compliance with the constitutional rights and liberties of persons participating in criminal procedures. Article 2 of the Law of the Republic of Azerbaijan on State Protection of Persons Involved in Criminal Procedures provides for the following: "the legislation on state protection of protected persons participating in criminal procedures consists of the Constitution of the Republic of Azerbaijan, the present Law and other legislative acts of the Republic of Azerbaijan". According to Article 5 of the same Law, principles of taking security measures in respect of protected persons include lawfulness, respect for human rights and liberties, fulfilment of security measures by authorities based on obligations of those authorities as well as protected persons. Article 11 provides for the securing of confidentiality of information concerning defendants. According to Article 3 of the Law of the Republic of Azerbaijan on Operative Investigation Activity, operative investigation activity is carried out according to the principles of lawfulness, humanism, respect for human rights and liberties, and by the harmonisation of undercover, secret and open methods of operation. Article 4 provides for the respect for human rights and liberties in the conduct of operative investigation activity, generally consisting of the following:

1. protection of human life, health, rights and liberties as well as legal interests of legal entities, etc. from criminal pursuits;
2. inadmissibility of dissemination of information concerning personal privacy, particularly personal and family secrecy and information

concerning the honour and dignity of any persons, without their consent.

In accordance with the provisions of the Law of the Republic of Azerbaijan on State Protection of Persons Involved in Criminal Procedures, security measures are applied by informing (Articles 19 and 20) protected persons, and in some cases on the bases of their consent (Articles 8, 10, 12, and 13) to the given procedures. Article 19 of the same Law stipulates the following rights of protected persons:
- to be aware of protection measures taken to ensure his/her security;
- to petition for the application or termination of protection measures;
- to demand the application of other measures prescribed by this Law, or the termination of one of them;
- to lodge a complaint in the Prosecutor's office or court against any illegal decisions or activities of authorities applying protection measures.

The latest legislative acts of the Republic of Azerbaijan stipulate legal provisions, which make obligatory the implementation of complex measures for the protection of victims. For example, the Law on Trafficking in Persons contains provisions in Chapter IV concerning the establishment of special institutions, shelters, and assistance centres aimed at the protection and rehabilitation of victims. According to the Law, assistance provided for victims covers legal, psychological and medical protection.

b. *Procedural measures*

9. At which stage(s), and in which context, is it possible for witnesses and *pentiti* to benefit from procedural measures of protection?

According to the requirements of Article 239.7 of the Criminal Procedure Code of the Republic of Azerbaijan, while personal identification as an investigative action is being conducted, the identification of a person based on a request of an identifying person may be conducted without his/her direct visual examination.

Rules of confrontation as an investigative action are set out in Article 235 of Criminal Procedure Code of the Republic of Azerbaijan. However, the disposition of the Article as well as the provisions of the remedial legislation do not provide for any alternative methods of protection from possible threats in cases of confrontation of accused persons with witnesses and victims of crime.

In addition, accused persons shall not leave the courtroom without the permission of the judge until recess is announced, and are obliged to comply with the rules of court sessions, in accordance with Articles 91.8.7 and 91.8.8 respectively. Furthermore, according to Article 310.6 of the Criminal Procedure Code of the Republic of Azerbaijan, appropriate measures may be taken upon a court decision in respect of persons coarsely violating the rules of court sessions after a warning has been given, with the exception of public prosecutor and advocate. According to Article 310.6.3 of the Criminal Procedure Code of the Republic of Azerbaijan, one of these measures is expelling from the courtroom for the whole or some period of court examination.

Under Article 18.2 of the Law on Combating Trafficking in Persons, the state body carrying out criminal procedures has to take necessary measures to ensure the security of victims who suffered from trafficking in persons. Such protection measures shall continue until the existing threat has vanished, including the preliminary investigation, trial and post-trial periods.

10. Is there the possibility for witnesses and *pentiti* to obtain legal assistance at this (these) stage(s)?

According to Article 61, paragraph 3, of the Constitution of the Republic of Azerbaijan, "every person has the right to be assisted by a lawyer from the moment of detention, arrest or accusation for a crime by competent state authorities". Furthermore, under Article 67 of the Constitution, "every person detained, arrested for and/or accused of the commission of a crime will be immediately informed by the competent state bodies about his/her rights, reasons of his/her detention, arrest and institution of criminal proceedings against him/her".

Articles 11 and 14 of the Law of the Republic of Azerbaijan on State Protection of Persons Involved in Criminal Procedures respectively envisage that the confidentiality of information concerning protected persons is preserved and closed sessions are held in cases of participation of defendants.

Furthermore, according to Article 19.3 of the Criminal Procedure Code of the Republic of Azerbaijan, during the interrogation of witnesses or victims of crime, the authority conducting the investigation has no right to prohibit the participation of the person invited as a defender in criminal procedures.

11. Are there alternative methods of giving evidence which allow the protection of witnesses and *pentiti* from intimidation resulting from face to face confrontation with the accused? If yes, please specify (e.g. full or partial anonymity, video-conference, disguise, exclusion of the defendant from the courtroom when the witness is giving evidence, exclusion of the media or the public from the trial, etc.) and indicate under which conditions these methods are used.

In accordance with the remedial legislation, statements of witnesses or victims of crimes and testimonies of anonymous witnesses or victims of crimes may not be considered as credible evidence prior to court examination. Accordingly, any evidence obtained in compliance with Article 145 of the Criminal Procedure Code of the Republic of Azerbaijan, is evaluated based on its pertinence, admissibility and reliability. Moreover, during the preliminary investigation, witnesses and victims of crime are interrogated in compliance with the provisions of Articles 230-231, whereas during the court examination they are interrogated in compliance with the provisions of Articles 328 and 330 of the Criminal Procedure Code of the Republic of Azerbaijan. Prior to interrogations they receive warnings about the responsibility for giving false testimonies provided for in Article 297 of the Criminal Code of the Republic of Azerbaijan. Only after that may testimonies of witnesses and victims of crime in criminal matters be considered as credible evidence.

12. On which grounds and on the basis of which criteria can anonymity be granted? Is there the possibility to obtain legal assistance at this stage?

Information given by victims of crime shall be executed upon their testimonies and only after that may it be considered as evidence in criminal matters.

13. Are pre-trial statements of witnesses and *pentiti* and testimonies of anonymous witnesses and *pentiti* regarded as valid evidence? If yes, under which conditions?

According to Article 91.5.18 of the Criminal Procedure Code of the Republic of Azerbaijan, accused persons have the right to raise objections against unlawful actions of the authority conducting criminal procedures, while according to Article 91.5.39 of the Criminal Procedure Code of the Republic of Azerbaijan, they also have the right to raise objections against unlawful actions of other parties participating in criminal procedures.

14. Is it possible, and if so, under which conditions, to use information provided by "*pentiti*"? How is their credibility assessed?

The possibility and conditions of the use of information provided by "*pentiti*" are evaluated on the bases of provisions of the Criminal Procedure Code of the Republic of Azerbaijan. If such information is obtained, collected and documented in accordance with the appropriate provisions of the Criminal Procedure Code then it is possible to use it.

15. Which are the opportunities for the defence to exercise its rights, including the right of the accused to challenge the witness'/*pentito*'s credibility in criminal proceedings (including at the pre-trial stage) and the respect of the "equality of arms" principle?

Under paragraph 3 of Article 63 of the Constitution, proof obtained illegally cannot be used for the purposes of justice. Furthermore, under Articles 7 and 13 of the Law on Courts and Judges (10 June 1997) based on constitutional Article 127, trials are held on the bases of principle of equality before the law and court, and the principle of contest.

c. Non-procedural measures

16. At which stage(s), and in which context, is it possible for witnesses and *pentiti* to benefit from a protection programme?

According to Article 6 of the Law of the Republic of Azerbaijan on State Protection of Persons Involved in Criminal Procedures, decisions on taking security measures in respect of protected persons are adopted by courts (judges), prosecutors and, upon prosecutor's approval, by investigators and investigation agencies, which conduct the investigation of criminal cases or have information concerning criminal cases. Article 17 of the same Law provides that where investigation agencies, investigators, prosecutors or courts (judges) have obtained information (request) about threats to the security of protected persons, they shall examine this information (request) and shall take decisions within at least three days, and in some cases immediately, on taking security measures or on refraining from taking security measures.

17. Is there the possibility for witnesses and *pentiti* to obtain legal assistance at this (these) stage(s)?

Please see the reply to question 9.

18. What is the procedure for admittance to a protection programme? Please specify, in particular, who takes the initiative, the criteria for admittance, the assessment of the relevance of a testimony and how admittance to the programme is formalised.

Please see the reply to question 4, paragraph 2.

19. Please indicate the measures that can be adopted for the protection of witnesses and *pentiti* (e.g. surveillance of the residence, physical protection, protection of personal records, relocation, change of identity, subsidies, assistance in job search, relocation of a detainee to another prison or to special units).

The Law of the Republic of Azerbaijan on State Protection of Persons Involved in Criminal Procedures of 11 December 1998 provides for security and social protection measures for victims and witnesses in criminal matters and other persons involved in criminal procedures. Article 7 of Part 2 of the same Law includes the list of security measures taken in respect of protected persons:

1) Protection of protected persons, their residence and property;
2) Providing protected persons with individual security facilities and notifying them of the existing threat;
3) Temporary accommodation of protected persons in safe places;

4) Securing the confidentiality of information concerning protected persons;
5) Providing protected persons with new jobs, new places of residence, and changing their workplaces or educational institutions;
6) Changing their documents and appearance;
7) Holding closed court examinations (hearings) in cases of protected persons' participation, in a manner determined by the legislation;

Furthermore, Article 16 of the same Law allows for the following measures to be taken so as to ensure the security of detained persons or persons serving the sentence of imprisonment:

1) Transfer from one place of detention, isolation ward or prison to another;
2) Keep them in separate or in one-man cells;
3) Change the preventive punishment in a manner set out in the remedial legislation of the Republic of Azerbaijan.

Article 17 of the Law of the Republic of Azerbaijan on Operative Investigation Activity also envisages the social and legal protection of persons co-operating with bodies dealing with operative investigation activity.

20. What can the duration of a protection programme be? Which are the procedures for assessing the degree of danger for the witnesses/*pentiti* and their compliance with the obligations of the programme? Is it possible to challenge a decision of suspension, revocation or termination of a protection programme?

According to Article 18 of the Law of the Republic of Azerbaijan on State Protection of Persons Involved in Criminal Procedures, security measures shall be cancelled in cases, where:

1) terms of taking security measures have expired;
2) the existing threat has vanished;
3) there is an application submitted by the person in respect of whom security measures are taken;
4) in spite of written notifications, protected persons do not comply constantly with well-grounded orders of authorities taking security measures.

Protected persons may lodge complaints in a court or prosecution office against adopted decisions. Complaints should be immediately reviewed. Complainants shall be notified in writing of the adopted decisions within three days.

d. International co-operation

21. Which measures (e.g. use of modern telecommunications means, assistance in relocating protected witnesses, exchange of information between witness protection authorities) have been

adopted in the context of mutual legal assistance in order to facilitate international co-operation? How are the financial implications of international co-operation activities dealt with?

The mentioned measures are restricted primarily to information exchange.

22. Has your country entered international (bilateral or multilateral) agreements on the protection of witnesses and *pentiti*? If so, please indicate what kind of provisions they include.

Generally, international agreements in the field of mutual legal assistance existing in the contractual experience of the Republic of Azerbaijan can be distinguished as follows:

1) Multilateral international agreements on mutual legal assistance (e.g. European Convention on Mutual Assistance in Criminal Matters 1959, and its Additional Protocol 1978; CIS Convention on Legal Assistance and Legal Relations in Civil, Family and Criminal Matters 1993, etc.);

2) Multilateral intergovernmental agreements on combating certain crimes (e.g. UN Convention Against Illicit Traffic in Narcotic Drugs and Psychotropic Substances 1988; Convention on the Prevention and Punishment of Crimes against Internationally Protected Persons, including Diplomatic Agents 1973; International Convention for the Suppression of Terrorist Bombings 1997);

3) Bilateral intergovernmental agreements on extradition and agreements on mutual assistance and legal relations in civil, family and criminal matters, namely: the Republic of Azerbaijan concluded 6 agreements on mutual assistance (with the Russian Federation, the Republic of Turkey, Georgia, the Republic of Uzbekistan, the Republic of Kazakhstan and the Republic of Lithuania), 3 agreements on extradition (with the Republic of Bulgaria, the Islamic Republic of Iran and the Republic of Kirghizistan) and 5 agreements on surrender of convicted persons (with the Russian Federation, the Republic of Kazakhstan, the Republic of Kirghizistan, Ukraine and the Republic of Uzbekistan).

23. How can international co-operation in the field of the protection of witnesses and *pentiti* be improved?
-

e. Statistics

-

f. Proposals and comments

-

Belgium

a. General information

1. **Please describe the framework (legal provisions and established practice) governing the use of measures protecting witnesses and** *pentiti*

Witness protection:

The legal framework governing witness protection is established by the Act of 7 July 2002 setting out rules relating to the protection of witnesses under threat and miscellaneous provisions (MB 10/08/2002). This act laid down the prescriptive and practical framework governing witness protection measures and established a special body enjoying exclusive competence, namely the Witness Protection Commission.

Witnesses under threat and members of their families can be afforded protection. The Act gives the following definitions:

- witness under threat: a person put at risk by statements made or to be made in the context of a criminal case during the preliminary investigation (*information*) or the judicial investigation (*instruction*), whether in Belgium, before an international court or – where reciprocal arrangements exist – abroad, who is prepared to confirm those statements in court on request;

- family members: the spouse of the witness under threat or the person with whom he/she cohabits and maintains a lasting emotional and sexual relationship, relatives – living under the same roof – of the witness under threat, of his/her spouse or of the person with whom he/she cohabits and maintains a lasting emotional and sexual relationship, their adoptive parents and adopted children living under the same roof and relatives of adoptive parents and adopted children living under the same roof;

- other relatives: relatives of the witness under threat up to the third degree not living under the same roof, relatives of his/her spouse or of the person with whom he/she cohabits and maintains a lasting emotional and sexual relationship, their adoptive parents and adopted children not living under the same roof and relatives of adoptive parents and adopted children up to the second degree not living under the same roof.

For details regarding the types of offence and circumstances in relation to which protection measures may be used, the procedure for the implementation of such measures and their nature, please refer to the questions below.

"Pentiti":

Belgium does not have a comprehensive system for the protection of *"pentiti"* or collaborators of justice. In the past, the Belgian government has introduced various bills intended to establish a set of legal rules relating to *"pentiti"*. As yet, these bills have not been passed by Parliament.

Nevertheless, a certain form of procedural co-operation is encouraged via the mechanism of grounds of excuse for denunciation:

Belgian law contains a number of provisions establishing grounds of excuse directly linked to the denunciation of accomplices or accessories. These provisions are set out in the Criminal Code and in specific Acts. The main grounds of excuse under Belgian law are found in two specific Acts.

- Section 6 of the Act of 24 February 1921 on trafficking in poisonous, soporific, narcotic, disinfectant and antiseptic substances provides for a number of grounds of excuse based on denunciation; these vary according to the seriousness of the offence of which the informer is guilty and the point at which the denunciation takes place. If the informer is subject only to penalties for lesser indictable offences, the denunciation will earn him/her complete exemption from punishment if it takes place prior to any prosecution and a reduced sentence if it takes place once a prosecution has commenced. If the informer is guilty of a serious indictable offence, however, the denunciation will only have an effect if it takes place before the prosecution has commenced, and will bring only a reduced sentence, never exemption from punishment.

- Section 10 of the Act of 11 July 1985 on the use of hormonal and anti-hormonal substances in animals established a system of reduced sentences or exemption from sentence more or less modelled on that found in the 1921 Act: anyone who reveals to the authorities, prior to any prosecution, the identity of the person having supplied him/her with the substances that enabled him/her to commit the offences of which he/she is accused is exempted from sentence; if the denunciation takes place once a prosecution has commenced, it will bring only a reduced sentence.

In practice, owing to the very stringent requirements laid down in the act and by the case-law for the application of grounds of excuse, denunciation under the terms of Section 6 of the Drugs Act very often appears to remain a dead letter. The main reasons for the ineffectiveness of these specific rules governing collaborators of justice appear to be:

- the fact that there is no opportunity for preliminary negotiation between the prosecuting authorities and collaborators of justice;
- the lack of sufficient guarantees that the collaborator of justice will actually receive a reduced sentence or exemption from sentence;
- the excessively stringent requirements imposed in relation to denunciations in order for grounds of excuse to be applicable;
- the lack of supplementary measures intended to protect the person of the collaborator of justice and of those close to him/her.

The last issue – the lack of protection measures for collaborators of justice – was not resolved by the 2002 Act on the protection of witnesses under threat, owing to its sensitive political nature (see below).

In conclusion, for the purposes of this questionnaire, we have concentrated on witness protection in the strict sense, as provided for under the 2002 Act. The explanatory memorandum confines the Act's scope to persons who have made statements in relation to a criminal case and are prepared to confirm those statements in court if requested to do so, without this necessarily being the case. It is theoretically irrelevant whether or not witnesses have criminal records. Police officers acting as witnesses can also receive protection if necessary.

2. **Please describe the framework (legal provisions and established practice) governing the use of measures encouraging witness and *pentito* to co-operate with the justice system.**

Three Acts passed by the previous government form the framework within which witnesses are encouraged to make statements in criminal cases relating to serious organised crime.

- The Act of 8 April 2002 on the anonymity of witnesses (MB 31/05/2002).
- The Act of 7 July 2002 setting out rules relating to the protection of witnesses under threat and miscellaneous provisions (MB 10/08/2002).
- The Act of 2 August 2002 on taking statements using audio-visual media (MB 12/09/2002).

3. **Can measures/benefits encouraging the co-operation of witnesses and *pentiti* be used in combination with protection measures (arrangements concerning trial proceedings, sentencing conditions, special penitentiary regimes, etc.)? If so, please specify and indicate under which conditions they are applied.**

The various possible measures (anonymity, protection, hearing by video-conferencing, tele-conferencing, etc.) are included in the three aforementioned Acts. There are also a number of practical measures to encourage testimony or statements.

For instance, Article 327 of the Code of Criminal Procedure provides that the president of the Assize Court may have one or more defendants withdrawn before, during or after the hearing of a witness, and examine them separately on particular facts of the case.

The Act of 28 November 2000 on the criminal protection of minors introduced provisions into the Code of Criminal Procedure concerning the audio-visual recording of hearings of minors who are victims or witnesses of certain offences. Records of examinations and tape recordings are produced before the investigating court and trial court rather than the appearing of the minor in person. However, the trial court may, in a reasoned decision, order the minor to appear should it consider such an appearance necessary in order to establish the truth. In such cases, the minor appears by video-conference, unless he/she expresses a desire to testify in court.

4. **For what kind of crime and under what circumstances can witness and *pentito* protection be applied? Can the measures be extended to the relatives or other persons close to the witness/*pentito*?**

4.1. Ordinary protection measures

The Witness Protection Commission may, with due regard to the principles of subsidiarity and proportionality, authorise ordinary protection measures for a witness under threat and, where necessary and insofar as they are put at risk by statements made or to be made by the witness, for family members and other relatives.

In particular, ordinary protection measures may include:

1. the protection of data relating to the person concerned kept by the population office and the registry of births, deaths and marriages;
2. the provision of advice in relation to prevention;
3. the installation of preventive technical equipment;
4. the designation of a contact official;
5. the devising of an alarm procedure;
6. the provision of psychological assistance;
7. the organisation of police patrols as a preventive measure;
8. the recording of incoming and outgoing calls;
9. the regular monitoring of consultations of the national register and/or the protection of data relating to the person concerned;
10. the provision of a secret telephone number;
11. the provision of a protected vehicle registration number;
12. the provision of a mobile phone for urgent calls;
13. close and immediate physical protection of the person concerned;
14. electronic protection of the person concerned;
15. relocation of the person concerned for up to 45 days;
16. accommodation in a specially protected section of the prison where a detainee is held.

In order for a witness to benefit from a protection measure, that protection must naturally be necessary. In particular, a witness may receive protection only if he/she is objectively put at risk by statements made as a witness in the context of a criminal case; a subjective feeling of insecurity is consequently not sufficient. This is consistent with the most stringent requirement set out in the Act on anonymous witnesses (see below). As in the case of totally anonymous witnesses, it also seems advisable to apply the principle of subsidiarity and to allow witnesses to make a statement, with all the repercussions this may have on their safety, only where this is necessitated by the examination of the facts and where other means do not appear to be sufficient in order to establish the truth. However, if the witness is at risk after making his/her statement, he/she must be able to receive protection, irrespective of whether the statement subsequently turns out to be crucial. The principle of proportionality must also be respected: the importance of the case must be weighed against the danger the statement will occasion and the protection measures that will consequently have to be taken.

Given that ordinary protection measures do not have a significant impact on a witness's family life, they may be authorised for family members only where the latter are also put at risk by the witness's statements.

4.2. Special protection measures

The Witness Protection Commission may, with due regard to the principles of subsidiarity and proportionality, exclusively authorise special protection measures for a witness under threat, including special protection for a witness whose protection cannot be ensured by ordinary protection measures and whose statements concern an offence coming under Article 90*ter*, §§ 2, 3 or 4 of the Criminal Code, an offence committed as part of a criminal organisation coming under Article 324*bis* of the Criminal Code or an offence coming under the Act of 16 June 1993 on the punishment of serious violations of international humanitarian law and, as the case may be, for family members and, insofar as they are put at risk by statements made or to be made, other relatives.

Special protection measures may include:
1. relocation of the person concerned for more than 45 days;
2. changing the identity of the person concerned.

Special protection measures automatically have a dramatic impact on those close to the witness. For this reason, the latter must also be able to receive special protection, irrespective of whether or not they are at risk. These measures cannot be granted unconditionally, however: only the witness's blood relatives and relatives by marriage living under the same roof may benefit from them. The witness's other blood relatives and relatives by marriage must be shown to be put at risk by his/her statements.

The Witness Protection Commission may, in the light of the specific situation of the person concerned, grant financial assistance to a witness under threat for whom special protection measures have been authorised.

Financial assistance may include:
1. a monthly payment intended to ensure the subsistence of the witness under threat and of family members and other relatives protected along with him/her, certain parts of which may be intended for specific purposes;
2. payment of a one-off sum to start up a self-employed business;
3. a special financial contribution set aside for specific purposes.

A person granted special protection measures is automatically entitled to psychological help, assistance in looking for work and intervention in the exercise of vested financial rights.

5. What urgent measures (e.g. immediate relocation to a secret place) can be taken in order to protect witnesses and *pentiti*?

Only ordinary protection measures may be granted as a matter of extreme urgency. If the witness needs to be accommodated in a safe place, short-term relocation (that is, up to 45 days) will have to suffice in the interim, since longer-term relocation constitutes a special protection measure.

The Chair of the Witness Protection Commission may, in consultation with the Director-General of the Criminal Investigation Division of the federal police, take a provisional decision in this respect. Such decisions must be confirmed by a plenary meeting of the Commission.

6. What institutions are involved in the protection of witnesses and *pentiti* and what is their role (e.g. law enforcement agencies, special independent agencies, prosecutor's offices, judicial authorities, etc.)? How does co-operation between the relevant institutions work in practice?

- Protection measures may be requested by the <u>Crown Prosecutor</u>, the <u>Principal Crown Prosecutor</u> or the <u>Federal Prosecutor</u>. In the context of a judicial investigation, the <u>investigating judge</u> may request protection measures.

- The regulations governing witness protection establish a special body enjoying exclusive competence, namely the <u>Witness Protection Commission</u>. This Commission is the only authority that can decide to grant, modify or withdraw protection measures and any financial assistance. The Commission's decisions are not subject to appeal.

The Witness Protection Commission is made up of:

- the Federal Prosecutor, who is its Chair. Cases in which the possibility of witness protection arises often have a transfrontier dimension, and are thus more likely to extend beyond district boundaries, meaning they fall within the jurisdiction of the Federal Prosecutor's Office. In addition, the Octopus agreement requires local judicial authorities to make contact with the federal level within their own judicial structure if need be, so that the Federal Prosecutor must be contacted where necessary;
- a Crown Prosecutor, designated by the Council of Crown Prosecutors. It is, in fact, recommended that Crown Prosecutors are represented, in so far as they too are entitled to initiate witness protection;
- the Principal Crown Prosecutor with specific responsibility for international relations. Where "relocation" abroad is necessary, it entails mutual assistance in criminal judicial matters. The presence of this Principal Crown Prosecutor is consequently a distinct advantage when it comes to the policy to be pursued;
- the Director General of the Criminal Investigation Division of the federal police, as the head and representative of the directorate general of this division, which is responsible for co-ordinating and organising protection;
- the Director General of Operational Support for the federal police, as the head and representative of the Directorate General of Operational Support, which is responsible for implementing protection measures;
- a representative of the Ministry of Justice, *inter alia,* in view of the budgetary implications for this ministry of granting witness protection;
- a representative of the Ministry of the Interior, to liaise with the officials responsible for administrative protection.

The Witness Protection Commission is not a standing body; it meets when called to do so by its Chair, thereby avoiding an excessive workload for its members. In addition, the latter may appoint proxies in accordance with the rules laid down in the internal regulations.

- Each of the Witness Protection Commission's decisions is preceded by a recommendation in writing from the Witness Protection Service. This is a special section set up within the Directorate General of the Criminal Investigation Division of the federal police, responsible for organising and co-ordinating witness protection. The Witness Protection Service must gather all the necessary information about the witness and the criminal case in order to establish whether or not a person qualifies for protection. The Director General of the Criminal Investigation Division of the federal police can then make a recommendation to the Witness

Protection Commission. This recommendation must be made within one month.

- The Witness Protection Service is responsible for co-ordinating and monitoring protection on an ongoing basis.

- The Directorate General of Operational Support within the federal police is responsible for the practical implementation of protection. Implementation of protection for witnesses detained in prison is the responsibility of the Directorate General of Prisons. Protection of detainees outside the prison (during transfers to the law courts, prison leave, etc.) is also the responsibility of the Directorate General of Operational Support, however. Once a detained witness has served his/her sentence, the Witness Protection Commission must decide whether there is any reason to continue granting protection measures to the person concerned.

7. **Are there any specific provisions governing the protection of witnesses and *pentiti* in relation to acts of terrorism? If so, please specify. Are there any specialised counter-terrorism institutions? If so, what is their role in the protection of witnesses and *pentiti* in relation to acts of terrorism?**

There are no specific provisions governing witness protection in relation to acts of terrorism, for the simple reason that terrorism is not (yet) established as a separate offence under Belgian criminal law.

It goes without saying that, in the context of investigations relating to acts of terrorism, witnesses under threat may be granted protection provided that these acts fall within the definitions of other criminal offences, and that those other offences come within the scope of ordinary or special protection measures.

There are no "specialised" counter-terrorism institutions at present. However, the National Security, the Military Information Department and the federal police all enjoy counter-terrorism powers.

A "Terrorism Unit" within the federal police concentrates on terrorism-related investigations.

8. **How does the framework governing the use of measures protecting witnesses and *pentiti* and encouraging them to co-operate with the judicial authorities guarantee respect for human rights and**

individual freedoms? Please indicate the procedures in place, if any, to monitor compliance with human rights standards.

- Subsidiarity and proportionality:
  The Witness Protection Commission must have due regard to principles of proportionality and subsidiarity in its decisions: the importance of the case must be weighed against the risk the statement will occasion and the protection measures that will consequently have to be taken (proportionality), and protection measures may be granted only where they are necessitated by an examination of the facts and where other means do not appear to be sufficient in order to establish the truth (subsidiarity).

- As far as special protection measures are concerned, proportionality is defined by the Act: firstly, special protection may be granted only if ordinary protection measures are not sufficient to ensure the witness's safety. In addition, by analogy with the provisions of the Act on anonymous witnesses, the witness's statement must concern an offence coming under Article 90*ter*, §§2, 3 or 4 of the Criminal Code, an offence committed as part of a criminal organisation coming under Article 324*bis* of the Criminal Code or an offence coming under the Act of 16 June 1993 on the punishment of serious violations of international humanitarian law.

- The principle of equality of arms and the rights of the defence are not jeopardised by the use of protection measures. The identity of a protected witness is known at each stage of the proceedings, and the defence has every opportunity to exercise its rights. Even in the event that a witness changes identity, his/her former identity is still known to all the parties, and testimony is given under that identity. The parties can therefore exercise their right to a fair hearing and question the witness.

b. Procedural measures

9. At what stage(s) and in what context is it possible for witnesses and *pentiti* to benefit from procedural measures of protection?

- Witness protection:
  The question of who can request protection measures depends on the stage in proceedings. Such requests may be made by the Crown Prosecutor. It is possible, however, that the judge may find protection measures are needed during the judicial investigation, and draw this to the Crown Prosecutor's attention.

  Under very exceptional circumstances, a witness may be granted protection when the case is referred to the trial court. The party in question must send a request to the Crown Prosecutor, who forwards it to the Witness Protection Commission.

Where such a situation arises before the Assize Court, the provisional measures for cases of extreme urgency make it possible to avoid this procedure. Moreover, the president of the Assize Court can take the necessary measures under his/her discretionary powers.

- Anonymity of witnesses:
  The Act of 8 April 2002 on the anonymity of witnesses provides for partial or total witness anonymity. Anonymity is a protection measure granted to a witness during the proceedings. It is a procedural form of protection. Anonymity is granted on the basis of subjective evidence. It is possible, however, that a protection procedure may be necessary once a witness's anonymity has been compromised, where it is clear that the witness is objectively at risk as a result of statements made.

  A witness is protected only if there are objective reasons for doing so. Such protection entails appreciable costs. This is more a post-procedural form of protection.

  The investigating judge may allow anonymous testimony, either as part of the preliminary police investigation for which he/she is responsible, or during the trial on the merits. For the circumstances under which a witness may be granted partial or total anonymity, please refer to the reply to question 12.

10. Can witnesses and *pentiti* obtain legal assistance at this (these) stage(s)?

Yes. Protected or anonymous witnesses may seek the assistance of a lawyer.

11. Are there alternative methods of giving evidence which allow the protection of witnesses and *pentiti* from intimidation resulting from face to face confrontation with the accused? If yes, please specify (e.g. full or partial anonymity, video-conference, disguise, exclusion of the defendant from the courtroom when the witness is giving evidence, exclusion of the media or the public from the trial, etc.) and indicate under which conditions these methods are used.

- The Act of 8 April 2002 on **the anonymity of witnesses** provides for partial or total anonymity of witnesses (see below).

- The Act of 2 August 2002 on taking statements using **audio-visual media** inserted hearings by video-conference, tele-conference and closed-circuit television into the Criminal Code.

Hearings by <u>video-conference</u> may be used for witnesses under threat to whom the Witness Protection Commission has granted a protection measure, as well as for witnesses, experts and charged persons (*inculpés*) resident abroad, on the basis of the principle of reciprocity. In other words, an accused person (*prévenu*) awaiting trial does not qualify. Witnesses under threat who have been subject to a protection measure may also be heard by <u>closed-circuit television</u>. For logical reasons, this means of telecommunication is not applicable to the hearing of witnesses, experts and charged persons resident abroad.

By analogy with the Convention on Mutual Assistance in Criminal Matters between Member States of the European Union, the preliminary draft of the act provides that hearings by video-conference or closed-circuit television may be allowed whenever it is not desirable or possible for the individual to be heard to appear in person.

The hearing of a witness by video-conferencing or closed-circuit television may be ordered by the Crown Prosecutor during the preliminary investigation (*information*) or by the investigating judge during the judicial investigation (*instruction*).

During the trial, the court, Court of Appeal or president of the Assize Court, on a reasoned request from the prosecuting authorities, decides whether or not to allow a hearing by vide-conferencing or closed-circuit television. The request must therefore state the reasons for which it is not desirable or possible for the witness or expert to appear in court in person.

A person can never be forced to make a statement by video-conference or closed-circuit television: his/ her agreement is always necessary.

In addition, the court, Court of Appeal or president of the Assize Court may, on a reasoned request from the prosecuting authorities, allow image or voice distortion. This procedure is not allowed in distance hearings during the preliminary judicial investigation, primarily because its use at this stage makes little sense, given that the preliminary judicial investigation is largely confidential. Image or voice distortion can afford a witness a certain form of anonymity. However, all details relevant to the identity of the person concerned must be disclosed. If these details are not to be disclosed, the rules on anonymous witnesses must be applied.

The record of a hearing by video-conference or closed-circuit television has the same evidential value as any other record of a hearing during a preliminary judicial investigation.

Statements made by video-conference or closed-circuit television during the trial are assessed freely by the trial court. If image or voice distortion is also used, the Act provides that the statements made may be taken into consideration as evidence only if they are strongly supported by other pieces of evidence. The concept of minimum statutory proof is therefore introduced in order to offset the restriction of the rights of the defence resulting from the partial anonymity of the person making the statements.

Tele-conference may be used in the hearing of witnesses under threat to whom the Witness Protection Commission has granted a protection measure and of witnesses and experts resident abroad, on the basis of the principle of reciprocity. Charged persons (*inculpés*) consequently cannot be heard by tele-conference.

A hearing by tele-conference may be allowed where it is not desirable or possible for the individual to be heard to appear in person, or to be heard by video-conference or closed-circuit television.

The procedure is the same as for hearings by video-conference or closed-circuit television.

Statements made by tele-conference may be taken into consideration by the trial court as evidence only if they are strongly supported by other pieces of evidence. This is because the restriction of the rights of the defence is more significant than in a hearing by video-conference or closed-circuit television, for instance, since the person heard cannot be observed while making his/her statements.

- Section 38 of the Act on **criminal protection of minors** introduces the possibility of making an audio-visual recording of the hearing of a minor who is a victim or witness of an offence coming under Article 91 of the Code of Criminal Procedure, and broadcasting it to the court rather than making the minor appear in person. Audio-visual recordings may also be ordered in view of serious, exceptional circumstances.

  In addition, Section 39 of this Act provides that an appearance by a minor may be arranged by video-conference if the court considers such an appearance necessary in order to establish the truth, unless the minor expresses a desire to testify in court. In the event of a hearing by video-conference, the minor is heard in a separate room, in the presence of a person of full age of his/her choice, his/her lawyer, one or more technicians and a psychiatric or psychological expert.

- Article 327 of the Code of Criminal Procedure provides that the president of the Assize Court may **have one or more defendants withdrawn** before, during or after the hearing of a witness, and examine them separately on particular facts of the case.

12. On what grounds and on the basis of which criteria can anonymity be granted? Is there the possibility to obtain legal assistance at this stage?

- **Partial anonymity:**

  The law provides for the suppression of certain details relevant to a witness's identity in the record of the hearing by the investigating judge or in court. In the first instance, this means the person's address and/or place of residence, but under certain circumstances it is possible that other details, such as the person's occupation and even name, may be suppressed.

  Partial anonymity may be granted to a witness only on the strict condition that he/she appear in court and be heard directly by the defence. In other cases, the system of total anonymity must be applied. Partial anonymity is useful primarily in the case of *ordinary witnesses* (*témoins occasionnels*) who are unknown to the suspects or those close to them, but nonetheless fear retaliation or intimidation.

  Only the judicial authorities – the investigating judge during the judicial investigation, and the court during the trial on the merits – have the power to grant or refuse partial anonymity to a witness in view of the specific circumstances of the case.

  This form of limited witness anonymity entails only a minimal, justified violation of the right to an adversarial hearing; the defence is scarcely impeded in its task. Indeed, it can put any questions to the witness other than those relating directly to the identity details to be kept confidential.

  The Act also provides that the place of residence of people who, in the course of their professional duties, are responsible for finding that an offence has been committed and investigating it, or who, in enforcing the law, become acquainted with the circumstances under which an offence was committed, and are heard as witnesses in this capacity, must not be disclosed. Instead, they may give their work address or the address at which they usually exercise their occupation.

- **Total anonymity:**

  Partial anonymity differs from total anonymity in that, in the case of the latter, all identity details (even external ones) are kept confidential, and the opportunity for both parties to be heard is indirect, rather than direct.

The investigating judge has the power to assess whether the witness wishing to maintain anonymity is actually entitled to this protected status. There is no provision for the parties to the trial to appeal an investigating judge's decision to grant or refuse (total) witness anonymity, given that such an appeal would excessively hinder the progress of the criminal investigation. The investigating judge also examines the reliability and credibility of the witness, and conducts the hearing itself. The investigating judge may allow anonymous testimony, either as part of the preliminary police investigation for which he/she is responsible, or during the trial on the merits. In the latter case, the court specifically instructs the investigating judge to examine the reliability and sincerity of the hearing of the anonymous witness, so that he/she can then report on the matter to the court.

The investigating judge him/herself must be informed of the witness's full identity, his/her relationship to the parties to the trial and his/her motivation for testifying. The hearing judge must clearly state the reasons for which maintenance of the witness's anonymity seems justified. The law stipulates two requirements to be applied in such cases.

A subjective requirement applies to civil witnesses. In practice, it is sufficient (within the bounds of reason) for the investigating judge to find that the witness (or a person close to him/her) wishing to remain anonymous feels threatened.

An objective requirement applies to police officers, however. According to this requirement, the police officer/witness (or a person close to him/her) must actually be at risk. Moreover, the rule of subsidiarity must be applied, even in such exceptional circumstances. Firstly, all other measures for protecting police officers' safety must have been exhausted; even where this is the case, limited anonymity must be preferred to total anonymity. The mere fact that the work of the police officers concerned may become complicated in the future is not a sufficient reason to maintain total anonymity.

As well as the hearing judge (who is aware of the identity of the anonymous witness) verifying the latter's reliability and credibility, the parties to the trial have the right to choose freely the questions to be put to the anonymous witness. By giving the parties the opportunity to have certain questions put to the anonymous witness via the investigating judge, and thereby subjecting the anonymous witness to cross-questioning, it is possible to test his/her reliability and credibility, which is an altogether necessary guarantee. Naturally, it is not essential that all the questions suggested by the parties to the trial actually be put by the investigating judge or that the witness answer them; nor is it necessary that all the answers to the questions put be communicated to the parties to the trial. This may be refused, within certain limits, where communication of the anonymous witness's answers is likely to lead to the disclosure of his/her identity. In such cases, the investigating judge acts as a filter, maintaining a careful balance between the witness's right to protection of his/her person, on the one hand, and the right of the parties to the trial to an adversarial hearing, on the other.

Within certain limits, the parties to the trial have the opportunity to see for themselves how the investigating judge conducts the hearing of the anonymous witness. Where appropriate, the investigating judge may require the parties to the trial (or their counsel) to follow the hearing in another room, via a telecommunications system.

Notwithstanding the application of the aforementioned guarantees, the judge cannot treat anonymous testimony as satisfying the requirement of proof of an offence unless it is substantially corroborated by other pieces of evidence. This consequently entails the introduction of a minimum degree of proof.

13. Are pre-trial statements of witnesses and *pentiti* and testimonies of anonymous witnesses and *pentiti* regarded as valid evidence? If yes, under which conditions?

This question has already been answered in the replies to the previous questions (particularly questions 11 and 12 on hearings using audio-visual media and anonymous testimony).

14. Is it possible and, if so, under which conditions to use information provided by *pentiti*? How is their credibility assessed?

Belgium does not have comprehensive regulations governing "*pentiti*" or collaborators of justice. As long as the statutory requirements are satisfied, information supplied by "*pentiti*" in the cases provided for by law (see the reply to question 1) may be used by the judicial authorities.

15. What opportunities are there for the exercise of the rights of the defence, including the right of the accused to challenge the witness'/*pentito*'s credibility in criminal proceedings (including at the pre-trial stage) and the respect of the "equality of arms" principle?

This question has already been answered in the replies to the previous questions (particularly questions 8 and 12).

c. *Non-procedural measures*

16. At what stage(s) and in what context is it possible for witnesses and *pentiti* to benefit from a protection programme?

See the reply to question 4.

17. Are witnesses and *pentiti* able to obtain legal assistance at this (these) stage(s)?

Yes. Protected or anonymous witnesses may seek the assistance of a lawyer.

18. What is the procedure for admittance to a protection programme? Please specify, in particular, who takes the initiative, the criteria for admittance, the assessment of the relevance of a testimony and how admittance to the programme is formalised.

- Where special protection appears to be advisable, consideration must be given to the extent to which the witness is capable of benefiting from such protection. Having checked that the statutory requirements are satisfied, the witness's personality must consequently be investigated in detail in order to assess his/her credibility, desire to co-operate, resistance to stress and flexibility. Above all, this investigation must make it possible to assess whether the witness is likely to retract in the long run, or to abandon the protection programme because he/she is not equal to it psychologically. The fact is special protection measures have a major impact on the witness's day-to-day life. In this connection, it should be emphasised that the acceptance of protection measures is always voluntary, and that the witness can therefore decide to terminate the protection programme at any time. It is consequently crucial that the witness be informed of the implications of his or decision in advance, so as to avoid any unpleasant surprises, either for him/her or for the authorities.

  If a witness has been found guilty of punishable offences in the past, the risk he/she may represent to the society in which he/she is to be "relocated" should also be assessed. This comment also applies to a witness's friends and family for whom the authorisation of special protection measures is envisaged. The law makes such an assessment mandatory for any person found guilty of an act liable to a penalty of one year in prison or a heavier penalty.

- Protection measures may be requested by the Crown Prosecutor, the Principal Crown Prosecutor or the Federal Prosecutor. In the context of a judicial investigation, the investigating judge may request protection measures. The Crown Prosecutor, Principal Crown Prosecutor and Federal Prosecutor send a written, reasoned request to the Chair of the

Witness Protection Commission. The investigating judge sends a request to the Crown Prosecutor, who immediately forwards it to the Chair of the Witness Protection Commission.

As soon as the Chair of the Witness Protection Commission receives a request for the authorisation of protection measures and, as the case may be, financial assistance, he/she asks the Director General of the Criminal Investigation Division of the federal police for a written recommendation.

If protection measures are necessary as a matter of extreme urgency, the Chair of the Witness Protection Commission may, after consulting the Director General of the Criminal Investigation Division of the federal police and pending the latter's recommendation, provisionally decide to authorise ordinary protection measures. Reasons must be given for this provisional decision, which must contain a precise description of the protection measures authorised. The witness under threat is notified of the provisional decision in writing.

Within one month of receiving the request, the Director General of the Criminal Investigation Division of the federal police makes a detailed recommendation as to whether the statutory requirements for authorising protection measures in respect of the persons for whom protection is requested are satisfied, and, as the case may be, where special protection measures are requested, on the personal suitability of the individuals concerned to receive the protection measures and any financial assistance requested.

As soon as the Chair of the Witness Protection Commission receives the recommendation of the Director General of the Criminal Investigation Division of the federal police, he/she calls a meeting the Commission to rule on the request.

- The witness under threat, to whom the decision to grant protection measures is delivered, signs a written memorandum in which he/she undertakes to make sincere and complete statements concerning the case in which he/she is to testify, and to testify each time he/she is asked to do so.

If special protection measures are granted, he/she also undertakes in the memorandum to make sincere and complete statements relating to all the civil obligations incumbent upon him/her or upon family members or other relatives who are also to be protected, and undertakes to comply with these obligations in their entirety.

He/she also gives a general authorisation to the Director General of the Criminal Investigation Division of the federal police. With the agreement of the witness, the Director General of the Criminal Investigation Division of the federal police may enter into contracts with other persons for the purpose of administering the assets of the witness under power of attorney.

19. **Please indicate the measures that can be adopted for the protection of witnesses and *pentiti* (e.g. surveillance of their residence, physical protection, protection of personal records, relocation, change of identity, subsidies, assistance with a job search, relocation of a detainee to another prison or to special units).**

See the reply to question 4.

20. **At what stages in proceedings (pre-trial investigation, during the trial, after the trial) can a protection programme be granted? What is the protection programme's duration? What are the procedures for assessing the degree of danger for the witnesses/*pentiti* and their compliance with the programme obligations? Is to possible to challenge a decision to suspend, revoke or terminate a protection programme?**

- It is possible to benefit from a protection programme at all the stages of proceedings mentioned above.

- At least every six months, the Witness Protection Service, on the request of the police, the Crown Prosecutor, the Federal Prosecutor, the investigating judge, the Director General of Prisons or the witness under threat, or *ex officio*, verifies whether there are grounds for modifying or withdrawing the protection measures and any financial assistance granted.

  The protection measures granted may be <u>modified</u> if they are insufficient or if less extensive measures are sufficient to ensure protection of the witness under threat, family members or other relatives, and in the cases in which they may be withdrawn.

  The protection measures granted to a person may be <u>withdrawn</u> if:

  (1) he/she is suspected of committing a misdemeanour or felony after the protection measures were granted;
  (2) he/she is found guilty, following the authorisation of protection measures, of an act carrying a penalty of one year in prison or a heavier penalty or if criminal proceedings against him/her for a similar act lapse;
  (3) he/she has committed any act detrimental to the protection measures granted to him/her;
  (4) the provisions of the memorandum are not complied with.

The protection measures granted to a person are withdrawn in any event when that person is no longer at risk.

Protection measures granted to a witness under threat are withdrawn in any event when he/she is formally charged or brought to court by the prosecuting authorities for the acts in respect of which he/she has testified.

- Financial assistance granted to a witness under threat may be modified if it is insufficient or if a lesser sum is sufficient to meet the needs of the witness under threat, family members protected along with him/her and other relatives, and in the cases in which it may be withdrawn. The Witness Protection Commission takes into account the specific situation of the person concerned.

Financial assistance granted to a witness under threat may be withdrawn

(1) if the witness under threat is able meet his/her own needs and those of family members and other relatives moved along with him/her, or if he/she was able to meet those needs but improper or negligent behaviour on his/her part has prevented him/her from doing so;
(2) where parts of the monthly allowance or of a special financial contribution intended for specific purposes have been used for purposes other than those stipulated by the Witness Protection Commission;
(3) if the witness under threat has died and the family members and other relatives moved along with him/her are able meet their own needs.

- If the Witness Protection Service decides that there are grounds for modifying or withdrawing the protection measures or financial assistance granted, the Director General of the Criminal Investigation Division of the federal police makes a reasoned recommendation, within one month, to the Chair of the Witness Protection Commission.

As soon as the Chair of the Witness Protection Commission receives the recommendation from the Director General of the Criminal Investigation Division of the federal police, he/she calls a meeting of the Commission to take a decision.

The decision of the Witness Protection Commission is not subject to appeal.

d. *International co-operation*

When it comes to international co-operation in the area of witness protection, a distinction should be made between, on the one hand, (one-off) technical assistance granted in the context of a foreign protection programme and, on the other hand, a request from the foreign authorities to admit the witness under threat to a <u>national</u> programme. This distinction is particularly important in terms of the procedure to be followed (whether or not a request for mutual judicial assistance is required, validation, competent authorities, etc.). It is equally important in terms of the financial implications. Where, in the context of a criminal case, a witness is prepared to make a decisive statement opening the way for the facts to be elucidated and/or a group of criminals broken up, all the costs inherent in any protection measures – whether these are arranged within national boundaries or abroad – are borne by the country in which the case was tried. The only variation in some instances is that certain countries (such as Canada) also expect the requesting State to reimburse the staff costs incurred as a result of the involvement of members of the witness protection service, whereas until now Belgium has charged such costs to the federal police budget.

21. What measures (e.g. use of modern telecommunications technology, assistance in relocating protected witnesses, exchange of information between witness protection authorities) have been adopted in the context of mutual legal assistance in order to facilitate international co-operation? How are the financial implications of international co-operation activities dealt with?

To date, Belgium has not yet received any requests for mutual judicial assistance seeking to have a witness under threat as a result of a criminal case tried abroad admitted to a Belgian protection programme. Two cases have given rise to police contact with foreign protection services with a view to the possible organisation of protection, however, but no further action was needed insofar as the "potential" witnesses under threat were able to be afforded sufficient protection via the judicial proceedings.

In such cases, the witness under threat may benefit from protection measures provided for under Belgian law for witnesses under threat. Depending on the nature and seriousness of the threat, these may be ordinary protection measures (the law contains a non-exhaustive list including, *inter alia*, close physical protection, installation of preventive technical equipment, protection of data kept in the national register, temporary relocation, see above) or special protection measures (long-term relocation and/or change of identity). Special protection measures also confer entitlement to financial and/or psychological assistance, help in seeking a job and assistance with a view to the exercise of financial rights.

Belgium has not (yet) concluded any bilateral/multilateral conventions intended to regulate this form of international co-operation. Pending a specific legislative framework in this area, the requesting State must <u>always make a request for mutual judicial assistance</u> to Belgium, either via diplomatic channels or directly to the Federal Prosecutor (in the case of Schengen countries).

In other witness protection cases, the requesting State seeks one-off assistance, but organises and retains responsibility for the protection in question. In such situations, there is no law setting out a fixed list of possible measures, and each request is considered separately according to its legal and technical feasibility. Such requests for assistance are generally made in the context of direct contacts established between the national witness services via an informal international (primarily European) network. In most cases, no request for mutual judicial assistance is required, but Belgium systematically submits the aforementioned requests for assistance to the decision of the Federal Prosecutor on the basis of a confidential report drafted by the Belgian Witness Protection Service. A request for mutual judicial assistance is required in certain exceptional cases, however, particularly for the organisation of hearings by video-conference insofar as there is already a specific legal framework in that area.

The following assistance has been granted to date in such cases:

- serving writs of the International Criminal Tribunal for the Former Yugoslavia, via the Witness Protection Service, intended to ensure the protection of witnesses during their stay;
- arranging contact with family members not admitted to a protection programme;
- organising transport for witnesses under threat;
- transferring sums of money to family members staying abroad who have not been admitted to a protection programme;
- temporary relocation in Belgium in view of an acute threat in the country organising the protection programme;
- discreet observation and escort for protection purposes;
- making a contact person available and organising a warning procedure in the event of an emergency;
- organising a holiday so that the psychological pressure on family members remains manageable;
- discreet relocation of a witness under threat and assistance in arranging a transfer to the International Criminal Tribunal.

22. Has your country entered international (bilateral or multilateral) agreements on the protection of witnesses and *pentiti*? If so, please indicate what kind of provisions they include.

No. However, it seems advisable, and indeed essential, for such agreements to be concluded so as to lay down clear, detailed rules in the area of co-operation. Definitions of the concept of "witness under threat" vary widely from one country to another, as do the rules governing the granting of protection (legality, subsidiarity and proportionality), the procedure followed and the criteria applied. In this connection, a clear decision should be made as to whether, in order to grant protection measures, the requested State must comply with its own legal framework or with the reference framework (regulated by law or otherwise) of the requesting State. A convention could also lay down clear rules regarding the financial implications of such co-operation.

23. How can international co-operation in the field of the protection of witnesses and *pentiti* be improved?

A series of significant social developments such as increasing globalisation and a rapid rise in the number of cases before international tribunals have, naturally, had an impact on how crime and related aspects are tackled. It is becoming increasingly necessary to relocate witnesses under threat beyond national boundaries. While international co-operation could undoubtedly be improved, it already operates in a fairly satisfactory manner at present. What is still problematic, however, is the establishment of an international regulatory framework for the organisation of witness protection. The exercise conducted by Europol (see document entitled "*Common Criteria for Taking a Witness into a Protection Programme*") shows that there are fairly significant differences among the various Member States, which also affect any co-operation.

e. Statistics

24. How many people currently benefit from witness or *pentito* protection measures/programmes and for how long? How many of them are foreigners? If the measures/programmes can be extended to relatives and other close persons, please indicate how many people are included in this category (and, if possible, specify the relationship with the witness/*pentito*). Please also provide figures on the different kinds of measures (procedural and non-procedural) adopted and on the number of cases involving international co-operation.

During the 2002-June 2003 period, the Witness Protection Service dealt with 37 cases. In 7 of these cases, no protection measures were taken, either because the statutory requirements were not satisfied, or because an examination of the initial evidence had shown that it was not appropriate to put a protection programme in place (lack of co-operation on the part of the victim, procedural difficulties, mental state, etc.).

As for the rest, protection measures were devised for 31 people under threat, including 9 foreign nationals. Protection programmes are not aimed solely at the witnesses under threat, but may be extended to family members or persons with whom the witness under threat maintains a lasting emotional relationship. With regard to the Belgian cases, this applies to 6 people at present (to whom another 8 may be added in the near future as a result of cases currently in preparation). As regards cases involving international co-operation, technical assistance was provided on behalf of 9 people, all family members of witnesses under threat. At the request of foreign authorities, Belgium has provided technical assistance in 7 protection cases to date. Lastly, two cases were initiated by the International Criminal Tribunal for the Former Yugoslavia.

f. Proposals and comments

25. Please provide any comments/proposals concerning the implementation of the terms of reference of the PC-PW and, in particular, instruments to be adopted to strengthen the protection of witnesses and *pentiti*.

See the reply to question 23: co-operation between States in relation to witness protection can be improved. There are fairly significant differences, which also affect any co-operation.

Bosnia and Herzegovina

a. General information

1. **Please describe the framework (legal provisions and established practice) governing the use of measures protecting witnesses and *pentiti*.**

Since Bosnia and Herzegovina adopted a new Criminal Procedure Code (which entered into force on 1 March 2003), introducing the possibility of the protection of witnesses, it has had no practical experience. Article 91 of the Criminal Code of Bosnia and Herzegovina stipulates that the position of protected witnesses is regulated by the provisions of a special law "the Law on Protection of Witnesses under Threat and Vulnerable Witnesses", which is the first Bosnia and Herzegovina State-level law regulating these issues.

The Law on Protection of Witnesses under Threat and Vulnerable Witnesses (hereinafter the Law) was enacted by the High Representative for Bosnia and Herzegovina with the Decision No. 102/03 of 24 January 2003. According to the aforesaid Decision the Law remained on an interim basis[1] until its adoption by the national Parliamentary Assembly in July 2003.[2]

Moreover, in 2004 the national Parliamentary Assembly adopted the Law on Witness Protection Programme.[3]

The status of "*pentiti*" was also introduced by the new Criminal Code of Bosnia and Herzegovina under Article 231 of the Criminal Procedure Code of Bosnia and Herzegovina.

2. **Please describe the framework (legal provisions and established practice) governing the use of measures encouraging witnesses and *pentiti* to co-operate with justice.**

Our law does not prescribe any special measures encouraging witnesses to co-operate with justice. There are only protection measures and they are stipulated in Articles 8, 9, 10, 11, 12, 13 and 14 of the Law on Protection of Witnesses under Threat and Vulnerable Witnesses.

---

[1] The Law was published in the Official Gazette of Bosnia and Herzegovina No. 3/03 of 10 February 2003 and entered into force on 1 March 2003.

[2] Cf. Offical Gazette of Bosnia and Herzegovina No. 21/03 of 24 July 2003. Amendments to the Law on Protection of Witnesses under Threat and Vulnerable Witnesses were adopted by national Parliamentary Assembly in 2004 and published in the Official Gazette of Bosnia and Herzegovina No. 61/04 of 29 December 2004.

[3] Official Gazette of Bosnia and Herzegovina No. 29/04 of 28 June 2004.

3. **Can measures/benefits encouraging the co-operation of witnesses and *pentiti* be used in combination with protection measures (arrangements concerning trial proceedings, sentencing conditions, special penitentiary regimes, etc.)? If so, please specify and indicate under which conditions they are applied.**

a) Protection measures for witnesses are listed hereinafter: a controlled interrogation of witnesses by the judge or president of the council; testifying by means of technical devices for sound and picture transmission (video-conference); removal of a defendant from the courtroom if his/her presence could influence a witness's ability to testify and give a full and accurate statement; limitation of the rights of the defendant and his/her defence attorney to examine papers and documents if this would reveal a witness's identity or endanger him/her; the court may decide that personal information about a witness stays confidential for as long as necessary and for no longer than 30 years once the decision becomes legally valid.

b) For *pentiti*, the prosecutor may propose to inflict a commuted penalty below the minimum of custodial sentence determined by the law for this crime (Article 231 of the Criminal Procedure Code of Bosnia and Herzegovina).

A written agreement between the *pentito* and the prosecutor must be approved by the court, i.e. it must be established that agreement was reached voluntarily, in all conscience and knowledge, if there is enough evidence on the crime of the *pentito*, if he/she waivers the right to trial and if he/she cannot appeal against a criminal legal sanction that would be pronounced against him/her.

4. **For which kind of crime and under which circumstances can witness and *pentiti* protection be applied? Can the measures be extended to the relatives or other persons close to the witness/*pentito*?**

Our law does not specify for what kind of crime a witness may be protected. He/she is protected if his/her personal security or the security of his/her family is in danger because of his/her participation in the proceedings, as the result of threats, intimidation or similar actions related to his/her testimony.

A vulnerable witness is a person who suffers from a serious physical or psychological trauma due to the circumstances in which a crime was committed or who is seriously disturbed psychologically, which has made him/her very sensitive.

5. **What urgent measures (e.g. immediate relocation to a secret place) can be taken in order to protect witnesses and *pentiti*?**

The law does not foresee any urgent measures.

6. Which institutions are involved in the protection of witnesses and *pentiti* and what is their role (e.g. law enforcement agencies, special independent agencies, prosecutor's offices, judicial authorities, etc)? How does co-operation between the relevant institutions work in practice?

Only institutions, such as the court, the prosecutor's office and social care organisations are involved in the protection of witnesses, by hiding the identity of witnesses and the way in which they are heard as well as by providing social care.

7. Are there any specific provisions governing the protection of witnesses and *pentiti* in relation to acts of terrorism? If so, please specify. Are there any specialised counter-terrorism institutions? If so, what is their role in the protection of witnesses and *pentiti* in relation to acts of terrorism?

There are no such provisions or specialised anti-terrorist institutions.

8. How does the framework governing the use of measures protecting witnesses and *pentiti* and encouraging them to co-operate with justice guarantee respect for human rights and individual freedoms. Please indicate the procedures in place, if any, to monitor compliance with human rights standards.

The reply to this question is contained in the replies to questions 1, 2 and 3.

b. *Procedural measures*

9. At which stage(s), and in which context, is it possible for witnesses and *pentiti* to benefit form procedural measures of protection?

It is possible to provide protection at any stage in the criminal procedure.

10. Is there the possibility for witnesses and *pentiti* to obtain legal assistance at this (these) stage(s)?

There is such a possibility.

11. Are there alternative methods of giving evidence which allow the protection of witnesses and *pentiti* from intimidation resulting from face to face confrontation with the accused? If yes, please specify

(e.g. full or partial anonymity, video-conference, disguise, exclusion of the defendant from the courtroom when the witness is giving evidence, exclusion of the media or the public from the trial, etc.) and indicate under which conditions these methods are used.

Article 13 of the Law on Protection of Witnesses under Threat and Vulnerable Witnesses stipulates that the court can allow the witness to testify behind a curtain or using an electronic device to change his/her voice or his/her appearance in order to protect his/her anonymity. The court allows this type of hearing once the statements of both parties (prosecutors and defence attorneys) have been taken.

12. On which grounds and on the basis of which criteria can anonymity be granted? Is there the possibility to obtain legal assistance at this stage?

The guarantee of anonymity comes from the court's obligation not to put a witness's personal details in the minutes of the hearing. In the event of the panel having to take a statement, it provides a guarantee that the witness will not show up at the trial in any other way than as a protected witness and that he/she will not have to answer any questions that may reveal his/her identity or the identity of other members of his/her family.

13. Are pre-trial statements of witnesses and *pentiti* and testimonies of anonymous witnesses and *pentiti* regarded as valid evidence? If yes, under which conditions?

This is only possible when there is a chance that the witness will not be present at the main trial.

14. Is it possible, and if so, under which conditions, to use information provided by "*pentiti*"? How is their credibility assessed?

Any information given by a *pentito* can be used if an agreement is reached between him/her and the prosecutor, and if the court approves this agreement. In this agreement the *pentito* guarantees that he/she will co-operate with the prosecutor and in return the prosecutor will suggest a commuted penalty.

15. Which are the opportunities for the defence to exercise its rights, including the right of the accused to challenge the witness'/*pentito*'s credibility in criminal proceedings (including at the pre-trial stage) and the respect of the "equality of arms" principle?

The possibility for the accused and the defence to challenge the credibility of the protected witness is limited to the absolute minimum.

c. Extra-procedural measures (physical protection)

16. At which stage(s), and in which context, is it possible for witnesses and *pentiti* to benefit from a protection programme?

17. Is there the possibility for witnesses and *pentiti* to obtain legal assistance at this (these) stage(s)?

18. What is the procedure for admittance to a protection programme? Please specify, in particular, who takes the initiative, the criteria for admittance, the assessment of the relevance of a testimony and how admittance to the programme is formalised.

19. Please indicate the measures that can be adopted for the protection of witnesses and *pentiti* (e.g. surveillance of the residence, physical protection, protection of personal records, relocation, change of identity, subsidies, assistance in job search, relocation of a detainee to another prison or to special units).

No, non–procedural measures exist with regard to questions 16, 17, 18 and 19. Our Law does not specify the possibility of surveillance, relocation, change of identity, assistance in finding a job or transfer of detainees to another prison. The Court has the right to protect the witness with the measures it considers appropriate.

20. What can the duration of a protection programme be? Which are the procedures for assessing the degree of danger for the witnesses/*pentiti* and their compliance with the obligations of the programme? Is it possible to challenge a decision of suspension, revocation or termination of a protection programme?

The protection programme has no time limits. There are no special procedures for assessing the degree of danger a witness may be exposed to.

d. International co-operation

21. Which measures (e.g. use of modern telecommunications means, assistance in relocating protected witnesses, exchange of information between witness protection authorities) have been adopted in the context of mutual legal assistance in order to facilitate international co-operation? How are the financial implications of international co-operation activities dealt with?

and

22. Has your country entered international (bilateral or multilateral) agreements on the protection of witnesses and *pentiti*? If so, please indicate what kind of provisions they include.

Our country has not yet ratified international agreements on the protection of witnesses.

23. How can international co-operation in the field of the protection of witnesses and *pentiti* be improved?

By introducing the possibility of relocation of protected witnesses outside their country, especially if that country is small, like Bosnia and Herzegovina, where their new address can easily be discovered.

e. Statistics

24. How many people currently benefit from witness or *pentito* protection measures/programmes, and for how long? How many of them are foreign people? If the measures/programmes can be extended to relatives and other close persons, please indicate (and, if possible, specify the relationship with the witness/*pentito*) how many people are included in this category. Please also provide figures on the different kinds of measures (procedural and non-procedural) adopted, and on the number of cases involving international co-operation.

There have been no cases of witness protection as the Law was only applied as of 1 March 2003.

f. Proposals and comments

25. Please provide any comments/proposals concerning the implementation of the terms of reference of the PC-PW and, in particular, instruments to be adopted to strengthen the protection of witnesses and *pentiti*.

The State Law should provide more concrete protection measures such as relocation, change of identity, help in finding a job, etc.

Czech Republic

a. *General information*

1. Please describe the framework (legal provisions and established practice) governing the use of measures protecting witnesses and *pentiti*.

In the Czech Republic, the protection of witnesses and persons co-operating with bodies involved in criminal proceedings is regulated, firstly, by the Code of Criminal Procedure (Section 55, clause 2) and secondly, by the Act on the Special Protection of Witnesses and Other Persons in connection with Criminal Proceedings (Act No. 137/2001, Collection of Laws).

a) The provisions of Section 55, clause 2 of the Code of Criminal Procedure provide for a witness, including his/her personal data (name and surname, employment, permanent address, etc.), to be concealed. The concealment is of course brought into effect on condition that there is an obvious threat to the health of the witness or of those close to him/her (any kind of threat to health is enough), and furthermore, on condition that they are threatened with other serious infringements of their basic rights and freedoms. The concealment of the witness's appearance and personal data only occurs after the fulfilment of additional conditions, i.e. if the protection of the witness cannot be reliably carried out in any other manner (e.g. police protection, temporary or long-term relocation to an unknown location, change of identity). If it is necessary to ensure the protection of these persons, the bodies that are involved in criminal proceedings will immediately take all the necessary measures.

Concealment, pursuant to the Code of Criminal Procedure, means measures to ensure that unauthorised entities, i.e. entities other than the bodies involved in criminal proceedings, do not gain information, particularly in relation to the examination of the witness. If the personal data of the witness is concealed, then his/her name and surname and other personal data are not included in the record of his/her examination or of other activities, but are recorded separately from the criminal records in a special record which can only be accessed by the bodies involved in criminal proceedings in which the witness was examined. This record must be labelled with the relevant degree of confidentiality and must be handled in accordance with the regulations concerning the manipulation of concealed records. No entity, other than bodies involved in criminal proceedings, may consult a record containing the personal data of a witness whose identity is concealed. The witness must be informed that he/she can sign the record using a pseudonym.

b) The special measures for protecting witnesses and persons close to them is laid down in Act No. 137/2001 on the Special Protection of Witnesses and

Other Persons in connection with Criminal Proceedings (hereinafter Act No. 137/2001). The purpose of this Act is to provide for the special protection of and assistance to witnesses and other persons who are threatened with bodily harm or in other grave danger in connection with criminal proceedings (endangered persons). This Act only comes into play if the safety of the endangered person cannot be ensured in any other manner. Whereas the above-mentioned provisions of the Code of Criminal Procedure only apply to the witness in criminal proceedings him/herself, protection pursuant to Act No. 137/2001 is provided to a wider circle of persons.

Act No. 137/2001defines the term "endangered person" as a person who has made or should make a statement, who testifies as a witness, who has testified or should testify as the accused or who in any other manner has helped or should help, pursuant to the Code of Criminal Procedure, to achieve the purpose of the criminal proceedings, or who is an expert or an interpreter, or who is the defendant, if accused, represented by the defending attorney, who has testified or should testify in favour of the criminal proceedings. Protection also applies to persons close to the above-mentioned persons.

Furthermore, Act No. 137/2001 defines the term "protected person" as an endangered person (see above) who is provided with special protection and assistance.

Special protection and assistance, pursuant to Act No. 137/2001, is a collection of measures that consist of:
- Personal protection,
- Relocation of the protected person, including the members of his/her household, and assistance to enable him/her to socially integrate in his/her new surroundings.
- Disguising the real identity of the protected person.

Special protection can be provided if the endangered person agrees to it, and the Minister of the Interior approves the proposal of the police, the judge or the prosecutor to provide the endangered person with special protection. The judge or the prosecutor submits such a proposal via the Minister of Justice.

2. **Please describe the framework (legal provisions and established practice) governing the use of measures encouraging witnesses and *pentiti* to co-operate with justice.**

The Criminal Code contains a provision (Section 40) that enables the judge to mitigate the term of imprisonment of a perpetrator who has co-operated with the bodies involved in criminal proceedings under the conditions stipulated in this provision.

Currently a Bill concerning so-called crown witnesses, which regulates measures to encourage witnesses to co-operate with bodies involved in criminal proceedings in greater detail (measures such as mitigation of sentence or granting of impunity), is being discussed in Parliament. The Bill takes the form of an amendment to the Criminal Procedure Code and Criminal Code.

3. **Can measures/benefits encouraging the co-operation of witnesses and *pentiti* be used in combination with protection measures (arrangements concerning trial proceedings, sentencing conditions, special penitentiary regimes, etc,)? If so, please specify and indicate under which conditions they are applied.**

Yes, encouraging measures can be used in combination with protection measures.

4. **For which kind of crime and under which circumstances can witness and *pentito* protection be applied? Can the measures be extended to the relatives or other persons close to the witness/*pentito*?**

The protection of witnesses or co-operating persons is not limited by Act No. 137/2001 to a certain type of crime. In reality, the provisions of witness protection are applied in cases concerning serious crime (organised crime, etc.). However, Act No. 137/2001 does not stipulate any limits in this sense of the Act.

Act No. 137/2001 is extended by a collection of protective measures for persons close to the endangered person. The following are considered to be close persons: relatives within one generation, adoptive parents, adopted children, siblings, and spouse. Other close persons are considered to be other persons within a family, or similar, relationship, whose injury would be felt by the endangered person as his/her own. In such cases, the bodies involved in criminal proceedings must investigate the actual relationship between these persons.

5. **What urgent measures (e.g. immediate relocation to a secret place) can be taken in order to protect witnesses and *pentiti*?**

If the endangered person is in immediate danger, the police, with the approval of the chief of police (or with the approval of the managing director of the penitentiary system, if the endangered person is in custody or serving a prison sentence) will provide special protection and assistance even before the Minister of the Interior has approved the proposal for the provision of special protection and assistance. In such cases, the special protection and assistance can even be provided without the endangered person's approval. As mentioned above, the protective measures are personal protection, relocation of the protected person and the members of his/her household, assisting the protected person to integrate socially into his/her new surroundings, and disguising the real identity of the protected person.

6. Which institutions are involved in the protection of witnesses and *pentiti* and what is their role (e.g. law enforcement agencies, special independent agencies, prosecutor's offices, judicial authorities, etc.)? How does co-operation between the relevant institutions work in practice?

The protection of endangered persons is provided and carried out by the police. The police, prosecutor or judge presents a proposal to the Minister of the Interior who approves it. The prosecutor or the judge submits such a proposal for protection via the Minister of Justice. If the endangered person is in police custody or is serving a prison sentence, the penitentiary system will provide special protection and assistance, with the approval of the managing director of the penitentiary system. However within the penitentiary system, the only measures which can be implemented are personal protection and the disguising of the real identity of the protected person (relocation cannot even be considered). The police and the penitentiary system are obliged to assist each other when carrying out these tasks.

7. Are there any specific provisions governing the protection of witnesses and *pentiti* in relation to acts of terrorism? If so, please specify. Are there any specialised counter-terrorism institutions? If so, what is their role in the protection of witnesses and *pentiti* in relation to acts of terrorism?

There are no special divisions in the Prosecutor's Office dedicated to the fight against terrorism in the Czech Republic. The police of the Czech Republic have a division specialised in the suppression of terrorism, within the Unit for the Detection of Organised Crime. There is no special law concerning the protection of witnesses in relation to terrorist attacks. The protection of witnesses or co-operating persons is not limited by Act No. 137/2001 to a certain type of crime.

8. How does the framework governing the use of measures protecting witnesses and *pentiti* and encouraging them to co-operate with justice guarantee respect for human rights and individual freedoms? Please indicate the procedures in place, if any, to monitor compliance with human rights standards.

Police bodies may allow the accused to participate in investigative activities and allow him/her to put questions to the investigated witnesses. From the start of the criminal prosecution, the accused's defending lawyer has the right to be present during any investigative activities whose results may be used as evidence during court proceedings. This means that even if the identity and appearance of the witness is concealed in the criminal proceedings, the defence has the right to put questions to the witnesses directly. The police bodies, the prosecutor or the court must make sure that there is no direct confrontation between the concealed witness and the accused or his/her defending lawyer. The appearance and personal data of the witness may not be revealed to entities other than the bodies that are involved in criminal proceedings. If the defending lawyer notifies police bodies, which are carrying out the investigation, that he/she wishes to participate in all the investigative activities, the police bodies are obliged to inform him/her in good time of the type, time and place of each investigative activity. Information on the examination of a witness whose identity is to remain secret must not contain any information that could lead to the ascertainment of the real identity of the witness.

b. *Procedural measures*

9. At which stage (s) and in which context is it possible for witnesses and *pentiti* to benefit from procedural measures of protection?

The protection of witnesses and other persons can be provided at any stage of the criminal proceedings, when they are in danger of bodily harm or threatened with other serious infringements of their basic rights and freedoms.

10. Is there the possibility for witnesses and *pentiti* to obtain legal assistance at this (these) stage (s)?

Pursuant to the Constitution of the Czech Republic and to the documents on basic rights and freedoms, which are a part of the Constitutional Order of the Czech Republic, everyone has the right to legal representation.

The Code of Criminal Procedure contains a more extensive wording concerning representation of the injured party. The injured party in criminal proceedings can be represented by an attorney who is authorised, on his/her behalf, to put forth proposals, make requests and protect his/her right of appeal. He/she also has the right to participate in all the activities in which the injured party is allowed to participate. If an injured party, who has claimed for the reimbursement of damages, is shown to not have enough means to pay for his/her representation by an attorney, the court may present a proposal for a decision concerning his/her right to be legally represented for free or represented for a reduced fee. The court, when coming to a decision, will take into consideration the amount or nature of the claim for the reimbursement of damages. During preliminary police procedures, the injured party puts forth his/her proposal via the prosecutor who will attach his/her statement to it. If the conditions are met, the court will assign an attorney to the injured party whose expenses in the given proceedings will be paid for by the State.

11. Are there alternative methods of giving evidence that allow the protection of witnesses and *pentiti* from intimidation resulting from face to face confrontation with the accused? If yes, please specify (e.g. full or partial anonymity, video-conference, disguise, exclusion of the defendant from the courtroom when the witness is giving evidence, exclusion of the media or the public from the trial, etc.) and indicate under which conditions these methods are used.

Witnesses or other persons can have full or partial anonymity in criminal proceedings. This can be the concealment of the witness's appearance and his/her personal information, or only partial concealment in cases where the name and surname of the witness is known to the accused but details of his/her residence, employment, etc. are changed and concealed in co-operation with the bodies involved in criminal proceedings. The conditions for concealing the appearance of the witness pursuant to Section 55, clause 2 of the Code of Criminal Procedure and disguising the real identity of the protected person pursuant to Act No. 137/2001 have been described above.

A recent amendment to the Code of Criminal Procedure allows for the use of video-conferencing within the framework of international co-operation (Section 444 – examination via video-telephone and telephone).

The anonymity of persons giving evidence can be protected using audiovisual technology when the accused and the defendant have the opportunity to put questions to the examined person. This is a situation comparable to video-conference, where the person testifying is separated from the other individuals present with the help of technical equipment and is not viewed directly.

If there is concern that the witness will not tell the truth in the presence of the accused at the main trial, or if the witness, or persons close to him/her, is threatened with an attack on his/her health, death or any other serious danger if he/she testifies, the court can take appropriate measures to ensure the witness's safety or that his/her identity is concealed, or it can exclude the accused from the courtroom during the examination of the witness. On his/her return to the courtroom, the accused must be informed of the contents of the witness's testimony and can express his/her opinion on it. The accused can also put questions to the witness through the court without having to meet this witness.

The court can decide to exclude the public during the main trial or for only part of the main trial. One reason for the exclusion of the public would be the safety or other important concerns of the witness. With prior court approval, it is possible to carry out visual or audio transmissions and to make pictorial records during court proceedings. The court can prohibit them if they disturb the course or the formality of the proceedings.

12. On which grounds and on the basis of which criteria can anonymity be granted? Is there the possibility to obtain legal assistance at this stage?

As was mentioned above, the concealment of the identity and appearance of a witness and his/her personal data means taking measures to ensure that these facts are not ascertained by not-authorised entities. This means entities other than the bodies involved in criminal proceedings, particularly those involved in criminal matters in which the witness was examined. Concealment of the appearance of the witness begins in the preliminary proceedings, particularly during activities in which the witness comes in contact with the accused, especially during identification, reconstruction or investigative activities, which must be carried out in such a manner that the witness and the accused and his/her lawyer, and possibly other persons, do not meet face to face. For instance, identification can be accomplished through a one-way see-through mirror; an investigative activity or reconstruction requiring the participation of the witness can be carried out via an audio or video connection, etc. In the case of the concealment of the witness's personal data, these data are not included in the record of his/her examination or in records of other activities, but are kept separately in a special record to which only the bodies that are involved in criminal proceedings have access. Other persons cannot consult these records.

Anonymity is also guaranteed by Act No. 137/2001 and in the provision of protection by disguising the real identity of the protected person. It is possible to invent a new identity in order to disguise the real identity of the protected person and place the personal data arising from this invented identity into the information system. These data are not identified in any special manner and are not kept separately from other personal data.

13. Are pre-trial statements of witnesses and *pentiti* and testimonies of anonymous witnesses and *pentiti* regarded as valid evidence? If yes, under what conditions?

It can generally be said that all evidence which is legally gathered after the criminal proceedings have been initiated against a specific person serves as valid proof. The police decide to initiate criminal proceedings against the accused if, during their investigations, they come to a justified conclusion that a crime has been committed by a specific person. The bodies involved in criminal proceedings, on the basis of careful, objective and multilateral deliberation, will evaluate all the evidence individually and as a whole. The testimonies of secret witnesses are also evaluated according to this principle.

The police may require explanations from certain persons before the initiation of the criminal prosecution of a specific person. These explanations allow the prosecutor and the accused to consider whether a person having provided explanations should be examined as a witness. This would also help the court determine whether or not to examine the individual in person. These explanations cannot be used in court proceedings as evidence unless they were urgent or could not be repeated and were given in the presence of the judge before the initiation of the criminal prosecution of a specific person. In this case they could be used as evidence to initiate the criminal prosecution in the preliminary proceedings and in the main trial.

14. Is it possible, and if so, under which conditions, to use information provided by "*pentiti*"? How is their credibility assessed?

It is possible to use the same conditions as stated in question 13.

15. What are the opportunities for the defence to exercise its rights, including the right of the accused to challenge the witness'/*pentito's* credibility in criminal proceedings (including at the pre-trail stage) and the respect of the "equality of arms" principle?

In the preliminary proceedings, the police may allow the participation of the accused in the investigative activities and allow him/her to put questions to the examined witnesses. From the initiation of the criminal prosecution, the defending attorney has the right to be present during any investigative activities whose results may be used as evidence in the court proceedings. He/she can put questions to the accused and to other examined persons. If the defending attorney informs the police bodies that he/she wishes to participate in the investigative activities, the police are obliged to inform him/her in good time about what kind of activity this will be and when and where it will take place. In the event of the examination of a witness whose identity should remain concealed, the police must take measures to ensure that the real identity of the witness is not discovered by the defending attorney or the accused. The same conditions apply in the phase in the court proceedings when both the accused and the defending attorney have the right to put questions to the examined person. However, in the case of a concealed witness, the court must ensure that no direct confrontation with this concealed witness occurs. The accused and the defending attorney can participate and put questions to the witness using audiovisual technology without directly viewing the person testifying. The accused and the defending attorney have the right to propose the presentation of any kind of evidence, including evidence that could confirm or undermine the credibility of the concealed witness.

c. Non-procedural measures

16. At which stage (s), and in which context, is it possible for witnesses and *pentiti* to benefit from a protection programme?

The same as in question 9.

17. Is there the possibility for witnesses and *pentiti* to obtain legal assistance at this (these) stage (s)?

See the reply to question 10.

18. What is the procedure for admittance to a protection programme? Please specify, in particular, who takes the initiative, the criteria for admittance, the assessment of the relevance of a testimony and how admittance to the programme is formalised.

The bodies involved in criminal proceedings are obliged to instruct the witness before he/she is examined that, among other things, he/she may request the concealment of his/her identity and appearance. If the witness decides to request the concealment of his/her identity and appearance, the Code of Criminal Procedure requires the witness to simultaneously state a specific reason that justifies doing so. One such reason would be, in particular, the existence of threats and other forms of intimidation against the witness or those close to him/her, if these threats of injury to health or other serious breach of basic rights are likely to be carried out. The police itself must take measures to conceal the identity and appearance of certain witnesses in its contacts with them. The police can also take a negative standpoint and prove that it is not necessary to conceal a witness. If the police do not comply with a witness's request, they must inform the prosecutor and have him/her re-examine their procedures. The prosecutor has the final say on this issue in the preliminary proceedings. If there is no danger due to delay, the police will postpone the examination of the witness until the prosecutor has given his/her decision. However, if there is danger due to a delay, the police will examine the witness and handle the record of the examination of the witness so that his/her identity remains concealed until the prosecutor's acceptance of the measures.

Pursuant to Act No. 137/2001, it is possible to provide special protection and assistance if the endangered person agrees with the terms and conditions for the provision of special protection and assistance and the Minister of the Interior has approved the proposal of the police, judge or prosecutor to provide special protection and assistance to the threatened person. The judge or the prosecutor makes its proposal via the Minister of Justice.

19. Please indicate the measures that can be adopted for the protection of witnesses and *pentiti* (e.g. surveillance of the residence, physical protection, protection of personal records, relocation, change of identity, subsidies, assistance in job search, relocation of a detainee to another prison or the special units).

Special protection and assistance includes:
a) Personal protection;

b)   Relocation of the protected person, including the members of his/her household, and assisting the protected person to socially integrate him/herself in his/her new surroundings;

c)   Disguising the real identity of the protected person.

The police and the penitentiary system provide special protection and assistance. They are obliged to mutually assist one another when fulfilling these tasks. It is possible to invent a new identity in order to disguise the real identity of a protected person and place the personal data arising from the new identity into the information system, where it is not kept separately from other personal data.

20. What can the duration of a protection programme be? What are the procedures for assessing the degree of danger for the witnesses/*pentiti* and their compliance with the obligations of the programme? Is it possible to challenge a decision of suspension, revocation or termination of a protection programme?

If circumstances indicate that the witness or persons close to him/her, or other persons connected with his/her testimony are obviously threatened with injury to health or other serious infringements of their basic rights, and it is not possible to guarantee the protection of the witness in any other manner, the bodies involved in criminal proceedings will take measures to conceal the identity and appearance of the witness, and will possibly provide special protection. Any kind of threat is sufficient, even of a slight injury to health or infringement of basic rights. However, this threat must be justified with specific ascertained circumstances.

If the reasons for concealing the appearance of the witness and his/her personal data no longer exist, the body that at that time is carrying out the criminal proceedings will attach his/her data to the criminal documents and the appearance of the witness will no longer be concealed.

Where the witness and other persons have been provided with special protection pursuant to Act No. 137/2001, he/she is obliged to comply with the conditions for the special protection. He/she must follow the instructions of the officers of the police and the penitentiary system, and must, without delay, inform them of any new circumstances and changes that could significantly affect the way he/she acts.

The provision of special protection ends obligatorily under two circumstances: if the protected person withdraws his/her approval concerning the terms and conditions of the special protection, or if the danger that threatened the protected person no longer exists. Moreover, the Minister of the Interior can facultatively decide to end the provision of special protection and assistance in the following cases: if the protected person refuses to help achieve the purpose of the criminal proceedings; if he/she deliberately commits a crime during the period when the special protection is being provided; if he/she does not fulfil his/her obligations; or if he/she violated the secrecy of secret facts. It is possible to appeal the decision of the Minister of the Interior within 15 days after his/her decision has been sent to the court, the appeal having a delaying effect.

d. *International co-operation*

21. Which measures (e.g. use of modern telecommunications means, assistance in relocating protected witnesses, exchange of information between witness protection authorities) have been adopted in the context of mutual legal assistance in order to facilitate international co-operation? How are the financial implications of international co-operation activities dealt with?

In the context of international legal assistance, it is possible to use the provisions on concealed witnesses pursuant to the Code of Criminal Procedure, as well as the provisions of Act No. 137/2001. In practice, a case has already occurred in which the Czech Republic examined a secret witness at the request of a foreign country. If, at the request of a foreign country, the Czech bodies in criminal proceedings examine a witness and come to the conclusion that there are conditions which justify the concealment of his/her appearance, and possibly his/her personal data, the requested legal assistance would be conveyed abroad on condition that even abroad the appearance, and possibly the personal data, of the witness be concealed.

Within the framework of international co-operation, concealed facts are provided abroad without the approval of the relevant State body. If necessary for the fulfilment of police tasks pursuant to Act No. 137/2001, it is possible to use an officer of the foreign security corps to fulfil this task on the basis of the international agreements by which the Czech Republic is bound, or if this kind of agreement has not been concluded then with the approval of the chief of police and with the approval of the relevant body of the foreign country. This officer of the foreign security corps has the rights and obligations of a police officer, as stated in Act No. 137/2001. He/she is appointed by the chief of police.

The expenses associated with the application of this Act No. 137/2001, including any financial means that may be provided to a protected person, are borne by the State.

22. Has your country entered international (bilateral or multilateral) agreements on the protection of witnesses and *pentiti*? If so, please indicate what kind of provisions they include.

Bilateral agreements have been concluded in the field of police co-operation which provide for specific procedures in police co-operation and which may also be used for the protection of witnesses and *pentiti* within the limits of legal regulations. Such bilateral agreements on police co-operation have been concluded with Austria, Germany, Poland and Slovakia.

23. How can international co-operation in the field of the protection of witnesses and *pentiti* be improved?

An amendment to Act No. 137/2001 has recently been approved by Parliament. The main aim of the amendment is to stipulate explicitly the conditions for the protection of witnesses and other persons in relation to foreign countries (co-operation on witness protection).

e. Statistics

24.How many people currently benefit from witness or *pentito* protection measures/programmes, and for how long? How many of them are foreign people? If the measures/programmes can be extended to relatives and other close persons, please indicate (and, if possible, specify the relationship with the witness/*pentito*) how many people are included in this category. Please also provide figures on the different kinds of measures (procedural and non-procedural) adopted, and on the number of cases involving international co-operation.

In the Czech Republic, precise statistics concerning the protection of witnesses or *pentiti* are subject to secrecy and cannot be disclosed. We can say that the explanatory report to Act No. 137/2001 presumed that the witness or *pentito* protection programme would be used for about 10 people a year.

f. Proposals and comments

25. Please provide any comments/proposals concerning the implementation of the terms of reference of the PC-PW and, in particular, instruments to be adopted to strengthen the protection of witnesses and *pentiti*.

The Czech Republic is aware that, apart from the above-mentioned instruments for the protection of witnesses, not all measures that are used in other countries have been taken yet. However, we can state that we are currently preparing the re-codification of the criminal substantive law and criminal procedure and, in relation to this, we intend to re-regulate the protection of witnesses and *pentiti*. The sense of the new legal regulation is to ensure the protection of these persons in criminal procedure, to strengthen their position, to detect and clear up the most serious forms of criminal activity. To achieve this, we also intend to use such instruments to guarantee the partial or full impunity of these persons, after meeting certain conditions, in the criminal proceedings in which they are to make a statement (see above – draft Act concerning so-called crown witnesses).

By adopting these changes, we expect an improvement in the effectiveness of criminal proceedings, in sanctioning the most serious forms of criminal activity, especially organised crime with an international element and criminal activities involving drug trafficking.

Finland

a. General information

1. Please describe the framework (legal provisions and established practice) governing the use of measures protecting witnesses and *pentiti*.

The Finnish legal system does not separate the concepts of "witness" and "*pentito*" in the sense that a person could be only either a witness or a *pentito*. As we have understood, the concept of *pentito* means a collaborator of justice in a situation where this person him/herself has also committed crimes, but still gives the relevant authorities information about a crime committed by either him/herself or someone else. When this kind of information is given as evidence in a criminal case, the *pentito* is also called or handled as a witness.

There are several legal provisions and established practices which are aimed at protecting witnesses (and *pentiti*). The main provisions and practices can be listed:

Legal provisions:

1) Intimidation of a witness or a person close to him/her is a separately criminalised act;
2) Restraining orders can be used to protect witnesses and *pentiti*;
3) Court hearings can be held *in camera* in order to protect witnesses and *pentiti*;
4) A witness or a *pentito* can be heard *ex parte* in the court hearing;
5) Court hearings can be held via video or telephone-conference;
6) Contact information on the witnesses (and parties) can be removed from the court and police files;
7) It is possible to change the witness's first and last (family) name. People can be relocated (if they so wish);
8) The police has the power to remove and arrest intimidating persons;
9) The police has the right to remain silent in order to protect informers. When being heard as a witness or otherwise, members of police personnel are not obliged to reveal the identity of any person who has provided them with confidential information during their employment or to reveal any confidential tactical or technical methods;
10) When being heard as a witness or otherwise, members of police personnel are not obliged to reveal the identity of a person who made a pseudo purchase or who was involved in undercover activities if disclosure of the information would endanger the success of the undercover activities concerned, or if it would significantly endanger the carrying out of similar duties in future by the person who made the

pseudo purchase or was involved in the undercover activities, or if there is another extremely weighty cause not to disclose such information;

11) For safety reasons, people may be subject to security checks before entering the courthouse;

12) When a prisoner or an arrested person is released from custody, any witness or *pentito* who may be in danger can be informed of the forthcoming release in advance.

Established practices:

1) Special penitentiary regimes can be used to separate those prisoners who co-operate with the authorities from other prisoners;

2) A police officer may be appointed to protect witnesses at any time.

2. Please describe the framework (legal provisions and established practice) governing the use of measures encouraging witnesses and *pentiti* to co-operate with justice.

In the framework of the Finnish legal system the measures which encourage witnesses and *pentiti* are not always distinguishable from the measures which protect witnesses and *pentiti*. It is generally understood that measures that protect also at the same time encourage witnesses and *pentiti* to co-operate with justice.

However, two separate legal provisions can be mentioned in this context:

1) The general rules of sentencing in the Penal Code define the mitigating and aggravating factors of which account must be taken in sentencing. A mitigating factor is the offender's co-operation with the authorities with regard to his/her own offence. This could, for example, mean a sincere attitude during questioning or turning him/herself in to the police. This ground for mitigation is limited to the offender's own offences;

2) Every relevant witness is entitled to a witness fee paid by the state. The fee covers reasonable expenses and loss of income.

3. Can measures/benefits encouraging the co-operation of witnesses and *pentiti* be used in combination with protection measures (arrangements concerning trial proceedings, sentencing conditions, special penitentiary regimes, etc.)? If so, please specify and indicate under which conditions they are applied.

Yes. See the reply to question 2.

4. For which kind of crime and under which circumstances can witness and *pentito* protection be applied? Can the measures be extended to the relatives or other persons close to the witness/*pentito*?

In Finnish legislation there are no such limitations as lists of crimes to which the protection measures can be applied. Therefore such measures can be applied in all cases where there is an existing need to protect a witness from intimidation.

Most of the measures can be applied to the relatives and other persons close to the witness/*pentito*.

5. What urgent measures (e.g. immediate relocation to a secret place) can be taken in order to protect witnesses and *pentiti*?

All of the measures mentioned can be taken urgently.

6. Which institutions are involved in the protection of witnesses and *pentiti* and what is their role (e.g. law enforcement agencies, special independent agencies, prosecutor's offices, judicial authorities, etc.)? How does co-operation between the relevant institutions work in practice?

Police, prosecutors, judges and prison officials. Through co-operation, in particular, the awareness of the existing possibilities provided by laws among the law enforcement officials has been improved. To improve the practical situation further, a working group consisting of the relevant authorities (police, prosecutors, judges and attorneys-at-law) was set up and their results were published in February 2003 (Report of the Working Party for the Protection of the Witnesses).

7. Are there any specific provisions governing the protection of witnesses and *pentiti* in relation to acts of terrorism? If so, please specify. Are there any specialised counter-terrorism institutions? If so, what is their role in the protection of witnesses and *pentiti* in relation to acts of terrorism?

There are no such specific provisions. All the general measures could also be applied, where appropriate, in relation to acts of terrorism.

8. **How does the framework governing the use of measures protecting witnesses and *pentiti* and encouraging them to co-operate with justice guarantee respect for human rights and individual freedoms? Please indicate the procedures in place, if any, to monitor compliance with human rights standards.**

All the measures in use guarantee respect for human rights and fundamental freedoms, as described in the European Convention on Human Rights and, in addition, in the Finnish Constitution. The monitoring of compliance with these requirements takes place at several different stages. Firstly, at the law-drafting stage: before any new legislation is proposed, its compliance with human rights is carefully considered. The Government's Bills for new legislation also go through a hearing procedure, where different practitioners and academics have the possibility to express their views. In Parliament, where necessary, the Constitutional Law Committee reviews Bills in the light of human rights issues.

Most of the measures can be taken only if a court of law so orders. The practical implementation or use of a particular measure in a specific criminal case is at the court's discretion. It is the duty of a court to protect human rights and individual freedoms. Decisions made by the courts or other authorities can be appealed.

All the measures in use in Finland can be used by either of the parties in the criminal procedure. This means that the witnesses called by the defence may enjoy the use of these protective measures as well. These are not only the privileges of the prosecutor's witnesses.

b. *Procedural measures*

9. **At which stage(s), and in which context, is it possible for witnesses and *pentiti* to benefit from procedural measures of protection?**

The measures mentioned above can be taken at different stages of the proceedings (before, during and after the court hearing) and also during the serving of the prison sentence.

10. **Is there the possibility for witnesses and *pentiti* to obtain legal assistance at this (these) stage(s)?**

If a witness or a *pentito* is also the accused or a victim of crime, he/she can obtain free legal assistance. Otherwise a witness or a *pentito* shall him/herself cover his/her lawyer's expenses. Legal assistance can be obtained at all stages of the procedure (pre-trial investigation and trial). After the trial, these expenses are not covered by the state.

11. **Are there alternative methods of giving evidence which allow the protection of witnesses and *pentiti* from intimidation resulting from face to face confrontation with the accused? If yes, please specify (e.g. full or partial anonymity, video-conference, disguise, exclusion of the defendant from the courtroom when the witness is giving evidence, exclusion of the media or the public from the trial, etc.) and indicate under which conditions these methods are used.**

See the reply to question 1. A witness or *pentito* cannot be granted full anonymity. Video-conference, removal of the defendant from the courtroom when the witness is giving evidence, exclusion of the media or the public from the courtroom are measures which can be used.

Partial anonymity is not a clear legal concept. If partial anonymity means, for example, the possibility that the contact information of a witness or *pentito* can be removed from the court and police files, this can be done.

12. **On which grounds and on the basis of which criteria can anonymity be granted? Is there the possibility to obtain legal assistance at this stage?**

Total anonymity cannot be granted to witnesses who are called to the court to testify. However, the police has the right to remain silent when questioned about the identity of a so-called informer (see the reply to question 1, point 9).

13. **Are pre-trial statements of witnesses and *pentiti* and testimonies of anonymous witnesses and *pentiti* regarded as valid evidence? If yes, under which conditions?**

The testimonies of anonymous witnesses and *pentiti* are not admissible and therefore cannot be regarded as valid evidence in court. The basic rule is that the witness must be heard in person in court. A statement made in the report of the pre-trial investigation (i.e. in a record of the police interrogation) is not, as a rule, in itself admissible and the person who made that statement must be heard again directly by the court. However, there are special circumstances permitting the use of statements made during the pre-trial investigation. An example could be a situation where the facts stated by the person in the trial differ from those given in the pre-trial investigation. The use of the pre-trial investigation report is permitted at least as comparative material for such purposes as to evaluate the weight of the new statement as evidence. The use of pre-trial statements also requires that the other party's right to cross-examine is ensured.

14. Is it possible, and if so, under which conditions, to use information provided by "*pentiti*"? How is their credibility assessed?

If a *pentito* is called as a witness to the court, his/her statements can be used as evidence in the case. His/her credibility is assessed in the normal manner. There are no special provisions on the evaluation of the witness's testimony. Free evaluation of the given evidence is applied.

15. Which are the opportunities for the defence to exercise its rights, including the right of the accused to challenge the witness'/*pentito*'s credibility in criminal proceedings (including at the pre-trial stage) and the respect of the "equality of arms" principle?

The defence always has the right to cross-examine the witness. The witnesses called by the defence may also benefit, where necessary, from protection measures.

c. Non-procedural measures

16. At which stage(s), and in which context, is it possible for witnesses and *pentiti* to benefit from a protection programme?

The systematic use of the measures mentioned in the replies to questions 1 and 2 can be called a protection programme. These different forms of protection are available, some before, some during and some after the trial stage of the proceedings.

17. Is there the possibility for witnesses and *pentiti* to obtain legal assistance at this (these) stage(s)?

See the reply to question 10.

18. What is the procedure for admittance to a protection programme? Please specify, in particular, who takes the initiative, the criteria for admittance, the assessment of the relevance of a testimony and how admittance to the programme is formalised.

In the context of the Finnish legal system, all the measures taken to protect a witness or *pentito* are considered according to the actual need. In Finnish legislation there is no such concept as a protection programme. As understood in Finland, the systematic use of two or more protection measures is a protection programme. Therefore there is no need to consider the procedure for admittance to a protection programme or to formalise it. The relevant question is which measures should be taken in a single case.

The initiative for measures can come from the witness him/herself, the police, prosecutor or judge. In practice, the initiative usually comes from the witness or from the police.

For the assessment of the relevance of a testimony, see the reply to question 13.

19. **Please indicate the measures that can be adopted for the protection of witnesses and *pentiti* (e.g. surveillance of the residence, physical protection, protection of personal records, relocation, change of identity, subsidies, assistance in job search, relocation of a detainee to another prison or to special units).**

See the reply to question 1.

20. **What can the duration of a protection programme be? Which are the procedures for assessing the degree of danger for the witnesses/*pentiti* and their compliance with the obligations of the programme? Is it possible to challenge a decision of suspension, revocation or termination of a protection programme?**

See the reply to question 18.

d. *International co-operation*

21. **Which measures (e.g. use of modern telecommunications means, assistance in relocating protected witnesses, exchange of information between witness protection authorities) have been adopted in the context of mutual legal assistance in order to facilitate international co-operation? How are the financial implications of international co-operation activities dealt with?**

Finland has signed, ratified or acceded to many international conventions and other instruments which include provisions aiming at the protection of witnesses. These instruments have been concluded in the context of the United Nations, the European Union and the Council of Europe and cover, for example, general obligations to protect witnesses with appropriate means and the use of video-conferencing in the hearing of witnesses.

22. **Has your country entered international (bilateral or multilateral) agreements on the protection of witnesses and *pentiti*? If so, please indicate what kind of provisions they include.**

See the reply to question 21.

23. How can international co-operation in the field of the protection of witnesses and *pentiti* be improved?

The areas where international co-operation is needed are:
- exchanges of information between relevant authorities;
- relocation of witnesses and *pentiti* to another country (including preconditions for relocation, who will bear the costs of relocation, reciprocity etc.);
- hearing of witnesses and *pentiti* in a country other than the place of the trial or investigation; questions relating to the taking of evidence via international mutual legal assistance, video-conferencing.

e. *Statistics*

24. How many people currently benefit from witness or *pentito* protection measures/programmes, and for how long? How many of them are foreign people? If the measures/programmes can be extended to relatives and other close persons, please indicate (and, if possible, specify the relationship with the witness/*pentito*) how many people are included in this category. Please also provide figures on the different kinds of measures (procedural and non-procedural) adopted, and on the number of cases involving international co-operation.

No such statistics are currently available.

f. *Proposals and comments*

25. Please provide any comments/proposals concerning the implementation of the terms of reference of the PC-PW and, in particular, instruments to be adopted to strengthen the protection of witnesses and *pentiti*.

In our view, in the implementation of the terms of reference the main focus should be how the protection of witnesses and *pentiti* could be improved by international co-operation in this field. It is not useful or even appropriate to try to create common methods to be used at national level in cases which do not involve cross-border aspects. Each Member State of the Council of Europe can, on the basis of its own legal traditions and practical needs, decide which kind of measure is needed in each situation. However, in the international context added value can be achieved in situations where the help of other Member States is needed. Therefore, the future work of the PC-PW should be concentrated on these international aspects of the protection of the witnesses and *pentiti*.

Having this approach in mind, the areas where international co-operation is needed are:

- exchanges of information between relevant authorities;
- relocation of witnesses and *pentiti* to another country (including preconditions for relocation, who will bear the costs of relocation, reciprocity, etc.);
- hearing of witnesses and *pentiti* in a country other than the place of the trial or investigation; questions relating to the taking of evidence via international mutual legal assistance, video-conferencing.

France

a. *General information*

1. Please describe the framework (legal provisions and established practice) governing the use of measures protecting witnesses and *pentiti*.

Witnesses

The Code of Criminal Procedure contains two types of provisions on the protection of witnesses:

- it is possible for the public prosecutor or investigating judge to authorise witnesses to give as their address that of the police station or *gendarmerie* (Article 706-57);

- if their examination may severely jeopardise their life or physical integrity, or that of members of their family, it is possible for the *juge des libertés et de la détention* (judge for civil liberties and detention), on referral by the public prosecutor or investigating judge, to authorise them to be heard without their identity being shown in the case file (Articles 706-58 to 706-63). Use of this procedure may be challenged by the defence, which may ask to be confronted with the witness concerned. No conviction may be based solely on such anonymous evidence.

Pentiti

Act No. 2004-204 of 9 March 2004 adapting the justice system to developments in the sphere of crime tightened up the specific legal framework applicable under French law to *pentiti* ("repentis").

The aim is to encourage individuals who have taken part in the preparation of an offence, have committed an offence or possess information enabling the commission of another offence to be prevented, to communicate this information to the administrative or judicial authorities. To this end, the law makes it possible for them to be spared punishment or have a lesser penalty imposed if they collaborate with the judicial system before being convicted, or to have the sentence imposed on them reduced if they collaborate either before or after their conviction.

Alongside the provisions of criminal law, machinery exists to protect persons who have collaborated with the administrative or judicial authorities.

1. Exemption from punishment or reduction of penalty

These are intended to be applied only to certain serious offences specified by the law (such as terrorist offences, drugs trafficking, kidnapping, aircraft hijacking, trafficking of human beings, blackmail by an organised group, etc.). In certain cases, only a reduction in penalty may be granted, and the person prosecuted cannot be completely spared punishment (e.g. certain offences relating to the possession or making of explosive devices).

In the cases for which the law provides, exemption from punishment may apply to anyone whose statements have made it possible to prevent the commission of an offence, in the preparation of which he/she had participated and to identify any other offenders or accomplices.

A penalty reduction may be granted to a person who has disclosed to the administrative or judicial authority, after an offence has been committed, information making it possible either to bring that offence to an end or for ensuing damage to be prevented, or to identify the other offenders or accomplices. Other potential beneficiaries are persons who make it possible to prevent the commission of a connected offence of the same kind as the crime or offence with which they have been charged, to bring such an offence to an end, to prevent any damage ensuing or to identify the offenders or their accomplices.

2. Penalty reduction subsequent to conviction

Such exceptional penalty reductions may be granted to convicted persons in the following circumstances:

- the *pentiti* made their statements prior to conviction, but
  - either the circumstances in which they gave their information did not meet the criteria for them to benefit from the aforementioned exemption from punishment or penalty reduction;
  - or the investigations needed to verify the truth of their statements were unable to be carried out before their trial.
- the *pentiti* made their statements after conviction, either remorseful about offences of which they were aware prior to their imprisonment or providing information of which they had become aware subsequent to their imprisonment.

In order for a *pentito* to benefit from an exceptional penalty reduction, his/her statements must have made it possible to bring to an end, or to prevent the commission of, one of the offences mentioned in Articles 706-73 and 706-74 of the Code of Criminal Procedure (offences connected with organised crime).

The penalty reduction granted by the judge responsible for the execution of sentences may be up to one-third of the sentence passed. Anyone sentenced to life imprisonment may, as a result of statements made, have a reduction of a maximum of five years of the term at the end of which they may be allowed to benefit from conditional release.

3. *Protection of pentiti*

The principle of protective measures for *pentiti* was laid down in Act No. 2004-204 of 9 March 2004 adapting the justice system to developments of delinquency. These provisions are to be supplemented by a decree - not yet issued - which will lay down the relevant practical arrangements.

This protection is enjoyed only by persons exempted from punishment or benefiting from a penalty reduction as described in paragraph 1 above.
Two types of protection are provided for:

- borrowed identity: *pentiti* may be authorised, by a reasoned order issued by the president of the *Tribunal de grande instance* (Regional Court), to use a borrowed identity. Such authorisation may also be given to members of the *pentito*'s family and to close relatives;

- protection and reintegration measures: these measures, which may also benefit members of the *pentito*'s family and close relatives, are laid down by a national commission, the membership and operation of which is to be laid down by decree.

The public prosecutor may *ex officio* make submissions with a view to a *pentito* being granted the benefit of protection and reintegration measures. Various measures may be requested by the person concerned or his/her lawyer, who may, depending on the circumstances, request the responsible judicial authority to authorise the use of borrowed identity or to ask the public prosecutor for a reference to the commission.

2. Please describe the framework (legal provisions and established practice) governing the use of measures encouraging witnesses and *pentiti* to co-operate with justice.

See the reply to question 1.

3. Can measures/benefits encouraging the co-operation of witnesses and *pentiti* be used in combination with protection measures (arrangements concerning trial proceedings, sentencing conditions, special penitentiary regimes, etc.)? If so, please specify and indicate under which conditions they are applied.

There are no other provisions in French criminal procedure enabling encouragement to be given to such co-operation.

4. For which kind of crime and under which circumstances can witness and *pentito* protection be applied? Can the measures be extended to the relatives or other persons close to the witness/*pentito*?

Witnesses

Use of police station address: all offences.

Anonymous evidence: all crimes and offences punishable by at least three years' imprisonment.

Pentiti

See the reply to question 1.

5. What urgent measures (e.g. immediate relocation to a secret place) can be taken in order to protect witnesses and *pentiti*?

In an emergency, the judicial authorities may require the police as administrative authorities, to provide such protection, i.e. for public order and safety purposes.

6. Which institutions are involved in the protection of witnesses and *pentiti* and what is their role (e.g. law enforcement agencies, special independent agencies, prosecutors' offices, judicial authorities, etc)? How does co-operation between the relevant institutions work in practice?

Witnesses

Use of police station address: this requires the consent of the public prosecutor at the inquiry stage, or the investigating judge where reference has been made to him/her. In practice, the investigator phones the responsible judge and obtains oral authorisation, published by the investigator in a record. The witness's actual address is recorded in an *ad hoc* register which is numbered, initialed and kept at the police station.

Anonymous evidence: authorisation is granted by a reasoned decision of the *juge des libertés et de la détention* to whom the public prosecutor or investigating judge has made a reasoned application. The *juge des libertés et de la détention* him/herself may decide to hear the witness. His/her decision, in which the person's identity is not revealed, is attached to the record of the witness hearing, which is not signed by the person concerned. The person's identity and address are shown in another record signed by the person concerned, which is kept in a file separate from the case file, in which the application from the public prosecutor or investigating judge is also kept. The person's identity and address are recorded in a numbered and initialed register created for this purpose at the *Tribunal de grande instance*. In practice, the investigator requests authorisation from the public prosecutor or investigating judge, who, if he/she considers such protection desirable, refers the matter to the *juge des libertés et de la détention*.

Pentiti

See the reply to question 1.

7. Are there any specific provisions governing the protection of witnesses and *pentiti* in relation to acts of terrorism? If so, please specify. Are there any specialised counter-terrorism institutions? If so, what is their role in the protection of witnesses and *pentiti* in relation to acts of terrorism?

There is no specific protection of witnesses and *pentiti* in connection with acts of terrorism. The rules explained above apply (see the reply to question 1).

Several police departments specialised in anti-terrorism: the DNAT (national directorate for the combating of terrorism), SAT (anti-terrorism section of the Paris police force), DST (territory surveillance directorate) and RG (general intelligence service). A specialised department of the *gendarmerie*, the anti-terrorist office, has also been set up within the national directorate-general of the *gendarmerie*. These departments have no specific role in the protection of *pentiti* and witnesses over and above those laid down in the procedural provisions applicable by all members of the police and *gendarmerie*.

8. How does the framework governing the use of measures protecting witnesses and *pentiti* and encouraging them to co-operate with justice guarantee respect for human rights and individual freedoms? Please indicate the procedures in place, if any, to monitor compliance with human rights standards.

Witness protection

The provisions allowing anonymous evidence are not applicable if, in the light of the circumstances in which the offence was committed or of the witness's personality, knowledge of the person's identity is vital to the exercise of the rights of the defence. Furthermore, the person under investigation may, within 10 days of the date on which he/she is told of the content of a hearing conducted anonymously, challenge the use of this procedure by applying to the president of the investigating section. The president rules in the light of the case file, in a reasoned decision not open to challenge. If he/she considers the challenge justified, he/she orders the hearing to be declared void. He/she also has the power to order the identity of the witness to be revealed, provided that the person concerned expressly accepts the loss of his/her anonymity.

The person under investigation or committed for trial may request to be confronted with the witness through a device enabling the witness to be heard remotely, with his/her voice being rendered unidentifiable.

Nobody may be convicted solely on the basis of statements collected anonymously.

The protection of pentiti

Nobody may be convicted solely on the basis of statements made by *pentiti*.

b. Procedural measures

9. At which stage(s), and in which context, is it possible for witnesses and *pentiti* to benefit from procedural measures of protection?

Witnesses

Use of police station address: at the inquiry and investigation stage.

Anonymous evidence: at the inquiry and investigation stage. A witness who has given anonymous evidence at these stages may be confronted with the accused in the trial court during the hearing. Arrangements must be made for the witness to be heard remotely, with his/her voice being rendered unidentifiable.

Pentiti

The relevant implementing regulations for the Act of 9 March 2004 not yet having been issued, it is difficult to reply on this point. Protective measures are potentially intended to apply during the inquiry, investigation and trial stages and/or subsequent to conviction.

10. Is there the possibility for witnesses and *pentiti* to obtain legal assistance at this(these) stage(s)?

No specific legal assistance arrangements are made for witnesses, as no provision is made in France for witnesses to be assisted by a lawyer. However, there is nothing to prevent witnesses from obtaining any legal advice they consider useful before deciding to give evidence anonymously.

Unlike witnesses, *pentiti* are involved in the case and may benefit from the assistance of a lawyer.

11. Are there alternative methods of giving evidence which allow witnesses and *pentiti* to be given protection from intimidation resulting from face-to-face confrontation with the accused? If yes, please specify (e.g. full or partial anonymity, video-conference, disguise, exclusion of the defendant from the courtroom when the witness is giving evidence, exclusion of the media or the public from the trial, etc) and indicate under what conditions these methods are used.

Witnesses

The president of the Assize Court may, before, during or following the hearing of a witness, have one or more of the accused taken out of court and examine them separately about certain facts, but the trial may be resumed only after the president has told all of the accused what happened during their absence and what the result was.

Where justified by the requirements of the inquiry or investigation, the hearing or examination of a person and the confrontation of several persons may be conducted at different places on French territory via telecommunications links secure enough to guarantee confidentiality. A record of the operations carried out there is then drawn up at each of these places.

A witness heard anonymously during the inquiry and investigation stage must, if confronted with the accused during the investigation or the trial hearing, be heard remotely, and his/her voice must be rendered unidentifiable by appropriate technical means.

Pentiti

There is no specific legal arrangement for *pentiti*, who may nevertheless benefit from the provisions enabling persons to be heard, examined and confronted with one another via telecommunications links secure enough to guarantee confidentiality.

12. On what grounds and on the basis of what criteria can anonymity be granted? Is it possible to obtain legal assistance at this stage?

See the reply to question 1. There is no legal aid system, as no provision is made in France for witnesses to be assisted by a lawyer.

13. Are pre-trial statements of witnesses and *pentiti* and testimonies of anonymous witnesses and *pentiti* regarded as valid evidence? If yes, under what conditions?

In French law evidence is free in criminal cases, and both the statements made by witnesses prior to the trial and anonymous evidence are admissible, subject to both parties having the opportunity to discuss them in the trial court.

The law nevertheless states that nobody may be convicted solely on the basis of anonymous statements.

14. Is it possible, and if so, under what conditions, to use information provided by *"pentiti"*? How is their credibility assessed?

Information provided by *pentiti* is considered to have the same value as conventional evidence. There is no credibility assessment criterion. The significance of the evidence is in practice evaluated at the trial stage. However, nobody may be convicted solely on the basis of statements by *pentiti*.

15. What are the opportunities for the defence to exercise its rights, including the right of the accused to challenge the witness'/*pentito's* credibility in criminal proceedings (including at the pre-trial stage) and respect of the "equality of arms" principle?

The evidential value of statements by *pentiti* and by witnesses, like any evidence, may be discussed between both parties during the trial.

During the investigation, a specific remedy against anonymous evidence is open to anyone under investigation, who may, within 10 days of being informed of the content of a hearing conducted anonymously, make an application to the president of the investigating section contesting the use of the procedure for which this Article provides. The president, on the basis of the case file, issues a reasoned decision not open to challenge. If the application is considered justified, the president orders the hearing to be declared void. He/she also has the power to order the identity of the witness to be revealed, provided that the witness concerned expressly accepts the loss of his/her anonymity.

The accused person may also ask to be confronted with the witness via a remote communication device, with his/her voice having to be rendered unidentifiable, or may have this witness examined via the same channel by his/her lawyer.

c. *Non-procedural measures*

16. At what stage(s), and in what context, is it possible for witnesses and *pentiti* to benefit from a protection programme?

See the reply to question 1.

The police may also provide protection to a witness, or even to a *pentito*. The criterion used is either the context of the case or the threats made against the person concerned.

17. Is it possible for witnesses and *pentiti* to obtain legal assistance at this (these) stage(s)?

See the replies to questions 10 and 12.

18. What is the procedure for admittance to a protection programme? Please specify, in particular, who takes the initiative, the criteria for admittance, the assessment of the relevance of a testimony and how admittance to the programme is formalised.

See the replies to the preceding questions.

19. Please indicate the measures that can be adopted for the protection of witnesses and *pentiti* (e.g. surveillance of the residence, physical protection, protection of personal records, relocation, change of identity, subsidies, assistance in job search, relocation of a detainee to another prison or to a special unit).

See the replies to the preceding questions.

20. At what stages of the proceedings (preliminary investigations, during the trial, after the trial) can the protection programme come into operation? What can the duration of a protection programme be? What are the procedures for assessing the degree of danger for the witnesses/*pentiti* and their compliance with the obligations of the programme? Is it possible to challenge a decision of suspension, revocation or termination of a protection programme?

See the replies to the preceding questions.

d. International co-operation

21. What measures (e.g. use of modern telecommunications means, assistance in relocating protected witnesses, exchange of information between witness protection authorities) have been adopted in the context of mutual legal assistance in order to facilitate international co-operation? How are the financial implications of international co-operation activities dealt with?

The provisions of the code of criminal procedure relating to hearings, examinations and "remote" confrontations via telecommunications links secure enough to guarantee confidentiality are applicable in the context of mutual legal assistance in criminal matters.

It is therefore possible to use these provisions for the simultaneous execution on national and foreign territory of requests for mutual assistance made by foreign judicial authorities or of mutual assistance activities carried out at the request of the French judicial authorities.

22. Has your country entered international (bilateral or multilateral) agreements on the protection of witnesses and *pentiti*? If so, please indicate what kind of provisions they include.

France is a Party to the United Nations Convention against Transnational Organized Crime, Article 24 of which contains provisions relating to witness protection. It has just transmitted its instruments of ratification of the United Nations Convention against Corruption, which contains some similar provisions (Articles 32 and 33).

23. How can international co-operation in the field of the protection of witnesses and *pentiti* be improved?

No specific comments about this as things stand.

e. Statistics

24.[2]How many people currently benefit from witness or *pentito* protection measures/programmes, and for how long? How many of them are foreign nationals? If the measures/programmes can be extended to relatives and persons close to them, please indicate (and, if possible, specify the relationship with the witness/*pentito*) how many people are included in this category. Please also provide figures on the different kinds of measures (procedural and non-procedural) adopted, and on the number of cases involving international co-operation.

No statistics are available as things stand.

f. Proposals and comments

25. Please provide any comments/proposals concerning the implementation of the terms of reference of the PC-PW and, in particular, instruments to be adopted to strengthen the protection of witnesses and *pentiti*.

No specific comments about this as things stand.

Georgia

The existing Georgian legislation, particularly the Criminal and Criminal Procedural Codes of Georgia does not provide for the protection of witnesses and *pentiti* in relation to acts of terrorism.

What Georgian legislation does regulate in relation to the protection of witnesses in general is that, in accordance with Article 335 of the Criminal Code, any unlawful methods used by law enforcement authorities to gain information (testimony) from persons involved in criminal proceedings (including witnesses) is punishable. Article 372 of the Criminal Code criminalises any act which aims at obtaining a false testimony by bribing or threatening a witness.

The Criminal Procedural Code of Georgia, namely its Article 109, provides the possibility for a witness to file an application in which "he/she may request the person or the authority in charge of the criminal case to protect him/her, members of his/her family and close relatives, their life, health, dignity and property if any illegal act has been committed against them or if there exists a real threat that such an act could be committed because of their participation in the criminal proceedings". But the details of how the authorities must proceed (legal and financial aspects) have not yet been regulated in the legislation. Although a newly established special inter-ministerial Commission is working on these issues, no real example of its findings can be presented at this stage.

It is envisaged that criminal procedural legislation shall also provide for the rights and responsibilities of witnesses during criminal proceedings; the examination of witnesses at the investigation phase; court proceedings; and, finally, the compulsory examination of witnesses at the request of the accused.

Germany

Foreword

Due to the federal structure of Germany an exhaustive description of the practice in all of the sixteen states of Germany (Länder) has not been possible in the short time within which this reply was to be furnished. The practice of the local police of Munich (Polizeipräsidium München) and the Central Police Authority of Bavaria (Bayerisches Landeskriminalamt) and its co-operation with other regional and federal authorities constitute the basis for the replies.

a. *General information*

1. Please describe the framework (legal provisions and established practice) governing the use of measures protecting witnesses and *pentiti*.

Protection from any threat whatsoever is a question of preventing danger and thus a traditional task of the police and not of justice; however, the danger to witnesses stems from criminal procedure and may be aggravated by adherence to the rules which regulate criminal procedure. So the main effort of protection has to be preventive in order to ensure complete and true information from the witness. The aspects of criminal law are mostly involved in safeguarding those preventive measures by modifying criminal procedure in such a way as to strike a balance between the needs of protection and needs of granting due process to the accused.

To accomplish these ends there exist several provisions and acts. The Federal Act on Harmonising Witness Protection (Zeugenschutz-Harmonisierungsgesetz, ZSHG) of 2001 has enlarged and clarified the tasks and the powers of witness protection agencies. Several recent amendments to the Code of Criminal Procedure (Strafprozessordnung, StPO) concern the improvement of the position of witnesses, especially victims, during the stages of the investigation and trial. Furthermore, there are administrative regulations concerning the granting of witness protection and concerning co-operation with the police and prosecuting, judicial and prison authorities involved. In addition, there are the general provisions on prevention of danger which come into play whenever the special conditions of witness protection do not cover the situation, for example when the danger arises only after a case has finally been closed.

2. **Please describe the framework (legal provisions and established practice) governing the use of measures encouraging witnesses and *pentiti* to co-operate with justice.**

a) Concerning *pentiti*, the most important question is obviously to what extent they can reduce their own sentence by collaborating with justice. For most crimes the law does not provide a fixed sanction but rather an extended frame of possible sanctions, ranging, for example, for taking hostages from five to fifteen years' imprisonment. Thus it is often possible to find a sanction within this range which sufficiently takes into account the collaboration of a criminal. This usually has to be done by the trial court, often with the prosecuting office suggesting a specific sanction which has already been discussed with the defence. The Federal Court (Bundesgerichtshof) has given a number of rules concerning this type of "plea bargaining" which do not, however, primarily concern the reduction of sanctions for *pentiti*. In addition, the law, in several provisions, allows the dismissal of the case against a criminal by the prosecutor's office, in more serious cases with the consent of the court, whenever it seems not necessary to convict him/her; the most usual of those provisions, however, are not applicable in the case of a felony (minimum sanction is one year's imprisonment or more).

The Narcotics Act provides for an additional substantial reduction of sanction for informants on drug offences by lowering the legal minimum sanction for their own drug crimes or, in certain less serious cases, allowing for a case to be dismissed.

In 1989, a legal provision concerning the reduction of punishment for participants of crimes concerning terrorist associations who give information on such crimes was introduced. Borrowing a term from the British legal system, it was called the Crown Witness Provision (Kronzeugenregelung). It was, however, abolished at the end of 1999 because its low practical relevance meant it was not considered worth the departure from normal sanctions. Because of the general possibility of taking into account the accused's collaboration, it would have been most important in murder cases in which, without special provisions, a life sentence is mandatory. Although the provision has been applied in several cases in which the accused, once apprehended, has helped with the investigations concerning past acts of terrorism, it has not been successful in motivating terrorists to prevent planned acts of terrorism or to help apprehend the co-authors of their crimes.

b) Apart from the question of sanctions for collaborators, a witness considering co-operating with the justice may request benefits from the administration. Wherever such acts are at the discretion of the administration, the possibility of taking into consideration the need to encourage co-operation with justice or to stabilise the witness in his/her new surroundings is not excluded. But in many cases this need cannot be considered sufficient to grant an act of administration which otherwise would not be granted. General rules cannot be given on this subject. However, there is a special regulation (Article 64, paragraph 3, of the Foreigners Act) that the expulsion or deportation of a foreigner who participates in a protection programme is only possible with the consent of the protection agency involved.

Payments for witnesses and *pentiti* benefiting from a witness protection programme are only allowed to the extent necessary for the protection (e. g. replacing the wages lost by relocation until the witness has found a new job). This is regulated in Article 8 ZSHG and expresses the general principle that the witness should not make an over-all profit from protection in order to avoid the impression of a "bought witness".

3. Can measures/benefits encouraging the co-operation of witnesses and *pentiti* be used in combination with protection measures (arrangements concerning trial proceedings, sentencing conditions, special penitentiary regimes, etc.)? If so, please specify and indicate under which conditions they are applied.

There is no rule excluding the combination of measures/benefits encouraging the co-operation of witnesses and *pentiti* and protection measures for those persons. Protection measures must moreover even be considered as one of the possible measures to encourage co-operation.

4. For which kind of crime and under which circumstances can witness and *pentito* protection be applied? Can the measures be extended to the relatives or other persons close to the witness/*pentito*?

There is no fixed catalogue of crimes which allow the application of protection measures. The importance lies in the quality and the extent of the danger to the witness/*pentito* or persons close to him/her. Since serious threats usually occur in cases of serious crimes, in practice protection measures are usually granted in felony cases, but not limited to those.

Protection measures can be extended to relatives of and other persons close to witnesses/*pentiti* if they are endangered and even to relatives and other persons close to the witness or his/her relatives if necessary for the purposes of witness protection e. g. all the members of a family if the whole family is to be relocated.

Since the prevention of danger is a general task of the police, even witnesses who will not testify in court can enjoy protection measures. This does, however, not happen within a protection programme (which aims at enabling the witness to stand up in court and testify) but within a more general framework.

5. **What urgent measures (e.g. immediate relocation to a secret place) can be taken in order to protect witnesses and *pentiti*?**

There is no fixed catalogue of possible measures to the exclusion of others. Whatever is deemed necessary will be done. Usually this means relocation to an hotel or a similar abode first of all; in this case it may also be necessary to assure the witness immediately that the costs for this will be borne by the protection agency because otherwise he/she could or would not agree to the measure.

6. **Which institutions are involved in the protection of witnesses and *pentiti* and what is their role (e.g. law enforcement agencies, special independent agencies, prosecutor's offices, judicial authorities, etc)? How does co-operation between the relevant institutions work in practice?**

The law enforcement agency investigating the case assesses the danger and informs the protection agency which is organised as an administratively separate part of the same law enforcement agency or part of another law enforcement agency, as the case may be. However, for reasons of objectivity and in order to avoid the charge of undue influence on the witness, the protection measures should never be implemented by officers immediately related to the case.

The protection agency evaluates the danger, including the importance of the witness's testimony with the consent of the prosecutor's office concerned, and implements adequate protection measures. Protection measures which can affect the detention of a person may only be implemented with the consent of the chief of the detention institution concerned (Article 11 ZSHG).

The co-operation between these institutions, as a rule, works smoothly due to adequate regulations based on former experience and shows no structural problems.

Public and private institutions can be involved in protection measures in as much as the protection agency can request that they treat the personal data of the protected person as confidential (e.g. social security institutions), that they inform the protection agency about any request for such data or that they issue documents necessary for a temporary change of identity.

7. **Are there any specific provisions governing the protection of witnesses and *pentiti* in relation to acts of terrorism? If so, please specify. Are there any specialised counter-terrorism institutions? If so, what is their role in the protection of witnesses and *pentiti* in relation to acts of terrorism?**

Terrorist cases fall within the responsibility of the Federal Prosecutor (Generalbundesanwalt) who entrusts the Federal Police Authority (Bunderkriminalamt) or – in regional cases – the relevant Central State Police Authority (Ländeskriminalamt) with the investigations. There are, however, no specific provisions governing the protection of witnesses and *pentiti* in this domain. The police authorities mentioned have witness protection agencies and use them in terrorist cases as in any other case within their responsibility.

8. **How does the framework governing the use of measures protecting witnesses and *pentiti* and encouraging them to co-operate with justice guarantee respect for human rights and individual freedoms? Please indicate the procedures in place, if any, to monitor compliance with human rights standards.**

The aim of a protection programme is to support the witness in such a way that he/she agrees to testify in court. Thus there is no material impairment of the rights of the defence in the case of a witness in a protection programme: the witness is available and can be challenged by the defence in the usual way.

Witnesses who are admitted to a protection programme as a rule have to commit themselves not to divulge any details of the protection measures which are considered to be official secrets. Since the witness protection agency does not release them from this commitment for the trial, the court and the defence cannot ask questions relating to those measures, e. g. the witness's new domicile or new job. This limitation, however, does not concern the essential part of the testimony and strikes an equitable balance between the rights of the accused and the witness's right to be protected from the adverse effects of his/her compliance with his/her duties as a witness.

Witnesses who do not wish to appear in court may be granted confidentiality and thus complete anonymity (in the sense that his/her identity is divulged neither to the defence nor to the court) with the consequence that they cannot be summoned for the trial. Informants may benefit from this in cases of serious or – exceptionally – medium crimes if the investigations would at least be seriously hampered without them, if they are endangered, they have not themselves participated in the crime and the prosecutor's office has consented. Undercover agents (i.e. covertly operating law enforcement officers), who are granted complete anonymity if they are endangered and the danger cannot be averted by other means, such as testifying by video-conference, may be employed in similar cases with the consent of the prosecutor's office or a judge. In both cases the information coming from the informant/undercover agent is introduced in the trial by an officer of the law enforcement agency testifying on what the anonymous witness has reported. The rights of the defence to challenge the witness at trial – the reporting officer – is only limited by the fact that he/she is not allowed to testify about official secrets such as the identity of the anonymous witness. This obviously is not sufficient for the purposes of the defence so the defence furthermore has the right to challenge the anonymous witness by listing questions in writing which are put to the anonymous witness by the officer who then reports the answers to the court at trial. Since this officer is but a hearsay witness, the court has to be extremely wary of the limited value of this testimony. The Federal Court (Bundesgerichtshof) has made it clear in several decisions that a conviction can usually only be founded on the information given by an anonymous witness if it has been corroborated by other important evidence. As a consequence, the aim of employing informants or undercover agents during investigations is primarily to obtain such evidence, if possible to the extent that the anonymous witness's testimony will not be necessary at all in the trial.

Witness protection measures, especially a change of identity, may factually influence the protected person's third party relations. However, there is no legal influence. Thus claims of third parties against the protected person are not affected by a change of identity; the protecting agency has to ensure that the protected person is still available to his/her creditors (Article 9 ZSHG). Likewise, the protected person keeps his/her claims, especially against the labour exchange, pension insurance institutions and social security institutions. There are special provisions for the assertion of those claims, obliging the protection agency to act on behalf of the protected person (Article 7 ZSHG).

Convictions which do not conform with human rights standards are liable to be reversed by appeal decisions. Thus compliance with those standards is monitored by the courts of appeal.

b. *Procedural measures*

9. **At which stage(s), and in which context, is it possible for witnesses and *pentiti* to benefit from procedural measures of protection?**

a) During the investigation stage, the following procedural protection measures are possible:

- Denying the defence access to the complete files (Article 147, paragraph 2, StPO); if, however, the accused has been arrested, the evidence which justifies the detention must be presented to the defence.

- Allowing the witness to give another address (e.g. his/her business head office) instead of the address of his/her domicile when interrogated (Article 68, paragraph 2, StPO); when admitted to a protection programme the witness has the same rights as in any other proceedings (Article 10, paragraph 1, ZSHG).

- Allowing the witness to give no information on his/her identity or only information on his/her former identity (Article 68, paragraph 3, StPO); when admitted to a protection programme the witness has the same rights as in any other proceedings (Article 10, paragraph 1, ZSHG).

- Videotaping the giving of evidence by the witness (Article 58a StPO). The tape can be shown at trial under the same – limited – conditions as a record of the interrogation can be read at trial (Article 255a StPO), the most important point being that the witness cannot be summoned for the trial. The tape may only be used for criminal prosecution purposes and has to be deleted once it is no longer necessary.

- Transmitting the examination of the witness by a judge electronically into another room where the accused and the defence (who are usually entitled to be present at judicial interrogations) can observe the proceedings and ask questions which are retransmitted to the judge and witness (Article 168e StPO). This can be combined with taping the interrogation; the tape may only be used for criminal prosecution purposes and has to be deleted once it is no longer necessary.

- The witness may granted confidentiality in accordance with the rules outlined in the reply to question 8.

b) During the trial stage, the following procedural protection measures are possible:

- Controlling the persons who constitute the audience of the trial (e.g. searching them for weapons, controlling their papers, noting their personal data, under certain circumstances even taking photographs of them; Article 176 Judicature Act [Gerichtsverfasungsgesetz, GVG]).

- Allowing the witness to give another address (e.g. his/her business head office) instead of the address of his/her domicile when interrogated (Article 68, paragraph 2, StPO).

- Allowing the witness to give no information on his/her identity or only information on his/her former identity; during trial, however, an undercover agent must divulge the fact that he/she learned the testified facts in his/her capacity as an undercover agent (Article 68, paragraph 3, StPO).

- Excluding the public from the courtroom for the time of the witness's interrogation (Article 172 GVG).

- Allowing a victim to have a person who enjoys his/her confidence present (Article 406f, paragraph 3, StPO); thus he/she can demand that a witness protection agent stays with him/her even if the public is excluded from the courtroom.

- Disallowing questions concerning the domicile or the identity of a witness (Article 241, paragraph 2, StPO).

- Excluding the accused from the courtroom while the witness is giving evidence. The court has to inform the accused afterwards about the essential content of the evidence (Article 247 StPO).

- Allowing the witness to be absent from the courtroom and to give evidence by video-conferencing; this can be combined with taping the interrogation (Article 247a StPO); the tape may only be used for criminal prosecution purposes and has to be deleted once it is no longer necessary.

- Introducing the information given by a witness to whom confidentiality has been granted in the way described in the reply to question 8.

It is not possible to hear a witness who is disguised or obscured from view in the courtroom (the "witness in the box").

10. Is there the possibility for witnesses and *pentiti* to obtain legal assistance at this (these) stage(s)?

If a witness does not yet have a legal counsel and it becomes obvious that he/she is not able to exercise his/her rights on his own, he/she may be assigned a lawyer paid by the state as counsel for the interrogation (but not outside of it; Article 68b StPO).

Victims of certain felonies (e.g. rape, attempted murder) and victims under the age of sixteen also in the case of sexual abuse crimes, can request a lawyer paid by the state to be assigned as a counsel. In other cases, victims can, under certain circumstances, request that the state finances a lawyer as a counsel; under certain circumstances, the state then can claim reimbursement in instalments from the victim (Articles 397a, 406g StPO).

The lawyer, as a counsel for a victim, has the right to be present during the interrogation of the victim as a witness by a prosecutor, a judge or at trial (Articles 406f and 406g StPO).

11. **Are there alternative methods of giving evidence which allow the protection of witnesses and *pentiti* from intimidation resulting from face to face confrontation with the accused? If yes, please specify (e.g. full or partial anonymity, video-conference, disguise, exclusion of the defendant from the courtroom when the witness is giving evidence, exclusion of the media or the public from the trial, etc.) and indicate under which conditions these methods are used.**

The possible measures, already mentioned in the reply b) to question 9, are:

- The public can be excluded from the courtroom during the witness's interrogation (Article 172 GVG) if there is reason to believe that giving evidence in the presence of the public in the courtroom may cause danger to the witness's life, health or freedom.

- The accused can be excluded from the courtroom while the witness is giving evidence (Article 247 StPO) if there is reason to believe that the witness will not tell the truth in the presence of the accused or that giving evidence in the presence of the accused may cause a serious danger of a grave detriment of their health; this includes danger to their health or life caused by their becoming known to the accused.

- The witness can be allowed to be absent from the courtroom and to give evidence by video-conferencing (Article 247a StPO) if there is serious danger of a grave detriment to the witness's well-being which cannot be countered by the measures mentioned above.

12. **On which grounds and on the basis of which criteria can anonymity be granted? Is there the possibility to obtain legal assistance at this stage?**

The circumstances under which confidentiality and thus complete anonymity (in the sense that his/her identity is divulged neither to the defence nor to the court) can be granted have already been described in the reply to question 8.

13. **Are pre-trial statements of witnesses and *pentiti* and testimonies of anonymous witnesses and *pentiti* regarded as valid evidence? If yes, under which conditions?**

As a rule, observations made by a person have to be introduced at trial by hearing this person as a witness (Article 250 StPO). This does not mean, however, that hearsay witnesses are excluded; they just give evidence on what they have heard. There is no rule that only the most immediate witness is permitted; however, the value of hearsay evidence usually is not strong enough to carry a conviction on its own without corroborating evidence.

There are exceptions from this general rule; with respect to questions of witness protection the following is of relevance: a witness's pre-trial statement can be used in trial if the witness cannot be interrogated by the court in the foreseeable future. This includes the case where the interrogation would cause serious danger to the witness's or his/her family's health or life.

14. Is it possible, and if so, under which conditions, to use information provided by "*pentiti*"? How is their credibility assessed?

A *pentito* is treated like any other witness and the information provided by him/her can be used in the same way as that of any other witness, in accordance with the principles already described. The court will, however, always have to bear in mind the special motivation of a *pentito* to obtain advantages for him/herself when evaluating the significance of the information. This is just a special case of the court's general duty to evaluate the evidence presented at trial.

15. Which are the opportunities for the defence to exercise its rights, including the right of the accused to challenge the witness'/*pentito*'s credibility in criminal proceedings (including at the pre-trial stage) and the respect of the "equality of arms" principle?

See the reply to question 8.

c. Non-procedural measures

16. At which stage(s), and in which context, is it possible for witnesses and *pentiti* to benefit from a protection programme?

A witness or *pentito* can be admitted to a protection programme from the beginning of an investigation until the case is finally closed. Since the aim of such a programme is to encourage a witness to testify in court, the benefits of such programmes are not granted if the danger appears for the first time after a case has been finally closed. However, a protection programme which has been initiated at an earlier stage can be continued after a case has been finally closed if the danger continues, since this is part of what has been promised to the witness in order to motivate him/her to testify.

The following preconditions are necessary for admittance to a witness protection programme:

- The witness's information must be of importance for clarifying the facts of the case or finding the accused;

- The witness, his/her relatives or other persons close to him/her must be endangered;

- Other measures are not sufficient to counter the danger;

- The person concerned (witness, relative or other person) must agree to his/her admittance in the programme;

- The person must be suitable for the programme. This includes the condition that he/she does not give false information (e.g. about third parties who have claims against the person), complies with the obligations of the programme (e.g. does not return to old – and often criminal – friends), keeps his/her involvement in a protection programme secret, and does not commit any crimes.

17. Is there the possibility for witnesses and *pentiti* to obtain legal assistance at this (these) stage(s)?

See the reply to question 10.

18. What is the procedure for admittance to a protection programme? Please specify, in particular, who takes the initiative, the criteria for admittance, the assessment of the relevance of a testimony and how admittance to the programme is formalised.

As described in the reply to question 6, the law enforcement agency investigating a case initiates the procedure for admittance to a protection programme by assessing the danger and informing the protection agency. The protection agency rates the danger with the consent of the prosecutor's office concerned which evaluates the importance of the witness's testimony and implements the adequate protection measures if the criteria described in the reply to question 16 are met. If the person to be protected is in detention the consent of the chief of the detention institution concerned is necessary as well.

Persons who are admitted to a protection programme as a rule have to commit themselves not to divulge any details of the protection measures which are considered to be official secrets.

19. Please indicate the measures that can be adopted for the protection of witnesses and *pentiti* (e.g. surveillance of the residence, physical protection, protection of personal records, relocation, change of identity, subsidies, assistance in job search, relocation of a detainee to another prison or to special units).

The possible measures are in principle:

- advising the protected person;

- causing public or private institutions to block personal records they have filed and respect the concerns of witness protection in their data processing; these institutions are legally bound to report any request for those records to the witness protection agency (Article 4 ZSHG);

- protecting the domicile and other abodes of the person;

- personal protection;

- relocation within the same state (Länder), another state (Länder) within Germany or a foreign country; this includes transfer to another prison or a special unit of the same prison;

- creating and using data and documents for a new identity for the protected person and witness protection agents (if necessary for protection e. g. if an agent has to pose as a member of the protected person's family); passports and other papers proclaiming the bearer to be of German nationality may only be issued to Germans;

- non-financial assistance in the new surroundings;

- financial assistance if and to the amount necessary for protection purposes; this is the case if the person does not have a sufficient income or has lost it because of the protection measures and does not (yet) have another revenue (e.g. unemployment benefit, social welfare benefits); as a rule the protected person should not profit economically from the protection measures.

20. What can the duration of a protection programme be? Which are the procedures for assessing the degree of danger for the witnesses/*pentiti* and their compliance with the obligations of the programme? Is it possible to challenge a decision of suspension, revocation or termination of a protection programme?

There is no fixed time limit for the duration of a protection programme; it can be continued as long as a sufficiently serious danger exists and the other criteria are met. The fact that the witness has given evidence and is no longer needed for the criminal proceedings is, of course, not in itself a reason for terminating a protection programme. Thus, protection programmes may well be in force for several years.

The continuation of the criteria is constantly supervised by the protection agency. If a certain measure (such as the use of false documents) or the programme as a whole is no longer necessary, it is terminated.

In principle, the decision on whether a witness is admitted to a protection programme or is excluded from it rests at the discretion of the protection agency. This means that a witness has no legal claim to be in a protection programme but only a claim that the agency exercises its discretion in an adequate fashion. However, this can be paramount to a claim to be admitted or kept in a protection programme in the rare cases in which no other decision would be adequate. Both the claim for correct exercise of discretion and the claim for admittance to a protection programme or its continuation can be asserted by legal action before the administrative courts.

d. International co-operation

21. **Which measures (e.g. use of modern telecommunications means, assistance in relocating protected witnesses, exchange of information between witness protection authorities) have been adopted in the context of mutual legal assistance in order to facilitate international co-operation? How are the financial implications of international co-operation activities dealt with?**

In general, international co-operation, including assistance in relocating protected witnesses, works well as long as an agreement on the sharing of costs can be reached. As with the co-operation between the different states (Länder) within Germany, it is expected that the initiating country bears the costs for the support of the protected person (e.g. accommodation and subsistence) and any current expenses for special measures requested by the initiating agency, whereas the assisting country bears the costs of its own personnel and material.

22. **Has your country entered international (bilateral or multilateral) agreements on the protection of witnesses and *pentiti*? If so, please indicate what kind of provisions they include.**

No such agreement has been entered.

23. **How can international co-operation in the field of the protection of witnesses and *pentiti* be improved?**

A general agreement on the distribution of costs could reduce friction in this area.

e. Statistics

24. **How many people currently benefit from witness or *pentito* protection measures/programmes, and for how long? How many of them are foreign people? If the measures/programmes can be extended to relatives and other close persons, please indicate (and, if possible, specify the relationship with the witness/*pentito*) how**

many people are included in this category. Please also provide figures on the different kinds of measures (procedural and non-procedural) adopted, and on the number of cases involving international co-operation.

There are only limited statistics available:

Federal or state witness protection cases	1996	1997	1998	1999	2000	2001
own cases	696	696	625	624	556	558
refused demands (1)					113	121
supporting measures (2)						155
protected persons	863	818	868	844	731	701

(1) Recorded since 2000.

(2) Support measures are short term measures for other agencies such as for trials, family reunions, etc.; they have been recorded since 2001.

f. *Proposals and comments*

25. Please provide any comments/proposals concerning the implementation of the terms of reference of the PC-PW and, in particular, instruments to be adopted to strengthen the protection of witnesses and *pentiti*.

Based on more than fifteen years' experience and the recent act on witness protection, the area of witness protection does not face major obstacles within Germany. On an international scale, an agreement on the distribution of costs could reduce friction.

Greece

a. *General information*

1. The legal framework on the protection of witnesses and collaborators of justice.

The only existing law on the protection of witnesses and collaborators of justice is Law 2928/01, which modified the legislation in the field of terrorism.

2. The measures encouraging witnesses and collaborators of justice to co-operate with justice.

Article 187B of the Penal Code[1] contains measures in favour of collaborators of justice in the field of organised crime (including terrorism), such as an acquittal being pronounced, a prosecution being dropped, a commuted penalty being imposed, or the execution of a penalty being suspended. There is also a provision encouraging victims to denounce actions committed against them by criminal organisations, since it is possible for the prosecutor to suspend (on a temporary or permanent basis) the prosecution of a victim of organised crime involved in illegal immigration or prostitution. In addition, the suspension of the expulsion of foreigners involved in illegal immigration is provided if he/she denounces acts committed by criminal organisations. Furthermore, Article 9 of Law 2928/01 refers to protection measures such as being guarded by trained police personnel, audio-visual testimony, witness anonymity, a change in the components making up an identity, and the relocation of civil servants.

3. Possibility of use of other measures encouraging witnesses and collaborators of justice to co-operate with justice.

According to the Greek legal system there are no possibilities of this kind.

4. Types of crimes and circumstances under which the measures encouraging witnesses and collaborators of justice are used. The possibility of the application of such measures to other persons.

Article 187B of the Penal Code provides for the use of measures encouraging witnesses and collaborators of justice to fight serious offences including organised crime, terrorist acts, and certain violations of humanitarian law. The exact meaning of these categories of crime is established by combining Articles 187, 187A and 187B of the Penal Code.

---

[1] It was renumbered from 187A of the Penal Code by means of Article 41 of Law 3251/04, but it contains the provisions of the former Article 187A of the Penal Code, supplemented by means of Article 2 of Law 2928/01.

The law makes no specific reference to people close to witnesses and collaborators of justice. The protection measures foreseen in Article 9 of Law 2928/01 indirectly cover people close to witnesses.

5. Urgent measures taken for the protection of witnesses and collaborators of justice.

The protection measures foreseen in Article 9 of Law 2928/01 are applied immediately because the sole ground for their implementation is a prosecutor's justified order or a ministerial decision, which does not require publication.

6. Institutions concerned by the protection of witnesses and collaborators of justice. Co-operation.

The institutions involved are the police, prosecutors and judges. Co-operation between these institutions is necessary to ensure the effective functioning of the law enforcement system.

7. Specific provisions for the protection of witnesses and collaborators of justice in relation to acts of terrorism.

The provisions of Law 2928/01 also cover organised crime and terrorism.

8. Respect for human rights and fundamental liberties. Instruments and procedures monitoring conformity.

Article 9 of Law 2928/01 stipulates that protection measures are taken with the consent of the witness – consent is necessary during the whole procedure – and that they do not limit the individual's liberty except if deemed necessary to safeguard his/her personal safety. In addition paragraph 4 of the same Article states that when anonymity has been granted to a witness, conviction cannot be based solely on his/her evidence.

b. *Procedural measures*

9. Timing and context of procedural measures for the protection of witnesses and collaborators of justice.

Protection is possible at any time in the procedure.

10. Possibility for witnesses and collaborators of justice to obtain legal assistance.

This is possible according to the general provisions (Articles 6 and 7 of Law 3226/04). Therefore the legal assistance provided to witnesses and collaborators of justice follows the difference between the accused and the civil party.

11. Alternative methods for the provision of evidence without confrontation with the accused.

Article 9 of Law 2928/01 refers, *inter alia,* to audio-visual testimony, witness anonymity and a change in the components that make an identity.

12. Criteria for anonymity. Legal assistance at this stage.

The law has not laid down specific criteria for granting anonymity or provisions for legal assistance in this particular case.

13. The value of pre-trial and anonymous testimonies.

The evidence is submitted to oral confrontation in court. When anonymity has been granted, the conviction cannot be based solely on the evidence given by this witness.

14. Use of information provided by collaborators of justice.

The evaluation of evidence is free (principle of free assessment of evidence).

15. Possibility of the accused to contest the credibility of witnesses and collaborators of justice.

During the procedure in court, the accused has the opportunity to challenge the alleged necessity for witness anonymity, his/her credibility and the origin of his/her knowledge (Article 9 of Law 2928/01).

c. Non-procedural measures

16. Timing and context for the protection of witnesses and collaborators of justice.

The police can protect witnesses and collaborators of justice if and when it considers it necessary.

17. Possibility of witnesses and collaborators of justice to obtain judicial assistance.

See the reply to question 10.

18. Procedure of admission to a protection programme.

There is no specific procedure.

19. Protection measures.

There are no specific measures, however, see the reply to question 2.

20. About protection programmes.

There are no specific programmes, however, see the reply to question 2.

d. International co-operation

21. Measures adopted in the context of legal assistance.

The existing international instruments for legal assistance can be applied in order to provide the effective protection of witnesses and collaborators of justice.

22. International instruments.

See the reply to question 21.

23. Possibility of improving international co-operation in the field of protection of witnesses and collaborators of justice.

Greece could examine the possibility of adapting existing instruments to new practices (e.g. examination of anonymous witnesses). In this respect, the European Convention on Mutual Assistance in Criminal Matters offers an effective medium. If this solution proved ineffective, Greece would then consider the possibility of adopting binding legal instruments or agreements.

e. Statistics

-

f. Proposals and comments

-

Hungary

a. *General information*

1. Please describe the framework (legal provisions and established practice) governing the use of measures protecting witnesses and *pentiti*.

The Hungarian laws – Act No. 19 of 1998 on the Code of Criminal Procedure, Act No. 85 of 2001 on the Protection Programme for those who participate in criminal proceedings and help justice, Government Decree No. 34/1999 (II. 26) on the personal protection of those who participate in criminal proceedings, as well as the rules and orders issued to promote the enforcement of the above acts – provide that protection shall be ensured for persons who expose themselves to danger by exercising their procedural rights and obligations in any phase of the criminal procedure.

In addition, the Hungarian laws provide, as a general obligation, that the Hungarian police forces shall protect everyone exposed to threat and shall prevent and deter crime. Thus, protection is not confined to those who provide actual help for the authorities in a given criminal case, either by providing information or in any other way – though the persons threatened are often those who have provided assistance to the authorities. The provision of practical protection is the task of the police forces.

The present situation is rather peculiar because at the time of the adoption of the Code of Criminal Procedure (Act No. 1 of 1973) there was no need for witness protection, this problem being unknown in Hungary. Rules on witness protection were later incorporated into the Code but they ceased to have effect on 30 June 2003 because the new Code of Criminal Procedure (Act No. 19 of 1998) entered into force on 1 July 2003. The new code (hereinafter referred to as "Be.") contains the procedural rules adopted so far. Therefore, its entry into force did not bring essential modifications into the substance of the law.

2. Please describe the framework (legal provisions and established practice) governing the use of measures encouraging witnesses and *pentiti* to co-operate with justice.

According to the rules of criminal procedure, a person against whom criminal proceedings have been instituted, i.e. who the authorities suspect of having committed the criminal offence which constitutes the subject matter of the proceedings, can testify in the capacity of either a suspect or a defendant (in the trial phase, after the charge has been preferred). Such persons are not obliged to testify but are entitled to do so and they must be given the opportunity to do so if they wish. A person suspected of having committed an offence may co-operate with the investigation authorities within the framework of which the perpetrator may contribute to the disclosure of the criminal offence (either of that in which he/she acted as a perpetrator or of other offences). His/her contribution to the interests of criminal prosecution may be so important that it may surpass the state's interest to establish criminal responsibility and punish the offenders. In such a situation, the criminal proceedings conducted against the perpetrator can, upon the decision of the public prosecutor, be discontinued, the charges against him/her can be dismissed and the criminal investigation can be discontinued. In such a situation, the information received within the framework of the co-operation may lead to evidence which renders the testimony of the co-operating perpetrator unnecessary. However, it may also happen that after obtaining evidence the perpetrator still has to testify. These questions can be arranged in advance, within the framework of the agreement on co-operation. According to the Constitution, the state's claim to criminal prosecution is enforced by the public prosecution therefore criminal proceedings cannot be dispensed with unless the prosecuting authority gives its consent. However, since the public prosecutor has no insight into the operative intelligence and reconnaissance positions of the investigation authority, he/she shall rely upon the information of the investigation authorities in assessing the value of the perpetrator's co-operation.

In respect of those witnesses who have not participated in the commission of a criminal offence but possess information about the fact which has to be proved, no specific means exist to encourage co-operation with justice; co-operation and giving testimony are civic obligations. To prevent compliance with these obligations by applying force, intimidation or by bribery are acts punishable under the law. This legal obligation is a kind of indirect means to encourage co-operation in respect of such persons.

In addition, the investigation authority is entitled to buy information (though not a formal testimony) and to offer a reward for the informer.

3. **Can measures/benefits encouraging the co-operation of witnesses and *pentiti* be used in combination with protection measures (arrangements concerning trial proceedings, sentencing conditions, special penitentiary regimes, etc.)? If so, please specify and indicate under which conditions they are applied.**

Certain incentives and protection measures, e.g. the purchase of information, the provision of physical protection or certain solutions of procedural protection, can be combined, but decisions related to sentences (the kind, length and weight of the punishment, the regime of the penitentiary institution, etc.) shall be taken by the court. Those questions which fall into the court's competence shall not be negotiated either by the public prosecution or by other authorities belonging to the executive powers.

4. **For which kind of crime and under which circumstances can witness and *pentito* protection be applied? Can the measures be extended to the relatives or other persons close to the witness/*pentito*?**

Certain witness protection measures, e.g. the confidential handling of the personal data or the name of the witness, can be applied in cases where the investigation authority, the public prosecutor or the trial court finds it appropriate in the interests of protecting the witness's life, physical integrity or personal freedom and of ensuring that the witness complies with his/her duty to testify without being intimidated (Section 95 of Be.). The application of a protection measure can be ordered either upon request of the witness or his/her counsel or *ex officio*. In the case of "*pentiti*" and their relatives, however, only programme-based protection can be ensured.

Co-operating perpetrators who have been arraigned or finally convicted may, by making reference to their co-operation, request the President to remit their punishment or to suspend the execution of their punishment for a probation period. The investigation authority may promise to support such a request for pardon but its promise shall not bind the decision-maker.

Procedural forms of witness protection – such as keeping personal data and even the name of the witness secret – may be applied in any criminal case, if necessary. The same holds true for physical protection.

A witness may only be granted anonymity or admission to the Protection Programme in cases of organised crime or extremely serious criminal offences.

5. **What urgent measures (e.g. immediate relocation to a secret place) can be taken in order to protect witnesses and *pentiti*?**

Urgent measures can be taken where there is a pressing necessity, if delay would endanger the person concerned and if the conclusion of an agreement on co-operation seems probable. In such cases, the head of the Witness Protection Service (hereinafter the Service) can order the personal protection of the person in danger, to ensure his/her safety by changing his/her place of residence or to transfer an endangered inmate to another penitentiary institution.

6. **Which institutions are involved in the protection of witnesses and *pentiti* and what is their role (e.g. law enforcement agencies, special independent agencies, prosecutor's offices, judicial authorities, etc.)? How does co-operation between the relevant institutions work in practice?**

The Witness Protection Service, organised within the police force, is responsible for the preparation and enforcement of the Protection

Programme. If protection should be granted to an inmate, the Service shall co-operate with the penitentiary institution in respect of the enforcement of the Programme. In the course of the enforcement, the Service shall contact and co-operate with the following bodies:

- investigation authorities;
- public prosecution;
- courts;
- Office of National Security;
- other public order bodies;
- the Central Data Processing Registration and Election Office of the Ministry of the Interior;
- the Board of Pension Insurance;
- the National Health Insurance Fund;
- the national tax authority;
- the labour authorities;
- the Hungarian Postal Service;
- local governments (public notaries);
- NGOs.

Co-operation is carried out partly on the basis of laws and partly on the basis of agreements on co-operation concluded with the above bodies.

The above bodies provide information, participate in the successful provision of protection and other measures, and exercise control.

7. Are there any specific provisions governing the protection of witnesses and *pentiti* in relation to acts of terrorism? If so, please specify. Are there any specialised counter-terrorism institutions? If so, what is their role in the protection of witnesses and *pentiti* in relation to acts of terrorism?

The Act on witness protection does not contain specific provisions on acts of terrorism. The bodies entrusted with the disclosure and prevention of acts of terrorism do not have specific tasks in connection with witness protection.

8. How does the framework governing the use of measures protecting witnesses and *pentiti* and encouraging them to co-operate with justice guarantee respect for human rights and individual freedoms. Please indicate the procedures in place, if any, to monitor compliance with human rights standards.

Witness protection measures may lead to the restriction of the defence's rights. Co-operation with the authorities may lead to ill-founded accusations in the hope of gaining more advantageous position.

Within the Hungarian criminal procedure system, witness protection measures, except for the institution of the "specially protected witness", do not affect the traditional criminal justice guarantees (principle of verbality, directness, hearing of both sides); the rules on physical protection do not have any effect on the procedural position of the accused person and the defence in general. If immunity is granted to a perpetrator in return for his/her co-operation with criminal justice, the state shall, under the law, compensate the injured party. Anonymity is regulated, in compliance with Recommendation No. R(97)13, as an exceptional procedure and due attention is paid to the "delicate balance" between the interests of criminal prosecution and the rights of the defence. Section 78 (4) of Be. provides that "a fact which derives from a means of evidence that the court, the public prosecution or the investigation authority obtained by restricting essentially the procedural rights of the participants shall not be admitted as evidence".

Protection may be granted to witnesses or collaborators of justice upon request and by their voluntarily entering an agreement on the conditions of the protection. The basis for their participation in the Programme is a contract.

b. *Procedural measures*

9. At which stage(s), and in which context, is it possible for witnesses and *pentiti* to benefit form procedural measures of protection?

Witness protection measures can be applied at any phase of the criminal procedure. According to the Hungarian laws, investigation forms part of the criminal procedure. Witnesses are entitled to request protection from the moment they are interrogated, even if they are perpetrators.

10. Is there the possibility for witnesses and *pentiti* to obtain legal assistance at this (these) stage(s)?

The law provides that witnesses may resort to the assistance of defence counsels if they find it necessary in order to protect their rights (Sections 59 and 80 of Be.). The application of a witness protection measure can be ordered *ex officio* or at the request of the witness or his/her counsel.

11. Are there alternative methods of giving evidence which allow the protection of witnesses and *pentiti* from intimidation resulting from face to face confrontation with the accused? If yes, please specify (e.g. full or partial anonymity, video-conference, disguise, exclusion of the defendant from the courtroom when the witness is giving evidence, exclusion of the media or the public from the trial, etc.) and indicate under which conditions these methods are used.

a) Sections 288 (2) and 292 (2) of Be. makes it possible to take a defendant who has already been heard by the court out of the courtroom while other defendants or witnesses are heard, if his/her presence might confuse them in giving their testimony.

b) Minors under the age of 14 shall not be heard as witnesses unless the testimonies given by them are indispensable.

c) Section 96 of Be. allows the confidential handling of the witness's personal data (date and place of birth, mother's name, address, profession). In this case, the defendant and the defence counsel shall not have access to the witness's personal data. The confidential handling of the witness's name can also be ordered if it is necessary (preconditions are specified under the reply to question 4).

d) Section 97 of Be. specifies the institution of the "specially protected witness". Such witnesses enjoy anonymity. According to Section 294 of Be. they cannot be summoned for hearings. During investigations, before the suspect has been arraigned, specially protected witnesses are interrogated by the investigation judge in the presence of the public prosecutor. The defence shall receive a copy of the minutes taken on the witness's testimony which, however, shall not contain the witness's personal data. On the basis of the minutes, further questions can be addressed to the specially protected witness or his/her anonymity can be challenged.

e) Section 244/A-D of Be. specifies the prerequisite conditions for and order of court hearings held through closed circuit television network.

12. On which grounds and on the basis of which criteria can anonymity be granted? Is there the possibility to obtain legal assistance at this stage?

Complete anonymity can be ensured if the witness's testimony refers to an essential circumstance of a very serious crime, if it cannot be substituted by any other evidence, if the witness's name, residence and the fact that the prosecution wishes to hear him/her as a witness is not known to the defendant or his/her defence counsel and, finally, if the disclosure of his/her identity would expose his/her or his/her relative's life, physical integrity or personal freedom to serious threat (Section 97 of Be.).

Anonymity may be granted if the testimony is related:

- to an important point of an extremely serious criminal case; and
- the testimony can not substituted by any other evidence; and
- the identity and/or the whereabouts of the witness, as well as the intention of the prosecution to call him/her as a witness, are not known to the defendant and the defence lawyer; and

- in a case where the identity of the witness is disclosed his/her – or his/her near relatives' – life, physical integrity or personal freedom will be exposed to serious threat.

(Article 97 of the Code of Criminal Procedure).

13. Are pre-trial statements of witnesses and *pentiti* and testimonies of anonymous witnesses and *pentiti* regarded as valid evidence? If yes, under which conditions?

From among the statements on facts, Hungarian criminal procedural rules admit expert opinions, witness testimonies and the testimony given by the defendant (suspect, accused person) as evidence. It is irrelevant in which phase of the proceedings the statement on facts was made. The testimonies given during the investigation are recorded in minutes; the witness is heard again orally at the hearing (this time by the court) but the minutes of the testimony given by him/her during the investigation can be read out if the witness refuses, without a lawful reason, to give testimony or if his/her testimony given before the court differs from that given during the investigation (Section 296 of Be.). Similar rules apply to testimonies given by defendants (Section 291 of Be.). Statements of facts made by persons who co-operate with justice shall not be admitted as evidence unless the statements have been given in the capacity of a defendant or a witness. It may happen that a person who was a suspect during the investigation gives testimony at the hearing as a witness because, as a result of a co-operation agreement concluded between him/her and the investigation authority, the proceedings instituted against him/her are discontinued with the consent of the public prosecutor (see the reply to question 2). The general rules shall apply to such witnesses.

14. Is it possible, and if so, under which conditions, to use information provided by "*pentiti*"? How is their credibility assessed?

The information provided by "*pentiti*" either must and can be corroborated by other sources, and in this case its value is to be assessed in the light of the other sources, or serves in itself as an independent source of evidence. In the latter case, the "*pentito*" is either a co-defendant whose testimony concerns a jointly committed offence and prejudices other persons as well or, as a result of the bargaining process described under question 2, a witness (perhaps a specially protected, i.e. anonymous witness).

The evaluation of the credibility of a testimony is the court's exclusive right and obligation; the public prosecutor, the defence counsel and the defendant may give their opinion but it is the judge who shall decide. The court is generally inclined to credit the testimony of a co-defendant who prejudices him/herself as well. The court shall examine and adjudge the credibility of the testimony given by the "*pentito*" as a witness. If the "*pentito*" is a specially protected (anonymous) witness, the investigation judge conducting the interrogation shall, if necessary with the participation of the investigation authorities, explore for the trial court "the witness's trustworthiness, the reliability of his/her testimony and the circumstances which affect the credibility of his/her testimony" (Section 213 (2) of Be.). In this case, too, it is the court which shall decide.

15. Which are the opportunities for the defence to exercise its rights, including the right of the accused to challenge the witness'/*pentito*'s credibility in criminal proceedings (including at the pre-trial stage) and the respect of the "equality of arms" principle?

According to the rules of Hungarian criminal procedure, the investigation authority shall interrogate all the suspects before they are taken to the prosecution authority. Everybody is entitled to have a defence counsel at each phase of the proceedings; the counsel has the right to be present at his/her client's interrogation and at several other stages of the investigation. The suspect and his/her counsel have the right to make observations and motions, including observations related to the testimonies (e.g. that the witness is not objective but biased, his/her testimony does not correspond to the facts, etc.), at both the investigation and the trial phase. At the investigation phase, observations can be made during the interrogations of the defendant and the presentation of the files which takes place when the investigation is closed. The investigation authority is obliged to make it possible for the suspect and his/her counsel to study the investigation documents and to make observations or motions (Section 193 of Be.). At the trial phase the defendant has the right to make a statement after the hearing of each witness. If the testimony of an anonymous witness is used in the proceedings, the defendant and his/her counsel shall be informed of this fact and the content of the anonymous witness's testimony in the course of the investigation, or at the presentation of the files when the investigation is closed or, at the latest, when the suspect is arraigned (Section 214 (4) of Be.) The defendant and his/her counsel may challenge the justifiability of the witness's anonymity, for example if they find out the witness's identity from the content of his/her testimony. They may also challenge the veracity of the facts alleged in the testimony of the anonymous witness, just as they can challenge the facts alleged in other testimonies. Since the identity of the witness is unknown, "*ad hominem*" argumentation is not applicable in such cases. Furthermore, since the defence cannot request the court to summon the anonymous witness the principle of the "equality of arms" is prejudiced.

c. Extra-procedural measures (physical protection)

16. At which stage(s), and in which context, is it possible for witnesses and *pentiti* to benefit from a protection programme?

The Protection Programme is applicable in the course of the criminal procedure, including at the phase of investigation, after the termination of the criminal proceedings (after deliverance of the judgment) and during the execution of the sentence as well.

17. Is there the possibility for witnesses and *pentiti* to obtain legal assistance at this (these) stage(s)?

Defence counsels can be involved in the Protection Programme (cf. the reply to question 10).

18. What is the procedure for admittance to a protection programme? Please specify, in particular, who takes the initiative, the criteria for admittance, the assessment of the relevance of a testimony and how admittance to the programme is formalised.

Those who meet the statutory requirements (see the appended text to the act) shall be admitted to the Protection Programme by a civil law contract.

19. Please indicate the measures that can be adopted for the protection of witnesses and *pentiti* (e.g. surveillance of the residence, physical protection, protection of personal records, relocation, change of identity, subsidies, assistance in job search, relocation of a detainee to another prison or to special units).

In the interests of preventing unlawful acts against a person's life, physical integrity and personal freedom, the following specific measures of protection shall be applied:

a) ensuring the safety of the person concerned by changing his/her place of residence or by placing an inmate admitted into the Protection Programme in another penitentiary institution;

b) ensuring personal protection;

c) confidential handling of the data recorded in the registrations and monitoring requests made with regard to the recorded data;

d) changing the person's name;

e) changing the person's identity;

f) participation in international co-operation.

In order to promote the social integration of the protected person, the Service shall see to it that psychological, social, economic and human support and legal advice are ensured for him/her. The rules on the provisions and supports ensured by the Service are specified under a separate Government decree. It is an important rule that the social and economic support provided for the protected person may not lead to his/her enrichment, but must be limited to the amount absolutely necessary for his/her subsistence and social integration.

20. What can the duration of a protection programme be? Which are the procedures for assessing the degree of danger for the witnesses/*pentiti* and their compliance with the obligations of the programme? Is it possible to challenge a decision of suspension, revocation or termination of a protection programme?

The temporal scope of the Protection Programme is not limited.

The degree of threat is determined in the light of the information gathered openly or, under statutory authorisation, in secret by paying due attention to all the relevant circumstances.

The performance of the obligations arising under the Programme shall be monitored by the Service in co-operation with the authority conducting the proceedings in which the need for protection has emerged. Persons deviating from the rules of conduct shall be warned or, in serious cases, excluded from the Programme

Disputes arising in connection with the agreement can be brought before a court if the parties cannot settle them.

d. *International co-operation*

21. Which measures (e.g. use of modern telecommunications means, assistance in relocating protected witnesses, exchange of information between witness protection authorities) have been adopted in the context of mutual legal assistance in order to facilitate international co-operation? How are the financial implications of international co-operation activities dealt with?

There is full international co-operation among the Witness Protection Services, which are in daily contact with each other. A protected person relocated in Hungary on the basis of international co-operation shall be provided for alimentation under the direction and with the financing of the foreign service, in compliance with the foreign programme.

22. **Has your country entered international (bilateral or multilateral) agreements on the protection of witnesses and *pentiti*? If so, please indicate what kind of provisions they include.**

Hungary is a Party to several international conventions. International obligations related to witness protection are coordinated by the National Headquarters of the Police.

23. **How can international co-operation in the field of the protection of witnesses and *pentiti* be improved?**

More intensive sharing of international experience and the joint training of the staff of the witness protection services would promote their work to a significant degree.

e. *Statistics*

24. **How many people currently benefit from witness or *pentito* protection measures/programmes, and for how long? How many of them are foreign people? If the measures/programmes can be extended to relatives and other close persons, please indicate (and, if possible, specify the relationship with the witness/pentito) how many people are included in this category. Please also provide figures on the different kinds of measures (procedural and non-procedural) adopted, and on the number of cases involving international co-operation.**

The Witness Protection Service started to operate on 1 April 2002. The figures related to its activity are secret and thus cannot be reported.

Italy

a. General information

1. Please describe the framework (legal provisions and established practice) governing the use of measures protecting witnesses and *pentiti*.

Under the Italian system the basic legislation on protection of witnesses and *pentiti* (or collaborators with justice) is Decree Law No. 8 of 15 January 1991, which was converted into a Law (No. 82) on 15 March 1991 and subsequently amended by Law No. 45 of 13 February 2001, "New provisions on kidnapping and on witness protection and protection and punishment of criminals collaborating with justice."

Earlier legislation aimed at encouraging members of criminal or terrorist organisations to collaborate did exist (see the reply to question 2), but no provision was made for a specific system of protection in their case. The ordinary police forces were responsible for protecting them from physical harm, but no form of economic or logistical assistance was provided. As a result, collaboration was a rare occurrence, and the few collaborators and their families were at risk of being threatened and suffering reprisals. The most significant cases of collaboration concerned individuals who had already cut off their links with a criminal or terrorist organisation for other reasons.

In contrast, the current system makes it possible to guarantee collaborators, and since 2001 witnesses, a high level of protection and assistance. This has led to considerable growth in co-operation. Since the amendments to the law came into force only a relatively short time ago, it is not yet possible to give a reliable picture of the situation as regards collaborators, but the number of witnesses is already quite high (see the reply to question 24).

Some clarification of the terminology used is necessary.

Nowadays, both collaborators and witnesses are covered by Law No. 82/91. The term "witness" refers to persons who give evidence of relevance to a preliminary investigation or trial proceedings but who have nothing to do with the offences concerned or with any criminal or terrorist organisation involved in their commission; their testimony is accordingly more disinterested since they have nothing to gain from it. Conversely, collaborators with justice (known as *pentiti*) are persons involved in a criminal or terrorist organisation who give evidence of relevance to a pending investigation into the organisation's activities; their aim is usually to obtain benefits such as remission of sentence, advantages while in prison, protection from the criminal organisation and economic assistance.

However, both witnesses and collaborators tend to play a similar role in trial proceedings. If they are not co-defendants or defendants in related proceedings, collaborators are subject to the same rules as witnesses.

They are accordingly under an obligation to tell the truth and any inconsistency between the evidence they give in court and their earlier statements that led to the collaboration can be challenged. If, on the other hand, the collaborator is a defendant in related proceedings other rules of evidence apply, since he/she may utilise the right to remain silent and not all earlier statements made by him/her are admissible as evidence. Collaborators are also assisted by counsel in the proceedings in which they are not a defendant.

Although the term "*pentito*" is frequently used to designate a criminal collaborating with justice, it does not appear in the legislation and is inappropriate since those concerned agree to collaborate without necessarily being in a state of repentance or resipiscence or officially dissociating themselves from the organisation in question. The sole criteria for determining whether they qualify as collaborators are objective ones (newness, completeness, credibility) and do not require the authorities to consider their inner convictions. The term may appear more appropriate to the incentive measures set out in the reply to question 2 since those measures apply only where the collaborator abandons the organisation and renounces violence. However, even then the measures are implemented without questioning the sincerity of the motives which led the collaborator to leave the organisation or contribute to its elimination.

Law No. 82/91 lays down the rules governing admittance to a protection programme, the programme's operation and termination and withdrawal of protection.

Stricter rules applicable in cases of collaboration were introduced in 2001.

These provide, *inter alia*, that collaborators have 180 days from the date on which they make known their desire to collaborate in order to give their testimony, which must be recorded in an explanatory transcript. The transcript must be kept confidential until the committal for trial. Collaborators must also provide information allowing the authorities to locate all their assets and pecuniary and other resources available to them for the purposes of seizure. Where the above time-limit is exceeded and in the event of failure to record the testimony in the explanatory transcript, the evidence is inadmissible in the trial proceedings and any protection measures already granted must be withdrawn. A collaborator who fails to countersign the explanatory transcript also cannot benefit from the mitigating circumstances provided for in cases of collaboration.

These amendments were made to avoid cases where collaborators varied their testimony over time or falsified it merely in order to obtain a prolongation of the protection programme. According to the case-law, the rules on the 180-day time-limit and the explanatory transcript do not apply to witnesses (Court of Cassation, Criminal Division, II, 18.12.2002, No. 42851). However, legal theorists disagree with this interpretation.

2. Please describe the framework (legal provisions and established practice) governing the use of measures encouraging witness and *pentito* to co-operate with the justice system.

Witnesses and *pentiti* are encouraged to co-operate with the judicial authorities by means of measures to protect them from physical harm and other measures of the nature of incentives.

As regards *pentiti*, the first incentive measures introduced in Italy in fact concerned offences linked to terrorism or attempted subversion of the constitutional system perpetrated in the 1970s and 1980s.

The first set of measures applicable to *pentiti* were set out in Decree Law No. 625 of 15 December 1979 (converted into Law No. 15 of 6 February 1980), entitled "Urgent measures to safeguard democracy and public safety", which introduced specific mitigating circumstances for persons who, having committed a terrorist or subversive offence, cut off their links with their co-perpetrators and sought to prevent the continuation of the criminal activity and its further consequences; the decree also introduced extenuating circumstances for those who prevented the commission of the offence. These rules are still in force and apply to offences committed at any time.

Subsequently, Law No. 304 of 29 May 1982, entitled "Measures to safeguard the constitutional system", was passed, which also applied to offences linked to terrorism and attempted subversion of the constitutional system, but solely where these had been committed before 31 January 1982. Under that law, persons who helped to eliminate a terrorist organisation or abandoned it while informing on its structure and organisation benefited from extenuating circumstances in respect of the offence of criminal association and certain less serious offences committed by the organisation; mitigating circumstances in respect of other offences; remission of sentence and broader access to certain advantages while in prison.

Lastly, Law No. 34 of 18 February 1987, entitled "Measures in favour of persons dissociating themselves from terrorism", introduced commutation or mitigation of sentence and advantages while serving a prison sentence for persons accused or convicted of terrorist or subversive offences who officially dissociated themselves from terrorism and rejected it as a means of political action. This law is solely applicable to offences perpetrated before 31 December 1983.

The legislation on persons collaborating with justice (Decree Law No. 8/91), which lays down the protection measures described in question 19, initially contained no measures to reward collaborators, who accordingly benefited from the ordinary incentive measures, including those provided for in the above-mentioned legislation on terrorist offences. Law No. 45/01 changed this by introducing Articles 16 *quater* – 16 *novies*, which, firstly, imposed more stringent conditions on collaborators, who benefit from the mitigating circumstances ordinarily provided for only if the co-operation they offer meets certain criteria (see the reply to question 1), and, secondly, made it possible to grant the advantages provided for by law (release on parole, leave, home imprisonment) also as a departure from the ordinary sentencing requirements on condition that the detainee has served a significant part of the sentence, co-operates in accordance with the above-mentioned criteria, does not pose any danger, has behaved well and has shown signs of resipiscence.

A special measure to encourage co-operation by nationals of non-European Union member states is set out in Legislative Decree No. 286 of 1998. Article 18 provides that a foreigner who is in danger and who decides to co-operate with the judicial authorities, or in any case shows a desire to break away from a criminal organisation, can be eligible for a special residence permit and may be admitted to an assistance and social integration programme.

Lastly, another incentive measure is laid down by Law No. 108 of 1996 for victims of usury. Those who declare themselves victims of this offence and are willing to testify against the perpetrator can obtain an interest-free loan from a special governmental fund.

3. **Can measures/benefits encouraging the co-operation of witnesses and *pentiti* be used in combination with protection measures (arrangements concerning trial proceedings, sentencing conditions, special penitentiary regimes, etc.)? If so, please specify and indicate under which conditions they are applied.**

Yes, the benefits described in the reply to question 2 can be combined with protection measures, under the conditions set out in the aforesaid answer.

4. **For what kind of crime and under what circumstances can witness and *pentito* protection be applied? Can the measures be extended to the relatives or other persons close to the witness/*pentito*?**

The conditions for granting protection measures vary for witnesses and for *pentiti*.

Witnesses are guaranteed protection where the ordinary security measures that may be taken by the police are inadequate and the witness is accordingly in serious, present danger on account of the testimony given. This may concern statements made in the course of a preliminary judicial investigation or during public trial proceedings in respect of any kind of offence.

For *pentiti* (or collaborators) the same conditions apply as regards the state of danger, but protection is guaranteed only in respect of certain serious offences, in particular where their testimony concerns offences of terrorism or subversion of the constitutional system or offences among those listed in Article 51, paragraph 3 bis, of the Code of Criminal Procedure (criminal association in a mafia-type organisation, kidnapping, criminal association for the purpose of drug trafficking, criminal association for the purpose of smuggling). They are also guaranteed protection solely on condition that their statements are intrinsically credible, adduce new evidence or can be seen to be particularly important for the conduct of an investigation or the outcome of a trial.

In the case of both witnesses and *pentiti* the protection measures can also be applied to persons living with them on a permanent basis, or persons who, while not living with them, are in real, serious, present danger. However, where *pentiti* are concerned, being related by blood or marriage or being a *pentito*'s spouse is not in itself sufficient to guarantee the extension of protection measures.

5. What urgent measures (e.g. immediate relocation to a secret place) can be taken in order to protect witnesses and *pentiti*?

In cases of urgency the Central Committee can, on the basis of summary information, adopt a provisional protection plan, making it possible to take all the ordinary protection measures in advance of an official decision. The committee subsequently re-examines the case in the light of a routine inquiry and may decide to cancel the provisional measures or to definitively adopt them. In cases of special urgency, where it is not possible even to wait for the committee to decide on a provisional plan, the Chief of Police may, pending the committee's decision, order immediate police measures for the enhanced protection of the person concerned and his/her relocation to a secret place. The rules governing the adoption and implementation of urgent measures are laid down in Ministerial Decree No. 161 (Article 4) issued by the Minister of the Interior on 23 April 2004.

6. **What institutions are involved in the protection of witnesses and *pentiti* and what is their role (e.g. law enforcement agencies, special independent agencies, prosecutor's offices, judicial authorities, etc.)? How does co-operation between the relevant institutions work in practice?**

The following are involved in the protection of witnesses and *pentiti*: the Central Committee for the Definition and Application of Special Protection Measures, the Central Protection Department, the Chief of Police, the Prefects, the Public Prosecutors, the District Anti-Mafia Prosecutors, the Principal Public Prosecutors at the Courts of Appeal, and the National Anti-Mafia Prosecutor. See the Minister of the Interior's Ministerial Decree No. 161 of 23 April 2004.

The Central Committee's role is to examine proposals concerning the granting of protection measures and admittance to a special protection programme, to take decisions thereon, to supervise the implementation of the protection measures and programme, and to take decisions on changes in or withdrawal of protection measures *ex officio* or on request. It is made up of an Under-Secretary from the Ministry of the Interior, two members of the judiciary and five public officials having the status of police officers.

The Central Protection Department's role is to assist the Committee with inquiries concerning proposals for the granting of protection and to implement the special protection programme decided by the committee. It is a police agency attached to the Ministry of the Interior.

Apart from taking the measures described in the reply to question 5, the Chief of Police has two roles: he/she has authority to propose that an individual be granted protection and is responsible for coordinating relations between the Prefects and the police as regards the special protection measures to be implemented in the protected individual's place of residence.

The Public Prosecutors and the District Anti-Mafia Prosecutors, whose offices bring prosecutions for the offences to which the individual at risk has testified, have authority to make admittance proposals. Where several offices are conducting related inquiries, the proposal is made by one office in agreement with the others. In the case of the offences covered by Article 51, paragraph 3 bis, of the Code of Criminal Procedure (see the reply to question 4), the proposal must be forwarded to the National Anti-Mafia Prosecutor, who is also responsible for settling any difference of opinion; where the offences are linked to terrorism the proposal is made in agreement with the relevant Principal Public Prosecutors.

7. **Are there any specific provisions governing the protection of witnesses and *pentiti* in relation to acts of terrorism? If so, please specify. Are there any specialised counter-terrorism institutions? If so, what is their role in the protection of witnesses and *pentiti* in relation to acts of terrorism?**

There are no specific provisions governing the protection of witnesses and *pentiti* in relation to acts of terrorism. Law No. 374 of 2001 gave the District Anti-Mafia Prosecutors jurisdiction concerning terrorist offences. However, their role with regard to the protection of witnesses and *pentiti* is not different from that described in the reply to question 6.

8. **How does the framework governing the use of measures protecting witnesses and *pentiti* and encouraging them to co-operate with the judicial authorities guarantee respect for human rights and individual freedoms? Please indicate the procedures in place, if any, to monitor compliance with human rights standards.**

The system for the protection of witnesses and *pentiti* guarantees full respect for human rights and fundamental freedoms. See the reply to question 15 as regards the principle of equality of arms and the rights of the defence. With regard to victims' rights, it can be noted that victims are entitled to appoint counsel to represent them during the preliminary investigation and trial, to challenge the authenticity of statements made by witnesses or *pentiti*, to object to any discharge order given at the investigation stage on the basis of the testimony of a witness or *pentito*, to request the public prosecutor to appeal against a judgment of conviction without punishment and to sue for damages.

The main responsibility for verifying that the above principles are upheld lies with the trial court handling the proceedings in which the witness or *pentito* gives evidence, since it must ensure that the rights of both defendants and victims are safeguarded. In addition, if false testimony is given, the court must transmit the case documents to the public prosecutor so that the relevant witness or *pentito* can be charged with perjury.

b. Procedural measures

9. **At what stage(s) and in what context is it possible for witnesses and *pentiti* to benefit from procedural measures of protection?**

Procedural protection measures may be granted to witnesses and *pentiti* at both the preliminary investigation and trial stages. Some procedural measures apply to anyone who is in danger, regardless of whether they have been admitted to a protection programme (see the reply to question 11 c), d), e), f), g)); conversely, other measures are dependent on admittance to the programme (see the reply to question 11 a), b)).

10. Can witnesses and *pentiti* obtain legal assistance at this (these) stage(s)?

Yes, witnesses and *pentiti* can obtain legal assistance at all stages in proceedings.

For witnesses, free legal assistance is available in respect of proceedings in which they give evidence where they are also a victim and wish to avail themselves of their procedural rights (submission of memorials, raising of objections, suing for damages); as regards other proceedings, legal assistance is part of the economic assistance measures that may be granted to a witness in order to ensure that his/her standard of living is unaffected by the testimony.

For *pentiti*, legal assistance is guaranteed in respect of the proceedings in which they give evidence.

11. Are there alternative methods of giving evidence which allow the protection of witnesses and *pentiti* from intimidation resulting from face to face confrontation with the accused? If yes, please specify (e.g. full or partial anonymity, video-conference, disguise, exclusion of the defendant from the courtroom when the witness is giving evidence, exclusion of the media or the public from the trial, etc.) and indicate under which conditions these methods are used.

Yes, there are many methods of safeguarding witnesses and *pentiti* from the intimidation resulting from face to face confrontation with the accused.

a)   Article 147 bis of the implementing provisions of the Code of Criminal Procedure provides that individuals who, in accordance with the law, are granted protection measures or admitted to a protection programme, even of an urgent or provisional nature, shall be heard during trial proceedings with all the precautions necessary to safeguard their persons. In particular, it is possible to have them testify from a remote location via an audiovisual link, simultaneously guaranteeing the visibility of all those present in the room where the person giving evidence is located. For the offences covered by Article 51, paragraph 3 bis, of the Code of Criminal Procedure (criminal association in a mafia-type organisation, kidnapping, criminal association for the purpose of drug trafficking, criminal association for the purpose of smuggling) and terrorist offences, and where the person giving evidence has changed his/her identity, this procedure is mandatory except where the court deems that the person's presence in the courtroom is absolutely necessary. If a person has changed identity, he/she must be able to give evidence without his/her face being visible.

b) Article 147 ter of the implementing provisions of the Code of Criminal Procedure provides for similar precautions to be taken as regards the identification of individuals who have changed identity or any other step entailing bodily observation.

c) Article 214 of the Code of Criminal Procedure lays down the general rule that, in cases of identification, where there is due reason to believe that the person required to make the identification may be intimidated or otherwise influenced by the presence of the person whose identity is being established, the procedure may take place without it being possible for the defendant or pre-trial detainee to see the person making the identification. This rule applies to both trial proceedings and preliminary investigations.

d) Where witnesses' anonymity must be protected, Article 472 of the Code of Criminal Procedure makes it possible to hold the hearing without the public being present. Proceedings concerning sexual offences perpetrated against minors are never held in public.

e) The defendant is entitled to be present at the hearing, but if his/her conduct is of a nature to disrupt the proceedings, the court may order his/her temporary or permanent removal from the courtroom.

f) Article 392 of the Code of Criminal Procedure provides for the possibility of a so-called advance hearing to take evidence (*incidente probatorio*), that is to say the taking of evidence in the same way as during the trial proceedings, and hence as described above, also at the investigation stage before the committal for trial. The circumstances in which this is permissible include where, on the basis of specific, tangible evidence, there is due reason to believe that the person concerned may be at risk of suffering violence, being threatened or being bribed, etc.

Article 398, paragraph 5 bis, of the Code of Criminal Procedure provides that advance taking of evidence in cases concerning sexual offences perpetrated against minors under the age of sixteen may take place under special conditions: the hearing may be held in a location other than the court, such as the minor's home or the premises of a specialist counselling agency; the minor's statements must be recorded in full by phonographic or audiovisual means.

12. On what grounds and on the basis of which criteria can anonymity be granted? Is there the possibility to obtain legal assistance at this stage?

Anonymity may be guaranteed within the limits specified in the reply to question 11.

13. Are pre-trial statements of witnesses and *pentiti* and testimonies of anonymous witnesses and *pentiti* regarded as valid evidence? If yes, under which conditions?

Pre-trial statements by witnesses and *pentiti* are admissible as evidence on the following conditions. Where the statements were made in the course of a so-called advance hearing to take evidence, that is to say at the investigation stage, in the presence of the defendant's counsel and before a judge other than the investigating judge, they are fully admissible as evidence for the purpose of the final verdict. As mentioned in the reply to question 11, the circumstances in which it is possible to hold an advance hearing to take evidence include where there is due reason to believe, on the basis of specific, tangible evidence, that the person concerned may be at risk of suffering violence, being threatened or being bribed, etc.

Where statements were made in the course of the investigation to the public prosecutor or the police, but the person testifying does not repeat them at the public hearing, they are admissible as evidence if there is tangible evidence to show that the witness was subjected to violence, threatened or bribed in order to prevent him/her from testifying or to cause him/her to falsify the testimony (Article 500, paragraph 4, of the Code of Criminal Procedure).

14. Is it possible and, if so, under which conditions to use information provided by *pentiti*? How is their credibility assessed?

As stated in the reply to question 1, in some circumstances *pentiti* are treated as having the same status as witnesses. This is the case:

a) where *pentiti* are not involved, directly or indirectly, in the proceedings concerning which they are testifying;

b) where they had the status of defendants in related proceedings and a final, irrevocable decision/judgment has been given concerning them;

c) where they are defendants in related proceedings and their testimony concerns the criminal liability of others.

In all of the above cases, *pentiti* are required to tell the truth and in circumstances b) and c) they are assisted by counsel (see Articles 64, 197 bis and 210 of the Code of Criminal Procedure). This is justifiable because, in Italian law, defendants are in principle entitled to remain silent and are not obliged to tell the truth. Treating *pentiti* on the same footing as witnesses exposes them to the consequences of a false testimony and prevents them from being able to make false allegations against others by taking advantage of their status of defendant.

However, where *pentiti* are co-defendants in the proceedings in which they are testifying they retain the status of defendant. They are not required to tell the truth. Statements they made during the preliminary investigation can be used against other defendants only if they reiterate them at the hearing, if the defendant in question consents thereto or if their repetition at the hearing has become impossible for objective, unforeseeable reasons (Article 513 of the Code of Criminal Procedure).

At all events, according to the case-law, if they are to be deemed credible and admissible as evidence, statements made by *pentiti* must be subject to very strict scrutiny and should be corroborated by other reliable evidence (documents, other testimonies, etc.).

15. What opportunities are there for the exercise of the rights of the defence, including the right of the accused to challenge the witness'/*pentito*'s credibility in criminal proceedings (including at the pre-trial stage) and the respect of the "equality of arms" principle?

Article 111 of the Italian Constitution expressly provides that:

a)   criminal proceedings shall be adversarial and based on equality between all parties;

b)   the defendant's representative shall systematically be entitled to cross-examine persons testifying against him/her;

c)   no defendant may be found guilty on the basis of testimony given by persons who avoided cross-examination by the defence, except in the cases expressly laid down by law.

These principles are reiterated in the Code of Criminal Procedure, which provides that evidence shall be taken in the course of the hearing, except in specific circumstances, and affords the defence considerable opportunities to challenge it. In particular, the defence may adduce exonerating evidence, challenge the admissibility of testimonies against the defendant, cross-examine witnesses and co-defendants and challenge the credibility of *pentiti* or witnesses at all stages in the proceedings (see the replies to questions 13 and 14).

During the pre-trial investigation, the defence cannot challenge statements made by a witness or a *pentito* to the public prosecutor or the police except where an advance hearing is held to take evidence (Articles 392 et seq. of the Code of Criminal Procedure), that is to say only in exceptional circumstances where the evidence is established before the trial proceedings.

However, compliance with the principle of equality of arms is guaranteed at the investigation stage by the rules on defence investigations (Articles 391 bis et seq. of the Code of Criminal Procedure), which entitle the defence to conduct its own investigation and to obtain certified statements from witnesses or defendants, which can be utilised at the hearing, in the same way as those taken by the public prosecutor and the police, in order to challenge testimonies given in court.

c. *Non-procedural measures*

16. At what stage(s) and in what context is it possible for witnesses and *pentiti* to benefit from a protection programme?

Witnesses and *pentiti* may be granted protection as soon as their testimonies expose them to danger, at any stage in criminal proceedings, during the investigation or the trial. The protection measures are implemented only following the completion of the administrative admittance procedure; however, in cases of urgency the procedure set out in the reply to question 5 may be followed.

17. Are witnesses and *pentiti* able to obtain legal assistance at this (these) stage(s)?

Other than during trial proceedings, there are no cases in which legal assistance is necessary.

18. What is the procedure for admittance to a protection programme? Please specify, in particular, who takes the initiative, the criteria for admittance, the assessment of the relevance of a testimony and how admittance to the programme is formalised.

The procedure for admittance to a protection programme is as follows.

An admittance proposal may originate from the Public Prosecutor or the District Anti-Mafia Prosecutor whose office is prosecuting the offences to which the persons in danger are testifying (Article 11, paragraph 1, of Law No. 89/91); where several offices are conducting related inquiries, the proposal is made by one office in agreement with the others. In the case of the offences covered by Article 51, paragraph 3 bis, of the Code of Criminal Procedure (see the reply to question 4), the proposal must be transmitted to the National Anti-Mafia Prosecutor, who is also responsible for settling any difference of opinion; in the case of terrorist offences, the proposal is also made in agreement with the relevant Principal Public Prosecutor (Article 11, paragraph 2, of Law No. 82/91). The proposal may also be made by the Chief of Police after seeking the public prosecutor's opinion (Article 11, paragraph 3, of Law No. 82/91). The practical aspects of the adoption and implementation of urgent measures are governed by Ministerial Decree No. 161 (Article 4) issued by the Minister of the Interior on 23 April 2004.

The admittance criteria vary for witnesses and *pentiti*. Witnesses are guaranteed protection where the ordinary protective measures that may be taken by the police are not enough and it can be seen that the witness is in serous, present danger as a result of his/her testimony.

Testimony may be given at the pre-trial investigation stage or during the public hearing, in respect of any category of offence. There is no credibility or newness requirement to be satisfied provided that the testimony is relevant. Admittance cannot be granted to witnesses in pre-trial detention on remand.

For *pentiti* the same conditions apply as regards the state of danger, but protection is guaranteed only in respect of certain serious offences, in particular where their evidence concerns offences of terrorism or subversion of the constitutional system or offences among those listed in Article 1, paragraph 3 bis, of the Code of Criminal Procedure (criminal association in a mafia-type organisation, kidnapping, criminal association for the purpose of drug trafficking, criminal association for the purpose of smuggling). They are also guaranteed protection solely on condition that their statements are intrinsically credible, adduce new evidence or can be seen to be particularly important for the conduct of an investigation or the outcome of a trial.

For the purposes of admittance to a protection programme, the testimony's significance or credibility is assessed by the Central Committee, which takes its decision on the basis of the proposal and the opinions of other advisory bodies.

Admittance to the programme is formalised by an administrative decision taken by the Central Committee. An appeal lies to the administrative courts against decisions refusing admittance. Following their admittance, witnesses and *pentiti* sign a document describing the programme's content and constituting an undertaking to comply with a number of obligations - failure to do so may result in the withdrawal or curtailment of the programme.

19. **Please indicate the measures that can be adopted for the protection of witnesses and *pentiti* (e.g. surveillance of their residence, physical protection, protection of personal records, relocation, change of identity, subsidies, assistance with a job search, relocation of a detainee to another prison or to special units).**

The protective measures that can be adopted in respect of *pentiti* are not imperative. Apart from those necessary in exceptional cases, the law provides for personal protection measures, technical security measures, relocation to a new place of residence, measures aimed at social rehabilitation, special conditions of detention, transfer or surveillance of prisoners, removal to a secret, protected place, personal assistance, change of identity, economic assistance. Economic assistance consists in providing persons unable to fend for themselves with accommodation, travel expenses, coverage of health care expenses, legal assistance, a subsistence allowance and educational fees for the *pentito* or for under-age family members. See also Ministerial Decree No. 161 issued by the Minister of the Interior on 23 April 2004 (Articles 4, 6, 7 and 8).

20. **At what stages in proceedings (pre-trial investigation, during the trial, after the trial) can a protection programme be granted? What is the protection programme's duration? What are the procedures for assessing the degree of danger for the witnesses/*pentiti* and their compliance with the programme obligations? Is to possible to challenge a decision to suspend, revoke or terminate a protection programme?**

The minimum duration of a protection programme is six months, and the maximum five years. Where the committee does not specify its duration, the programme is for one year. The Committee verifies that the danger exists and the obligations have been complied with before the expiry of the programme and whenever requested to do so by the authority which submitted the protection request. An appeal lies to the administrative courts against decisions to withdraw or suspend a programme. Ministerial Decree No. 161 issued by the Minister of the Interior on 23 April 2004 (Article 10) laid down in very precise terms the procedure for periodic verification of collaborators' or witnesses' compliance with their duties under a protection programme.

d. International co-operation

21. **What measures (e.g. use of modern telecommunications technology, assistance in relocating protected witnesses, exchange of information between witness protection authorities) have been adopted in the context of mutual legal assistance in order to facilitate international co-operation? How are the financial implications of international co-operation activities dealt with?**

Where a foreign authority issues a letter rogatory requesting assistance entailing the taking of evidence from a person covered by a protection programme in Italy, it is executed by the competent authorities in the normal manner. The only particularity is that the Ministry of Justice, which is the central authority dealing with letters rogatory sent to or received from foreign authorities, does not know the protected person's place of residence. Consequently, when the Ministry of Justice receives a request concerning a protected person it usually forwards it to the Office of the Principal Public Prosecutor at the Rome Court of Appeal, which liaises with the Central Protection Department at the Ministry of the Interior in order to initiate the procedure and locate the Italian judicial authority competent for execution. As regards other measures aimed at facilitating co-operation while guaranteeing the protected person's safety, Italian law allows the use of audiovisual links for the remote taking of evidence (video-conference) also in cases of execution of letters rogatory received from foreign authorities. To that end, Law No. 367/2001 of 5 October 2001 introduced an Article 205 ter in the implementing provisions of the Code of Criminal Procedure, which extends the use of video-conferencing, already provided for in Article 147 bis of the implementing provisions, to evidence to be taken in execution of letters rogatory (see the reply to question 11). This technology has already been used in certain cases to allow the German judicial authorities to question persons granted protection in Italy. According to information supplied by the Central Protection Department, there have been two cases, both confidential in nature, where mutual assistance consisted in sending persons under protection in Italy to a foreign country. Lastly, Italy is participating in a Europol working party which studies and pools information on good practices in the field of witness management.

22. Has your country entered international (bilateral or multilateral) agreements on the protection of witnesses and *pentiti*? If so, please indicate what kind of provisions they include.

Italy has not concluded international, bilateral or multilateral, agreements specifically concerned with protection of witnesses or *pentiti*. However, a bilateral agreement between Italy and Switzerland of 10 September 1998, supplementing the Strasbourg Convention of 20 April 1959, which was ratified by Law 367/01 and has been operational since 1 June 2003, sets out arrangements for video-conferences in Article VI. Under that agreement video-conferences can be used where it is inappropriate or impossible for the person giving evidence to be heard in person. A video-conference is naturally an optimum means of satisfying the security and confidentiality requirements surrounding the hearing of protected witnesses or *pentiti*. As already mentioned in question 21, the ratification law introduced an Article 250 ter in the implementing provisions of the Code of Criminal Procedure, which extends the use of video-conferencing, already provided for in Article 147 bis, to evidence to be taken in execution of letters rogatory (see the reply to question 11).

23. How can international co-operation in the field of the protection of witnesses and *pentiti* be improved?

Apart from suggesting an extension of the already existing international activities for the study of these matters and the pooling of information, on the basis of its positive experience so far in both a domestic and an international context, Italy is convinced that broader use of video-conferencing could allow huge progress in co-operation between states and also lead to considerable savings of time and human and financial resources.

e. *Statistics*

24. How many people currently benefit from witness or *pentito* protection measures/programmes and for how long? How many of them are foreigners? If the measures/programmes can be extended to relatives and other close persons, please indicate how many people are included in this category (and, if possible, specify the relationship with the witness/*pentito*). Please also provide figures on the different kinds of measures (procedural and non-procedural) adopted and on the number of cases involving international co-operation.

According to information provided by the Central Protection Department at the Ministry of the Interior, the figures for people benefiting from protection measures are presently 1,091 collaborators (with 3,664 members of their families) and 63 witnesses (with 187 members of their families). 23 of them, all collaborators, are foreigners. It is not possible to provide statistical data on the duration of the protection programme for each individual concerned, since the committee does not always set a given duration and, in any case, reserves the right to re-examine all cases on an annual basis, with the possibility of withdrawing, prolonging or reducing the protection programme (see the reply to question 20). Information on the nature of the relationship between the protected family members and the collaborator or witness is not yet available.

f. *Proposals and comments*

25. Please provide any comments/proposals concerning the implementation of the terms of reference of the PC-PW and, in particular, instruments to be adopted to strengthen the protection of witnesses and *pentiti*.

Italy considers that the experience so far has been very positive. At the same time, it feels able to propose the system described above as a generally very effective model, albeit open to improvement, for the protection of witnesses and *pentiti*.

Latvia

a. General information

1. Please describe the framework (legal provisions and established practice) governing the use of measures protecting witnesses and *pentiti*.

The legal framework governing the use of measures protecting witnesses and *pentiti*, is Criminal Procedure Code of the Republic of Latvia (hereinafter CPC). CPC prescribes the special procedural protection of persons giving evidence in criminal cases (for the purposes of this activity: witnesses and *pentiti*). CPC determines:

1) persons who can benefit from special procedural protection (hereinafter SPP);
2) bases and grounds for applying SPP;
3) persons who can be admitted as subjects for SPP;
4) obligation to perform in due form the procedure for application of SPP;
5) withholding of protected persons identity data;
7) special provisions of procedural action in relation to protected persons;
8) prohibition on using evidence of protected person;
9) the rights of persons concerning SPP;
10) termination of the SPP of a person;
11) termination of criminal prosecution in relation to a person who has assisted in the disclosure of a serious or a particularly serious crime committed by another person;
12) reduction of penalty in exceptional cases.

The Law on Investigation Operations also prescribes all the necessary activities which must be carried out for the execution of a decision made by the general prosecutor regarding the provision of special procedural protection to a person.

2. Please describe the framework (legal provisions and established practice) governing the use of measures encouraging witnesses and *pentiti* to co-operate with justice.

The measures used to encourage witnesses and *pentiti* to co-operate with justice are the following:

1) the person testifying can be granted SPP;
2) the fact that an offender has helped to detect the crime of another person can be a palliative circumstance in the consideration of his/her liability;
3) the criminal prosecution of the defendant can be dismissed;

4) the penalty of a convicted person, stated in the judgment, may be reduced.

3. **Can measures/benefits encouraging the co-operation of witnesses and _pentiti_ be used in combination with protection measures (arrangements concerning trial proceedings, sentencing conditions, special penitentiary regimes, etc.)? If so, please specify and indicate under which conditions they are applied.**

The above-mentioned circumstances may be used in combination with protection measures.

Upon receipt of a decision by the general prosecutor regarding the provision of special procedural protection for a person, the body performing investigation operations must carry out all the necessary activities for the execution of the decision, utilising appropriate methods and means (as described in the reply to question 19).

In association with the above-mentioned measures, imprisoned persons may be subject to the following SPP:

1) transfer of a protected person to another cell or to another place of imprisonment specifically chosen for this purpose;
2) keeping the protected person isolated from other prisoners;
3) removal of a person who endangers or may endanger the protected person to another place of imprisonment;
4) reinforced control over the protected person's contacts with other prisoners.

A convoy, in isolation from other prisoners may also be applied to prisoners or sentenced persons (not yet imprisoned).

4. **For which kind of crime and under which circumstances can witness and _pentito_ protection be applied? Can the measures be extended to the relatives or other persons close to the witness/_pentito_?**

Protection can be applied to witnesses and _pentiti_ if these persons are testifying in serious offences or particularly serious offences in relation to which there is a real danger to their life, health, property or legal interests, or there is an imminent threat or there are sufficient grounds to believe that the danger may occur. SPP can also be applied to persons (relatives, etc.) whose endangerment may influence witnesses or _pentiti_. The legal basis for the granting of SPP is an application by the said persons.

5. What urgent measures (e.g. immediate relocation to a secret place) can be taken in order to protect witnesses and *pentiti*?

The Law on Investigation Operations prescribes that in urgent cases, in order to prevent an actual threat to a person, the bodies performing investigation operations can carry out special activities even before this person has been declared a person requiring special procedural protection and before the receipt of a relevant decision.

The above-mentioned activities are as follows:

- to guard the person to be protected and his/her residence (property);
- to secure the conversations of the person to be protected against unsanctioned wiretapping and his/her correspondence against unsanctioned monitoring;
- to issue special technical devices and weapons to such a person and train him/her in their use;
- to provide lodging for the required period of time to the person to be protected in guarded residential premises unknown to others (confidential);
- to organise, according to the prescribed procedures, the issuing to such a person of a passport and other documents with different personal identity data, as well as change of permanent residence and place of work;
- other necessary activities.

From 1 October 2005, the same provision is provided by the Law on Special Protection of Persons, however the new law provides for more special protection measures in addition to those mentioned above. The additional measures are the following:

- to provide for the protection of such a person's data and to ensure such data is not released from state information systems;
- to transfer the person to be protected to another country in accordance with concluded international treaties or an agreement with the country in question;
- to provide for the insurance of the property of the person to be protected, if necessary;
- to provide to imprisoned and sentenced persons to be protected the convoy in isolation from other prisoners.

6. **Which institutions are involved in the protection of witnesses and *pentiti* and what is their role (e.g. law enforcement agencies, special independent agencies, prosecutor's offices, judicial authorities, etc.)? How does co-operation between the relevant institutions work in practice?**

The institutions involved in the protection of witnesses and *pentiti* are:

*   the relevant person responsible for the procedure (prosecutor, judge, etc.), who applies to the general prosecutor with a proposal to grant the witness or *pentito* SPP;
*   the relevant person responsible for the procedure when an appropriate criminal case is entered in his/her records (at the pre-trial investigation stage or at the hearing);
*   the general prosecutor or a prosecutor who is specially authorised by the general prosecutor (he/she prepares and takes the decision on whether to grant a person SPP);
*   the State SPP department in the General Criminal Police Board and other defensive institutions (the subject of operative action), who receive decisions from the general prosecutor and enforce them.

Upon the entry into force of the Law on Special Protection of Persons (1 October 2005), detention places also have special units dealing with special protection.

7. **Are there any specific provisions governing the protection of witnesses and *pentiti* in relation to acts of terrorism? If so, please specify. Are there any specialised counter-terrorism institutions? If so, what is their role in the protection of witnesses and *pentiti* in relation to acts of terrorism?**

No, there are no specific provisions governing the protection of witnesses and *pentiti* in relation to acts of terrorism and there is no specific counter-terrorism institution. The fight against terrorism is within the scope of the Security Police.

8. **How does the framework governing the use of measures protecting witnesses and *pentiti* and encouraging them to co-operate with justice guarantee respect for human rights and individual freedoms? Please indicate the procedures in place, if any, to monitor compliance with human rights standards.**

To ensure the protection of testifying persons, operative and other measures may be implemented as well as the measures prescribed in the Law of Investigation Operations.

Respect for human rights and individual freedoms and the principles of subsidiarity and proportionality are guaranteed and embodied in the principles of investigation operations.

The principles of investigation operations are as follows:

- Investigation operations must be organised and performed on a lawful basis, observing overall human rights, and in co-operation with and relying on the assistance of the general public.
- In performing investigation operation activities, it is prohibited to cause physical harm or material damage to persons, to endanger the life and health of people, to threaten the use of or use physical means of coercion, to incite people to criminal acts, and to cause significant harm to the environment.
- The manner, scope and intensity of investigation operation activities shall be commensurate to the form and danger level of the threat. Investigation duties shall be conducted so as to interfere as little as possible in the sphere of human rights.
- Investigation operation activities must be performed in accordance with the general method if the tactics, form and scope of their performance do not significantly infringe on the constitutional rights of persons. An official, with the approval of his/her immediate manager (supervisor) or deputy manager (Section 7 (2)), shall initiate such activities.
- Investigation operation activities must be initiated and performed only if the functions mentioned in Section 2 of this Law are fulfilled and it is not possible or would be significantly more difficult to achieve the objectives by other means.
- Investigation operation activities must be performed without regard to the person's citizenship, gender, nationality, age, residence, education, or social, employment or financial status and office, political and religious views, or affiliation with parties or other public organisations.

If a person believes that a body performing investigation operations has, through its actions, infringed his/her lawful rights and freedoms, he/she is entitled to submit a complaint to the prosecutor who, after conducting an examination, shall provide an opinion on whether the actions of the officials of the body performing the investigation operations were in conformity with the law; or the person may bring an action in court (Section 5).

If, in the course of investigation operations, the rights and interests of persons have been unlawfully infringed and as a result harm has been caused, the obligation of the relevant official, prosecutor or court shall be to restore such rights and to compensate for or allay the inflicted material or moral harm in accordance with the procedures prescribed by law (Section 29).

b. Procedural measures

9. At which stage(s), and in which context, is it possible for witnesses and *pentiti* to benefit from procedural measures of protection?

Witnesses and *pentiti* can benefit from procedural protection measures before criminal proceedings are initiated, which may take place during the period of the investigation of a criminal matter and continue after its termination. The right of victims, witnesses, suspects, accused and convicted persons (for the purposes of this activity: witnesses and *pentiti*) to acquire SPP can be applied if these persons are testifying in serious offences or particularly serious offences in relation to which there is a real danger to their life, health, property or legal interests, or there is an imminent threat or there are sufficient grounds to believe that the danger may occur.

10. Is there the possibility for witnesses and *pentiti* to obtain legal assistance at this (these) stage(s)?

Under the conditions stated in CPC, the protected person has the right to legal assistance – an attorney, who has the right to represent the interests of the protected person, can participate in pre-trial examination actions, in the hearing, in Courts of Appeal and Courts of Cassation and may declare rejections, submit petitions and appeals.

11. Are there alternative methods of giving evidence which allow the protection of witnesses and *pentiti* from intimidation resulting from face to face confrontation with the accused? If yes, please specify (e.g. full or partial anonymity, video-conference, disguise, exclusion of the defendant from the courtroom when the witness is giving evidence, exclusion of the media or the public from the trial, etc.) and indicate under which conditions these methods are used.

To exclude any possibility of the protected person being identified and to guarantee his/her security, the following methods of testifying may be adopted:

1) The identity data of the protected person may not be indicated in the materials of the criminal case (protocols, decisions, etc.). These data are replaced with a pseudonym, and the name and telephone (fax) number is replaced with the name and telephone number of the institution with whose mediation the protected person can be invited to the pre-trial examination or to the court. In the court examination of a person, whose identity cannot be revealed, special visual and acoustic interference can be created with the effect that the other parties in the proceedings do not identify this person.

2) If the necessity arises to prevent contradictions between the testimonies of two formerly examined persons and one of these two persons is a

subject of SPP, they can both be examined at the same time using special equipment, which prevents the protected person from being identified.

3) During the hearing, the person responsible for the procedure or the representative of protected person may reject any questions if the answer to such questions may make it possible to identify the protected person, but the protected person has the right not to answer these questions.

4) The court may examine the protected person in the meeting room or in another room, using technical equipment, providing the other participants in the proceedings can hear the questions and the answer to these questions, and can ask questions themselves.

5) If the protected person is not located in a court building, the court may examine him/her, using technical equipment and providing the other participants in the proceedings can see the person, ask questions and hear the answers. In this case there must be a specialist with the protected person, who is an authority of the institution responsible for the distribution of passports in order to check and certify the identity of the person.

12. On which grounds and on the basis of which criteria can anonymity be granted? Is there the possibility to obtain legal assistance at this stage?

Anonymity can be granted only in cases where there is well-founded information that the offenders (persons, who can endanger the person to be examined) are not informed about the identity of the protected person. If, in the ongoing procedure, the data relating to the person's identity has been included in the documents, CPC determines that to conceal this person's real identity data, these documents must be rewritten changing only the data relating to the person's identity. The original documents are withdrawn from the case and kept together with the decision on the application of SPP to this person. Only the person responsible for the procedure in the appropriate case (prosecutor, judge, etc.) and the prosecutor who is specially authorised by the general prosecutor may view these documents.

There is a possibility to obtain legal assistance at this stage. Under the conditions stated in CPC, the protected person has the right to legal assistance – an attorney, who has the right to represent the interests of the protected person and can participate in pre-trail examination actions, in the hearing, etc.

13. **Are pre-trial statements of witnesses and *pentiti* and testimonies of anonymous witnesses and *pentiti* regarded as valid evidence? If yes, under which conditions?**

The testimony of protected persons as well as those of persons whose identity data is replaced with a new identity are considered as evidence.

14. **Is it possible, and if so, under which conditions, to use information provided by "*pentiti*"? How is their credibility assessed?**

The testimony of a suspect (defendant, etc.) is considered as evidence, because, as it is stated in the CPC, the evidence in a criminal case is any fact, on the basis of which, as stated by the law (under Criminal Law), the existence or non-existence of a criminal offence, the guilt of persons who have committed an offence or any other conditions, which are significant for the correct adjudication of the case, can be proved.

The person responsible for the procedure evaluates the credibility of the evidence on the basis of a complete, unbiased and independent review of all the circumstances of the case and their interrelationship, according to the law and juridical sense. No evidence can be considered as a binding evidence on the court, the judge, the prosecutor and investigator.

15. **Which are the opportunities for the defence to exercise its rights, including the right of the accused to challenge the witness'/*pentito*'s credibility in criminal proceedings (including at the pre-trial stage) and the respect of the "equality of arms" principle?**

The defendant has the right to consider all the materials of the case from the moment of the completion of the pre-trail examination, including the identification data of persons who are testifying in that case, except where the person testifying has acquired a pseudonym. In this case, the rights of the defendant are restricted to protect persons, who are the subject of SPP, against possible endangerment.

c. *Non-procedural measures*

16. **At which stage(s), and in which context, is it possible for witnesses and *pentiti* to benefit from a protection programme?**

It is possible for witnesses and *pentiti* to benefit from a protection programme before criminal proceedings are initiated, during the period of the investigation of the criminal matter and after its termination.

Witnesses and *pentiti* can benefit from a protection programme in this context:

1) these persons are subject to SPP;
2) the criminal case against the person can be dismissed if he/she has helps to disclose a serious or a particularly serious crime committed by another person, which is more serious or more dangerous than the one committed by this person;
3) the penalty stated in the judgment may be reduced if the convicted person helps to disclose a serious or a particularly serious crime committed by another person, which is more serious or more dangerous than the one committed by this person.

17. Is there the possibility for witnesses and *pentiti* to obtain legal assistance at this (these) stage(s)?

Under the conditions stated in CPC, the protected person has the right to legal assistance – an attorney, who has the right to represent the interests of the protected person, can participate in pre-trial examination actions, in the hearing, in Courts of Appeal and Courts of Cassation and may declare rejections, submit petitions and appeals.

18. What is the procedure for admittance to a protection programme? Please specify, in particular, who takes the initiative, the criteria for admittance, the assessment of the relevance of a testimony and how admittance to the programme is formalised.

The legal basis for the granting of SPP is an application from the endangered person. If the person responsible for the procedure has approved his/her application, he/she applies to the general prosecutor with a proposal to grant the endangered person SPP.

After the general prosecutor, on the basis of application from the person responsible for the procedure, has considered the materials and has listened to the endangered person, he/she takes a decision on whether to grant him/her SPP.

The person responsible for the procedure takes the initiative, but the decision is made by the general prosecutor. The assessment of the relevance of a testimony and the evaluation of the possible danger is carried out by the person responsible for the procedure as well as by the general prosecutor.

19. Please indicate the measures that can be adopted for the protection of witnesses and *pentiti* (e.g. surveillance of the residence, physical protection, protection of personal records, relocation, change of identity, subsidies, assistance in job search, relocation of a detainee to another prison or to special units).

In order to provide SPP, the following measures can be implemented:

- guarding the person to be protected and his/her residence (property);
- securing the conversations of the person to be protected against unsanctioned wiretapping and his/her correspondence against unsanctioned monitoring;
- issuing special technical devices and weapons to such a person and training him/her in their use;
- provision of lodging for the required period of time to the person to be protected in guarded residential premises unknown to others (confidential);
- organisation, according to the prescribed procedures, of the issuing to such a person of a passport and other documents with different personal identity data, as well as of a change of permanent residence and place of work;
- other necessary activities.

From 1 October 2005, the same provision is provided by the Law on Special Protection of Persons, however the new law provides for more special protection measures in addition to those mentioned above.

The additional measures are the following:

- to provide for the protection of such a person's data and ensure that such data are released from state information systems;
- to transfer the person to be protected to another country in accordance with concluded international treaties or an agreement with the country in question;
- to provide for the insurance of the property of the person to be protected, if necessary;
- to provide to imprisoned and sentenced persons to be protected the convoy in isolation from other prisoners.

20. What can the duration of a protection programme be? Which are the procedures for assessing the degree of danger for the witnesses/*pentiti* and their compliance with the obligations of the programme? Is it possible to challenge a decision of suspension, revocation or termination of a protection programme?

The duration of SPP is not determined in law, though protection measures must continue while the possible danger exists or while the protected person has not renounced it him/herself, or while this person's actions have not made the protection measures impossible.

A decision of the general prosecutor to grant (or refuse) a witness admittance to SPP, can be appealed to the Criminal Case Department of Supreme Court by the person to whom this decision relates, or the defender or the legal representative of these persons.

d. International co-operation

21. Which measures (e.g. use of modern telecommunications means, assistance in relocating protected witnesses, exchange of information between witness protection authorities) have been adopted in the context of mutual legal assistance in order to facilitate international co-operation? How are the financial implications of international co-operation activities dealt with?

CPC provides the following measures of mutual legal assistance in order to facilitate international co-operation:

1) use of modern telecommunication means;
2) use of video and audio and photographic means;
3) use of specific technical, chemical and biological means;
4) use of information systems;
5) assistance in relocating protected witnesses;
6) exchange of information between witness protection authorities;
7) etc.

22. Has your country entered international (bilateral or multilateral) agreements on the protection of witnesses and *pentiti*? If so, please indicate what kind of provisions they include.

The Republic of Latvia has entered international agreements on the protection of witnesses and *pentiti*, e.g. bilateral agreements with the Republic of Lithuania, the Republic of Estonia and the Republic of Slovenia. Agreements with the Czech Republic and Austria are in the stage of elaboration. These agreements provide details on how to relocate protected persons to another country for an appropriate period of time. These persons may also be relocated to other countries subject to mutual arrangements with the appropriate authorities of justice.

23. How can international co-operation in the field of the protection of witnesses and *pentiti* be improved?

International co-operation in field of the protection of witnesses and *pentiti* may be improved by extending the number of concluded agreements with other countries.

e. *Statistics*

24. How many people currently benefit from witness or *pentito* protection measures/programmes, and for how long? How many of them are foreign people? If the measures/programmes can be extended to relatives and other close persons, please indicate (and, if possible, specify the relationship with the witness/*pentito*) how many people are included in this category. Please also provide figures on the different kinds of measures (procedural and non-procedural) adopted, and on the number of cases involving international co-operation.

-

f. *Proposals and comments*

25. Please provide any comments/proposals concerning the implementation of the terms of reference of the PC-PW and, in particular, instruments to be adopted to strengthen the protection of witnesses and *pentiti*.

On 1 October 2005, a new Criminal Procedure Law entered into force in Latvia which repeals the Criminal Procedure Code and which in turn is the main legal framework governing the use of measures protecting witnesses and *pentiti*. It provides a more strengthened system for the protection of witnesses and *pentiti*. This new Law defines the substance of SPP more precisely; the cause and the basis of SPP; the order of consideration of an application for the granting of SPP to an appropriate person; proposition of the person responsible for the procedure to determine SPP; determination of a person to be the subject of SPP; decision on the granting of SPP; realisation of decision on SPP; the rights and obligations of the protected person; the rights and obligations of representatives or other persons; individuality of procedural action in pre-trial stage; the individuality of hearings; discontinuance of SPP and non-usage of the testimony of protected persons.

On 19 May 2005, a new Law on Special Protection of Persons was adopted which entered into force together with the Criminal Procedure Law. This law repeals the provisions on special procedural protection contained in the Law on Investigation Operations since it provides for more detailed and specific procedures, rights, guarantees, and duties with regard to providing special procedural protection to persons testifying in criminal proceedings or participating in the disclosing, investigation, or trial of serious or especially serious crimes.

Lithuania

a. *General information*

1. Please describe the framework (legal provisions and established practice) governing the use of measures protecting witnesses and *pentiti*.

The main laws and regulations relating to witness protection in Lithuania are listed hereafter:

1. Specialised laws and regulations:
    1.1. the Republic of Lithuania's Law on the Protection from Criminal Influence of the Participants in Criminal Proceedings and Clandestine Activities, Law Enforcement Officers and Members of the Judiciary (13-02-1996 No. I-1202).
    1.2 Lithuania's Government Resolution on the Approval of the Temporary Regulations on the Protection from Criminal Influence (13-02-1997 No. 119).

2. General laws and regulations (which regulate the implementation of protection measures, a secrecy regime, etc.):
    2.1. the Republic of Lithuania's Law on State Secrets (25-11-1999 No. VIII-1443).
    2.2. the Republic of Lithuania's Law on Clandestine Activities (20-06-2002 No. IX-96).
    2.3. the Republic of Lithuania's Penal Code (26-09-2000 No. VIII 1968).
    2.4. the Republic of Lithuania's Criminal Proceeding Code (14-03-2002 No. IX-785).
    2.5. the Republic of Lithuania's Law on Law Courts (24-01-2002- No. IX-732).
    2.6 Lithuania's Government Resolution on the Physical Protection of Judges and their Family Members (22-12-2002 No. 1957).
    2.7. the Republic of Lithuania's Law on Public Prosecutors (22-04-2003 No. IX-1518).

Detailed information on the use of measures protecting witnesses (further — protected persons) is confidential and cannot be provided; as a result, only indicative data is given hereafter:

1) Protected persons by citizenship are:

    - 89 percent — Lithuanians;
    - 6 percent — foreign;
    - 5 percent — stateless.

2) 15 percent — protected persons on international cooperation cases, 85 percent — on domestic cases.

3) 30 percent of protected persons are relatives of witnesses; 5 percent — participants of the clandestine activities; other — participants of criminal proceedings:
   - 30 percent — witnesses;
   - 25 percent — suspects and accused;
   - 10 percent — victims.

4) The use of measures protecting witnesses was initiated during period 1999-2002 by:
   - Public prosecutor office — 68 percent;
   - Police department — 28 percent;
   - Police commissariats — 4 percent.

2. Please describe the framework (legal provisions and established practice) encouraging the use of measures protecting witnesses and *pentiti* to co-operate with justice.

Witnesses and *pentiti* are encouraged to co-operate with justice by being offered the possibility of being protected from threats to their health, their lives and their property. In addition, *pentiti* are encouraged by being given the possibility of a mitigated sentence or avoiding punishment thanks to their co-operation with justice.

The legal provisions in the Republic of Lithuania's Penal Code are the following:

- Article 32 (performance of assignment of a law enforcement institution);
- Article 391 (pardon from punishment in cases where an individual has actively assisted in disclosing crimes committed by an organised crime group or members of an organised crime association).

1. The person suspected of participating in crimes committed by an organised crime group or organised crime association or belonging to an organised crime association may be exempted from punishment if he/she confesses to such a crime or to belonging to an organised crime association, or by actively assisting in disclosing crimes committed by an organised crime group or organised crime association.

2. The 1st part of this article is not applied to a person having participated in the commitment of a homicide, or if he/she was previously pardoned from punishment, or to the leaders of an organised crime group or organised crime association.

Article 59 (extenuating circumstances) and in particular part 1 of Article 2 (the perpetrator pleads guilty, expresses repentance, or helps to resolve the crime or identify the person responsible for the crime).

Article 61 (assignment of penalty in cases of extenuating and/or aggravating circumstances) part 4 (if the perpetrator voluntarily pleads guilty, expresses sincere repentance, actively assists in resolving the crime, and if there are no aggravating circumstances, the court punishment should not be more than the average imprisonment or no imprisonment).

Article 62 (assignment of a commuted penalty with respect to the one defined by law).

Article 114 (State takeover), part 3 (the person is pardoned from punishment for this crime if he/she voluntarily provides valuable information on this crime).

Article 227 (bribery), part 4 (the person is pardoned from punishment for bribery if the bribe was demanded, provoked and he/she offered the bribe in full knowledge of the law enforcement institution).

Article 233 (influence on a witness, victim, expert, specialist or interpreter).

Article 234 (influence on a victim in order for he/she to accept reconciliation).

Article 259 (illegal possession of drugs), part 3 (the person is pardoned from punishment for illegal possession of drugs, if he/she voluntarily consulted a doctor or called a law enforcement institution in order to return the illegal drugs).

3. **Can measures/benefits encouraging the co-operation of witnesses and *pentiti* be used in combination with protection measures (arrangement concerning trial proceedings, sentencing conditions, special penitentiary regimes, etc.)? If so, please specify and indicate which conditions they are applied.**

Yes, measures/benefits encouraging the co-operation of witnesses and *pentiti* can be used in combination with protection measures.

Conditions are described in the reply to question 4.

4. For which kind of crime and under which circumstances can witness and *pentito* protection be applied? Can the measures be extended to the relatives or other persons close to witnesses and *pentiti*?

Witness and *pentito* protection measures can be applied in cases of severe and very severe crimes (homicide, property extortion, organised crime association, etc.).

The conditions for applying protection measures are:

1) Threats to a witness's health or life;
2) Threats to a witness's property;
3) Threats to a witness's constitutional rights and freedoms.

The mandatory condition for witnesses and *pentiti*, who actively co-operate with judiciary institutions, is to assist in resolving crimes or to provide law enforcement officers and judiciary institutions with other valuable information.

The protection measures can be applied during a clandestine activity, a pre-trial investigation, a case hearing in court and once the hearing or clandestine activity is over.

Yes, protection measures can be applied to kinsfolk's parents, children, siblings, foster children, foster parents, grandparents, grandchildren and spouses. In addition, protection measures can by applied to judges, prosecutors, interrogators, investigators and bailiffs.

5. What urgent measures (e.g. immediate relocation to a secret place) can be taken in order to protect witness and *pentito*?

Protection measures can be applied as a matter of urgency. Urgent protection measures might be:

- the physical protection of the witness or *pentito*, as well as their property, at their place of residence, or
- their temporary relocation to a safe place.

6. Which institutions are involved in the protection of witnesses and *pentiti* and what is their role (e.g. law enforcement agencies, special independent agencies, prosecutor's office, judicial authorities, etc.)? How does co-operation between relevant institutions work in practice?

The protection of witnesses and *pentiti* in the Republic of Lithuania is carried out by a specialised police force, the Lithuania Police Witnesses and Victims' Protection Service. Their mission is to ensure the complex implementation of different means of protection from criminal influence and operational activities, inside the country and abroad, on the basis of international and interdepartmental agreements. Witnesses and *pentiti* protection is also carried out by other police agencies. The relevant institutions are the prosecutor's office and other law enforcement institutions.

Practical co-operation among relevant institutions is implemented according to the Republic of Lithuania's law on the Protection from criminal influence of the participants in criminal proceedings and clandestine activities, law enforcement officers and members of the judiciary (13-02-1996 No. 1-1202) and Lithuania's Government Resolution on the Approval of the temporary regulations on the protection from criminal influence (13-02-1997 No. 119).

7. **Are there any specific provisions governing the protection of witnesses and *pentiti* in relations to act of terrorism? If so, please specify. Are there any specialised counter-terrorism institutions? If so, what is their role in the protection of witnesses and *pentiti* in relation to acts of terrorism?**

There are no specific provisions governing the protection of witnesses and *pentiti* in relation to acts of terrorism, but terrorism is qualified as a very severe crime and is covered by the reply to question 4.

Specialised counter-terrorism institutions are the Lithuanian police SWAT "Aras" and the Lithuanian State Security Department.

8. **How does the framework governing the use of measures protecting witnesses and *pentiti* and encouraging them to co-operate with justice guarantee respect for human rights and individual freedoms? Please indicate the procedures in place, if any, to monitor compliance with human rights standards?**

A protected person is entitled to sign a written agreement, which outlines his/her rights and obligations.

A protected person has the following responsibilities:

1. to actively co-operate with the officers of law enforcement and judiciary institutions, to assist in resolving crimes or to provide officers of law enforcement and judiciary institutions with other valuable information (this duty is not applied to experts, defendants and officers of law enforcement and judiciary institutions).
2. not to commit wrongdoings in the future.
3. in case of need, to delegate contacts with third parties to other persons.
4. to comply with all lawful requests made by the officer carrying out the protection.
5. to inform the protection officer of every threat against him/her or other unlawful act against him/her.

6. not to disseminate information about the methods of protection from criminal influence applied to him/her, unless permitted to do so by the officer carrying out the protection.
7. to fulfil the conditions as laid down in the agreement.

All protection measures are only implemented once a person has given his/her consent.

b. *Procedural measures*

9. At which stage(s), and in which context, is it possible for witness and *pentito* to benefit from procedural measures of protection?

According to the agreement, a witness'/*pentito's* personal security and individual constitutional rights and freedoms must be ensured as well as his/her change of job and place of residence.

10. Is there the possibility for witnesses and *pentiti* to obtain legal assistance at this (these) stage(s)?

Yes, according to the reply to question 8.

11. Are there alternative methods of giving evidence, which allow the protection of witnesses and *pentiti* from intimidation resulting from face to face confrontation with the accused? If yes, please specify (e.g. full or partial anonymity, video-conference, disguise, exclusion of the defendant from the courtroom when the witness is giving evidence, exclusion of media or the public from the trial, etc.) and indicate under which conditions these methods are used.

The following alternative methods of giving evidence are described in the Republic of Lithuania's Criminal Proceeding Code (hereinafter referred to as CPC): anonymity, video-conference, disguise, exclusion of the defendant from the courtroom when the witness is giving evidence, exclusion of the media or the public from the trial.

A video-conference can only be used for a protected person for protection reasons (part 4 of Article 183 of the CPC). The video-conference might be applied to an anonymous witness in conjunction with video and audio interferences. Part 4 of Article 282 of the CPC stipulates that in cases where the arrival of an anonymous witness in a courtroom might endanger him/her or his/her relatives' life, health or freedom, according to Article 203, he/she might not be cited to court trial, and his testimony, given to the pre-trial investigation judge, might be read aloud during the trial. In such cases, the witness might have testified by means of a video-conference in conjunction with video and audio interferences.

A disguise is used in conjunction with video and audio interferences for witnesses having to testify.

To avoid a face-to-face confrontation with the accused, parts 2 and 3 of Article 282 of the CPC stipulate that:

1. An anonymous witness can testify in a closed-door trial in conjunction with video and audio interferences, which should prevent him/her from being identified.
2. If it is not possible to use video and audio interferences, the anonymous witness testifies in a different place to where the trial is to take place, without other trial participants being present. The participants in the trial provide the chairman of the trial with a question in writing, which they would like to ask the witness. Such testified witness testimony is read aloud during the trial.

Exclusion of the media or the public from the trial: According to Article 9 of the CPC (case publicity in court), all cases in all courts are public unless state, professional or commercial secrets are at stake.

A closed-door trial is permitted when the anonymous witness or victim is testifying.

Use of audio-video-recording devices (Article 260 of the CPC):

1. During a court trial, it is forbidden to use TV and cinema cameras, photo cameras, and other audio-video-recording equipment.
2. These equipments can be used by the court.
3. Participants may use audio recording devices as long as they do not interfere with criminal proceedings.
4. There are fines foreseen in case of violation of these rules.

12. On which rounds and the basis of which criteria can anonymity be granted? Is there the possibility to obtain legal assistance at this stage?

Grounds (Article 199 of the CPC):

1. Anonymity can be granted to a victim or witness if:

   1) There is a real danger to his/her life, health, freedoms or property, or to that of his/her family or relatives.
   2) The victim's or witness's testimony is crucial to the criminal case.
   3) The victim or witness testifies in severe or very severe crime cases.

2. Anonymity is applied to a victim or witness if all grounds are present.

Conditions (part 2 of Article 200 of the CPC):

The prosecutor or investigator also has the obligation to check if the victim or witness:

1) suffers from no physical or mental disorders, which prevent him/her from testifying.
2) has no convictions for perjury.
3) has no self-interests.

13. Are pre-trial statements of witnesses and *pentiti* and testimonies of anonymous witness and *pentito* regarded as valid evidence? If yes, under which conditions?

Yes.

Article 184 of the CPC. Interview of the witness by the pre-trial judge. This article enacts a witness's pre-trial testimony as valid evidence.

Article 189 of the CPC. Interview of the suspect by the pre-trial judge. This article enacts a suspect's pre-trial testimony as valid evidence.

Article 203 of the CPC. Interview of the anonymous witness by the pre-trial judge. This article enacts the anonymous witness's pre-trial testimony as valid evidence. In addition, it is possible to use video and audio interferences.

14. Is it possible, and if so, under which conditions, to use information provided by "*pentiti*"? How is their credibility assessed?

The use of information provided by "*pentiti*" is permitted. *Pentiti* can be interviewed in the same way as witnesses according to part 7 of Article 158 of the CPC.

Their credibility is assessed by confronting their testimony with other evidence. According to Article 301 of the CPC, no conviction must be pronounced solely on the testimony of anonymous witnesses and *pentiti*.

15. Which are the opportunities for the defence to exercise its rights, including the right of the accused to challenge the witness'/*pentito*'s credibility in criminal proceedings (including at the pre-trial stage) and the respect of the "equality of arms" principle?

According to Article 203 of the CPC, the pre-trial judge informs the accused on the witness'/*pentito*'s testimony and afterwards the accused may question the witness'/*pentito*'s testimony through the pre-trial judge. If these questions could disclose the witness'/*pentito's* identity, they may be not asked or should be reworded.

According to Article 204 of the CPC, a confrontation and an identity parade must be accomplished by using video and audio interferences.

c. Non-procedural measures

16. At which stage(s), and in which context, is it possible for witnesses and *pentiti* to benefit from a protection programme?

The personal security and the individual's constitutional rights and freedoms are ensured at all stages.

17. Is there the possibility for witnesses and *pentiti* to obtain legal assistance at this (these) stage(s)?

Yes, according to the contract signed by the witness.

18. What is the procedure for admittance to a protection programme? Please specify in particular, who takes the initiative, the criteria for admittance, the assessment of the relevance of a testimony and how admittance to the programme is formalized.

Grounds for the application of protection means:

The means for the protection from criminal influence may be applied to witnesses and *pentiti* if there are sufficient grounds to believe that:

1) there is a threat to the individual's life or health;
2) the individual's property may be damaged or destroyed;
3) there is a threat to the individual's constitutional rights and freedoms.

"1. Having grounds, the individuals indicated in points 1-2 of paragraph I of Article 3 of this Law shall be entitled to apply to the Head of the Police Department of the Ministry of Interior, the Head of a City (District) Police Station, the Prosecutor General or his Vice Prosecutors, the Regional Chief Prosecutor or his Vice Prosecutors, or the Area Chief Prosecutor with a request to prescribe protection from criminal influence.

2. Having grounds, the individuals indicated in point 3 of paragraph I of Article 3 of this Law shall be entitled to apply to the Prosecutor General or his Vice Prosecutors, the Regional Chief Prosecutor or his Vice Prosecutors, or the Area Chief Prosecutor with a request to prescribe protection from criminal influence.

3. In the three days (in exceptional cases, immediately) following the receipt of the request of the individual, the Head of the Police Department of the Ministry of Interior, the Head of a City (District) Police Station, the Prosecutor General or his Vice Prosecutors, the Regional Chief Prosecutor or his Vice Prosecutors, or the Area Chief Prosecutor shall review the request and adopt the decision on the prescription of or denial of protection from criminal influence. The decision on the prescription of protection from criminal influence shall include: the date and place of the final decision; the full name and position of the officer having adopted the decision; the circumstances in support of the prescription of protection from criminal influence; the full name of the individual for whom protection from criminal influence is prescribed. The individual to whom the protection from criminal influence is prescribed shall be informed of the above-mentioned decision.

4. Having sufficient information about the actual threat to the protected individual's life, health, property or constitutional rights and liberties, the Head of the Police Department of the Ministry of Interior, the Head of a City (District) Police Station, the Prosecutor General or his Vice Prosecutors, the Regional Chief Prosecutor or his Vice Prosecutors, or the Area Chief Prosecutor must inform the threatened individual, and recommend to him/her the prescription of means for the protection from criminal influence. In the event of an individual turning down the offer of protection from criminal influence, a memorandum is drawn up, putting this in writing. The memorandum shall be signed by the individual having refused the protection and the officer having offered the protection.

5. In the event of the request to prescribe protection from criminal influence being denied, the individual concerned shall be entitled to appeal against this decision to the Prosecutor General within a period of five days. The Prosecutor General shall adopt the final decision to satisfy or deny the request within a period of three days".

19. **Please indicate the measures that can be adopted for the protection of witnesses and *pentiti* (e.g. surveillance of the residence, physical protection, protection of personal records, relocation, change of identity, subsidies, assistance in job search, relocation of a detainee to another prison or to special units).**

The following means of protection from criminal influence can be applied to witnesses and *pentiti*:

- Physical protection of an individual's person and property;
- Temporary relocation of the individual to a safe place;
- Provision of special procedures for obtaining data on the individual from passport offices and other formal information keeping agencies;
- Changing of an individual's place of residence, work or study;

- Changing of an individual's personal records, curriculum vitae;
- Changing of an individual's appearance through plastic surgery;
- Provision of the individual with a firearm or other special security measures.

20. What can the duration of a protection programme be? Which are the procedures for assessing the degree of danger for the witnesses/*pentiti* and their compliance with the obligations of the programme? Is it possible to challenge a decision of suspension, revocation or termination of a protection programme?

The duration of a protection programme is not limited in time and may be terminated if:

- The threat to the person's security no longer exists;
- The protected person violates the terms of the contract;
- The protected person refuses to be protected.

The threat is determined on the grounds of information collected from official and confidential sources.

An appeal against the decision to suspend, revoke or terminate a protection programme may be addressed to the Prosecutor General.

d. International Co-operation

21. Which measures (e.g. use of modern telecommunications means, assistance in relocating protected witnesses, exchange of information between witness protection authorities) have been adopted in the context of mutual legal assistance in order to facilitate international co-operation? How are the financial implications of international co-operation activities dealt with?

International co-operation is implemented by specialised witness protection services executing witness protection measures. The requesting party usually covers all the expenses relating to the relocation of protected witnesses.

22. Has your country entered international (bilateral or multilateral) agreements on the protection of witnesses and *pentiti*? If so, please indicate what kind of provision they include.

Yes, the Trilateral Agreement between the Government of the Republic of Lithuania, the Government of the Republic of Latvia and the Government of the Republic of Estonia on Co-operation in the Protection of Witnesses, was ratified on 24.05.2001 (No. IX-342).

23. How can international co-operation in the field of witnesses and *pentiti* be improved?

International co-operation in the field of witnesses and *pentiti* can be improved by preparing agreements between specialised witness protection services of the countries concerned.

e. *Statistics*

24. How many people currently benefit from witnesses and *pentiti* protection measures/programmes, and how long? How many of them are foreign people? If the measures/programmes can be extended to relatives and other close persons, please indicate (and, if possible, specify the relationship with the witness *(pentito)* how many people are included in this category. Please also provide figures on the different kinds of measures (procedural and non-procedural) adopted, and on the number of cases involving international co-operation.

Detailed information on the use of measures protecting witnesses (further — protected persons) is confidential and cannot be provided; as a result, only indicative data is given hereafter:

1) Protected persons by citizenship are:
- 89 percent — Lithuanians;
- 6 percent — foreign;
- 5 percent — stateless.

2) 30 percent of protected persons are relatives of witnesses; 5 percent — participants of the clandestine activities; other — participants of criminal proceedings:
- 30 percent — witnesses;
- 25 percent — suspects and accused;
- 10 percent — victims.

3) The frequency of use of measures protecting witnesses:
- Physical protection — 70 percent of protected persons;
- Temporary relocation to the secure place — 90 percent;
- Changing of individual's place of residence, work or study — 15 percent;
- Changing of individual's personal records, curriculum vitae — 10 percent;
- Provide for special procedures for obtaining data on the individual from passport offices and other formal information keeping agencies — 5 percent.

4) The duration of use of measures protecting witnesses (1999-2000):
  - Less than 6 months — 36 percent.
  - 6 months - 1 year — 19 percent.
  - 1 year - 2 years — 29 percent.
  - More than 2 years — 16 percent.

f. Proposals and comments

25. Please provide any comments/proposals concerning the implementation of the terms of reference of the PC-PW and, in particular, instruments to be adopted to strengthen the protection of witnesses and *pentiti*.

We propose to sign regional agreements (e.g. among North European countries, the three Baltic states, etc.) in order to strengthen co-operation between these countries.

Our practice of implementing witness protection measures within the Baltic States suggests that it would be advisable for the Council of Europe to adopt rules, which could regulate co-operation between specialised witness protection services in its member states. This would simplify the adoption of protection measures.

Luxembourg

General comments

As things currently stand, Luxembourg legislation has only a few provisions relating to the protection of witnesses and *pentiti.* These provisions apply in general to all criminal offences and are not specific to terrorism.

The Law of 12 August 2003 (1) on the suppression of terrorism and the financing of terrorism and (2) approving the International Convention for the Suppression of the Financing of Terrorism, opened for signature in New York on 10 January 2000, transposed into Luxembourg law, apart from the provisions of the said Convention, the Framework Decision of the Council of the European Union of 13 June 2002 on combating terrorism. In the present document that Law will be referred to as "the Law of 12 August 2003 on terrorism". It should also be noted that this Law also introduced a general definition of terrorism into Luxembourg law.

Moreover, in the light of the particular situation of victims and witnesses with regard to organised crime and terrorism, on 20 May 2003 the Government tabled Bill No. 5156 entitled "Bill strengthening the rights of victims of criminal offences and improving the protection of witnesses" aimed at reforming Luxembourg law in this domain. In the present questionnaire, this Bill, which will be referred to as the "Victims and Witnesses Bill" in the remainder of this document, will be thoroughly analysed.

In the replies to the various questions, reference will primarily be made to these two instruments.

a. *General information*

1. **Please describe the framework (legal provisions and established practice) governing the use of measures protecting witnesses and** *pentiti.*

In Luxembourg positive law, there are as yet no *specific* measures relating to the protection of witnesses and *pentiti.*

Article 282 of the Criminal Code currently provides for prison sentences and fines where witnesses have been subject to abuse or physical attack as a result of their testimony.

Under Article 326 of the Criminal Code, the penalties provided for in the Chapter of the Criminal Code relating to a criminal association or organisation shall not apply to persons found guilty who, prior to any attempted crime or offence by the said association or organisation, and before any proceedings have commenced, have provided the authorities with information on the existence of such groups and the names of their leaders or subordinates.

In addition, Section 31 of the amended law of 19 February 1973 on the sale of medicinal substances and the fight against drug addiction provides that those found guilty of certain categories of drug offences shall be exempt from imprisonment or fines where they have revealed to the authorities the identity of those responsible for the offences or the fact that such offences had taken place. For certain offences, the above law makes provision for a reduction in custodial sentences or fines.

The Law of 12 August 2003 on terrorism introduced into Luxembourg law exemptions from penalties for those who, prior to any attempted offence under Sections 135-1 (act of terrorism), 135-2 (act of terrorism resulting in the death of one or more persons) and 135-5 (funding of terrorism) and before any proceedings have commenced, provide information to the authorities on plans to commit the above offences or the identity of those implicated.

Similarly, custodial sentences will be reduced in pursuance of Article 52 of the Criminal Code in line with the scale provided for with regard to those who, after proceedings have commenced, reveal to the authorities the identity of those who had hitherto remained unknown.

Under the terms of Article 135-8 of the Criminal Code, exemption from penalties are provided for those found guilty of being part of a terrorist group who, prior to any attempted terrorist act by the group, and before any proceedings have commenced, inform the authorities of the existence of the said group and the names of its leaders or subordinates.

2. **Please describe the framework (legal provisions and established practice) governing the use of measures encouraging witnesses and *pentiti* to co-operate with the justice system.**

Apart from the current provisions providing exemptions from penalties, described under the reply to question 1, there are no special provisions aiming at encouraging witnesses or *pentiti* to collaborate with the justice system.

3. **Can measures/benefits encouraging the co-operation of witnesses and *pentiti* be used in combination with protection measures (arrangements concerning trial proceedings, sentencing conditions, special penitentiary regimes, etc.)? If so, please specify and indicate the conditions under which they are applied.**

The Victims and Witnesses Bill provides that under certain conditions, the courts may agree to hear a witness who is under threat or a witness or expert residing abroad, via video-conference or any other appropriate means of remote audio-visual communication, with the witness's agreement, if it is not possible or desirable for the latter to appear at the trial in person.

Under the terms of this Bill, a witness under threat is considered to be an individual in circumstances in which it may legitimately be presumed that he/she or a person of his/her circle may feel under serious threat on account of the evidence to be given, and who has indicated that he/she does not intend to testify because of that threat (the future Article 158-2 of the Code of Criminal Procedure)

For further details on the conditions under which these measures will be applied, please refer to the reply to question 11.

4. **For what kind of crime and under what circumstances can witness and *pentito* protection be applied? Can the measures be extended to the relatives or other persons close to the witness/*pentito*?**

The protective measures established by the Victims and Witnesses Bill, i.e. the recording of the hearing of a witness or minor, the use of video-conferencing or the removal of the accused from the courtroom, are not limited to a certain kind of crime.

At present there is no general protection scheme for *pentiti;* the general witness protection provisions described above also apply to relatives or other close persons when they give evidence.

5. **What urgent measures (e.g. immediate relocation to a secret place) can be taken in order to protect witnesses and *pentiti*?**

Under the Victims and Witnesses Bill, the recording of statements or the use of video-conferencing may be ordered by the State Prosecutor at the preliminary investigation stage. The Bill does not foresee other specific measures to be taken in case of emergency.

6. **What institutions are involved in the protection of witnesses and *pentiti* and what is their role (e.g. law enforcement agencies, special independent agencies, prosecutor's offices, judicial authorities, etc.)? How does co-operation between the relevant institutions work in practice?**

Under the terms of the Victims and Witnesses Bill, the authorities required to take the measures provided for in the Bill are the State Prosecutor, the investigating judge and the trial court.

As it is just a Bill at present, there is no practical experience of how the provisions are applied.

7. **Are there any specific provisions governing the protection of witnesses and *pentiti* in relation to acts of terrorism? If so, please specify. Are there any specialised counter-terrorism institutions? If so, what is their role in the protection of witnesses and *pentiti* in relation to acts of terrorism?**

There are no specific measures concerning witness protection in relation to acts of terrorism. However, the offences classified as terrorist offences by the Law of 12 August 2003 satisfy the conditions specified by the Victims and Witnesses Bill, with the result that the protection measures contained therein will apply to witnesses of acts of terrorism. The agencies involved in the fight against terrorism (primarily in the police and state intelligence service) will not play a role in witness protection.

8. **How does the framework governing the use of measures protecting witnesses and *pentiti* and encouraging them to co-operate with justice guarantee respect for human rights and individual freedoms? Please indicate the procedures in place, if any, to monitor compliance with human rights standards.**

The provisions foreseen in the Victims and Witnesses Bill have been drawn up so as to strike a balance between (i) the fight against terrorism and organised crime and (ii) respect for human rights and fundamental freedoms.

In order to ensure compatibility between the measures foreseen in the Victims and Witnesses Bill and the right to a fair trial, reference was made during the drafting of the Bill to a series of judgments delivered by the European Court of Human Rights, including the Doorson v. the Netherlands judgment of 26 March 1996 and the Van Mechelen v. the Netherlands judgment of 23 April 1997, and to Recommendation No. R (97) 13 of the Committee of Ministers to member states of the Council of Europe concerning the intimidation of witnesses and the rights of the defence.

The Victims and Witnesses Bill does not provide for the creation of specific bodies and procedures as the current procedures of common law were judged sufficient to assert defendant's rights.

b. *Procedural measures*

9. At what stage(s), and in what context, is it possible for witnesses and *pentiti* to benefit from procedural measures of protection?

Under the Victims and Witnesses Bill, the procedural protection measures contained therein can be ordered at the preliminary investigation stage by the State Prosecutor, or by the investigating judge during the investigation stage. They can also be taken or maintained at the trial stage.

10. Is it possible for witnesses and *pentiti* to obtain legal assistance at this (these) stage(s)?

Under the amended Legal Aid Act of 18 August 1995, legal aid shall be granted to an individual for the purposes of defending his/her interests. Given that a witness has no *prima facie* interests to defend within the meaning of the criminal proceedings, the aforementioned Act makes no provision for legal aid for witnesses. However, where an investigating judge, in the course of questioning, charges a person initially called as a witness, the latter is immediately (and before any further steps in the case are taken) entitled to legal aid.

11. Are there alternative methods of giving evidence which allow witnesses and *pentiti* to be given protection from intimidation resulting from face to face confrontation with the accused? If yes, please specify (e.g. full or partial anonymity, video-conference, disguise, exclusion of the defendant from the courtroom when the witness is giving evidence, exclusion of the media or the public from the trial, etc.) and indicate under what conditions these methods are used.

The Victims and Witnesses Bill seeks to introduce in the Code of Criminal Procedure a series of provisions relating to the recording of statements given by witnesses and victims, the use of video-conferencing, the removal of the accused from the courtroom when certain witnesses are testifying, and hearings *in camera*.

With the exception of the last two measures, which are matters solely for the trial courts, such steps can be taken under virtually identical conditions in both the investigation and trial stages.

a. Total or partial witness anonymity:

It is foreseen that a separate bill will deal with the question of the total or partial anonymity of witnesses.

b. Remote questioning and hearings:

The investigating judge and the trial courts could decide to take evidence from a witness who is under threat or a witness or expert residing abroad, via video-conference or any other appropriate means of remote audio-visual communication, with the witness's agreement, if it is not possible or desirable for latter to appear at the trial in person.

It could also be decided to take evidence via a tele-conference from a witness who is under threat or a witness or expert residing abroad, with the latter's agreement, if it is not possible or desirable for the individual who is to give evidence to appear at the trial in person.

c. Distortion of the image and/or voice of the person giving testimony:

It is foreseen that a separate bill will deal with the question of the distortion of the image and/or voice of the person giving testimony.

d. Departure of the accused from the courtroom during certain testimonies:

The new Article 158-3 of the Code of Criminal Procedure, as foreseen by the Victims and Witnesses Bill, would enable the trial court to order the accused to exit the courtroom if there was reason to fear that a witness would not tell the truth in his/her presence or if there would be an immediate risk of serious harm for the health of the witness if the latter was heard in the presence of the accused, or if the witness was a minor and there was reason to believe that his/her well-being would be in danger if the testimony was given in the presence of the accused.

In order to avoid any objections regarding compliance with the rights of the defence, it is provided that when statements are gathered using tele-conferencing, the statements cannot be considered as evidence unless they are corroborated by other evidence.

e.   Hearings *in camera*:

The Victims and Witnesses Bill seeks to amend Article 190 of the Code of Criminal Procedure whereby trials are held in public, in that it proposes stipulating that where the court finds that there would be a danger to the safety of a witness if he/she testified in a public hearing, it can order the trial to be held *in camera*, as the danger to the safety of witnesses is considered to be a threat to public order.

12.   On what grounds and on the basis of what criteria can anonymity be granted? Is it possible to obtain legal assistance at this stage?

As regards the question of anonymity, please refer to the reply above under question 11a.

As regards the conditions for the granting of legal aid, please refer to the reply above under question 10.

13.   Are pre-trial statements of witnesses and *pentiti* and testimonies of anonymous witnesses and *pentiti* regarded as valid evidence? If yes, under what conditions?

Under the Victims and Witnesses Bill, statements made before and during the trial that are recorded or which use video-conferencing shall be considered as evidence. However, they must be corroborated by other evidence.

14.   Is it possible, and if so, under what conditions, to use information provided by *"pentiti"*? How is their credibility assessed?

At present there is no legislation specific to *pentiti*. They will therefore be considered as witnesses to whom the general provisions relating to witnesses as well as those set out above shall apply. The question of the credibility of a witness shall be left to the discretion of the judges.

15.   What are the opportunities for the defence to exercise its rights, including the right of the accused to challenge the witness'/*pentito's* credibility in criminal proceedings (including at the pre-trial stage) and respect of the "equality of arms" principle?

The Victims and Witnesses Bill provides that an individual could not be convicted solely on the basis of statements gathered by recording or video-conferencing. The latter must be corroborated by other evidence.

In application of customary criminal procedure, it is for the investigating judge and the trial courts to evaluate and ascertain the credibility of the witness, which may be challenged, in both procedural stages, by the accused.

c. Non-procedural measures

16. At what stage(s), and in what context, is it possible for witnesses and *pentiti* to benefit from a protection programme?

Under the Victims and Witnesses Bill, the protection measures in question could be provided at the preliminary investigation stage, as well as during the investigation stage, i.e. when the matter is referred to the investigating judge, and during the trial stage in the trial court.

17. Is it possible for witnesses and *pentiti* to obtain legal assistance at this (these) stage(s)?

Please refer to the reply to question 10.

18. What is the procedure for admittance to a protection programme? Please specify, in particular, who takes the initiative, the criteria for admittance, the assessment of the relevance of a testimony and how admittance to the programme is formalised.

Please refer to the reply to question 11.

19. Please indicate the measures that can be adopted for the protection of witnesses and *pentiti* (e.g. surveillance of the residence, physical protection, protection of personal records, relocation, change of identity, subsidies, assistance in job search, relocation of a detainee to another prison or to special units).

At present, none of the specific protection measures mentioned in this question have been provided for by the Victims and Witnesses Bill.

20. At what stages of the proceedings (preliminary investigations, during the trial, after the trial) can the protection programme come into operation? What can the duration of a protection programme be? What are the procedures for assessing the degree of danger for the witnesses/*pentiti* and their compliance with the obligations of the programme? Is it possible to challenge a decision of suspension, revocation or termination of a protection programme?

Please refer to the reply to question 16.

d. International co-operation

21. What measures (e.g. use of modern telecommunications means, assistance in relocating protected witnesses, exchange of information between witness protection authorities) have been adopted in the context of mutual legal assistance in order to facilitate international co-operation? How are the financial implications of international co-operation activities dealt with?

As at present there are no provisions in national legislation specific to the protection of witnesses and *pentiti,* there are as yet no international co-operation measures in this field.

22. Has your country entered international (bilateral or multilateral) agreements on the protection of witnesses and *pentiti*? If so, please indicate what kind of provisions they include.

The Grand Duchy of Luxembourg has not yet concluded any specific international agreements in this field.

23. How can international co-operation in the field of the protection of witnesses and *pentiti* be improved?

International co-operation in the field of witnesses and *pentiti* could be improved in particular by introducing transnational protection programmes enabling a person in danger to be relocated to another country.

e. Statistics

24. How many people currently benefit from witness or *pentito* protection measures/programmes, and for how long? How many of them are foreign nationals? If the measures/programmes can be extended to relatives and persons close to them, please indicate (and, if possible, specify the relationship with the witness/*pentito*) how many people are included in this category. Please also provide figures on the different kinds of measures (procedural and non-procedural) adopted, and on the number of cases involving international co-operation.

In view of the fact that the measures and provisions detailed in the replies to this questionnaire are still at the Bill stage, it is not possible at present to provide any statistics in this field.

f. Proposals and comments

25. Please provide any comments/proposals concerning the implementation of the terms of reference of the PC-PW and, in particular, instruments to be adopted to strengthen the protection of witnesses and *pentiti*.

The Grand Duchy of Luxembourg has no particular comments or proposals to make on this matter.

Moldova

a. General information

1. Please describe the framework (legal provisions and established practice) governing the use of measures protecting witnesses and *pentiti*.

The use of measures protecting the persons who contributed to the detection, prevention, interruption, investigation and discovery of the crimes to the judiciary examination of the criminal cases is legalised by Law of the Republic of Moldova No. 1458-XIII dating from 28 January 1998 On State Protection of the victims, witnesses and other persons who assist in the criminal procedure, some articles of the Criminal Code, as well as the departmental directives of the bodies that carry out measures of state protection.

2. Please describe the framework (legal provisions and established practice) governing the use of measures encouraging witnesses and *pentiti* to co-operate with justice.

In accordance with Article 110 of the Criminal Procedure Code, if there are serious reasons that the witness's life, bodily integrity or freedom are in danger because of his/her testimonies in a criminal case regarding a serious, very serious or extremely serious criminal offence, the examining magistrate or the court may allow the witness to be heard without being present at the place of the criminal proceeding body or in the law court during the trial. The witness may be examined with the help of the relevant technical means. The examined witness is allowed to declare some other facts about his/her identity than the real ones. In order not to be recognized, the witness can also be examined through a video-conference with distorted voice and image.

Measures encouraging witnesses and *pentiti* to co-operate with judicial bodies are stipulated in Article 19, Chapter V of the above-mentioned Law No. 1458-XIII.

3. Can measures/benefits encouraging the co-operation of witnesses and *pentiti* be used in combination with protection measures (arrangements concerning trial proceedings, sentencing conditions, special penitentiary regimes, etc.)? If so, please specify and indicate under which conditions they are applied.

According to Article 46, paragraph 6, of the Criminal Code, a member of a criminal organisation is exempt from criminal charges if he/she voluntarily declares about the existence of the criminal organisation and contributes to the detection of the criminal offences or the exposure of the organisers, leaders or members of the relevant organisation.

Articles 506-511 of the Criminal Procedure Code also stipulate the possibility to make an agreement recognizing the guilt with the guilty person who contributed to the detection of the criminal offence committed by him/her. The agreement recognizing the guilt can be made in cases of light, less serious and serious criminal offences.

4. **For which kind of crime and under which circumstances can witness and *pentito* protection be applied? Can the measures be extended to the relatives or other persons close to the witness/*pentito*?**

According to Law of the Republic of Moldova No. 1458-XIII dating from 28 January 1998 the use of measures of state protection does not depend on the category of offence. It is suitable to use the measure of protection when there is a direct link between the person, who is supposed to be protected, and the possibility to detect, prevent, interrupt, investigate and discover the crimes as well as to proceed with judiciary examination of the criminal cases connected with organised crime.

Protection can be applied for the following categories of persons:

a) the persons who declared about the committed crimes, contributed to their detection, prevention, interruption, investigation and discovery;
b) the witnesses;
c) the suspects, the accused persons, the defendants and their legal representatives at the trial, the convicted persons;
d) the relatives of the persons mentioned in a), b), c) and d) (husband/wife, parents and children, the adopters and the adopted, brothers and sisters, grandparents, nephews and nieces), but also, in extreme cases, other persons by whom the persons mentioned above are constrained.

5. **What urgent measures (e.g. immediate relocation to a secret place) can be taken in order to protect witnesses and *pentiti*?**

Urgent measures of protection can be physical protection and surveillance of the residence, temporary displacement in a secret place. The witness can be provided with special techniques of individual defence and communication regarding the danger.

6. **Which institutions are involved in the protection of witnesses and**
   pentiti **and what is their role (e.g. law enforcement agencies,**
   special independent agencies, prosecutor's offices, judicial
   authorities, etc)? How does co-operation between the relevant
   institutions work in practice?

According to Article 3 of Law of the Republic of Moldova No. 1458-XIII dating from 28 January 1998 the following institutions are involved in the protection of the persons mentioned above:

a)   those that decide the use of state protection;
b)   those that apply the measures of state protection.

The chief of the institution responsible for the testimony (information) about the crime or the criminal case takes the decision regarding the use of the protection measures.

The chiefs of the institutions that have special operative subdivisions take the decision regarding the use of the protection measures that are considered extraordinary measures. The special subdivisions apply the protection measures on the basis of a motivated ruling released by the judge, the General Attorney, the inquiry body or the investigator who is responsible for the testimony (information) about the crime or the criminal case and – when the sentence is final – by the institution where the protected person expiates from penalty. The ruling must contain information about the possibility of detecting, preventing, interrupting, investigating and discovering the crime as well as the possibility of the judiciary examination of the criminal case from the point of view of the protected person.

The institutions applying protection measures towards protected persons in the cases they are responsible for are: the Ministry of Internal Affairs, the Security and Information Service of the Republic of Moldova, the Centre for Corruption and Economic Crime Control, as well as other state institutions that have the right to apply such measures according to the legislation in force. The above-mentioned institutions have special subdivisions responsible for the protection of witnesses.

The protection measures regarding persons protected in relation to criminal cases for which the court or the General Attorney's Office are responsible, are applied, on the basis of the judge's decision or the General Attorney's decision, by the bodies of the Ministry of Internal Affairs, regional institutions of the Security and Information Service of the Republic of Moldova or the Centre for Corruption and Economic Crime Control. Protection measures regarding the military and their relatives are applied by the headquarters of the appropriate military unit, and protection measures regarding the persons under arrest or in prison – the bodies of the appropriate institutions.

7. **Are there any specific provisions governing the protection of witnesses and *pentiti* in relation to acts of terrorism? If so, please specify. Are there any specialised counter-terrorism institutions? If so, what is their role in the protection of witnesses and *pentiti* in relation to acts of terrorism?**

At present, there is a special subdivision "Antiteror" within the General Department for the Fight against Organised Crime of the Ministry of Internal Affairs.

8. **How does the framework governing the use of measures protecting witnesses and *pentiti* and encouraging them to co-operate with justice guarantee respect for human rights and individual freedoms? Please indicate the procedures in place, if any, to monitor compliance with human rights standards.**

Protection measures can be applied only with the agreement of the protected person and without violating his/her rights, liberties and personal dignity (Article 8 of Law No. 1458-XIII dating from 28 January 1998).

The protected person has the right:

a) to submit a declaration about the application of the protection measures and about their cancellation;
b) to be informed about the applied protection measures;
c) to request for supplementary protection measures or to ask for their cancellation;
d) to contest the illegal actions and decisions of the institutions applying protection measures in a superior hierarchical body or in the court.

b. Procedural measures

9. **At which stage(s), and in which context, is it possible for witnesses and *pentiti* to benefit from procedural measures of protection?**

State protection of witnesses and persons can be applied at any stage of the criminal procedure inclusively before it starts and after the judicial sentence is passed.

10. **Is there the possibility for witnesses and *pentiti* to obtain legal assistance at this (these) stage(s)?**

Yes, the persons who help during the criminal procedure can obtain legal assistance at any stage of the criminal procedure.

11. Are there alternative methods of giving evidence which allow the protection of witnesses and *pentiti* from intimidation resulting from face to face confrontation with the accused? If yes, please specify (e.g. full or partial anonymity, video-conference, disguise, exclusion of the defendant from the courtroom when the witness is giving evidence, exclusion of the media or the public from the trial, etc.) and indicate under which conditions these methods are used.

Reply to question 2 contains the partial answer to this question.

The examination of the case within a closed judiciary sitting, on the basis of a motivated ruling of the judge, is allowed if the interests of the protected person require this.

12. On which grounds and on the basis of which criteria can anonymity be granted? Is there the possibility to obtain legal assistance at this stage?

See the reply to question 2. It is possible to obtain legal assistance at this stage.

13. Are pre-trial statements of witnesses and *pentiti* and testimonies of anonymous witnesses and *pentiti* regarded as valid evidence? If yes, under which conditions?

If the witness's presence at the trial is impossible because of his/her leaving for some other countries or because of some other reasons the General Attorney can request the examining magistrate to hear the witness. The suspect, the accused and his/her defender, the victim and the attorney should have the possibility to ask the examined witness questions.

Testimonies of anonymous witnesses are not regarded as valid evidence. With a view to protecting the witness, he/she is allowed not to present the real information about his/her identity. The examining magistrate registers the information about the real identity of the witness in a separate report, which is kept at the headquarters of the appropriate institution in a sealed envelope in conditions of maximum safety of confidentiality. Testimonies of the witnesses examined in these conditions can be regarded as valid evidence only in cases where they are justified by other testimonies.

14. Is it possible, and if so, under which conditions, to use information provided by "*pentiti*"? How is their credibility assessed?

The information provided by *pentiti* has the conditions of the witnesses' testimonies. Their credibility does not differ from the credibility of other such testimonies.

15.Which are the opportunities for the defence to exercise its rights, including the right of the accused to challenge the witness'/*pentito*'s credibility in criminal proceedings (including at the pre-trial stage) and the respect of the "equality of arms" principle?

The accused and his/her defender are guaranteed the possibility to ask the protected witness questions at any stage of the criminal procedure.

c. Non-procedural measures

16. At which stage(s), and in which context, is it possible for witnesses and *pentiti* to benefit from a protection programme?

See the reply to question 9.

17. Is there the possibility for witnesses and *pentiti* to obtain legal assistance at this (these) stage(s)?

See the reply to question 10.

18. What is the procedure for admittance to a protection programme? Please specify, in particular, who takes the initiative, the criteria for admittance, the assessment of the relevance of a testimony and how admittance to the programme is formalised.

The reason for admittance to a protection programme is the protected person's testimony and the operative information about the threat to the person's security.

The reason for admittance to a protection programme is the information about the existence of the death threat, use of violence, property destruction or deterioration or other illegal actions in connection with the person's contribution to the criminal procedure.

The inquiry body, the investigator, the attorney or the judge, after receiving information about the threat to protected person's security, is obliged to verify this information and in three days or in cases of urgent need, immediately, to take the decision about the application or suspension of the protection measures of the person. A motivated ruling is released regarding the decision taken. The bodies applying the protection measures should execute this ruling and it can be challenged in the higher hierarchical body, at the General Attorney's Office or in court.

As a result of concrete circumstances the body responsible for the application of the protection measures establishes the necessary measures and the possibilities for their implementation.

If it is necessary to take a decision concerning the application of the protection measures, the protected person and the institution applying the protection measures draw up an agreement that establishes the conditions of application of protection measures, the rights and obligations of parties.

19. Please indicate the measures that can be adopted for the protection of witnesses and *pentiti* (e.g. surveillance of the residence, physical protection, protection of personal records, relocation, change of identity, subsidies, assistance in job search, relocation of a detainee to another prison or to special units).

Depending on concrete circumstances, the following measures of protection can be adopted in order to guarantee the protected persons' security:

1) ordinary:
   a) physical protection, surveillance of the residence and property;
   b) the witness can be provided with special techniques of individual defence and communication regarding the danger;
   c) temporary relocation to safe places;
   d) protection of personal records;

2) extraordinary:
   a) change of the place of work or study;
   b) change of residence with obligatory allocation of a dwelling place (house, apartment);
   c) change of identity (name, surname, appearance);
   d) the examination of the case at a closed judiciary sitting.

With a view to guaranteeing protection measures, operative investigation measures can also be applied.

20. What can the duration of a protection programme be? Which are the procedures for assessing the degree of danger for the witnesses/*pentiti* and their compliance with the obligations of the programme? Is it possible to challenge a decision of suspension, revocation or termination of a protection programme?

The duration of a protection programme is not established. The character of the protection measures depends on the danger to the protected person's life, health and estate, the concrete circumstances and is determined by the institution responsible for the application of the protection measures.

The protected person is obliged:

a) to collaborate with the legal institutions on detection, prevention, interruption, investigation and discovery of the crime, as well as on the judiciary examination of the criminal case;

b) to fulfil the conditions of use of the protection measures and the legitimate requests of the institutions applying the protection measures;
c) to take care of the temporary property and documents issued according the legislation;
d) to inform immediately the relevant institutions every time there is a threat to personal security;
e) to not reveal information about the protection measures applied to him/her.

The protected person can challenge the decision regarding the suspension of the protection measures to the higher hierarchical body of the institution applying the protection measures or to the court.

d. *International co-operation*

21. Which measures (e.g. use of modern telecommunications means, assistance in relocating protected witnesses, exchange of information between witness protection authorities) have been adopted in the context of mutual legal assistance in order to facilitate international co-operation? How are the financial implications of international co-operation activities dealt with?

We had no international co-operation activities on the protection of witnesses and *pentiti* because of the lack of bilateral or multilateral agreements.

22. Has your country entered international (bilateral or multilateral) agreements on the protection of witnesses and *pentiti*? If so, please indicate what kind of provisions they include.

The Republic of Moldova will be party to the Agreement of collaboration among the member states of the Commonwealth of Independent States on the protection of witnesses and *pentiti*, that at the moment is being finalised.

23. How can international co-operation in the field of the protection of witnesses and *pentiti* be improved?

With a view to improving and facilitating international co-operation in the field of the protection of witnesses and *pentiti* it is necessary to issue an international or European Convention that will oblige the signatory states to adopt measures regarding the protection of the above-mentioned persons, to establish the essential principles of international co-operation in the referred field.

e. *Statistics*

24. **How many people currently benefit from witness or *pentito* protection measures/programmes, and for how long? How many of them are foreign people? If the measures/programmes can be extended to relatives and other close persons, please indicate (and, if possible, specify the relationship with the witness/*pentito*) how many people are included in this category. Please also provide figures on the different kinds of measures (procedural and non-procedural) adopted, and on the number of cases involving international co-operation.**

Beginning with the year 2000 up to now, protection measures have been applied regarding 28 persons in accordance with 20 ordinances, but out of those 13 regarding 16 persons were annulled in order to apply protection measures in 12 cases of transgression of contract conditions. There were two cases where 4 children of victims were placed under protection and one case of implementation of protection measures of 44 foreign citizens. There are no cases of international co-operation.

f. *Proposals and comments*

25. **Pease provide any comments/proposals concerning the implementation of the terms of reference of the PC-PW and, in particular, instruments to be adopted to strengthen the protection of witnesses and *pentiti*.**

Elaboration of agreements, financing of programmes.

The Netherlands

Preliminary notes

At present, Dutch criminal law only contains regulations with regard to threatened witnesses (Articles 226a-f Dutch Code of Criminal Procedure (DCCP)), that deal with the anonymity of the threatened witness vis-à-vis the defence. These regulations were already described in detail during the elaboration of *Recommendation R(97)13 on intimidation of witnesses and the rights of the defence*. For the sake of completeness, the reader is referred to this Recommendation.

A Bill on suspected and criminal witnesses (i.e. witnesses who are suspects or who have already been convicted, so-called collaborators of justice) has been accepted by Parliament and will come into force in 2006. It regulates the negotiations between the suspect, assisted by his/her lawyer, and the public prosecutor on the possible reduction of his/her sentence in exchange for an incriminating statement against another suspect. The agreement is subject to the approval of a judge. At the same time, a new instruction on pledges given to witnesses in criminal cases will be sent to public prosecutors. Until its date of commencement, the pledges to collaborators of justice are regulated by the Temporary instruction on pledges given to witnesses in criminal cases (*Tijdelijke aanwijzing toezeggingen aan getuigen in strafzaken*), an instruction that was drawn up by the Board of General Procurators, the public prosecution service's highest authority. The temporary instruction is generally based on the Bill in anticipation of its acceptance. Where relevant, reference will be made to the Bill and to this instruction.

Apart from these procedural measures for the benefit of threatened and criminal witnesses, there are also the typical witness protection measures. This is a broader ranger of measures: for example, they can be applied to informants who are at risk because of the State, or to "ordinary" witnesses.

a. *General information*

1. Please describe the framework (legal provisions and established practice) governing the use of measures protecting witnesses and *pentiti*.

Threatened witnesses (full anonymity) (Articles 226a-f DCCP)

On 1 February 1994 new provisions were added in the Dutch Code of Criminal Procedure regarding the protection of witnesses, who have suffered threats or undue influence to change their testimonies in court (Articles 226a – f DCCP). It contains procedural safeguards, by which a witness can be heard out of court before an investigating judge, the *rechter-commissaris*, who is the judicial authority in charge of the pre-trial investigation.

The object of the pre-trial investigation is to ascertain whether there are sufficient grounds to continue prosecution and start a trial. During this investigation the identity of the witness is not disclosed to the defendant or his/her counsel. The defence is entitled to put questions to the witness by handing them to the judge, who decides whether they are admissible and whether the witness is allowed to answer. This separate procedure, in the context of a pre-trial investigation, may be invoked by the witness or by the public prosecution, if there are circumstances which suggest that by testifying in public the witness's or another person's life, health or personal safety would be endangered. Another circumstance would be a serious risk of the witness's or another person's family life or social-economic existence being disrupted.

The judge has to investigate the credibility and the reputation of the witness, whose identity is known to him/her, before he/she decides to comply with the request for the witness to be heard without his/her identity being revealed to the defence. If he/she decides to comply, the witness is sworn in. The witness is exempted from appearing at the trial in a public court. The defence has a right to appeal the decision of the judge that a witness must be considered as a threatened witness.

Testimonies given in this manner are admissible as evidence at the trial, provided that the defence has had an adequate and proper opportunity to challenge and question the witness. The rules of evidence are adjusted so that no conviction can be based solely on the statement of an anonymous witness. The European Court of Human Rights (hereinafter the Court), in its judgment in the Kostovski case[1] clearly stated that procedural safeguards during the pre-trial stage can compensate any deficiencies at the trial stage.

This special procedure may be used in more serious cases, usually connected with organised crime.

The confined anonymous witness (Article 190 Sv)

It is usually sufficient for police officers who have infiltrated criminal organisations to submit their written statements in the case without divulging their full identities. If the defence wishes to put questions to these officers, it has to submit the questions to the *rechter-commissaris* who decides whether they are admissible. When no specific threat has been made, but the witness may expect difficulties with his/her professional functioning (e.g. undercover agents), the trial judge can rule certain questions inadmissible. Technical provisions such as heavy make-up, beards and glasses may be used to prevent the defence from discovering the identity of the witness. The witness

---

[1] *Kostovski v. The Netherlands* , Op. cit., p. 46.

cannot be excused from appearing at the trial, if the defence wishes to question him/her.

Collaborators of justice

It can be understood from the Temporary instruction on pledges for witnesses in criminal cases that collaborators of justice can also qualify for witness protection. Measures will be taken according to the Dutch basic instruction for witness protection. Apart from that, it should be noted that collaborators of justice are questioned on trial like any other witness. According to the Bill, they cannot be given full anonymity, which means that they cannot be questioned pre-trial like a threatened witness (Article 226j-2). However, it is possible to keep their identity temporarily hidden from the defendant (for the duration of the pre-trial investigation, Article 226j-4).

Witness protection programme

A special witness programme was set up in 1995, following a report by a special working group. The Witness Protection Department, organised under the Dutch National Police Agency (KLPD), is responsible for the implementation of the programme. The department is staffed with specially trained personnel. A public prosecutor is specifically entrusted with nation-wide authority over the department and its activities. The development and implementation of the witness protection programme started in 1994 and has been functioning since then. The measures that can be taken within the framework of this programme are very varied and range from a witness "going into hiding" in a safe place for a short time, to moving the witness and his/her family to a different country, and temporary change of identity.

2. **Please describe the framework (legal provisions and established practice) governing the use of measures encouraging witnesses and *pentiti* to co-operate with justice.**

Witnesses are given the opportunity to testify in a criminal case by offering them protection (in exchange for their testimony) provided that there is a threat which relates directly to the co-operation of the witness with the police and Justice. For the relevant regulations, please refer to the reply to the first question.

Under certain circumstances, an agreement can be made with a collaborator of justice on testifying in exchange for having his/her sentence reduced (see also the reply to the third question).

3. **Can measures/benefits encouraging the co-operation of witnesses and *pentiti* be used in combination with protection measures (arrangements concerning trial proceedings, sentencing conditions, special penitentiary regimes, etc.)? If so, please specify and indicate under which conditions they are applied.**

Threatened witnesses: see the replies to the first and second questions.

The confined anonymous witness (Article 190 Sv): see the replies to the first and second questions.

Collaborators of justice: the Temporary instruction on pledges for witnesses in criminal cases prescribes that the public prosecutor is not allowed to pledge witness protection measures, other than that the public prosecutor will ensure that measures will be taken according to the basic instruction for witness protection. In this situation, the public prosecutor is not allowed to act on his/her own authority.

4. **For which kind of crime and under which circumstances can witness and *pentito* protection be applied? Can the measures be extended to the relatives or other persons close to the witness/*pentito*?**

In the application of witness protection measures, no distinction is made in terms of the seriousness of the criminal offence. However, in real terms measures are usually applied in cases of serious forms of (organised) crime. When it comes to threatened witnesses, the witness protection measures can also be applied to family members, close relatives or to other persons who are related directly or closely to the threatened person. In future, it is expected to be applicable to collaborators of justice as well.

Apart from this, the instructions also prescribe when someone does not qualify for witness protection (in any case): when he/she is responsible for creating the threat by his/her own actions or when he/she is mentioned in an instruction regarding persons who fill a public office, which is related to the (criminal) administration of justice (*Ministeriële regeling inzake het optreden bij dreiging tegen personen die een openbaar ambt vervullen dat is gerelateerd aan de strafrechtspleging*).

5. **What urgent measures (e.g. immediate relocation to a secret place) can be taken in order to protect witnesses and *pentiti*?**

When it has not yet been decided whether a witness is a "threatened witness" (as in Article 226a DCCP), it is important to take measures to conceal the identity of the witness. Therefore, Article 226f DCCP prescribes that the *rechter-commissaris* is allowed to take these measures, insofar as is possible by mutual agreement with the public prosecutor.

Also, various witness protection measures can be taken for confined anonymous witnesses and collaborators of justice before, during and after the trial.

6. **Which institutions are involved in the protection of witnesses and** *pentiti* **and what is their role (e.g. law enforcement agencies, special independent agencies, prosecutor's offices, judicial authorities, etc)? How does co-operation between the relevant institutions work in practice?**

Threatened witnesses
- *rechter-commissaris*: judges if someone can be regarded as a threatened witness (Article 226a DCCP).

Witness protection programme
- (Head) public prosecutor: requests the Board of Procurators General to take witness protection measures.
- Board of Procurators General: takes the decision on whether or not to take witness protection measures.
- Witness Protection Department of the Dutch National Police Agency (KLPD): advises about and carries out witness protection measures.

7. **Are there any specific provisions governing the protection of witnesses and** *pentiti* **in relation to acts of terrorism? If so, please specify. Are there any specialised counter-terrorism institutions? If so, what is their role in the protection of witnesses and** *pentiti* **in relation to acts of terrorism?**

There are no specific legal provisions governing the protection of witnesses in relation to acts of terrorism.

8. **How does the framework governing the use of measures protecting witnesses and** *pentiti* **and encouraging them to co-operate with justice guarantee respect for human rights and individual freedoms? Please indicate the procedures in place, if any, to monitor compliance with human rights standards.**

The legal provisions governing threatened witnesses were designed following the Kostovski case. A few years later, in 1996, these provisions were tested in the Doorson case.[2] In this case, the Court decided that the regulations comply with respect for human rights and fundamental freedoms, provided that no conviction is based either solely or to a decisive extent on evidence provided by anonymous witnesses. The Court also decided that the importance of the protection of the witness can also influence the decision on whether or not to grant anonymity.

---

[2] *Doorson v. The Netherlands,* Op. cit., p. 46.

Regarding collaborators of justice, it should be noted that no harm is done to the rights of the defence, as long as there is complete openness about the contents of the pledge, and as long as the defence is given the opportunity to examine the witness. This can be done during the trial or during the pre-trial investigation.

The rights of a suspected and/or convicted witness are in principle the same as those of any other witness. He/she has the obligation to appear on trial, the obligation to be put on oath, the obligation to testify and the obligation to tell the truth. Regarding the right to refuse to testify, the explanatory memorandum of the Bill recommends that the agreement with the collaborator of justice mentions the persons with regard to whom the witness refuses to testify. The witness cannot be asked to relinquish his/her right of refusal to testify unconditionally and for the entire duration of the criminal procedure.

b. *Procedural measures*

9. At which stage(s), and in which context, is it possible for witnesses and *pentiti* to benefit from procedural measures of protection?

Protective measures can be taken before, during and after the trial. However, they last no longer than for the duration of the threat. It must be a serious threat which relates directly to the witness's co-operation with the police and justice for there to be a duty on the part of the Dutch authorities to provide for the protection of the person in question for the duration of the threat.

10. Is there the possibility for witnesses and *pentiti* to obtain legal assistance at this (these) stage(s)?

A witness can be legally assisted at all times. However, the current law does not yet contain a provision on legal assistance for threatened witnesses. This will change when the Bill is accepted by Parliament. The Bill contains the provision that a lawyer will be provided to any witness who does not yet have one in relation to the procedure for obtaining the status of "threatened witness" or for negotiating an agreement with the public prosecutor on the possibility of a reduced sentence in exchange for an incriminating statement against another suspect.

Article 226h-1 of this Bill prescribes that a collaborator of justice can also be legally assisted when making an agreement with the public prosecutor. If he/she does not yet have a lawyer, the state will provide him/her with one.

When witness protection measures are taken, an agreement is made with the person who will be protected. This agreement sets out the rights and duties of both the witness and the authorities. When making this agreement, the witness can have legal assistance.

11. Are there alternative methods of giving evidence which allow the protection of witnesses and *pentiti* from intimidation resulting from face to face confrontation with the accused? If yes, please specify (e.g. full or partial anonymity, video-conference, disguise, exclusion of the defendant from the courtroom when the witness is giving evidence, exclusion of the media or the public from the trial, etc.) and indicate under which conditions these methods are used.

Threatened witnesses

Threatened witnesses can also be questioned in the absence of the suspect and/or his/her lawyer (Article 226d DCCP). Furthermore, the questioning of the witness will always take place during the pre-trial investigation, which is not public. The media and the public are not therefore involved.

The confined anonymous witness (Article 190 DCCP)

A confined anonymous witness is questioned during the pre-trial investigation or during the trial. In principle, the suspect and/or his/her lawyer are present during the questioning. Under Article 190 DCCP, the witness will not be asked for his/her name and address. Furthermore, other measures can be taken to conceal the identity of the witness from the suspect, such as using make up or disguising the witness, or concealing the witness during questioning. If the witness is questioned in a different location to the suspect and/or his/her lawyer, telecommunications can be used in order to give the defence the opportunity to question the witness.

Collaborators of justice

A collaborator of justice is questioned in court, in the presence of the defence. In principle, he/she has no right to anonymity – that is only possible during the pre-trial investigation (see also the reply to the first question of this questionnaire). Naturally protective measures can be taken where there is a threat that can be related directly to the co-operation of the collaborator with the police and justice.

12 On which grounds and on the basis of which criteria can anonymity be granted? Is there the possibility to obtain legal assistance at this stage?

For the answer to this question please refer to the reply to the first question.

13. Are pre-trial statements of witnesses and *pentiti* and testimonies of anonymous witnesses and *pentiti* regarded as valid evidence? If yes, under which conditions?

The questioning of a threatened witness (whose identity is not known) can be regarded as valid evidence, provided that no conviction is based either solely or to a decisive extent on evidence provided by such an anonymous witness (Article 342-2 DCCP). This provision also applies to other anonymous witnesses.

Suspected and convicted witnesses are questioned during the trial. Their testimonies can therefore be regarded as evidence (Article 342-1 DCCP). However, the main rule is that the conviction cannot be based on the testimony of just one witness (Article 342-3 Sv, *unus testis nullus testis).*

14. Is it possible, and if so, under which conditions, to use information provided by "*pentiti*"? How is their credibility assessed?

The collaborator of justice testifies in court. The information that is provided by this testimony can be used as evidence in the criminal case on which the testimony has been given. The credibility of the testimony can be challenged by the defence during the trial; it is, however, up to the judge to decide whether or not the testimony can be used as evidence.

15. Which are the opportunities for the defence to exercise its rights, including the right of the accused to challenge the witness'/*pentito*'s credibility in criminal proceedings (including at the pre-trial stage) and the respect of the "equality of arms" principle?

The investigating judge has to enquire about the credibility and reputation of the witness, whose identity is known only to him/her, before he/she decides to grant anonymity to the witness (Article 226e DCCP). The defence, as well as the prosecutor and the witness, will be heard before this decision is made (Article 226a lid 2 DCCP). If he/she grants it, the witness is sworn in and shall be excused from appearing at the trial. The testimony thus given will be admissible in court, provided that the defence has been given adequate opportunity to challenge and question the witness. The rules of evidence have also been modified so as to ensure that no conviction is based solely on the statement of an anonymous witness. The defence has the right to appeal against the decision of the *rechter-commissaris* granting anonymity to a witness (Article 226b DCCP).

Because collaborators of justice are heard in court (and the defence is allowed to question the witness as well), the defence is given enough opportunity to challenge the credibility of the witness. It is also already possible to question the witness during the pre-trial investigation.

c. Non-procedural measures

16. At which stage(s), and in which context, is it possible for witnesses and *pentiti* to benefit from a protection programme?

See the reply to the ninth question.

17. Is there the possibility for witnesses and *pentiti* to obtain legal assistance at this (these) stage(s)?

See the reply to the tenth question.

18. What is the procedure for admittance to a protection programme? Please specify, in particular, who takes the initiative, the criteria for admittance, the assessment of the relevance of a testimony and how admittance to the programme is formalised.

If a request for protective measures is made, the (head) public prosecutor, who is responsible for the criminal investigation or the prosecution in which this request is made, sends a written request for a threat analysis and a request for advice on which protective measures should be taken, to the office of the national public prosecutor. The national public prosecutor sends the request together with his/her advice to the board of the procurators-general. This board decides whether protective measures should be taken. Which measures should be taken depends partly on the threat analysis. When it has been decided that a witness should be protected, a written agreement is concluded with the witness about the execution of the measures.

19. Please indicate the measures that can be adopted for the protection of witnesses and *pentiti* (e.g. surveillance of the residence, physical protection, protection of personal records, relocation, change of identity, subsidies, assistance in job search, relocation of a detainee to another prison or to special units).

Different kinds of measures can be taken to protect a threatened person. These measures vary from the electronic protection of the witness's house and temporary relocation to providing the witness with a temporary change of identity.

20. What can the duration of a protection programme be? Which are the procedures for assessing the degree of danger for the witnesses/*pentiti* and their compliance with the obligations of the programme? Is it possible to challenge a decision of suspension, revocation or termination of a protection programme?

Participation in a witness protection programme is temporary. The threat analysis contains a judgement on the nature and seriousness of the threat and the person(s) against whom the threat is aimed. Furthermore, it contains advice on the person(s) who must be protected, an outline of the proposed protective measures and the feasibility of these measures. When it has been decided that a witness should be protected, an agreement is made with him/her (reply No. 10). Any possible dispute will not be tested by a judge, but will be resolved by means of arbitration.

d. *International co-operation*

21. Which measures (e.g. use of modern telecommunications means, assistance in relocating protected witnesses, exchange of information between witness protection authorities) have been adopted in the context of mutual legal assistance in order to facilitate international co-operation? How are the financial implications of international co-operation activities dealt with?

The measures that can be taken are very different. They include not only mutual exchanges of knowledge, but also the actual transfer of the execution of protective measures. The operational costs for the exchange of witnesses between different services will be paid by the country that sends such witnesses. The costs of staff will be paid by the host country. This co-operation will be put down in writing in a mutual "gentleman's agreement".

22. Has your country entered international (bilateral or multilateral) agreements on the protection of witnesses and *pentiti*? If so, please indicate what kind of provisions they include.

The Netherlands has not finalised any agreements to make international co-operation in the field of witness protection possible. It is sufficient that in a given criminal case a request for legal assistance is made, which can be based on general regulations concerning the extension of help and rendering of assistance from applicable treaties of international legal assistance. When the criminal case is closed, there are no technical requirements for this request. At Europol, people work with a standard witness protection document. This document mentions several standard issues, such as threat, group of suspects, compound of the family, health of the witness, etc. This document is supplied by the requesting country. This way of working has not yet been implemented in (European) law.

23. How can international co-operation in the field of the protection of witnesses and *pentiti* be improved?

–

e. Statistics

24. How many people currently benefit from witness or *pentito* protection measures/programmes, and for how long? How many of them are foreign people? If the measures/programmes can be extended to relatives and other close persons, please indicate (and, if possible, specify the relationship with the witness/*pentito*) how many people are included in this category. Please also provide figures on the different kinds of measures (procedural and non-procedural) adopted, and on the number of cases involving international co-operation.

Since the witness protection programme was established in 1995, dozens of witnesses have used the programme. A minority of the witnesses is from abroad. The measures are usually restricted to the witness, his/her partner, children and parents.

f. Proposals and comments

25. Please provide any comments/proposals concerning the implementation of the terms of reference of the PC-PW and, in particular, instruments to be adopted to strengthen the protection of witnesses and *pentiti*.

–

Norway

a. General information

1. Please describe the framework (legal provisions and established practice) governing the use of measures protecting witnesses and *pentiti*.

The Criminal Procedure Act, the General Criminal Act and Act relating to the Courts of Justice stipulate provisions regarding protection of witnesses.

These provisions apply in general, and there are no specific provisions regarding terrorism. The provisions embrace a lot of different measures, and cover measures during investigation, during court proceedings and after court proceedings.

The General Criminal Section 132 a establishes a penal provision which is based on witness protection.

According to Section 132 a, any person shall be liable to a penalty for obstruction of the administration of justice who, by means of violence, threats, damage or other unlawful conduct aimed at a participator in the administration of justice or any of his next-of-kin:

a)   behaves in such a way as is likely to influence the participator to perform or omit to perform an act, task or service in connection with a criminal or civil case, or
b)   retaliates for any act, task or service which the participator has performed in connection with a criminal or civil case.

Witness protection according to the Criminal Procedure Act covers a lot of different measures.

Measures during investigation

According to Section 130 a, the court may on the application of the public prosecutor's order decide to hear the evidence of an anonymous witness if knowledge of the witness's identity may entail a risk:

a)   of a serious felony that will impair the life, health or liberty of the witness or any person to whom the witness has such a relationship as is specified in Section 122, or
b)   that a witness playing an undercover part in the investigation of other cases of the kind specified above will encounter considerable difficulty.

279

This provision applies to certain criminal acts, e.g. the General Criminal Code Section 151 a: any person who on board of a ship or aircraft, by violence, threats or otherwise, unlawfully and forcibly takes control of the vessel or aircraft or otherwise interferes with its sailing or flying shall be liable to imprisonment for a term of not less than two years and not more than 21 years. The same penalty shall apply to any person who by similar means unlawfully and forcibly takes control of any installation or construction on the continental shelf. Section 130 a may also be applied to cases concerning Section 233: any person who causes another person's death, or is accessory thereto.

In addition, the Parliament passed a new bill in 2003, which limits access to documents by the defence.

According to Section 242 a, the court may on the application of the public prosecutor's order decide to limit the defence access to documents if access may entail a risk:

a) of a serious felony that will impair the life, health or liberty of the witness or any person to whom the witness has such a relationship as is specified in Section 122, or
b) that the possibility of a witness playing an undercover part in the investigation of other cases of the kind specified above will encounter considerable difficulty, or
c) that the possibility for the Police to prevent or investigate felonies will encounter considerable difficulty due to information about police methods being well-known, or
d) police co-operation with foreign authorities will encounter considerable difficulty.

The court may only make a decision according to Sections 130 a and 242 a if it is strictly necessary and does not entail considerable misgivings in regard to the defence of the person charged.

Measures during hearings

According to the Act relating to the Courts of Justice, Section 125, the court may decide to close a hearing, e.g. when a witness is being examined.

Furthermore, the Criminal Procedure Act, Section 245 says the court may decide that the person charged shall leave the courtroom while a witness is being examined if there is special reason to fear that an unreserved statement will not otherwise be made. The court may also decide that the person charged shall leave the courtroom during the hearing of an application for hearing the evidence of an anonymous witness, cf. Sections 130 a and 234 a, and when an anonymous witness is being examined. Other persons may for the same reasons be ordered to leave the courtroom during the examination of a witness or a person charged.

In addition, (according to Section 130) the witness shall, as a point of departure give his/her name, date of birth, occupation, place of residence and relationship to the person charged and the aggrieved person. Instead of his/her place of residence the witness may state his/her workplace. However, if there is a risk that the witness or any person to whom the witness has such a relationship, as specified in Section 122, may be exposed to a felony impairing life, health or liberty, or to considerable material loss of another kind, the president may decide that information concerning the place of residence or workplace shall only be given in writing to the court.

Section 109 a is also a part of the provisions that establish protection for witness. According to Section 109 a the Court of Appeal and the District Court may examine witnesses at a distance.

Measures at all stages

According to Section 222 a of the Criminal Procedure Act, the prosecuting authority may impose a ban on visits if there is reason to believe that a person will otherwise:

a)   commit a criminal act against another person,
b)   pursue another person, or
c)   in any other way disturb another person's peace.

The ban may be imposed if the person who is to be protected by the ban has requested it, or if it is required in the public interest. Section 107 a shall apply correspondingly.

The ban on visits may entail that the person who is to be subject to the ban is prohibited from:

a)   being present at a specific place, or
b)   pursuing, visiting or in any other way contacting another person.

If there is any imminent risk of any act specified in the first paragraph item a) being committed, the person concerned may be banned from staying in his own home.

The ban on visits may be restricted by the imposition of further conditions.

The ban on visits shall apply for a specific period of time, not exceeding one year at a time. A ban on visits to one's own home may not last for more than three months at a time. A ban on visits may be maintained only so long as the conditions are fulfilled.

The prosecuting authority shall as soon as possible, and as far as possible no later than five days after the serving of a decision to impose a ban on visits on any person, bring the decision before the court.

2. **Please describe the framework (legal provisions and established practice) governing the use of measures encouraging witnesses and *pentiti* to co-operate with justice.**

and

3. **Can measures/benefits encouraging the co-operation of witnesses and *pentiti* be used in combination with protection measures (arrangements concerning trial proceedings, sentencing conditions, special penitentiary regimes, etc.)? If so, please specify and indicate under which conditions they are applied.**

Under Norwegian law measures have not been established in order to encourage witnesses to collaborate with the police.

In addition, witnesses do not have any obligation to make a statement or to collaborate with the police. However, a witness is obliged, on receiving a summons, to attend a police station or district sheriff's office in the police district where he/she resides or is staying in order to declare whether he/she is willing to make a statement to the police, according to the Criminal Procedure Act 230. This provision applies to a criminal procedure.

Furthermore, every person summoned to attend as a witness is bound to do so and to give evidence before the court, unless otherwise provided by statute, according to Section 108. And according to Section 137: "if a witness refuses to give evidence after being ordered to do so by a legally enforceable court order, the court may by a new order decide that the witness shall be kept in custody until he/she fulfils his/her obligation."

4. **For which kind of crime and under which circumstances can witness and *pentito* protection be applied? Can the measures be extended to the relatives or other persons close to the witness/*pentito*?**

With regard to when measures of witness protection apply, see the reply to question 1.

In order to elaborate further needs for measures to prevent crime and combat terrorism, the Ministry of Justice has set up two committees. The terms of reference of the two committees are, among other, to consider new provisions concerning witness protection.

As mentioned in the reply to question 1, the Criminal Procedure Act Sections 130, 130 a, 242 a also apply when there is a risk of a serious felony that will impair the life, health or liberty of any person to whom the witness has such a relationship as is specified in Section 122. The latter Section reads:

"The spouse, relatives in a direct line of ascent or descent, siblings and equally close relatives by marriage of the person charged are exempted from the duty to testify. The spouse of a relative by marriage is also regarded as such a relative."

The provision concerning spouses also applies to divorced persons and persons who live together in a marriage-like relationship.

The court may exempt the fiancé(e), foster parents, foster children or foster siblings of the person charged from the duty to testify.

5. What urgent measures (e.g. immediate relocation to a secret place) can be taken in order to protect witnesses and *pentiti*?

The police may relocate immediately, if necessary, at a safe and secret place and also provide armed police as guard.

6. Which institutions are involved in the protection of witnesses and *pentiti* and what is their role (e.g. law enforcement agencies, special independent agencies, prosecutor's offices, judicial authorities, etc.)? How does co-operation between the relevant institutions work in practice?

In Norway there is only one police force. Co-operation with the Prosecutors Office and other judicial authorities is not considered to create any problems. The lowest level of the prosecutor authority is within the police. The communication between the prosecutor, the court and the police in matters of witness protection should be of no problem.

The practical protection will be performed either by the local police force, or the National Police Directorate when it comes to relocation and/or change of identity. If the National Police Directorate has the responsibility for the protection of the witness, all strings to the former life are cut off and all communication goes through the Directorate. The Directorate will hence be the link between the witness and those who need to get in touch with the witness.

7. **Are there any specific provisions governing the protection of witnesses and *pentiti* in relation to acts of terrorism? If so, please specify. Are there any specialised counter-terrorism institutions? If so, what is their role in the protection of witnesses and *pentiti* in relation to acts of terrorism?**

The same set of laws and protection applies for witnesses in relation to terrorism as for witnesses in relation with serious organised crime, trafficking in women and victims of domestic violence.

8. **How does the framework governing the use of measures protecting witnesses and *pentiti* and encouraging them to co-operate with justice guarantee respect for human rights and individual freedoms? Please indicate the procedures in place, if any, to monitor compliance with human rights standards.**

See the replies to questions 2 and 3. The Criminal Procedure Act Section 137 does not, as a point of departure, raise any questions regarding human rights. However, according to Section 4 the court shall apply all provisions in the Criminal Procedure Act subject to such limitations as are recognized in international law or which derive from any agreement made with a foreign State. This reservation includes human rights and individual freedoms.

b. *Procedural measures*

9. **At which stage(s), and in which context, is it possible for witnesses and *pentiti* to benefit from procedural measures of protection?**

See the replies to questions 1 and 4.

10. **Is there the possibility for witnesses and *pentiti* to obtain legal assistance at this (these) stage(s)?**

According to Section 107 a of the Criminal Procedure Act, in cases concerning any contravention of Section 222 a of the Criminal Procedure Act, the aggrieved person is entitled to the assistance of an advocate if the said person so desires. In other cases the court may on application appoint an advocate for the aggrieved person if there is reason to believe that as a result of the criminal act the said person will suffer considerable harm to body or health and there is deemed to be a need for an advocate.

When a case concerning a ban on visits to a person's own home (cf. Section 222 a, second paragraph, second sentence) is brought before the court, the person who is to be protected by the ban is entitled to have a defence counsel. The provisions of this chapter shall apply correspondingly in so far as they are appropriate.

The police shall inform the aggrieved person of the right to have an advocate when the matter is reported to the police.

In other cases the witness is entitled to have the assistance of a lawyer of his/her own choice at every stage of the case. However, the lawyer does not have the right to take part in the criminal procedures, e.g. hearings.

11. Are there alternative methods of giving evidence which allow the protection of witnesses and *pentiti* from intimidation resulting from face to face confrontation with the accused? If yes, please specify (e.g. full or partial anonymity, video-conference, disguise, exclusion of the defendant from the courtroom when the witness is giving evidence, exclusion of the media or the public from the trial, etc.) and indicate under which conditions these methods are used.

According to Section 130 a of the Criminal Procedure Act the evidence of an anonymous witness may be given on one or more of the following measures:

a) the witness's name shall not be revealed,
b) no other information shall be given which may lead to the witness's identity becoming known, or
c) physical or technical measures shall be instituted to keep the witness's identity secret.

12. On which grounds and on the basis of which criteria can anonymity be granted? Is there the possibility to obtain legal assistance at this stage?

As mentioned above, the court may on the application of the public prosecutor's order decide to hear the evidence of an anonymous witness, according to Section 130 a of the Criminal Procedure Act, if knowledge of the witness's identity may entail a risk:

a) of a serious felony that will impair the life, health or liberty of the witness or any person to whom the witness has such a relationship as specified in Section 122, or
b) that the possibility of a witness playing an undercover part in the investigation of other cases of the kind specified above will encounter considerable difficulty.

This provision applies concerning contraventions of e.g. Sections 132 a, 147 a,151 a, 229 third alternative penalty, 231 and 233 of the Penal Code.

A decision to hear the evidence of an anonymous witness may only be made if it is strictly necessary and does not entail considerable misgivings in regard to the defence of the person charged.

13. **Are pre-trial statements of witnesses and *pentiti* and testimonies of anonymous witnesses and *pentiti* regarded as valid evidence? If yes, under which conditions?**

According to Section 130 a, paragraph 6, of the Criminal Procedure Act the court may decide to admit that evidence of an anonymous witness shall be made during the preparatory proceedings. This statement can be used as evidence during the main hearing. The decision shall be taken by three professional judges, or by the president of the court if the case is prosecuted for the District Court.

14. **Is it possible, and if so, under which conditions, to use information provided by "*pentiti*"? How is their credibility assessed?**

See the replies to questions 2 and 3 regarding "*pentiti*".

In principle, witnesses who can give evidence that is deemed to be of significance in the case should be examined orally during the main hearing if special circumstances do not prevent this, according to Section 296 of the Criminal Procedure Act. The provision secures the defence a possibility to exam the witness.

15. **Which are the opportunities for the defence to exercise its rights, including the right of the accused to challenge the witness'/*pentito*'s credibility in criminal proceedings (including at the pre-trial stage) and the respect of the "equality of arms" principle?**

See the reply to question 14.

When the court, during the main hearing or pre-trail state, decides to hear the evidence of an anonymous witness, the defence counsel shall be informed of the witness's name and shall be apprised of other matters that are significant for the case according to the Criminal Procedure Act Section 130 a, paragraph 5.

c. *Non-procedural measures*

16. **At which stage(s), and in which context, is it possible for witnesses and *pentiti* to benefit from a protection programme?**

See the replies to questions 1 and 4.

17. **Is there the possibility for witnesses and *pentiti* to obtain legal assistance at this (these) stage(s)?**

See the reply to question 10.

18. **What is the procedure for admittance to a protection programme? Please specify, in particular, who takes the initiative, the criteria for admittance, the assessment of the relevance of a testimony and how admittance to the programme is formalised.**

and

19. **Please indicate the measures that can be adopted for the protection of witnesses and *pentiti* (e.g. surveillance of the residence, physical protection, protection of personal records, relocation, change of identity, subsidies, assistance in job search, relocation of a detainee to another prison or to special units).**

First of all it is important to point out that witness protection is voluntary and that the police are depending on total co-operation with the witness in order to be successful. If the witness responds positively the police will assist the witness with advice about how to protect him/herself, such as:

- remove the name from the front door;
- install an alarm;
- secure doors and windows;
- change of daily routines;
- seek support from trusted friends/neighbours;
- change bank and bank account;
- new phone number;
- secret phone number;
- remove or restrict access to the name and address in all official registers;
- in the more severe cases; relocation outside the local area or in another police district or abroad;
- permanent relocation with change of identity.

The police will ensure it, in co-operation with other official authorities, that the witness will receive the social benefits he/she are entitled to. The police will be the link for other authorities to get in touch with the protected witness.

If a detainee needs to be relocated from one prison to another that will be done, as the system works today.

20. **What can the duration of a protection programme be? Which are the procedures for assessing the degree of danger for the witnesses/*pentiti* and their compliance with the obligations of the programme? Is it possible to challenge a decision of suspension, revocation or termination of a protection programme?**

The duration can be for lifetime. However, situations may occur that might make the police terminate their protection, or other circumstances will end it.

E.g. if a witness behaves in a way that makes it impossible for the police to provide the needed level of safety, or if the witness breaches any of the rules listed in the MoU, the police might terminate his/her protection.

The protection might also be terminated if:

1) The witness in writing says that he/she does not want to be protected any more;
2) The witness has intentionally failed to inform or given false information of conditions which is crucial for the protection;
3) The Police Directorate has pointed out breaches of the MoU;
4) There is no need for protection any more (e.g. the source of the threat is dead).

Our guidelines stipulate that there shall always be an updated threat assessment. The threat assessment consists of three assessments that lead to a risk analysis. It is the threat, evidence and personal assessment put together that lead to the risk analysis, which will indicate what measures should be taken.

If it is decided to terminate the protection, the witness is to be notified in writing and given the reason for the decision. He/she will also have the opportunity to file a complaint about this.

d. *International co-operation*

21. Which measures (e.g. use of modern telecommunications means, assistance in relocating protected witnesses, exchange of information between witness protection authorities) have been adopted in the context of mutual legal assistance in order to facilitate international co-operation? How are the financial implications of international co-operation activities dealt with?

In the Nordic Council of Ministers the five Nordic states have a long-standing co-operation in the judicial field. And regarding witness protection, the Nordic states are developing co-operation in order to facilitate protection of witnesses.

In addition, Norway may on request assist foreign authorities in order to protect witness.

22. Has your country entered international (bilateral or multilateral) agreements on the protection of witnesses and *pentiti*? If so, please indicate what kind of provisions they include.

Norway has not entered any specific international agreements on the protection of witnesses. However, as mentioned above, in the reply to question 21, we are developing a Nordic co-operation in order to facilitate protection of witnesses.

In addition, Norway has signed a co-operation agreement with the European Police Office (Europol) and takes part in Europol efforts to protection witness.

e. *Statistics*

24. How many people currently benefit from witness or *pentito* protection measures/programmes, and for how long? How many of them are foreign people? If the measures/programmes can be extended to relatives and other close persons, please indicate (and, if possible, specify the relationship with the witness/*pentito*) how many people are included in this category. Please also provide figures on the different kinds of measures (procedural and non-procedural) adopted, and on the number of cases involving international co-operation.

There are no statistics available on how many people benefit from protection measures or programmes, due to the reasons explained previously.

In the guidelines we point out that a witnesses accepted in the Witness Protection Programme will also include the person's closest family.

Poland

a. *General Information*

1. Please describe the framework (legal provisions and established practice) governing the use of measures protecting witnesses and *pentiti*.

The Polish Code of Criminal Procedure currently in force contains various provisions concerning protection of a witness' identity:

- Article 184 of the Code of Criminal Procedure provides possibilities to impose secrecy on the identity of a witness,

- Article 191 item 3 of the Code of Criminal Procedure provides the possibility to reserve information concerning a witness's place of residence, exclusively for the prosecutor or the court. This may be applied to each witness, when a justified assumption of threat exists against the life, health, freedom or property of the witness or those close to the witness.

The Crown Witness Act was adopted by the Parliament on 25 June 1997. It provides a possibility for perpetrators to act as witnesses in organised crime or in cases of conspiracy aimed at committing certain crimes, specified in the Act. The act provides a possibility to include such a witness in a special protection programme.

2. Please describe the framework (legal provisions and established practice) governing the use of measures encouraging witnesses and *pentiti* to co-operate with justice.

The concept of measures encouraging witnesses to co-operate with the administration of justice does not exist in Polish law. As far as crown witnesses are concerned, as a measure of this type we could consider the possibility of escaping criminal responsibility where, according to Article 7 of this Act, if a court issues a decision on the admissibility of evidence from the crown witness's testimony, the prosecutor prepares copies of the materials relating to the person indicated in the decision and excludes them for separate proceedings. Subsequently, such materials are suspended in relation to the crown witness. The suspension lasts until the proceedings against the remaining offenders reach a legally valid conclusion. In this way, the crown witness is not liable for punishment for crimes, in which he/she has participated and which he/she has disclosed as a suspect. After delivering a legally valid verdict in relation to the remaining offenders, a decision on the discontinuance of the legal proceeding against the crown witness is issued within 14 days from the day on which the verdict ending the penal proceedings becomes legally valid. In Polish criminal law, we can also find an institution of the so-called small crown witness. This relates to suspects, who decide to co-operate with the administration of justice, but the institution of crown witness cannot be applied to them since they have attempted or committed a murder or participated in this type of crime, incited other persons to commit a forbidden act in order to direct criminal proceeding against that person or formed an organised group or criminal alliance, or perhaps managed such a group or alliance. Under Article 60.3 of the Polish Penal Code, the court uses an extraordinary mitigation of penalty with regard to such a person and even suspends its execution conditionally if the offender acting together with other people discloses to a body of justice administration information on the persons taking part in committing the crime and important circumstances of its perpetration. According to Section 4 of this Article, upon the prosecutor's request the court can apply extraordinary mitigation of penalty and even suspend its execution with regard to an offender who, besides making statements on his case, provides an investigating body with the information relating to a crime liable to a penalty of imprisonment in excess of 5 years and presents significant circumstances, unknown to the investigating body until now.

3. **Can measures/benefits encouraging the co-operation of witnesses and *pentiti* be used in combination with protection measures (arrangements concerning trial proceedings, sentencing conditions, special penitentiary regimes, etc.)? If so, please specify and indicate under which conditions they are applied.**

The above-mentioned measures, relating to crown witnesses and the so-called small crown witnesses, can be applied together with other protection measures. The agreement between the administration of justice and a crown witness or a small crown witness permits the use of both measures at the same time. The conditions for conviction or impunity result from the binding regulations. The action connected with legal proceedings are arranged and conducted in specific circumstances, for example, during a trial it is obligatory to conduct the hearings in afternoon hours, in an empty and examined court building and after ensuring police protection. As far as possible there are also special conditions provided for staying in penal institutions, most frequently separate cells and selected penal institutions.

4. **For which kind of crime and under which circumstances can witness and *pentito* protection be applied? Can the measures be extended to the relatives or other persons close to the witness/*pentito*?**

The Crown Witness Act is applicable in organised crime cases or in cases of conspiracy aimed at committing the following types of crime: assassination of the President of the Republic of Poland, murder, causing a catastrophy or a general danger, causing a direct threat of catastrophy or general danger, causing an epidemiological threat, illegal trade in radioactive substances, kidnapping of a person with the aim at forcing her/him to deal with prostitution abroad, trafficking in human beings, illegal trade in arms, robbery and extortion, money laundering, falsification of currency, damage to property, causing considerable losses, fiscal offences causing considerable losses, fiscal offences causing considerable decrease of dues to the State Treasury, illegal production and trafficking in narcotics and psychotropic substances, selected offences against the Excise Act, participation in an organised group or conspiracy aimed at committing crime. Application of this institution is explicitly excluded in cases of murderers and organisers or leaders of criminal groups. The witness protection measures can be extended to the relatives or other persons close to the crown witness.

5. **What urgent measures (*e.g.* immediate relocation to a secret place) can be taken in order to protect witnesses and *pentiti*?**

The place where a crown witness and persons nearest to him/her stay can be changed immediately and a 24-hours physical protection can be provided.

6. **Which institutions are involved in the protection of witnesses and *pentiti* and what is their role (*e.g.* law enforcement agencies, special independent agencies, prosecutor's offices, judicial authorities, etc.)? How does co-operation between the relevant institutions work in practice?**

The protection of a crown witness is entrusted to the police; its role is limited to executing the decisions issued by a prosecutor with regard to the form of the witness protection and the extent of the financial aid granted. Co-operation between these two institutions works correctly through exchange of information, consultations and meetings.

7. **Are there any specific provisions governing the protection of witnesses and *pentiti* in relation to acts of terrorism? If so, please specify. Are there any specialised counter-terrorism institutions? If so, what is their role in the protection of witnesses and *pentiti* in relation to acts of terrorism?**

There are no rules relating to the protection of witnesses in the cases of terrorism acts.

8. **How does the framework governing the use of measures protecting witnesses and *pentiti* and encouraging them to co-operate with justice guarantee respect for human rights and individual**

freedoms? **Please indicate the procedures in place, if any, to monitor compliance with human rights standards.**

In terms of principles, the applied methods of protecting crown witnesses guarantee that human rights and personal freedom are observed. Restrictions occur only in situations where a 24-hour physical protection is required due to a danger or due to the need for immediate relocation.

b. Procedural measures

9. At which stage(s), and in which context, is it possible for witnesses and *pentiti* to benefit from procedural measures of protection?

a) At the stage of the investigation:
- at the time of the filing of the proposal to allow him/her to testify in the form of a crown witness, his/her testimonies will be made latent;
- incognito witness – see the reply to question 12;
- the option exists of filing in the protocols, the address of employment instead of the home address (e.g. police officers).

b) In the court:
- the witness can request that he be questioned during the absence of the defendant in the courtroom;
- exclusion of an open trial at the request of the witness (obligatory in the case of the crown witness).

10. Is there the possibility for witnesses and *pentiti* to obtain legal assistance at this (these) stages(s)?

The Polish legal procedure does not foresee such a possibility.

11. Are there alternative methods of giving evidence which allow the protection of witnesses and *pentiti* from intimidation resulting from face to face confrontation with the accused? If yes, please specify (e.g. full or partial anonymity, video-conference, disguise, exclusion of the defendant from the courtroom when the witness is giving evidence, exclusion of the media or the public from the trial, etc.) and indicate under which conditions these methods are used.

In Polish law, there are alternative methods for collecting evidence, which allow the protecting of witnesses and crown witnesses regarding the fear associated with a confrontation:

- the institution of witness incognito permits the concealing of the personal data of such persons, and the subsequent conducting of an investigation in a secret place. During a trial at bar, a witness incognito is heard in the presence of a judge, usually the judge from the bench. The testimony is heard by the parties present at the court, who can pose questions. In

294

order to prevent identification during the testimony, the witness's voice is changed by technical means;
- disguise with regard to witnesses incognito and persons nearest to a crown witness;
- crown witness - exclusion of an open trial is obligatory. Parties to the proceeding participate in this hearing;
- provisions of the code of penal proceedings, binding as of 1 July 2003, introduced the possibility of interrogating a witness from a distance (video-conference). In practice, this does not function yet.

12. On which grounds and on the basis of which criteria can anonymity be granted? Is there the possibility to obtain legal assistance at this state?

According to Article 184 of the Code of Penal Proceedings if there is a reasonable apprehension of danger to life, health, freedom or property of considerable value of the witness or a person nearest to the witness, it is the public prosecutor during preparatory proceeding or the court during court proceedings, who decides to keep secret the data which could disclose the witness's identity. In such a case, the personal data is known only to the prosecutor and the court and, in justified cases, to the police officer carrying out the criminal investigation. The deposition of the witness should be made available for the accused or his/her defence lawyer in a manner preventing the disclosure of the witness's identity.

Technically, the copies of a witness's deposition are made omitting the personal data and signatures. Once a decision on keeping a witness's data secret is issued, such data constitutes a state secret. It is not possible to give a witness other help apart from the help in arranging the hearings.

13. Are pre-trial statements of witnesses and *pentiti* and testimonies of anonymous witnesses and *pentiti* regarded as valid evidence? If yes, under which conditions?

According to our procedure, the first testimony of a crown witness is the statements he makes as a suspect during the preliminary investigation. Only upon issuing a decision on the admissibility of evidence from the crown witness's testimony by a court, appropriate for hearing the case, does his/her role in the proceeding change. He/she becomes a witness, to whom the provisions of Articles 182-185 of the Code of Penal Proceedings do not apply, i.e. he/she does not have the right to refuse a deposition referring to the suspension of proceedings and cannot avoid giving an answer.

The deposition of a witness incognito established by a prosecutor has the same force of evidence as a testimony before the court.

Statements of a crown witness are also considered as such evidence.

14. Is it possible, and if so, under which conditions, to use information provided by "*pentiti*? How is their credibility assessed?

The Polish law permits using the evidence provided by a crown witness and it is treated as any other evidence. The credibility of a witness and his/her testimony is checked by admitting other evidence during the preparatory proceeding. Those are open depositions of other witnesses, documents and objects as well as secured traces. Statements of suspects in the case, in which the crown witness was appointed, also play a significant role.

15. Which are the opportunities for the defence to exercise its rights, including the right of the accused to challenge the witness'/*pentito*'s credibility in criminal proceedings (including at the pre-trial stage) and the respect of the "equality of arms" principle?

The restrictions in applying the principle of "equality of arms" are due to the very nature of the institution of crown witness and witness incognito, mainly in a preparatory proceeding, where in the case of witness incognito it is practically impossible to carry out a confrontation with such a person. According to Article 184.4 of the Penal Code, the hearing of a witness with the participation of the accused or his/her defence lawyer can take place only and exclusively in circumstances that preclude the possibility of disclosing the witness's identity. In case of an accused, which, when making statements applies to testify as a crown witness, his/her statements are kept secret.

They remain secret until the court issues a decision on the admissibility of the crown witness's testimony. Therefore, checking the circumstances, indicated by the crown witness gives the advantage to the plaintiff. If the court does not admit evidence from the crown witness's testimony, the minutes of the statements must be destroyed.

c. Non-procedural measures

16. At which stage(s), and in which context, is it possible for witnesses and *pentiti* to benefit from a protection programme?

Once the suspect applied for allowing him/her to give a deposition as a crown witness, he/she can already take advantage of the protection program. This requires the prosecutor to issue an appropriate decision and means an immediate change of residence, personal protection and financial aid.

As soon as the court issues a decision on the crown witness, a prosecutor conducting the preparatory proceeding issued a decision on granting protection and financial aid on the basis of information held.

The duration of the protection programme depends on the evaluation of the degree of endangerment. In the Polish procedure, the suspension of the protection programme is not possible - it can only by withdrawn. The withdrawal of the protection or aid can occur, in accordance with the cited ordinace, if the danger to the life or health of the protected person ceased, or if the protected person applies for the withdrawal of the granted aid and protection, in the case of purposeful violation of the principles or recommendations with regard to protection or persistent failure to fulfil the duties, in the event of taking up the suspended proceedings in relation to a crown witness, in the event of gross violation of the granted protection and aid conditions by the protected person. This relates to failure to observe legal order, suppressing material information significant for the protection, not complying with the recommendations of policemen providing the protection and using the protection and aid contradictory to its purpose. The issue of a decision on withdrawing the protection and aid is within the competence of a prosecutor. The protected person and persons nearest to him/her can appeal against the decision.

17. Is there the possibility for witnesses and *pentiti* to obtain legal assistance at this (these) stage(s)?

The Polish legal procedure does not foresee such a possibility.

18. What is the procedure for admittance to a protection programme? Please specify, in particular, who takes the initiative, the criteria for admittance, the assessment of the relevance of a testimony and how admittance to the programme is formalised.

The condition for application of protective measures and support specified by the Act is a written statement, made by an adult person, making it obligatory to follow the rules and recommendations concerning implementing protective measures, and fulfilling all obligations specified by the Act, and following all decisions issued on the basis of the Act – when protected or assisted in changing the place of residence or when ID documents allowing the use of a different identity issued. Application of personal protection and support is decided upon by a prosecutor on request of the crown witness or an individual close to him/her.

A prosecutor may also, on his own initiative take a decision in that extent, with the consent of those persons. The witness protection programme in Poland must be based on the voluntary participation and consent of the witness.

19. **Please indicate the measures that can be adopted for the protection of witnesses and *pentiti* (*e.g.*, surveillance of the residence, physical protection, protection of personal records, relocation, change of identity, subsidies, assistance in job search, relocation of a detainee to another prison or to special units).**

The protection and assistance measures used in Poland are the following:

- personal protection (physical) - that takes place only in emergency situations because of the fact, that it requires engaging a lot of manpower and is possible only for short period of time.

- change of the crown witness's place of residence – this method is more efficient and safer than the previous one. But at the same time it is more expensive, especially when the change of place is necessary several times.

- assisting the crown witness to find a new job or to increase his/her qualifications by providing a training course.

- providing the crown witness with other personal data and sometimes (in justified situations) with new identity documents, including documents allowing the crossing of state borders.

- economic and medical assistance – used in cases of lack of possibilities to earn money by the crown witness and his/her family.

20. **What can the duration of a protection programme be? Which are the procedures for assessing the degree of danger for the witnesses/*pentiti* and their compliance with the obligations of the programme? Is it possible to challenge a decision of suspension, revocation or termination of a protection programme?**

The duration of protection measures is dependent on the evaluation of the threat situation.

d. International co-operation

21. **Which measures (*e.g.*, use of modern telecommunications means, assistance in relocating protected witnesses, exchange of information between witness protection authorities) have been adopted in the context of mutual legal assistance in order to facilitate international co-operation? How are the financial implications of international co-operation activities dealt with?**

The Polish law provides for adopting the protection programme from abroad and relocating the protected persons outside the Polish frontiers. In the event of transferring a protection programme to Polish territory, the country effecting such a transfer shall cover the costs of transport to the border, costs of renting and maintaining accommodation as well as the costs of supporting the witness and medical care.

Costs of relocations on Polish territory and costs of protection forces are covered by Poland. From amongst measures facilitating the co-operation, the possibility of using video-conference facilities was used.

22. Has your country entered international (bilateral or multilateral) agreements on the protection of witnesses and *pentiti*? If so, please indicate what kind of provisions they include.

The exchange of witness protection programmes takes place under the international agreements on overcoming organised crime.

23. How can international co-operation in the field of the protection of witnesses and *pentiti* be improved?

International co-operation could be improved by:

- unifying legal regulations;
- organising a contact point at the institution effecting protection of witnesses in each country.

e. Statistics

24. How many people currently benefit from witness or *pentito* protection measures/programmes, and for how long? How many of them are foreign people? If the measures/programmes can be extended to relatives and other close persons, please indicate (and, if possible, specify the relationship with the witness/*pentito*) how many people are included in this category. Please also provide figures on the different kinds of measures (procedural and non-procedural) adopted, and on the number of cases involving international co-operation.

Presently we are dealing with:

- 56 cases
- 135 protected people (53 crown witnesses and 80 family members)
- 2 programmes we have exchanged abroad and 1 we have accepted.

f. Proposals and comments

25. Please provide any comments/proposals concerning the implementation of the terms of reference of the PC-PW and, in particular, instruments to be adopted to strengthen the protection of witnesses and *pentiti*.

In order to strengthen the institution of witness protection, using the Polish example, the following is recommended:

-   to apply this institution also to victims and eye witnesses. This would permit taking fuller advantage of this institution and giving victims and eye witnesses a right to protection and aid equal to the right of a crown witness;

-   to introduce it on a permanent basis and not temporarily as is the case in Poland - this would increase the effectiveness of its application and would eliminate the mass criticism of this institution by the lawyers' circles;

-   the crown witness status to be granted by a commission - this would help to avoid further disappointments on the part of a crown witness and the administration of justice;

-   to create special teams in penal institutions, allowing protection of witnesses sentenced to imprisonment.

Portugal

a. General information

1. Please describe the framework (legal provisions and established practice) governing the use of measures protecting witnesses and *pentiti*.

Portugal has a single legal framework governing the protection of witnesses and *"pentiti"*, owing to the fact that the relevant legislation – Act 93/99, of 14 July 1999 – does not distinguish protection measures according to the role played in the proceedings by the individuals to be protected. They are always described as witnesses, in the broad sense of the word.

The methods used to protect such individuals so as to enable them to give evidence are consequently identical, and involve safeguarding the witness's identity by means of voice concealment and distortion and testimony by video-conference.

This legislation also deals with special protection and safety measures, which may be short-term in nature – during the stage of proceedings in which the witness is involved – or take the form of a special safety programme, in the event that the threat is expected to continue once the proceedings are over.

These measures are extended to the witness's relatives and other people close to him/her. The use of special safety programmes is allowed only in cases relating to terrorism, drug trafficking, terrorist organisations, criminal association and trafficking in human beings, and in those cases in which there is clearly a serious threat to the life, person, freedom or valuable property of the people concerned.

The following measures may be included in the special safety programme: provision of false identities; changes in physical appearance; changes of address (including abroad); transportation of people and property; help to find new jobs; and temporary grants.

2. Please describe the framework (legal provisions and established practice) governing the use of measures encouraging witness and *pentito* to co-operate with the justice system.

The Portuguese criminal justice system has not traditionally enabled suspects to negotiate their sentences according to the extent to which they have co-operated in the proceedings. The judicial authorities are even somewhat averse to making the principles of legality and involvement in the running of criminal proceedings more flexible. We consequently do not have what could be described as a legal framework for encouraging co-operation in criminal proceedings.

Admittedly, we do have separate measures used in the prevention of the serious crimes mentioned above (except for trafficking in human beings), which allow for special sentence reductions, or even, in extreme cases, non-application of sentences.

Defendants may be eligible for these measures where they make a serious effort to stop the criminal activity continuing. However, the effects of their repentance or efforts to co-operate with the authorities cannot be guaranteed in advance.

As far as witnesses are concerned, they are bound by a duty to co-operate and to testify truthfully; encouragement is confined to the aforementioned protection measures.

3. **Can measures/benefits encouraging the co-operation of witnesses and *pentiti* be used in combination with protection measures (arrangements concerning trial proceedings, sentencing conditions, special penitentiary regimes, etc.)? If so, please specify and indicate under which conditions they are applied.**

As explained, we do not have active measures to encourage co-operation. We do have more flexible sentence-serving regimes, however, which are applied – depending on the specific circumstances of the case – on the basis of the prisoner's conduct, rather than any prior co-operation with the authorities. In any event, such a regime is not applied as a reward for a prisoner's co-operation. In this connection, prisoners may be eligible for a special penitentiary regime on safety grounds.

4. **For what kind of crime and under what circumstances can witness and *pentito* protection be applied? Can the measures be extended to the relatives or other persons close to the witness/*pentito*?**

The protection and safety measures provided for by law (identity protection, video-conferencing, voice concealment and image distortion) may be applied to all types of criminal proceedings, on the condition that, in the specific case in question, there is a genuine threat to the witness, those close to him/her and/or his/her valuable property. Special protection and safety programmes may be implemented only in respect of the offences of criminal association, terrorist organisation, terrorism, drug trafficking and trafficking in human beings. All the measures mentioned above may be extended to relatives and other people close to the witness.

5. **What urgent measures (e.g. immediate relocation to a secret place) can be taken in order to protect witnesses and *pentiti*?**

We do not have any specific urgent measures, given that these measures are adopted by the investigating authorities on an *ad hoc* basis. This excludes the procedure for implementing protection and safety measures, which is separate from the investigation procedure; it is urgent in nature, and the time limit for appeals is halved.

6. **What institutions are involved in the protection of witnesses and *pentiti* and what is their role (e.g. law enforcement agencies, special independent agencies, prosecutor's offices, judicial authorities, etc.)? How does co-operation between the relevant institutions work in practice?**

The Public Prosecutor's Office always has the power to apply for the measures provided for; in some cases, the parties or the judge may apply for such measures, depending on the stage in the proceedings.

Where special safety and protection programmes are implemented, there is a Special Safety Programmes Committee comprising two members appointed by the Ministry of Justice (the Chair and secretary of the Committee), a judge and a public prosecutor, appointed by the Higher Magistrates' Council and the Higher Public Prosecutors' Council respectively, and a fifth member appointed by the Ministry of Internal Administration.

This Committee has the power to adopt, and ensure the effective implementation of, the necessary measures for the proper application of the programmes. Particularly in the preliminary stages of proceedings, there is also considerable involvement of the criminal investigation division of the police, which is responsible for conducting investigations.

7. **Are there any specific provisions governing the protection of witnesses and *pentiti* in relation to acts of terrorism? If so, please specify. Are there any specialised counter-terrorism institutions? If so, what is their role in the protection of witnesses and *pentiti* in relation to acts of terrorism?**

No. Specific, more drastic measures are applied to the offences listed in the reply to question 4. As regards the existence of specialised counter-terrorism institutions, Portuguese law stipulates that investigations into terrorist offences are conducted exclusively by the police's criminal investigation division, which has a central department specialising in counter-terrorism (the DCCB). As far as protection of witnesses (including *"pentiti"*) is concerned, this department's role is to ensure – in close co-operation with the Public Prosecutor's Office – that urgent measures are taken to guarantee the safety of the people involved, and to help with the safety programmes implemented. In the past, given that there was no specific legal framework, the department performed this role on a more informal basis, while complying with the strict legal rules in force at the time.

8. **How does the framework governing the use of measures protecting witnesses and *pentiti* and encouraging them to co-operate with the judicial authorities guarantee respect for human rights and individual freedoms? Please indicate the procedures in place, if any, to monitor compliance with human rights standards.**

Measures intended to guarantee human rights and individual freedoms are stipulated in Act 93/99, which includes witness protection measures. In addition to respect for the principles of proportionality and subsidiarity, decisions giving rise to protection measures must guarantee the suspect the opportunity to be heard. As an example, testimony by video-conference must be given in the presence of a judge other than the trial judge.

Likewise, the judge ruling on an application for protection measures cannot be the same judge as gave rulings against the defendant during the judicial investigation stage of the proceedings in question.

Even more protective is the measure prohibiting any conviction based solely on evidence given by persons subject to protection measures. In addition to the statement of reasons, and alongside the obligation to justify any decisions that affect defendants' rights – including those making proceedings subject to special measures – the general rules set out in the Code of Criminal Procedure afford the defence considerable powers of scrutiny during the trial stage (in which the evidence leading to the final decision is produced).

b. Procedural measures

9. **At what stage(s) and in what context is it possible for witnesses and *pentiti* to benefit from procedural measures of protection?**

At any stage in the proceedings, provided they have already been registered as such. Only situations involving police prevention work remain outside the trial framework. As already mentioned, these measures may be extended beyond the close of the proceedings.

10. **Can witnesses and *pentiti* obtain legal assistance at this (these) stage(s)?**

Yes, although outside the specific legal framework governing witness protection. Our legal order includes a system of general legal aid, which is applied in specific cases if/when the individuals involved satisfy the necessary requirements.

11. Are there alternative methods of giving evidence which allow the protection of witnesses and *pentiti* from intimidation resulting from face to face confrontation with the accused? If yes, please specify (e.g. full or partial anonymity, video-conference, disguise, exclusion of the defendant from the courtroom when the witness is giving evidence, exclusion of the media or the public from the trial, etc.) and indicate under which conditions these methods are used.

Yes, those mentioned above. Total (in cases involving the most serious offences mentioned in the reply to question 4) or partial concealment of identity, tele-conferencing and voice and image distortion. These methods are used in any case in which there is a threat to the giving of full and frank testimony.

12. On what grounds and on the basis of which criteria can anonymity be granted? Is there the possibility to obtain legal assistance at this stage?

Whenever there is evidence that the life or person of the witness or of people close to him/her is in danger, or that there is a risk of loss of valuable property belonging to the witness, measures to protect his/her identity may be applied. According to the general rule set out in the Portuguese Criminal Code, such a judgment is subjective, as there is no such thing as typical valid evidence. Even so, insofar as these exceptions restrict the rights of the defence, they must be subsidiary and proportional in nature, and reasons must be given for the decision ordering them. In addition, the evidence warranting such exceptions must be part of the proceedings. Legal aid is governed by the same general rules applicable to all other proceedings.

13. Are pre-trial statements of witnesses and *pentiti* and testimonies of anonymous witnesses and *pentiti* regarded as valid evidence? If yes, under which conditions?

As a rule, no. The Portuguese Code of Criminal Procedure stipulates that only evidence given in court is valid. The sole exception to this principle – a situation not contained in the framework governing witness protection – is in the case of statements for "future record", which are taken (*inter alia*) when it is known in advance that a particular witness is to travel abroad. By analogy, however, this measure may be applied to someone under a protection programme who has to be moved before the hearing.

14. Is it possible and, if so, under which conditions to use information provided by *pentiti*? How is their credibility assessed?

The principle of free assessment of evidence by the courts is the general rule followed. Statements by *"pentiti"* are analogous to evidence given by witnesses; they are freely assessed, bearing in mind, naturally, the circumstances in which they were made. Wherever possible, the reliability of a witness's evidence must be confirmed by other types of evidence, particularly when it is given in the context of a witness protection programme. Reliability is therefore assessed case by case, given that there are no pre-defined requirements or parameters on which to base this assessment.

15. What opportunities are there for the exercise of the rights of the defence, including the right of the accused to challenge the witness'/*pentito*'s credibility in criminal proceedings (including at the pre-trial stage) and the respect of the "equality of arms" principle?

The stage of proceedings prior to the trial must in all cases include the preliminary investigation, conducted by the Public Prosecutor's Office; where requested, this is followed by the judicial investigation, conducted by the investigating judge, which sets out to validate the decisions of the preliminary investigation. Only at this stage can the accused be confronted with the accusations against him/her; these accusations may be contested and/or the credibility of witnesses, including *"pentiti"*, can be challenged. Given that the judgment is based solely on evidence given in court, equality of arms is thereby guaranteed; witnesses covered by a protection programme may be questioned extensively during the proceedings and confronted with evidence that might contradict their testimony, thereby guaranteeing the adversarial principle.

c. Non-procedural measures

16. At what stage(s) and in what context is it possible for witnesses and *pentiti* to benefit from a protection programme?

In accordance with the Act, protection and safety measures may be implemented on behalf of witnesses only as part of criminal proceedings, bearing in mind that these measures are only legal in the context of a trial.

17. Are witnesses and *pentiti* able to obtain legal assistance at this (these) stage(s)?

Only in accordance with the general legislation governing legal aid.

18. What is the procedure for admittance to a protection programme? Please specify, in particular, who takes the initiative, the criteria for admittance, the assessment of the relevance of a testimony and how admittance to the programme is formalised.

Notice of situations eligible for protection and safety measures may be given unofficially – the judge may order such measures during the judicial investigation or the trial if he/she deems them necessary – or at the request of the Public Prosecutor's Office, the parties, witnesses or "*pentiti*". There is no specific procedure for implementing protection and safety measures. The requirements are subjective, and are assessed empirically. As far as the application of special protection and safety measures is concerned, the person(s) protected simply has (have) to undertake to fulfil the stipulated obligations relating to safety, failing which the programme will be terminated. In cases entailing a total concealment of identity, an additional procedure is followed, intended to ensure the rights of the defence: the bar association is asked to appoint a suitable barrister to ensure the rights of the defence in the specific proceedings in question. Such witnesses are then known by an identification code until the close of the proceedings.

19. Please indicate the measures that can be adopted for the protection of witnesses and *pentiti* (e.g. surveillance of their residence, physical protection, protection of personal records, relocation, change of identity, subsidies, assistance with a job search, relocation of a detainee to another prison or to special units).

All the standard personal safety measures that may be necessary, depending on the threat to witnesses, people close to them and their property.

Portuguese law specifies all the measures mentioned in the question.

20. At what stages in proceedings (pre-trial investigation, during the trial, after the trial) can a protection programme be granted? What is the protection programme's duration? What are the procedures for assessing the degree of danger for the witnesses/*pentiti* and their compliance with the programme obligations? Is to possible to challenge a decision to suspend, revoke or terminate a protection programme?

The measures alluded to in the reply to question 19 apply primarily to safety programmes of limited duration, which are evaluated every three years by the authority that ordered them. Where a dangerous situation is likely to continue indefinitely, special safety programmes authorise the provision of official documentation including various identity papers, changes in physical appearance, a new home in Portugal or abroad, free transportation to that new home, creation of the necessary conditions to make it possible to earn a living and a short-term subsistence grant. These measures are extended to relatives and people close to the witness, and must be agreed to before they can be implemented. Since there is no provision for any specific procedure, the suspension, revocation or termination of a special safety programme can always be appealed in accordance with the general statutory requirements.

d. *International co-operation*

21. What measures (e.g. use of modern telecommunications technology, assistance in relocating protected witnesses, exchange of information between witness protection authorities) have been adopted in the context of mutual legal assistance in order to facilitate international co-operation? How are the financial implications of international co-operation activities dealt with?

There is no provision for any specific measures in this area. Although Portugal has the technical wherewithal to conduct video-conferences with foreign countries, there is no provision for them in the Witness Protection Act.

22. Has your country entered international (bilateral or multilateral) agreements on the protection of witnesses and *pentiti*? If so, please indicate what kind of provisions they include.

No.

23. How can international co-operation in the field of the protection of witnesses and *pentiti* be improved?

By pooling experience, sharing support structures, possibly providing assistance in obtaining documentation, helping to monitor the fulfilment of obligations by protected persons placed abroad and helping such persons to find jobs.

e. *Statistics*

24. How many people currently benefit from witness or *pentito* protection measures/programmes and for how long? How many of them are foreigners? If the measures/programmes can be extended to relatives and other close persons, please indicate how many people are included in this category (and, if possible, specify the relationship with the witness/*pentito*). Please also provide figures on the different kinds of measures (procedural and non-procedural) adopted and on the number of cases involving international co-operation.

–

f. *Proposals and comments*

25. Please provide any comments/proposals concerning the implementation of the terms of reference of the PC-PW and, in particular, instruments to be adopted to strengthen the protection of witnesses and *pentiti*.

The suggestions made in the reply to question 23 call for special attention, given that we are faced with a threat of a transnational nature. The ever-increasing mobility of criminal networks – terrorist or otherwise – means that the response capacity of protection programmes, including in the area of mobility, must be stepped up. Moreover, bearing in mind that it is the State in which the proceedings are held that has to pay relocation costs, the latter will be huge if it is not possible to make use of existing arrangements in other States. The use of such arrangements does not entail significant additional costs, at least in comparison with the amounts paid by a single country. Supplying documentation to other States is a simple, low-cost measure; where provision is made for it, there are no legal impediments. It becomes very difficult to monitor the implementation of programmes when relocations are involved, and these tasks could be shared with the receiving States. It would also be entirely appropriate for such States to possess in-depth information about those they accept as protected witnesses, and under what conditions.

Russian Federation

There is no such concept as *"pentiti"* in Russian legislation, therefore the following responses refer only to witnesses.

According to Article 56 ("Witness") of the Code of Criminal Procedure of the Russian Federation of 18 December 2001, No. 174-ФЗ (hereinafter CCP), a witness is a person who may be aware of any facts relevant to the investigation or the prosecution of a crime and is summoned to give evidence.

Witnesses are summoned and interrogated under the procedure provided for by Articles 187-191 of the CCP.

The following persons shall not be called to testify:

1) a judge or a juror - about any facts in the criminal case he/she became aware of through his/her participation in the criminal proceedings;
2) a counsel for the defendant, suspect - about any facts he/she became aware of through his/her participation in criminal proceedings;
3) a lawyer - about any facts he/she became aware of when rendering legal assistance;
4) a clergy person - about any facts he/she became aware of in connection with confession;
5) a member of the Federation Council or a deputy of the State Duma without his/her consent - about any facts he/she became aware of in the performance of his/her duties.

A witness has the right:

1) not to testify against him/herself, his/her spouse and other close relatives specified in paragraph 4 of Article 5 of the CCP. If a witness agrees to testify, he/she shall be warned that his/her testimony may be used as evidence at the trial, even if he/she withdraws his/her evidence in the future;
2) to testify in his/her native language or any language he/she knows;
3) to obtain an interpreter free of charge;
4) to waive the interpreter who takes part in interrogation;
5) to file motions and complaints regarding any acts (omissions) and decisions by the inquiry officer, investigator, prosecutor or the court;
6) to be interrogated in the presence of his/her lawyer as defined in paragraph 5 of Article 189 (General Rules of Conducting Questioning) of this Code;
7) to claim the protection measures provided for in paragraph 3 of Article 11 ("Protection of Human and Civil Rights and Freedoms in Criminal Proceedings") of the CCP.

A witness may not be submitted to forensic examination or inspection except as provided in paragraph 1 of Article 179 of the CCP.

A witness has no right:

1) to ignore a summons from the inquiry officer, investigator, prosecutor or a summons to appear in court;
2) to deliberately give false evidence or refuse to give evidence;
3) to disclose preliminary investigation data learnt in connection with his/her involvement in the criminal proceedings if he/she has been appropriately forewarned under the procedure established by Article 161 of the CCP.

In the case of non-appearance without a valid reason, a witness may be brought by force.

A witness is liable for deliberately giving false evidence or refusing to give evidence under Articles 307 ("Perjured Evidence, Expert's Opinion or Incorrect Translation") and 308 ("Witness's or Victim's Refusal to Give Evidence") of the 1996 Criminal Code of the Russian Federation. A witness is liable for the disclosure of preliminary investigation data under Article 310 ("Disclosure of Preliminary Investigation Data") of the 1996 Criminal Code of the Russian Federation.

a. *General information*

1. **Please describe the framework (legal provisions and established practice) governing the use of measures protecting witnesses and *pentiti*.**

The legal status of participants in criminal proceedings, including witnesses, is determined by the CCP. This document complies with the European standards and experts from 13 European countries were involved in its examination.

The protection measures for witnesses and the procedure for their enforcement are determined by Articles 11, 166, 186, 193, 241 and 278 of the CCP.

Thus, under paragraph 3 of Article 11 ("Protection of Human and Civil Rights and Freedoms in Criminal Proceedings") of the CCP if there exist sufficient information that a victim, witness or other participants in criminal proceedings or their immediate relatives, relatives or intimate persons are facing threats of murder, violence, or destruction of or damage to their property, or other dangerous unlawful actions, the court, procurator, investigator, inquiry agency, or inquiry officer shall, within their subject-matter jurisdiction, take security measures to protect the said persons, as envisaged by Articles 166 (paragraph 9), 186 (paragraph 2), 193 (paragraph 8), 241 (paragraph 2, sub-paragraph 4), 278 (paragraph 5) of the CCP.

On 6 June 2003, the State Duma of the Russian Federation approved in the first reading the draft Federal Law "On the Public Protection of Victims, Witnesses and other Participants in the Criminal Proceedings", tabled by the President of the Russian Federation on 17 March[1]. This Bill was developed by the working group established by the President of the Russian Federation under the Security Council of the Russian Federation. The bill was drafted taking into account foreign experience, including that of other European states. It is aimed at protecting participants in criminal proceedings, including witnesses, first of all those involved in cases concerning grave crimes and felony, including terrorist cases. The system of state protection measures includes security measures and social protection measures. Security measures may include, in particular, physical protection of the protected person, protection of his/her residence and property; providing him/her with special means of individual protection, communication and danger warning; ensuring confidentiality of the information concerning the protected person; his/her relocation to another place of residence; change of his/her identity; change of his/her appearance; change of his/her place of work; his/her temporary relocation to a secure place, as well as applying additional security measures to the protected person in custody or in the place he/she is serving his/her sentence, including his/her transfer from his/her place of detention or the place he/she is serving his/her sentence to another. The draft also determines the procedure and grounds for applying security and social protection measures, as well as the procedure for revoking security measures.

4. **For which kind of crime and under which circumstances can witness and *pentito* protection be applied? Can the measures be extended to the relatives or other persons close to the witness/*pentito*?**

Under the provisions of the CCP, security measures shall apply to witnesses in the course of investigating criminal cases concerning all grades of offences. According to Article 11 (Protection of Human and Civil Rights and Freedoms in Criminal Proceedings) of the CCP, the above-mentioned measures may also be extended to their close relatives (i.e. spouses, parents, children, adoptive persons, adoptees, siblings, grandparents, grandchildren), relatives or their close persons (i.e. persons who have an affinity with the victim or witness, other than their close relatives and relatives, as well as persons whose life, health and well-being are dear to the victim or witness by virtue of existing personal relations).

---

[1] Entered into force on 1st January 2005.

7. **Are there any specific provisions governing the protection of witnesses and *pentiti* in relation to acts of terrorism? If so, please specify. Are there any specialised counter-terrorist institutions? If so, what is their role in the protection of witnesses and *pentiti* in relation to acts of terrorism?**

In Russian legislation there are no specific provisions governing protection of witnesses in connection with acts of terrorism. The general rules for the protection of witnesses in criminal proceedings apply to witnesses connected with the acts of terrorism.

Under Article 6 of the 1998 Federal Law on Combating Terrorism, counter-terrorist committees are established at the federal and regional levels in order to organise activities to combat terrorism; however, the protection of witnesses does not fall within the jurisdiction of these committees.

8. **How does the framework governing the use of measures protecting witnesses and *pentiti* and encouraging them to co-operate with justice guarantee respect for human rights and individual freedoms? Please indicate the procedures in place, if any, to monitor compliance with human rights standards.**

Russian criminal procedure laws contain norms which establish the principles of legality in course of proceedings in criminal case (Article 7 of the CCP), respect for honour and dignity of individual (Article 9 of the CCP), protection of human and civil rights and freedoms in criminal proceedings (Article 11 of the CCP). Thus, for instance, according to Article 11 ("Protection of Human and Civil Rights and Freedoms in Criminal Proceedings") of the CCP, the court, the prosecutor, the investigator and the inquiry officer are obliged to expound to the parties in criminal proceedings their rights, obligations and responsibilities, and secure facilities to exercise those rights. Moreover, any damage caused to a person as a result of the violation of his/her rights and freedoms by the court, or by the officials carrying out criminal prosecution, is to be compensated on the grounds and in accordance with the procedure set by this Code.

9. **At which stage(s), and in which context, is it possible for witnesses and *pentiti* to benefit from procedural measures of protection?**

In accordance with the CCP, witnesses may benefit from procedural measures of protection as early as during pre-trial proceedings, at the stage of preliminary investigation. Thus, according to paragraph 9, Article 166, when it is necessary to provide security of the witness, their immediate relatives and intimate persons, the investigator shall have the right not to refer to the information on their identities in the official record of the investigative action, in which they participated. In this instance the investigator, acting with the consent of a prosecutor, shall render a ruling which shall set forth the reasons of making the decision to keep this information confidential, refer to the alias of a participant in the investigative action, and produce the specimen of the signature, that he/she shall use in the official records of investigative actions conducted with his/her participation. The ruling shall be placed in an envelope that shall be then sealed and included to the criminal case file.

10. Is there the possibility for witnesses and *pentiti* to obtain legal assistance at this (these) stage(s)?

The possibility to obtain legal assistance (in particular, the services of an attorney) is guaranteed by the Constitution of the Russian Federation (Articles 45, 46, 48), as well as by the CCP.

11. Are there alternative methods of giving evidence which allow the protection of witnesses and *pentiti* from intimidation resulting from face to face confrontation with the accused? If yes, please specify (e.g. full or partial anonymity, video-conference, disguise, exclusion of the defendant from the courtroom when the witness is giving evidence, exclusion of the media or the public from the trial, etc.) and indicate under which conditions these methods are used.

Such methods are provided for by paragraph 8 of Article 193 ("presentation for Identification") of the CCP, according to which the investigator, in order to provide security of a person making identification, presentation of a person for identification, pursuant to the investigator's decision, may be conducted in the conditions excluding the possibility of visual observation of the person making identification by a person presented for identification

Under paragraph 1 of Article 241 ("Transparency") of the CCP, criminal proceedings in all courts are held in public, except in cases stipulated in this Article. However, sub-paragraph 4 of paragraph 2 of the said Article provides that private hearings are possible upon judicial declaration or decision in cases where there is a need to protect the parties in criminal proceedings (including witnesses), their close relatives, relatives or close persons. Under paragraph 5 of Article 278 ("Examination of Witnesses") of the CCP, if it is necessary to provide for security of a witness, his/her close relatives, relatives or intimate persons, the court may, without disclosing the real information on the identity of the witness, examine him/her out of view of other participants in the court proceedings, with a court finding or ruling rendered to that effect.

12. On which grounds and on the basis of which criteria can anonymity be granted? Is there the possibility to obtain legal assistance at this stage?

Under Article 11 ("Protection of Human and Civil Rights and Freedoms in Criminal Proceedings") of the CCP, the criterion is the availability of sufficient information proving that the witness, or his/her immediate relatives, relatives or intimate persons, are threatened with murder, violence, destruction or damage to their property, or other dangerous unlawful actions.

13. Are pre-trial statements of witnesses and *pentiti* and testimonies of anonymous witnesses and *pentiti* regarded as valid evidence? If yes, under which conditions?

Such statements are of evidential value if no provision of the CCP has been violated. Under Article 75 ("Inadmissible Evidence") of the CCP, evidence obtained in violation of the requirements of the Code is inadmissible. Inadmissible evidence has no legal validity and may not form the basis of the prosecution. Under the same Article 75, neither the testimony of a witness, based on his/her guesses, supposition or rumours, nor the testimony of a witness who cannot identify the source of his/her knowledge is admissible.

15. Which are the opportunities for the defence to exercise its rights, including the right of the accused to challenge the witness'/*pentito*'s credibility in criminal proceedings (including at the pre-trial stage) and the respect of the "equality of arms" principle?

The criminal procedure laws provide ample opportunities for the defence.

For example, a suspect is entitled in particular to offer explanations and to testify as regards suspicions against him/her or to refuse to provide any explanations or testify; to present evidence; to make applications or objections; to file complaints against action (or inaction) and decisions taken by the court, prosecutor, investigator or the inquiry officer; to defend him/herself by other means and methods consistent with the CCP.

The accused is entitled in particular to defend his/her rights and legitimate interests and have sufficient time and conditions to prepare his/her defence, to present evidence; to make applications or objections; to see all the criminal case materials after the preliminary investigation has been completed and to take written notes of any information from his/her criminal case file, whatever its length; to file complaints against action (or inaction) and decisions by the investigator, inquiry officer, prosecutor or the court and to take part in the trial of his/her case by the court.

As soon as the attorney for the defence is allowed to take part in criminal case proceedings, he/she is entitled in particular to collect and present the evidence necessary to render legal assistance in accordance with the procedure set forth in paragraph 3 of Article 86 ("Collection of Evidence") of the Code; to see the detention writ, the decision concerning his/her pre-trial conditions, the records of investigation activities carried out with participation of the suspect or accused and other instruments that have been or should have been presented to the suspect or accused; to see all criminal case materials after the preliminary investigation has been completed, to take written notes of any information from the criminal case file, whatever its length, to make, at his/her own expense, copies of criminal case materials including copies made with the use of technical means; to make applications or objections; to file complaints against action (or inaction) and decisions made by the investigator, the inquiry officer, prosecutor, or the court and to take part in the trial of his/her case by the court; and to use other defence means and remedies consistent with the Code.

(Note: this answer refers only to those rights of the suspect, the accused or attorney for the defence that may relate to evidence. That is why such fundamental rights as the right of the suspect or the accused to demand to participate in the hearings of his/her attorney or an interpreter, etc., are not mentioned.)

d. *International co-operation*

The Meeting of the Plenipotentiary Representatives and Experts from the Commonwealth of Independent States member countries (Minsk, April 2001) reached consensus on the text of the draft agreement on protection of the parties in criminal proceedings and recommended that it be submitted to the Council of Ministers of Foreign Affairs and the Council of Heads of State of the Commonwealth for consideration.

Spain

a. *General information*

1. **Please describe the framework (legal provisions and established practice) governing the use of measures protecting witnesses and *pentiti*.**

Spanish legislation regulates the protection of witnesses and *pentiti* under Implementing Act 19/1994 of 23 December 1994 on the Protection of Witnesses and Experts in Criminal Proceedings, published in the Spanish Official Gazette of 24 December 1994. The explanatory memorandum to this Act acknowledges that its main purpose is to ensure the effective protection of witnesses and experts, allowed by the European Court of Human Rights and United Nations Security Council Resolution 827/1993, of 25 May 1993.

2. **Please describe the framework (legal provisions and established practice) governing the use of measures encouraging witness and *pentito* to co-operate with the justice system.**

In view of the foregoing, solely the desire of the person in question to co-operate or his/her genuine repentance may be taken into account. At present, courts can take a number of protection measures (hearings in separate rooms, voice distortion, sittings *in camera*, etc.), but these apply only during the proceedings or before the investigating judge.

There is no common practice, as each district can deal with these aspects in its own way.

3. **Can measures/benefits encouraging the co-operation of witnesses and *pentiti* be used in combination with protection measures (arrangements concerning trial proceedings, sentencing conditions, special penitentiary regimes, etc.)? If so, please specify and indicate under which conditions they are applied.**

Spanish legislation also regulates measures intended to encourage witnesses and *pentiti* to assist in the administration of justice. In particular, Article 21 of the Spanish Criminal Code of 23 November 1995 provides that "circumstances mitigating criminal responsibility shall include: 4) The fact that an offender admitted the offence to the authorities before being notified of the bringing of judicial proceedings against him/her; 5) The fact that an offender has taken steps to repair the damage caused to the victim, or to reduce its impact, at any time during the proceedings prior to the hearing".

4. **For what kind of crime and under what circumstances can witness and *pentito* protection be applied? Can the measures be extended to the relatives or other persons close to the witness/*pentito*?**

Under Section 1 of Implementing Act 19/1994, the protection measures prescribed by Spanish law may be ordered "for those involved in criminal proceedings as witnesses or experts"; this provision stipulates that "in order for protection measures to be applicable, the judicial authorities must rationally find a serious danger to the person, freedom or property of the individual desiring such protection, his/her spouse or the person to whom he/she is bound by an analogous emotional relationship, or his/her ascendants, descendants or brothers or sisters". Protection measures may thus be ordered for any offence, provided that the aforementioned serious danger is found, and adopted not only in respect of the witness, but also of his/her spouse or the person to whom he/she is bound by an analogous emotional relationship, and of his/her ascendants, descendants, brothers or sisters.

5. **What urgent measures (e.g. immediate relocation to a secret place) can be taken in order to protect witnesses and *pentiti*?**

Where there is a serious danger as described in Section 1.2 of Implementing Act 19/1994, police protection for witnesses may be ordered at the request of the prosecuting authorities; in exceptional cases, witnesses may be given new identity papers and financial assistance to change their place of residence or work. Witnesses and experts may ask to be driven to court premises, places where they are to complete any procedural formalities or their homes in official vehicles; while on court premises, they are to be provided with a properly supervised area for their exclusive use, all without prejudice to other protection measures of a procedural nature. These measures may also be adopted once the criminal proceedings are over, should the serious danger in question continue.

6. **What institutions are involved in the protection of witnesses and *pentiti* and what is their role (e.g. law enforcement agencies, special independent agencies, prosecutor's offices, judicial authorities, etc.)? How does co-operation between the relevant institutions work in practice?**

The institutions involved in adopting the protection measures discussed are members of the security forces and corps, the prosecuting authorities and the judicial authorities. Procedural protection measures are ordered by the investigating judge or committal judge, either *ex officio* or at the request of one party; other protection measures are requested by the prosecuting authorities, who will ask for police co-operation if need be. This system and co-operation between the institutions involved work extremely well in practice.

7. **Are there any specific provisions governing the protection of witnesses and *pentiti* in relation to acts of terrorism? If so, please specify. Are there any specialised counter-terrorism institutions? If so, what is their role in the protection of witnesses and *pentiti* in relation to acts of terrorism?**

Implementing Act 19/1994 may be applied in respect of any offence, without any specific measures in relation to acts of terrorism.

8. **How does the framework governing the use of measures protecting witnesses and *pentiti* and encouraging them to co-operate with the judicial authorities guarantee respect for human rights and individual freedoms? Please indicate the procedures in place, if any, to monitor compliance with human rights standards.**

As the explanatory memorandum to Implementing Act 19/1994 states, this Act is based on the case-law of the European Court of Human Rights; Section 4 of Implementing Act 19/1994 expressly provides that protection measures, where necessary, are to be adopted "after weighing the constitutionally protected interests, conflicting fundamental rights and attendant circumstances of the witnesses and experts in relation to the criminal proceedings in question". The principle of proportionality is thereby safeguarded. The Act also provides that "the measures adopted shall be subject to appeal before the same court" and that "without prejudice to the foregoing, should any of the parties make a reasoned request in its provisional charge sheet, indictment or written defence pleadings for disclosure of the identities of proposed witnesses or experts whose statements or reports are considered relevant, the judge or court to hear the case must, in the very order declaring the relevance of the proposed evidence, state the first names and surnames of the witnesses and experts, while respecting the other guarantees secured to the latter under this Act". The Act also allows any of the parties to propose fresh evidence intended to substantiate any fact that might affect the probative value of the witnesses' testimony, thereby ensuring respect for the rights of the defence. Lastly, the adversarial principle and the principle of equality of arms are respected, since the Act provides that "the statements or reports of witnesses and experts who have been subject to protection in application of this Act during the investigation may have evidential value, for the purposes of the judgment, only if they are authenticated during the trial, in the form prescribed by the Criminal Procedure Act, by those who gave them", that is, publicly and in the presence of all the parties. The Act also states that, "should they be considered impossible to reproduce (...) they must be authenticated on the basis of a literal reading so that they can be contested by the parties".

b. Procedural measures

9. At what stage(s) and in what context is it possible for witnesses and *pentiti* to benefit from procedural measures of protection?

Under Spanish legislation, protection measures may be adopted at any stage in criminal proceedings or once the proceedings are over, insofar as the serious danger is substantiated.

10. Can witnesses and *pentiti* obtain legal assistance at this (these) stage(s)?

Legal aid is provided to anyone considered to be an accused person or a defendant, and an interpreter is appointed if the witness does not understand or speak Spanish (Sections 384 and 440 of the Criminal Procedure Act).

11. Are there alternative methods of giving evidence which allow the protection of witnesses and *pentiti* from intimidation resulting from face to face confrontation with the accused? If yes, please specify (e.g. full or partial anonymity, video-conference, disguise, exclusion of the defendant from the courtroom when the witness is giving evidence, exclusion of the media or the public from the trial, etc.) and indicate under which conditions these methods are used.

The measures established by Spanish legislation in order to ensure witnesses' privacy are as follows:

a) Procedural documents shall not contain their first name, surname, address, workplace or occupation, or any other details that might serve to identify them; a number or any other code may be used for this purpose.
b) Any method of making normal visual identification impossible shall be used during appearances to complete any procedural formalities.
c) For the purposes of summonses and services, witnesses' addresses shall be set down as the seat of the court concerned, which shall forward such documents discreetly to the addressee.

Section 2 of Implementing Act 19/1994 provides that all of these measures shall be adopted "without prejudice to adversarial action assisting the accused's defence".

12. On what grounds and on the basis of which criteria can anonymity be granted? Is there the possibility to obtain legal assistance at this stage?

The investigating judge may order anonymity, stating reasons, either *ex officio* or at the request of one party, where he/she deems it necessary in view of the degree of risk or danger; this includes the necessary measures to safeguard the identities, addresses, occupations and workplaces of witnesses and experts, if a serious risk to the person, freedom or property of those wishing to be protected by such measures is found.

13. **Are pre-trial statements of witnesses and *pentiti* and testimonies of anonymous witnesses and *pentiti* regarded as valid evidence? If yes, under which conditions?**

As far as the value of witnesses' testimonies is concerned, Section 4.5 of Implementing Act 19/94 provides that "the statements or reports of witnesses and experts who have been subject to protection in application of this Act during the investigation may have evidential value, for the purposes of the judgment, only if they are authenticated during the hearing, in the form prescribed by the Criminal Procedure Act, by those who gave them", that is, publicly and in the presence of all the parties. The Act then states that, "should they be considered impossible to reproduce (…) they must be authenticated on the basis of a literal reading so that they can be contested by the parties".

14. **Is it possible and, if so, under which conditions to use information provided by *pentiti*? How is their credibility assessed?**

The same Section of the Act provides that testimony shall be subject to the adversarial principle, without prejudice to the rights of the defence or the rights of the parties to propose other types of evidence.

15. **What opportunities are there for the exercise of the rights of the defence, including the right of the accused to challenge the witness'/*pentito*'s credibility in criminal proceedings (including at the pre-trial stage) and the respect of the "equality of arms" principle?**

The rights of the defence and the right to equality of arms are guaranteed at all stages of the proceedings; if protection measures are ordered during the investigation stage, reasons must be given; such measures are adopted, where necessary, "without prejudice to adversarial action assisting the accused's defence" (Section 2 of Implementing Act 19/1994). In addition, during the indictment stage, provision is made for the competent court to rule, stating reasons, on the need to continue, adopt or modify measures ordered "after weighing the constitutionally protected interests, conflicting fundamental rights and attendant circumstances of the witnesses and experts in relation to the criminal proceedings in question", subject to appeal before the same court, all without prejudice to what is said earlier about ensuring the adversarial principle and the rights of the defence in respect of the probative value of the statements given.

c. Non-procedural measures

16. At what stage(s) and in what context is it possible for witnesses and *pentiti* to benefit from a protection programme?

Section 3 of Act 19/1994 allows non-procedural protection measures to be ordered during the course of the proceedings or once they are over.

17. Are witnesses and *pentiti* able to obtain legal assistance at this (these) stage(s)?

Accused persons and defendants are entitled to legal aid during the proceedings, without prejudice to the right enabling every citizen to request advisory services from the bar association, particularly where an application is made for free legal aid (Section 22 of Act 1/1996, of 10 January 1996, on Free Legal Aid).

18. What is the procedure for admittance to a protection programme? Please specify, in particular, who takes the initiative, the criteria for admittance, the assessment of the relevance of a testimony and how admittance to the programme is formalised.

The basis for non-procedural protection is the existence of a "serious danger to the person, freedom or property of the individual desiring such protection, his/her spouse or the person to whom he/she is bound by an analogous emotional relationship, or his/her ascendants, descendants or brothers or sisters".

19. Please indicate the measures that can be adopted for the protection of witnesses and *pentiti* (e.g. surveillance of their residence, physical protection, protection of personal records, relocation, change of identity, subsidies, assistance with a job search, relocation of a detainee to another prison or to special units).

As specific protection measures, the law states that "new identity papers and financial assistance to change his/her place of residence or workplace may be provided". Witnesses and experts "may ask to be driven to court premises, places where any procedural formalities are to be completed or their homes in official vehicles; while on court premises, they shall be given a properly supervised area for their exclusive use" (Section 3.2 of Implementing Act 19/1994). In addition, "members of the security forces and corps, the prosecuting authorities and the judicial authorities shall endeavour to prevent photos being taken of the witnesses and experts, or their images being captured by any other means; anyone breaching this prohibition shall have their photographic, film, video or any other type of equipment confiscated. This equipment shall be returned to its owner once it has been determined that there is no trace of any shots in which the witnesses or experts appear in such a way that they may be identified" (Section 3.1).

20. At what stages in proceedings (pre-trial investigation, during the trial, after the trial) can a protection programme be granted? What is the protection programme's duration? What are the procedures for assessing the degree of danger for the witnesses/*pentiti* and their compliance with the programme obligations? Is to possible to challenge a decision to suspend, revoke or terminate a protection programme?

The measures described above may be ordered at any point in the criminal proceedings and last for as long as the danger warranting them exists; as the explanatory memorandum to the Act states, "the system put in place requires the judge or court to make a rational assessment of the degree of risk of danger (...) measures which, within the framework of the law, are subject to appeal."

d. International co-operation

21. What measures (e.g. use of modern telecommunications technology, assistance in relocating protected witnesses, exchange of information between witness protection authorities) have been adopted in the context of mutual legal assistance in order to facilitate international co-operation? How are the financial implications of international co-operation activities dealt with?

At the international level, Spain is a signatory to the European Union Convention of 29 May 2000 on Mutual Assistance in Criminal Matters between member states of the European Union.

22. Has your country entered international (bilateral or multilateral) agreements on the protection of witnesses and *pentiti*? If so, please indicate what kind of provisions they include.

-

23. How can international co-operation in the field of the protection of witnesses and *pentiti* be improved?

-

e. Statistics

24. How many people currently benefit from witness or *pentito* protection measures/programmes and for how long? How many of them are foreigners? If the measures/programmes can be extended to relatives and other close persons, please indicate how many people are included in this category (and, if possible, specify the relationship with the witness/*pentito*). Please also provide figures on the different kinds of measures (procedural and non-procedural) adopted and on the number of cases involving international co-operation.

–

f. Proposals and comments

25. Please provide any comments/proposals concerning the implementation of the terms of reference of the PC-PW and, in particular, instruments to be adopted to strengthen the protection of witnesses and *pentiti*.

–

Sweden

General comments

For the time being, Sweden has no protection programme or specific framework governing protection of witnesses and *pentiti*, whether in general or in relation to acts of terrorism. The Swedish Code of Judicial procedure (SFS 1942:740) regulates procedural measures protecting witnesses and *pentiti* in a very general way.

According to Chapter 29, Section 5 of the Swedish Penal Code, on the Determination of Punishment and Exemption from Sanction, the court shall, when determining the appropriate punishment, give reasonable consideration to whether the accused gave him/herself up.

The replies given below are therefore general and only follow the main outlines of the questionnaire. The specific questions do not really apply in Sweden's case.

In December 2001 the Swedish government assigned an investigator the task of preparing a national programme for witness/victim protection. The assignment included drawing up a proposal for a suitable organisation and administration within the police authority and others involved. The investigator was also asked to consider whether witnesses ought to receive compensation for any incurred costs. The investigator presented his results and conclusions in December 2003.

However, there is legislation in place which is intended to afford protection to persons who are subject to threat. These rules can also be applied to witnesses and *pentiti*. Here follows a short description of this legislation.

Police protection

According to the Police Act (1984:387) it is the duty of the police to prevent crime and provide the public with protection. This regulation governs the police's duty to protect a person who is exposed to a threat from someone else. One part of such protection can be to provide an alarm device and in exceptional cases, bodyguard protection. The police can also arrange relocation to a secret place and afford assistance in matters like protection of personal records and change of identity.

Protection of population registration data

Most of the information kept in the population registration database is, under the principle of public access to information, normally accessible to the general public. If it is assumed that disclosure of information about a person could lead to the persecution of that person, a secrecy classification can be entered into the database. The classification applies to all information about the person and serves as a signal, aimed at ensuring that a careful secrecy assessment is actually made before any information about the person is disclosed.

Another form of protection is for the tax authority (which keeps the population registration database) to decide, based on the provisions of the Population Registration Act (1991:481), to grant a person who has moved to a new residence, or intends to do so, the right to remain registered at the former place of residence. This can be granted for a period not exceeding 3 years. Instead of the actual (new) residence, the address of the tax authority is entered into the database as the person's postal address. The tax authority can only decide not to register the new residence if there are strong indications of a threat to the person that require more protection.

If there is found to be a particularly strong threat to a person, he/she can be granted the right to use a fictitious identity in accordance with the provisions of the Law on Fictitious Personal Identification Data (1991:483). For this to be done, it is required that other protective measures, such as secrecy classification or non-registration of new residence, are deemed to be insufficient. The competent authority for these issues is the Stockholm District Court, which makes its decision upon a request by the National Police Board. Once the court has authorised the use of fictitious data, the National Police Board decides about the identification data to be entered into the population registration database.

Contact person

According to the Social Services Act, the social services may appoint a contact person to assist individuals in the local community with personal matters. The Social Services Act also states that the local community has an obligation to help victims and their families to deal with the consequences of the crime.

Support person

In view of the strain and discomfort an injured party may suffer during a court hearing, the victim can choose to be accompanied by a support person when visiting the police and appearing in court. The support person has no judicial powers, and is chiefly intended to provide moral support. A support person is not reimbursed from public funds. The support person may attend the preliminary investigation if his/her presence causes no inconvenience.

Although the victim may request the presence of a particular support person, the court of law ultimately decides who is suitable. Representatives from the victim services, social welfare officers, contact persons appointed by the social services and relatives may act as support persons.

Counsel for the injured party

The injured party may have a legal representative in court. Such assistance is known as counsel for the injured party, "målsägandebiträde", or, in some contexts, a complainant's counsel or victim assistant. It is the most extensive form of support yet available to the injured party.

The victim is entitled to information about the rules relevant to this form of appointment.

The counsel has an unconditional right to be present during the questioning at the preliminary investigation and the hearing. His/her appointment may continue if the case is appealed. The provisions on counsel can be found in the Act on Counsel for the Injured Party 1988:609 and its amendments. In broad terms, the Act permits the court to appoint a counsel when the injured party has been subjected to sexual offences, unless this is obviously unnecessary, violent offences and other crimes punishable by a prison sentence and/or when the injured party is in a great need of assistance.

The counsel's main duty is to safeguard the general legal needs of the victim, according to the law to "act for the interests of the injured party and provide him/her with help and support." For instance, the counsel may explain the legal system, prepare the injured party for questioning and provide personal support during the procedure. In practice, the counsel's most important task is to assist the injured party in claiming for damages, and to assess and arrange the evidential situation in that respect.

Procedural matters

There are possibilities for procedural protection during the trial.

If the *pentito* is a defendant, he/she may be assisted by the defence counsel (Chapter 21, Section 3, of the Code of Judicial procedure). Under certain conditions a public defence counsel can be appointed (Chapter 21, Section 3, of the Code of Judicial procedure).

If there are grounds to believe that, in the presence of a party or any listener, a witness or a *pentito* would not tell the truth openly, through fear or any other cause, or if a party or a listener hinders the witness or the *pentito* from testifying by interrupting or otherwise, the court may order the party or listener to be excluded from the courtroom during the examination (Chapter 36, Section 18 and Chapter 37, Section 3, of the Code of Judicial procedure).

Sweden has a system whereby witnesses, under certain conditions, can testify through video-conference (Chapter 5, Section 10, of the Code of Judicial procedure). This possibility has so far been limited to a small number of courts but will be extended to all general courts.

A hearing may be held behind closed doors if secrecy applies under the Secrecy Act. The examination of anyone under the age of fifteen years, or of anyone who suffers from a mental disturbance, may be held behind closed doors (Chapter 5, Section 1, of the Code of Judicial procedure).

A witness or *pentito* cannot testify anonymously. The identity of a witness or *pentito* giving testimony must always be revealed to the defendant. According to Chapter 36, Section 10 and Chapter 37, Section 3, of the Code of Judicial procedure, a witness or *pentito* who is not a party shall state his/her full name. The uncodified principle of a party's right to access all the information held by the court in a case implies that the defendant has a right to this information.

Anonymity cannot be granted by the court.

A statement made in writing or by way of a recording by a person by reason of a pending or contemplated proceeding, or a record of a statement that, by reason of such a proceeding, a person has rendered to a prosecutor or a police authority or else outside court, may be admitted as proof if it is specifically authorised by law, if the examination of the person who made the statement cannot be held at, or outside, the main hearing or otherwise before the court, or if there are special reasons with regard to the costs or inconvenience that an examination at, or outside, the main hearing can be assumed to imply, and also to what can be assumed to be attained by such an examination, the importance of the statement, and other circumstances (Chapter 35, Section 14, of the Code of Judicial procedure).

During the trial the witness or *pentito* must give his/her testimony orally. The written statements of witnesses may not be invoked. During the witness's examination, statements previously made by the witness before a court, prosecutor, or police authority may be brought forward only when the witness's testimony during the examination departs from what previously has been stated, or when the witness declares him/herself unable or unwilling to testify (Chapter 36, Section 16, of the Code of Judicial procedure). It has recently been decided that all testimonies given in the court of first instance (District court) shall be video-recorded, unless there is a special reason to prevent it. Furthermore, in the Court of Appeal and the Supreme Court it will be possible, but not mandatory, to video-record testimonies (Chapter 6, Section 6, of the Code of Judicial procedure). The use of video-recordings will to a greater extent make it unnecessary to recall witnesses that were heard in the District court. The Court of Appeal will instead play the video-recording when deciding the case. The technology will also enable the extended use of the taking of evidence outside the main hearing.

The Code of Judicial procedure rests on two principles of importance in this regard (Chapter 35, Section 1). The first principle is that anything that may have a value as evidence may be freely submitted by the parties in a case. The second principle relates to the evaluation of the evidence by the competent courts, namely that they are entitled to evaluate the evidence at their own discretion. There are, however, certain exceptions to the rule, one of which is related to a principle established by doctrine; the principle of "the best evidence". This principle means that the piece of evidence to be used shall normally be that which guarantees the most reliable proof. The fact that written testimonies and the reading of statements made during the preliminary investigation in a criminal case are not allowed, ordinarily, shall be seen against this background (Chapter 35, Section 14).

The main feature to protect the rights of the defence with regard to information given by a witness or *pentito* is the right to put questions to them and to question their credibility. At the pre-trial stage, the suspect and/or the defence counsel are entitled to attend interviews of witnesses or *pentiti*. The suspect or his/her defence counsel may put questions to the person who is being questioned (Chapter 23, Sections 10 and 11).

At the witness's examination, the suspect shall always be afforded an opportunity to ask the witness or *pentito* questions. A testimony delivered in the absence of a party (pursuant to Chapter 36, Section 18, first paragraph, of the Code of Judicial procedure) shall be read to the extent necessary when the party is present again (Chapter 36, Section 18, second paragraph). If it is possible, however, the party shall have the possibility to view and listen to the testimony by way of transmission.

International co-operation

The Swedish law includes no specific regulations regarding international judicial co-operation specifically dealing with protection of witnesses in relation to acts of terrorism. However, according to the Swedish International Legal Assistance Act, measures such as hearing by means of tele-conference or by means of video-conference can be afforded to foreign authorities upon request. These are examples of available measures to Swedish prosecutors and judges in a Swedish criminal investigations or proceedings.

The Swedish International Legal Assistance Act is, as a general rule, applicable only in relation to judicial assistance in criminal matters, i.e. assistance for the purpose of criminal investigations or criminal proceedings. Consequently police and customs co-operation is not governed by this Act.

In 1998 a treaty between Sweden and the International Tribunal for the Prosecution of Persons Responsible for Serious Violations of International Humanitarian Law Committed in the Territory of Former Yugoslavia entered into force. The treaty includes provisions on the protection of witnesses at the Tribunal and their relatives. No other agreements specifically dealing with protection of witnesses has been entered.

All international co-operation can be improved by using the most efficient and direct channels when it comes to making contacts. Furthermore, an improved knowledge of languages is desirable.

Switzerland

a. General information

1. Please describe the framework (legal provisions and established practice) governing the use of measures protecting witnesses and pentiti.

In Switzerland, although substantive criminal law comes under the Confederation's jurisdiction, criminal procedure is still mainly a matter for the cantons. We accordingly have 26 different cantonal codes of procedure. Procedural provisions are also contained in certain federal laws: the Law on Federal Criminal Procedure (for offences under the Confederation's jurisdiction), the Law on Criminal Procedure in Court Marshal Proceedings (for offences under the Military Criminal Code) and a Law on Criminal Procedure in Administrative Matters. Switzerland thus has 29 laws on criminal procedure.

On 12 March 2000 Swiss voters approved an amendment to the Federal Constitution (Article 123), which transferred jurisdiction for criminal procedure from the cantons to the Confederation. The Federal Office of Justice is therefore now drafting a Unified Code of Criminal Procedure.

As a result, there is currently no specific federal law that deals with the protection of witnesses or *pentiti* in general. Provisions on witness protection are nonetheless to be found in the cantonal codes of procedure, the law on federal procedure, the Law on Secret Investigations (LFIS), since 1 June 2004, the Code of Military Criminal Procedure and the Law on Assistance for Victims of Offences (LAVI).

A number of cantons recently - mostly in around 2000 - adopted procedural provisions designed to guarantee the protection of certain witnesses. However, these provisions are extremely diverse in nature as regards both the persons concerned (in particular undercover agents, chance witnesses, victim-witnesses, professional witnesses and informers) and the protection measures themselves (including non-disclosure of identity, *in camera* hearings, concealment of the witness's face, protection measures during confrontation procedures, disguising of the witness's voice and presence in a separate room during the hearing). They also differ in respect of the guarantees afforded regarding defendants' rights, which must be weighed against those of the person being protected.

Rules allowing witnesses to refuse to testify, where doing so would compromise their honour or would have serious consequences for them, are very widespread and effectively guarantee the protection of witnesses but sometimes jeopardise the discovery of the truth.

Moreover, physical measures to protect witnesses and other persons (police protection) are already possible without express legislation to that end. On the other hand, Switzerland does not apply extrajudicial protection measures, such as changes of identity. It can be noted that protecting witnesses outside the courts is part of the general duties conferred on the police (protection of the public), but there is no specialist unit or any specific legislation.

The Federal Law on Secret Investigations (LFIS) and the relevant implementing regulations (OIS) came into force on 1 January 2005. A number of provisions of these two legal instruments concern specific protection measures for both undercover agents (regarded as professional witnesses) and third parties who have participated in a covert investigation. These measures include non-disclosure of identity, action by the authority in charge to guarantee the promised secrecy, changes of appearance and disguising of the person's voice, questioning in a separate room, holding of the hearing *in camera* where the person's identity cannot be kept secret by other means, and exclusion of the defendant where face-to-face confrontation would endanger the undercover agent.

Through an amendment of 19 December 2003, the Swiss parliament introduced specific provisions on witness protection into the law on military criminal procedure, which make it possible, *inter alia*, to guarantee the anonymity of witnesses and third parties providing information.[1] Furthermore, where there is a danger, protection measures (in particular police protection) may be taken before the person participates in proceedings, and even before he/she makes any formal statement. The protection measures must not end with the official closing of the proceedings. The Federal Council's message of 22 January 2003 gives full information on these aspects of witness protection.[2]

The Law on Assistance for Victims of Offences (LAVI) also provides for a number of measures aimed at protecting victims in the course of criminal proceedings, where they have been physically, mentally or sexually abused by an offender. In particular, they may request that a person of trust be present when they give evidence or supply information (Article 7, paragraph 1, of the LAVI), ask not to be brought face-to-face with the defendant (Article 5, paragraph 4, of the LAVI) or benefit from other protection measures (hearing *in camera*, Article 5, paragraph 3, of the LAVI). Specific rules apply to minors (Article 10a-10d of the LAVI). These provisions of the LAVI solely concern witnesses who are also victims within the meaning of Article 2, paragraphs 1 and 2, of the law.

---

[1] Articles 98a et seq. of the *Procédure Pénale Militaire* (PPM), RS 322.1, http://www.bk.admin.ch/ch/f/rs/3/322.1.fr.pdf.

[2] See *Feuille fédérale* (FF) 2003 693, http://www.bk.admin.ch/ch/f/ff/2003/693.pdf.

The Swiss preliminary draft Unified Code of Criminal Procedure (AP-CPP) largely reiterates the regulations in force at cantonal and federal level and the relevant case-law.

As regards *pentiti*, unlike in Italy there is no legislation proper which expressly provides that an offender who has actively co-operated with the authorities conducting a criminal investigation may be exempted from punishment or discharged. It would indeed be contrary to the fundamental principles governing our system of law (primarily the principles of the rule of law and of equal treatment) if some defendants were treated more favourably than others. Under our system there are accordingly no "crown witnesses", and defendants willing to testify in criminal proceedings against a third party are regarded as mere witnesses, or persons providing information. They receive no favours or advance promises regarding the outcome of their own trial.

However, under certain provisions of the Swiss Criminal Code a degree of repentance by a person charged with an offence can be taken into consideration. Article 260ter, paragraph 2, of the Criminal Code (criminal organisations) provides, for instance, that "the court may freely mitigate the penalty (Article 66) imposed on a person who has attempted to prevent the continuation of the organisation's criminal activities."

Article 66 of the Criminal Code stipulates "where the law provides for free mitigation of penalties, the court shall not be bound by either the nature of the penalty laid down for the offence or the minimum sentence required."

Again on the subject of Article 260ter of the Criminal Code, it can be noted that this Article permits the courts to pronounce a substantially mitigated sentence even where the defendant has been a member of a criminal organisation or has aided and abetted that organisation's activities. Consideration will be given not only to the defendant's efforts to foil the organisation's further criminal activities, but also to all the relevant information he/she has given the prosecuting authorities in the course of the proceedings. In addition, there is no requirement that the authorities must succeed in dismantling the organisation, since the legislation refers to the efforts and resolve of the person concerned, not to the absolute need for a result.

Apart from in these circumstances, Article 64 of the Criminal Code (mitigating circumstances) allows the courts to mitigate a penalty where the defendant's behaviour shows sincere repentance.

2. **Please describe the framework (legal provisions and established practice) governing the use of measures encouraging witnesses and *pentiti* to co-operate with the justice system.**

In the light of the above, the sole considerations are the person's willingness to co-operate and his/her sincere repentance. The courts may currently take a number of protection measures (questioning on separate premises, disguising of the witness's voice, holding of the session *in camera*, etc.), but these apply only during trial proceedings or questioning by an investigating judge.

It should also be pointed out that there is no common practice, since each canton may adopt its own specific rules in such matters.

3. **Can measures/benefits encouraging the co-operation of witnesses and *pentiti* be used in combination with protection measures (arrangements concerning trial proceedings, sentencing conditions, special penitentiary regimes, etc.)? If so, please specify and indicate under which conditions they are applied.**

Apart from protection measures and the prospect of being given a mitigated sentence, there are no other benefits for *pentiti*, such as a special penitentiary regime.

4. **For what kind of crime and under what circumstances can witness and *pentito* protection be applied? Can the measures be extended to relatives or other persons close to the witness/*pentito*?**

Witness protection measures usually apply whatever the nature of the offence, since all that is necessary is for there to be a serious threat.

As regards possible measures concerning *pentiti*, as mentioned above (see the reply to question 1), Article 260ter, paragraph 2, of the Criminal Code (criminal organisations) makes express provision for free mitigation of penalties; otherwise, Article 64 (mitigating circumstances) allows the courts to mitigate a sentence in all cases where the guilty party has shown sincere repentance through his/her behaviour.

The procedural provisions on protection apply solely to persons having a role in proceedings, such as witnesses, victims, experts and so on.

Under military criminal procedure a general provision (Article 98a of the Code of Military Criminal Procedure) applies to all participants in proceedings, such as witnesses, third parties required to supply information, defendants, experts, interpreters or translators, in respect of whom all the necessary protection measures can be taken.

More specific protection measures which interfere with the defendant's rights, such as anonymity guarantees, solely concern witnesses and third parties required to supply information. Here, the proceedings must concern an offence punishable by more than five years' imprisonment and there must be a "serious risk of grave damage to one of the legally protected assets" of the witness or third party concerned (see Articles 98b to 98d of the Code of Military Criminal Procedure).

5. **What urgent measures (e.g. immediate relocation to a secret place) can be taken in order to protect witnesses and *pentiti*?**

This is part of the police's general role (protection of persons at risk). Any other measures must be decided upon on a case-by-case basis, regard being had to the circumstances. For example, it is possible for an accomplice co-operating with the judicial authorities to be transferred, for his/her own safety, to a different prison from that where the co-perpetrators are being detained.

6. **What institutions are involved in the protection of witnesses and *pentiti* and what is their role (e.g. law enforcement agencies, special independent agencies, prosecutor's offices, judicial authorities, etc.)? How does co-operation between the relevant institutions work in practice?**

The institutions concerned are those responsible for security (the police) and those dealing with the judicial aspects of proceedings (investigating judges, trial courts).

Under military criminal procedure, the authority competent for granting a guarantee of anonymity is the investigating judge or the President of the court hearing the case. The approval of the President of the Military Court of Cassation (TMC - Tribunal Militaire de Cassation) must be sought within thirty days (Article 98c of the Code of Military Criminal Procedure).

7. **Are there any specific provisions governing the protection of witnesses and *pentiti* in relation to acts of terrorism? If so, please specify. Are there any specialised counter-terrorism institutions? If so, what is their role in the protection of witnesses and *pentiti* in relation to acts of terrorism?**

The Federal Police Office (fedpol) includes anti-terrorism units, but these units and their staff have no possibilities or powers beyond those already mentioned above with regard to the protection of witnesses.

8. **How does the framework governing the use of measures protecting witnesses and *pentiti* and encouraging them to co-operate with the judicial authorities guarantee respect for human rights and individual freedoms? Please indicate the procedures in place, if any, to monitor compliance with human rights standards.**

In the light of past experience and given the relative lack of legislation on these matters, this problem is dealt with by means of the rules of procedure applicable to the usual judicial channels, and the proportionality principle must be upheld. This aspect is being taken into account in the drafting work on the future legislation referred to above.

Under military criminal procedure, specific measures, such as the guarantee of anonymity, are subject to review by the TMC, which weighs the interests of the defendant, the proceedings and the witnesses.

b. Procedural measures

9. **At what stage(s) and in what context is it possible for witnesses and *pentiti* to benefit from procedural measures of protection?**

Although each canton's rules of procedure are different, generally speaking protection measures are mainly taken where there is a serious threat to life, a risk of physical harm or other serious implications. As regards specific measures for the protection of witnesses, see the reply to question 1.

10. **Can witnesses and *pentiti* obtain legal assistance at this (these) stage(s)?**

There are no restrictions on legal assistance for witnesses, but as a general rule witnesses are not represented by counsel during proceedings. They appear alone before the trial court or the investigating judge. They are naturally free to seek legal advice before and after a hearing.

Pentiti who are also defendants in proceedings benefit from legal assistance, which may be compulsory, depending on the seriousness of the offence. A legal aid system allows defendants without the necessary resources to have counsel appointed *ex officio*.

Under Article 3 of the LAVI, counselling centres may provide victims with legal assistance.

The AP-CPP expressly provides that persons in need of protection may be accompanied by counsel when attending hearings in which they are required to participate. In some exceptional cases counsel may be appointed for them free of charge.

11. Are there alternative methods of giving evidence which allow the protection of witnesses and *pentiti* from intimidation resulting from face-to-face confrontation with the accused? If yes, please specify (e.g. full or partial anonymity, video-conference, disguise, exclusion of the defendant from the courtroom when the witness is giving evidence, exclusion of the media or the public from the trial, etc.) and indicate under which conditions these methods are used.

The methods listed in the question exist, but their use is currently left to the discretion of the President of the court or the investigating judge, and the situation differs from one canton to another. At all events the constitutional rights of the defendant must be taken into consideration, as must the procedural guarantees set out in the European Convention on Human Rights.

Rules allowing witnesses to refuse to testify where doing so would have serious consequences for them are very widespread and effectively guarantee the protection of witnesses but sometimes jeopardise discovery of the truth. The Federal Court has also given a number of leading decisions on the conditions in which anonymous testimonies are admissible.

The Code of Military Criminal Procedure makes express provision for appropriate restrictions of the defendant's procedural rights, notably the holding of hearings in the parties' absence or *in camera*, performance of identification procedures outside the parties' presence, guarantees of anonymity, disguising of a person's appearance or voice or concealment of the person to be protected, reading out of statements made to the prosecuting authorities rather than direct questioning of the person concerned at the hearing or questioning in writing rather than orally (Article 98d of the Code of Military Criminal Procedure).

The AP-CPP includes all of these measures. Where they do not suffice to guarantee the protection of the person concerned, he/she may be released from the obligation of testifying (Article 163).

12. On what grounds and on the basis of which criteria can anonymity be granted? Is there the possibility to obtain legal assistance at this stage?

The Federal Court has given a number of rulings on the admissibility of anonymous testimonies. It has, *inter alia,* accepted that undercover police officers may testify by means ensuring that they cannot be seen, nor their voices recognized, after their identity has been duly verified (judgment ATF 118 Ia 331 ground 2c).

The AP-CPP provides that public prosecutors and the courts may take measures to guarantee the anonymity of persons in need of protection, where the circumstances so require (Article 162). Granting of anonymity must be approved by a review body, whose decision is final. Where approval is not requested within 30 days or is refused, the evidence obtained must be removed from the case-file. Anonymity is permissible only where no other protection measure can be envisaged and where justified by the importance of what is at stake and the role to be played by the protected person.

The AP-CPP does not confine anonymity guarantees to proceedings concerning serious offences.

13. Are pre-trial statements of witnesses and *pentiti* and testimonies of anonymous witnesses and *pentiti* regarded as valid evidence? If yes, under which conditions?

Yes. If pre-trial statements by witnesses were recorded, confirmed and signed in the presence of an investigating judge or public prosecutor they are admissible where cantonal legislation so provides or where appropriate measures exist. If evidence is given anonymously the defence must have the possibility of cross-examining the witness under conditions guaranteeing his/her protection, with the court's approval (see above).

14. Is it possible and, if so, under which conditions to use information provided by *pentiti*? How is their credibility assessed?

As mentioned above, in Switzerland *pentiti* have no special status in proceedings (apart from what is provided for in Article 260ter of the Criminal Code - see the reply to question 1). If they are themselves defendants in a court case, they are treated as such. Failing that, they may be heard as witnesses and benefit from the protection rules set out above.

15. What opportunities are there for the exercise of the rights of the defence, including the right of the accused to challenge the witness'/*pentito*'s credibility in criminal proceedings (including at the pre-trial stage) and the respect of the "equality of arms" principle?

It goes without saying that, for example, evidence adduced by hearing witnesses - or persons providing information - anonymously or outside the presence of the parties is admissible only if the parties, in particular the defendant and his/her counsel, have an opportunity to assert their rights. For instance, the defence must at all events be allowed to ask additional questions.

The AP-CPP provides that the parties' right to be heard must be respected before granting a protection measure (Article 160, paragraph 3). A decision to guarantee anonymity must also be approved by the higher authority.

Lastly, in each particular case it is for the authorities concerned to strike a balance between the defendant's interests and those of the person in need of protection. The proportionality principle must also be upheld.

c. *Non-procedural measures*

16. At what stage(s) and in what context is it possible for witnesses and *pentiti* to benefit from a protection programme?

Since there is no legislation on witness protection outside judicial proceedings, in practice the criteria applied are the same as for procedural measures, that is to say where there is an immediate, serious threat, where the witness's presence is essential to the conduct of the proceedings and where the offence qualifies as a serious one. However, certain cantons have established their own witness protection programmes.

17. Are witnesses and *pentiti* able to obtain legal assistance at this (these) stage(s)?

Yes, and some cantons also grant assistance in connection with the activities of so-called professional witnesses (police officers). As part of the immediate and more long-term assistance available under the federal Law on Assistance for Victims of Offences (Article 3 of the LAVI), witnesses who are also victims within the meaning of Article 2 of the LAVI may be granted legal aid.

18. What is the procedure for admittance to a protection programme? Please specify, in particular, who takes the initiative, the criteria for admittance, the assessment of the relevance of a testimony and how admittance to the programme is formalised.

Since there is no law on witness protection, there is also no real protection programme. Decisions are taken on a case-by-case basis according to the circumstances.

19. Please indicate the measures that can be adopted for the protection of witnesses and *pentiti* (e.g. surveillance of their residence, physical protection, protection of personal records, relocation, change of identity, subsidies, assistance with a job search, relocation of a detainee to another prison or to special units).

The range of measures taken by the police is aimed at guaranteeing the witness's personal physical and mental wellbeing, essentially during the trial proceedings. In practice, assistance by specialist psychological counsellors is also fairly frequent.

20. At what stages in proceedings (pre-trial investigation, during the trial, after the trial) can a protection programme be granted? What is the protection programme's duration? What are the procedures for assessing the degree of danger for witnesses/*pentiti* and their compliance with the programme obligations? Is it possible to challenge a decision to suspend, revoke or terminate a protection programme?

There is no centralised witness protection programme. Each case is dealt with individually, and the measures taken depend on the situation. The measures are primarily governed by three considerations: "the existence of a serious, immediate threat", "the importance of the case being heard" and "the importance of the witness's testimony."

As to duration, it is the degree of danger that is taken into account and the witness's own behaviour (co-operation, compliance with instructions, personal discretion, etc.).

d. International co-operation

21. What measures (e.g. use of modern telecommunications technology, assistance in relocating protected witnesses, exchange of information between witness protection authorities) have been adopted in the context of mutual legal assistance in order to facilitate international co-operation? How are the financial implications of international co-operation activities dealt with?

a)   At an international level there are no specific instruments on judicial co-operation in criminal matters which solely concern acts of terrorism. The European Convention on Extradition of 13 December 1957[3] and the protocols thereto and the European Convention on Mutual Assistance in Criminal Matters of 20 April 1959[4] and its protocols apply to all proceedings concerning offences under the general law. Among the Council of Europe's instruments, mention should be made of the Second Additional Protocol of 8 November 2001 to the European Convention on Mutual Assistance in Criminal Matters.[5]

-     This protocol includes an Article 23 on protection of witnesses, which allows a state to request special protection measures for a person subject to - or at risk of - intimidation in connection with criminal proceedings. It calls on the states concerned to agree on measures capable of

---

[3] European Convention on Extradition of 13 December 1957, ETS No. 024, http://conventions.coe.int.

[4] European Convention on Mutual Assistance in Criminal Matters of 20 April 1959, ETS No. 030, http://conventions.coe.int.

[5] Second Additional Protocol to the European Convention on Mutual Assistance in Criminal Matters of 8 November 2001, ETS No. 182, http://conventions.coe.int.

guaranteeing the threatened individual's safety. The term "witness" may also encompass experts and interpreters.

- The protocol also provides for the hearing of witnesses and experts by video-conference (Article 9). Use of this new method of conducting hearings is subject to the condition that hearing by video-conference is not contrary to fundamental principles of the requested state's law and that essential procedural rights are upheld. The Article concerns cases where a person's appearance at a hearing held in another state is not desirable or is impossible. Video-conferences can therefore help to guarantee improved protection of witnesses and victims.

- The protocol allows use of modern means of telecommunication (e.g. fax or e-mail) for the transmission of requests for mutual assistance and other communications provided that the requesting authority is capable of producing at any time the original of the request or document transmitted and documentary proof of its transmission (Article 4).

- The protocol also contains provisions on cross-border observations, controlled delivery and covert investigations (Articles 17 to 19).

In addition mention can be made of the Council of Europe Convention on Cybercrime of 23 November 2001,[6] which also makes it possible to use modern means of telecommunication and other modern forms of judicial co-operation in criminal matters allowing states to take very rapid, effective action in this area (Articles 23 et seq.).

In this connection, reference should also be made to the instruments governing co-operation with international courts, namely

- the Rome Statute of the International Criminal Court of 17 July 1998, which also contains provisions on witness protection (Article 68);

- the statutes of the *ad hoc* International Criminal Tribunals dealing with the war crimes perpetrated in former Yugoslavia and Rwanda,[7] which contain articles on witness protection (Articles 22 and 21 respectively).

b) How are the financial implications of international co-operation activities dealt with?

Judicial assistance in criminal matters is in principle free of charge. However the European Convention on Mutual Assistance in Criminal Matters and its second protocol provide for departures from this rule. Under Article 20 of the

---

[6] Convention on Cybercrime of 23 November 2001, ETS No. 185, http://conventions.coe.int.

[7] United Nations Security Council Resolutions 827 (1993) and 955 (1994), http://www.un.org.

Convention and Article 5 of the Protocol (which replaces Article 20 of the Convention), the requested state may ask the requesting state to refund costs incurred for the attendance of experts and costs of a substantial or extraordinary nature.[8] This provision could apply, for example, where a state requests protection measures for a witness or to costs incurred for a hearing by video-conference.[9] In the latter case, the requesting state must also bear all the costs, unless the two states agree otherwise.

22. Has your country entered into international (bilateral or multilateral) agreements on the protection of witnesses and *pentiti*? If so, please indicate what kind of provisions they include.

To date the Swiss Federal Council has concluded one agreement with the International Criminal Tribunal for Former Yugoslavia on the relocation of witnesses. Under this agreement Switzerland is committed to take in a number of relocated witnesses and their families each year. It contains clauses defining the concepts of relocation, witness, persons dependent on the witness and relocated person(s).

The agreement also determines the procedure for relocating witnesses and for the transfer of responsibility for them from the ICTFY to the Swiss authorities. In particular, the international tribunal is required to complete a form requesting the Swiss authorities to take in a witness and his/her family. On the basis of that form and the information set out in it, the Swiss authorities competent in matters of asylum can freely decide how to deal with the matter on an individual basis and in accordance with the Federal Law on Asylum.

The agreement provides that persons charged with offences before the tribunal, persons who have been convicted of an offence in Switzerland or persons prohibited from entering Swiss territory shall be excluded from the relocation procedure. In addition to these grounds for exclusion, the Swiss authorities apply their own criteria to assess the risks posed in specific cases, which may lead them to refuse a request by the international tribunal where they are unable to guarantee relocation of a witness without excessive risks for the person concerned.

Under the agreement Switzerland undertakes to provide the persons concerned with protection equivalent to that enjoyed by Swiss nationals. Relocated persons are also guaranteed the same welfare rights.

The agreement also deals with the status of a relocated witness. Where the Swiss authorities accept the tribunal's relocation request, the witness and his/her family, as defined in the agreement, are granted asylum under the relevant procedure laid down in the Federal Law on Asylum. In addition the

---

[8] Article 5, paragraph 1, of the Protocol.
[9] Article 5, paragraph 2, of the Protocol.

witness and his/her family members are issued with residence permits and, after five years, establishment permits, where they fulfil the conditions. The tribunal reviews the situation of the witness and any family members after six months, and then on an annual basis, in order to determine whether relocation must be continued. It informs the Swiss authorities of the outcome of its review, and they then decide, on that basis, whether to prolong or revoke the asylum measure.

The revocation procedure is also provided for in the agreement. It is consistent with the relevant provisions of the law on asylum. However, the Swiss authorities cannot return a relocated person, or any family members, to former Yugoslavia without the tribunal's approval.

Should Switzerland consider that relocation is no longer necessary and envisage sending away the person concerned, the tribunal has ninety days in which to find another host state for relocation purposes. After this time-limit the relevant rules of Swiss law are applied to the person, who can be sent to a third state. If relocation is no longer necessary, Switzerland can revoke the asylum measure. Decisions on withdrawal or extension of residence permits are taken separately from asylum revocation decisions. The same applies in the case of the agreement.

Switzerland bears the cost of relocation in Switzerland. As refugees, the persons concerned are entitled to the benefits provided for in the Federal Law on Asylum, which stipulates that these costs shall be covered. The tribunal itself bears the cost of travel between Switzerland and The Hague and of accommodation and subsistence in The Hague when the persons concerned are called to testify. The agreement accordingly does not entail any additional expense for Switzerland.

The agreement has been in force since 22 November 2003.

23. How can international co-operation in the field of the protection of witnesses and *pentiti* be improved?

The Second Additional Protocol to the European Convention on Mutual Assistance in Criminal Matters is aimed at improving co-operation between States Parties by supplementing and updating existing regulations in the field of judicial assistance in criminal matters. As compared with the Convention of 1959, the Protocol contains innovations allowing swift, efficient co-operation between states. Along with the European Union's Convention on Mutual Assistance in Criminal Matters, this new instrument of the Council of Europe constitutes a modern basis for international co-operation in Europe.

It is important that States Parties to the Convention of 1959 accede as soon as possible to the Protocol, so that the innovations it makes can become effective in practice. Once it is in force, the Protocol will enable States Parties to intensify their efforts to combat crime, and in particular terrorism, at an international level. As a result of its provisions expediting international judicial co-operation in criminal matters, the Council of Europe Convention on Cybercrime also allows progress to be made.

e. *Statistics*

24. How many people currently benefit from witness or *pentito* protection measures /programmes and for how long? How many of them are foreigners? If the measures/programmes can be extended to relatives and other close persons, please indicate how many people are included in this category (and, if possible, specify the relationship with the witness/*pentito*). Please also provide figures on the different kinds of measures (procedural and non-procedural) adopted and on the number of cases involving international co-operation.

Unfortunately we have no statistics concerning witnesses owing, in particular, to the disparity and recent nature of the few pieces of legislation in force in the cantons and also to the fact that a unified procedural law - including provisions in this field - is currently being drawn up.

f. *Proposals and comments*

25. Please provide any comments/proposals concerning the implementation of the terms of reference of the PC-PW and, in particular, instruments to be adopted to strengthen the protection of witnesses and *pentiti*.

In conclusion, it can be pointed out that Switzerland is aware of the issues raised by the implementation of witness protection measures, which is why this matter is dealt with a length in the AP-CPP. However, as mentioned above, there are no plans at this stage to introduce genuine extrajudicial protection programmes, which, in a small country like Switzerland, would pose practical difficulties.

It must nonetheless be pointed out that the AP-CPP gives the cantons and the Confederation discretion to go beyond the measures proposed (Article 165).

As regards *pentiti* or crown witnesses, the AP-CPP does not introduce any specific protection measures, since Switzerland considers this would be too great an infringement of fundamental rights.

It can also be added that, although this falls outside the scope of anti-terrorism measures, consideration is being given to legislation making it possible for victims of trafficking in human beings to no longer be treated as offenders and to be granted a residence permit under certain conditions, at least in order to allow them to testify.

"The former Yugoslav Republic of Macedonia"

a. General information

1. Please describe the framework (legal provisions and established practice) governing the use of measures protecting witnesses and *pentiti*.

The protection of witnesses and collaborators of justice is regulated by the Law on Criminal Procedure and the Law on Witness Protection.[1] The Law on Criminal Procedure encompasses the procedural measures while the Law on Witness Protection defines non-procedural measures.

The Law on Criminal Procedure[2] (Chapter XX, Articles 293-294) provides the basis for non-procedural protection (Article 294) and also defines methods for special examining witnesses (Article 293). Namely, "the public prosecutor, or the investigative judge or the President of the Council during the proceedings shall undertake measures and activities to secure the effective protection of witnesses, collaborators of justice and victims appearing as witnesses in the proceedings, at any time they are intimidated, threatened with revenge or there is a threat to their lives or physical integrity or there is a need for them to be protected. The protection of the above-mentioned persons is ensured by adapting the way in which they are questioned or participate in the proceedings. In such cases, the witness will only be questioned in the presence of the public prosecutor and the investigative judge or the President of the Council, in a place where the protection of his/her identity can be guaranteed, except in cases where, with the consent of the witness, the Council decides to hold the hearing in a different way through the court or to use technical equipment and other appropriate means of communication. A transcript of the minutes with the witness's statement, without the witness's signature, shall be delivered to the accused and his/her lawyer, who may put questions to the witness via the court."

Apart from the above-mentioned protection measures, Article 294 of the Law on Criminal Procedure provides the framework for the implementation of non-procedural measures. "The implementation of non-procedural measures is carried out through a Witness Protection (hereinafter Programme).

---

[1] The Law on Witness Protection was adopted by Parliament at the Session held on 5 May 2005 and entered into force on 1 January 2006. In this period secondary legislation was enacted and its bodies were established, namely the Witness Protection Council, which has already had its first constitutive session, and the Department for Witness Protection within the Ministry of the Interior.

[2] Novelties in this law regarding witness protection were introduced in November 2004 with the adoption of the Amendments to the Law on Criminal Procedure.

Programme. Requests for inclusion in the Programme may be submitted to the State Public Prosecutor by the competent public prosecutor, the investigative judge or the President of the Council. If there are grounds for inclusion in the Programme, the State Public Prosecutor will submit a proposal to the competent state body (the Witness Protection Council) which makes a decision on inclusion in the Programme. The Law on Witness Protection determines the composition and the responsibilities of the Witness Protection Council, as well as the protection measures and the manner of their implementation."

The Law on Witness Protection regulates the procedure and conditions for providing protection and assistance to witnesses, defines the protection measures and establishes the Witness Protection Council and the Department for Witness Protection within the Ministry of the Interior (hereinafter Department for Witness Protection). The provisions of this Law are also applied to collaborators of justice and to victims appearing as witnesses, as well as to persons close to witnesses, collaborators of justice and victims appearing as witnesses.

2. **Please describe the framework (legal provisions and established practice) governing the use of measures encouraging witnesses and *pentiti* to co-operate with justice.**

According to Article 156 of the Law on Criminal Procedure, the public prosecutor is not obliged to undertake criminal prosecution, i.e. can abandon prosecution, if the suspect is a member of an organised group, gang or other criminal association and voluntarily co-operates before or after disclosure or during the criminal proceedings and if his/her co-operation and statement is important for the disclosure of a criminal act and its perpetrator.

3. **Can measures/benefits encouraging the co-operation of witnesses and *pentiti* be used in combination with protection measures (arrangements concerning trial proceedings, sentencing conditions, special penitentiary regimes, etc.)? If so, please specify and indicate under which conditions they are applied.**

The legal framework of "the former Yugoslav Republic of Macedonia" pays special attention to the specific benefits that can be given to witnesses and especially to collaborators of justice who are serving prison sentences. For that purpose, the Director of the Directorate of Prison Administration is *ex officio* a member of the Witness Protection Council.

Article 38 of the Law on Witness Protection provides collaborators of justice involved in the Programme (with whom the Department has concluded an Agreement, and who are serving prison sentences) with special privileges and conditions in prison, in accordance with the Law. In the part of the Law that regulates the implementation of measures, it is prescribed that if the recommended protection measure for a collaborator of justice serving a prison sentence in "the former Yugoslav Republic of Macedonia" is relocation, he/she can be transferred to another country to serve his/her prison sentence, in accordance with a ratified international agreement.

Privileges, special penitentiary regimes, etc. are also the subject of various relevant laws. Therefore, in order to have consistent legislation on this matter "the former Yugoslav Republic of Macedonia" has initiated the procedure to introduce the above-mentioned issues into the Law on Execution of Sanctions. A working group has been established within the Ministry of Justice that will draft the new Law on Execution of Sanctions, which will comprise provisions on sentencing conditions, special penitentiary regimes, etc. for collaborators of justice who are serving prison sentences.

4. For which kind of crime and under which circumstances can witness and *pentito* protection be applied? Can the measures be extended to the relatives or other persons close to the witness/*pentito*?

Article 3 of the Law on Witness Protection regulates the circumstances under which the Law may be applied. Namely, this Law is applied if it would be extremely difficult or impossible to prove a criminal act without a statement from a person who, due to the risk of being exposed to intimidation and threats of revenge or danger to his/her life, health, freedom, physical integrity or property, does not agree to give statement as a witness on the following crimes:

- crimes against the state;
- crimes against humanity and international law;
- organised crime for which the Criminal Code stipulates a sentence of at least 4 years' imprisonment.

5. What urgent measures (e.g. immediate relocation to a secret place) can be taken in order to protect witnesses and *pentiti*?

The Law on Witness Protection defines urgent measures as well as procedures for their implementation. According to the Law, the following urgent measures can be used:

- keeping the identity secret;
- providing personal protection; and
- relocation.

Procedure for the implementation of urgent measures:

If the Public Prosecutor of "the former Yugoslav Republic of Macedonia" considers that the life, health, freedom, physical integrity or property of the witness, collaborator of justice or victim appearing as a witness, and of their close persons is exposed to a serious danger that cannot be removed with the normal police protection measures, he/she will simultaneously propose the persons admittance to the Programme and notify the Department of the need for the application of urgent measures. On receipt of the above-mentioned notification and within a period of 24 hours, the Department shall enact a decision on the implementation of measures and shall implement them, and shall notify the Council and the Public Prosecutor of "the former Yugoslav Republic of Macedonia" in order to do so. Before undertaking urgent measures, the Head of the Department shall obtain the written consent of the person in respect of whom the urgent measures are to be applied. The urgent measures last until the Council has enacted a decision on the admittance of the person to the Programme, or at most three months from the date of their implementation.

After the decision on the implementation of urgent measures has been taken and the type of measures has been defined, the Head of the Department will ask the person to whom the urgent measures are to be applied to undergo a medical examination and to fill out a questionnaire (personal data, property, obligations towards third parties and other information).[3]

6. **Which institutions are involved in the protection of witnesses and** *pentiti* **and what is their role (e.g. law enforcement agencies, special independent agencies, prosecutor's offices, judicial authorities, etc)? How does co-operation between the relevant institutions work in practice?**

The two key institutions in the witness protection process are the Witness Protection Council and the Department for Witness Protection. The Council has the main role in the procedure for inclusion in the Programme, while the Department is responsible for the implementation of protection measures. Besides these two institutions, there are numerous actors which are also involved in witness protection (judges, public prosecutors, prison administration, social institutions, etc.).

The Witness Protection Council consists of five members: a representative of the Supreme Court of "the former Yugoslav Republic of Macedonia" from the row of judges; a representative of the Public Prosecutor's Office of "the former Yugoslav Republic of Macedonia" from among the deputy public prosecutors; the Director of the Directorate for Executing Sanctions at the Ministry of Justice; a representative of the Ministry of the Interior; and the Head of the Department for Witness Protection. All of the above-mentioned members have deputies who are representatives of the same bodies as the members they are replacing. The members of the Council and their deputies are appointed and dismissed by the official in charge of the body they represent. The members of the Council, with the exception of the Head of

---

[3] The form and the content of the questionnaire are prescribed by the Minister of the Interior.

the Department and the Director of the Directorate for Executing Sanctions and their deputies, are appointed for a term of five years with the right to be re-elected. The President of the Council and his/her deputy are representatives of the Supreme Court of the "the former Yugoslav Republic of Macedonia". The administrative and technical work of the Council is carried out by the Department.

The Council is authorised to:

- make a decision on the inclusion of a person in the Programme;
- make a decision on the removal of a person from the Programme; and
- make a decision on the application of a "change of identity" as a protection measure.

Article 12 regulates the work of the Department for Witness Protection:

- to involve the persons in Article 2 paragraph 1, lines 1, 2, 3 and 4 of this Law in the Programme, upon a Decision made by the Council;
- to decide on protection measures, except "change of identity" as a measure;
- to implement protection measures;
- to give legal aid to the persons in Article 2, paragraph 1, lines 1, 2, 3 and 4 of this Law;
- to implement the Programme;
- to make an agreement on protection with the person involved in the Programme;
- to establish and record the data of protected persons;
- to manage the financial resources allocated for the implementation of the Programme;
- to co-operate with the appropriate services on witness protection in other countries;
- to organise the continuous education and training of the persons employed in the Department;
- to keep the original documents on the identity of the persons from Article 2, paragraph 1, items 1, 2, 3 and 4 of this Law;
- to draft operative guidelines and instructions on the implementation of protection measures.

7. Are there any specific provisions governing the protection of witnesses and *pentiti* in relation to acts of terrorism? If so, please specify. Are there any specialised counter-terrorism institutions? If so, what is their role in the protection of witnesses and *pentiti* in relation to acts of terrorism?

Among other criminal offences, the Law on Witness Protection is applied in the field of organised crime, which also includes all forms of terrorist acts.

Pursuant to the current laws, the following bodies are competent in the fight against terrorism in "the former Yugoslav Republic of Macedonia":

- Public Prosecutor's Office of "the former Yugoslav Republic of Macedonia", established as a state body that prosecutes perpetrators of crimes, including terrorism and crimes related to terrorism (Law on Public Prosecutor's Office, Official Gazette of "the former Yugoslav Republic of Macedonia" No. 38/04);
- Intelligence Agency (Law on Intelligence Agency, Official Gazette of "the former Yugoslav Republic of Macedonia" No. 19/95);
- Ministry of the Interior (Official Gazette of "the former Yugoslav Republic of Macedonia" Nos. 19/95, 55/97, 38/02, 33/03 and 19/04) through:
    - Directorate for Security and Counter-intelligence (Article 13 of the Law on Internal Affairs and the Rulebook on the Operation of the Directorate, Official Gazette of "the former Yugoslav Republic of Macedonia" No. 48/98), established as a body within the Ministry of the Interior;
    - Section on Anti-terrorism; and
    - Special Forces (Special Tasks Unit and Rapid Deployment Unit), which are specially trained and responsible for acting in crisis situations, such as hostage situations, airplane hijacking, etc., as well as suppressing direct resistance.
- Ministry of Defence:
    - Section on Security and Intelligence; and
    - Directorate on the Prevention of Money Laundering, which represents the administrative model of a financial intelligence unit, and acts as a mediator between the law-enforcement bodies and the private sector in preventing the financing of terrorism (Law on the Prevention of Laundering Money and other Proceeds of Crime, Official Gazette of "the former Yugoslav Republic of Macedonia" No. 46/04).

8. How does the framework governing the use of measures protecting witnesses and *pentiti* and encouraging them to co-operate with justice guarantee respect for human rights and individual freedoms? Please indicate the procedures in place, if any, to monitor compliance with human rights standards.

For a person to be included in the Programme, the Law on Witness Protection requires the written consent of the person. For the inclusion of a minor in the Programme, the written consent of his/her parents, legal representative or guardian is required. Furthermore, a person deprived of his/her legal capacity may only be admitted into the Programme with the written consent of his/her legal representative or guardian.

In Article 25, Chapter V, of the Law, the obligations of the Department towards the protected person are prescribed. These obligations are also elements in the Memorandum of Understanding. There are two main obligations:

- that during the whole Programme, legal, psychological and any other necessary help will be provided to the protected person;
- that the person will be economically and socially assisted until his/her independence. This support cannot be greater than the amount necessary to cover the living expenses for the protected person to integrate him/herself into his/her new surroundings.

b. *Procedural measures*

9. At which stage(s), and in which context, is it possible for witnesses and *pentiti* to benefit from procedural measures of protection?

According to the normative framework of "the former Yugoslav Republic of Macedonia", procedural measures may be used in the pre-trial and trial procedure.

It is possible for a witness to refuse to give a statement, if there is a probability that by giving a statement or answering certain questions, he/she will expose him/herself or another person close to him/her to a serious threat of danger to his/her life, health or physical integrity. Where a witness refuses to give a statement for these reasons and the public prosecutor, investigative judge or presiding judge finds that his/her refusal is justified, he/she will stop the questioning and will take appropriate actions to protect the witness within 24 hours.

10. Is there the possibility for witnesses and *pentiti* to obtain legal assistance at this (these) stage(s)?

The right to legal assistance is regulated in Chapter VI of the Law on Criminal Procedure. Article 63 provides everyone with the right to counsel at the pre-trial and trial stage. Furthermore, before the initial questioning, the person under suspicion in the pre-trial procedure, i.e. the accused, must be instructed that he/she has the right to have counsel of his/her own choice and that counsel may attend his/her questioning. The following persons may act as counsel for the accused: his/her legal representative, marital i.e. common-law spouse, blood relatives of the first degree, adoptive parents, adopted children, siblings.

The Law prescribes that only a lawyer (attorney at law) can be counsel for the defence.

11. Are there alternative methods of giving evidence which allow the protection of witnesses and *pentiti* from intimidation resulting from face to face confrontation with the accused? If yes, please specify (e.g. full or partial anonymity, video-conference, disguise, exclusion of the defendant from the courtroom when the witness is giving evidence, exclusion of the media or the public from the trial, etc.) and indicate under which conditions these methods are used.

Witnesses and experts situated on the territory of another country may be examined via telephone or video-conference. The examination of such witnesses and experts is conducted in accordance with the provisions of this Law and the provisions of the Second Additional Protocol of the European Convention on Mutual Assistance in Criminal Matters.

From the beginning to the end of the trial, the Council may at any time *ex officio* or on a proposal by one of the parties, but always after their hearing, exclude the public from the trial or from a part of it, if it is necessary to maintain secrecy, to restore public order or to protect a person's reputation, the personal and private life of the accused, the witness or the victim, or the interests of a minor.

12. On which grounds and on the basis of which criteria can anonymity be granted? Is there the possibility to obtain legal assistance at this stage?

According to Article 270-a, during the proceedings the public prosecutor, the investigative judge or the President of the Council shall take measures and action to secure the effective protection of witnesses, collaborators of justice and victims appearing as witnesses, at any time they are intimidated, threatened with revenge or there is a threat to their lives or physical integrity or when there is a need for them to be protected. The protection of the above-mentioned persons is ensured by adapting the way in which they are questioned or participate in the proceedings. In such cases, the witness will only be questioned in the presence of the public prosecutor and the investigative judge or the President of the Council, in a place where the protection of his/her identity can be guaranteed, except in cases where, with consent of the witness, the Council decides to hold the hearing in a different way through the court or to use technical equipment and other appropriate means of communication. A transcript of the minutes with the witness's statement, without the witness's signature, shall be delivered to the accused and his/her lawyer, who may put questions to the witness through the court.

13. Are pre-trial statements of witnesses and *pentiti* and testimonies of anonymous witnesses and *pentiti* regarded as valid evidence? If yes, under which conditions?

According to Article 152, paragraph 4, the public prosecutor can call the person who has reported a crime, as well as the suspect, in the presence of his/her attorney, and any other persons who have any knowledge that may contribute to his/her evaluation of the authenticity of the statements in the criminal report. The public prosecutor will advise the person he/she has called of his/her rights. The minutes on information gathered from citizens, given in presence of the public prosecutor and signed by them, may be used as evidence in criminal proceedings.

Furthermore, when the public prosecutor summons other persons whose information may contribute to his/her evaluation of the authenticity of the statements in the criminal report, and the perpetrator is known to the authorities, he/she summons the perpetrator and his/her defence attorney. The minutes on the collected information, compiled in the presence of the public prosecutor, the perpetrator and his/her defence attorney and signed by the summoned person, may be used as material evidence in criminal proceedings.

c. *Non-procedural measures*

16. At which stage(s), and in which context, is it possible for witnesses and *pentiti* to benefit from a protection programme?

All of the non-procedural measures defined in the Law on Witness Protection can be undertaken before, during and after the criminal proceedings.

The conditions for the protection measures are defined by the Law as criteria that should be taken into account when deciding on a person's inclusion in the Programme. Namely:

- the importance of the information possessed by the person whose protection is proposed concerning a committed crime, its perpetrator and other important circumstances, i.e. data and information relevant for the criminal proceedings which are necessary or essential to prove the criminal act;
- the information possessed by the person whose protection is proposed is important for the criminal proceedings and cannot be obtained in any other way;
- the seriousness of the intimidation;
- the willingness of the person whose protection is proposed to co-operate with the judicial bodies, and with the Department in the implementation of protection measures.

17. Is there the possibility for witnesses and *pentiti* to obtain legal assistance at this (these) stage(s)?

Among other possibilities, in the Memorandum of Understanding signed between the Department and the person to be included in the Programme, one of the obligations of the Department towards the person is the duty to provide legal, psychological and any other necessary help during the whole Programme.

18. What is the procedure for admittance to a protection programme? Please specify, in particular, who takes the initiative, the criteria for admittance, the assessment of the relevance of a testimony and how admittance to the programme is formalised.

There are three stages in the procedure for admittance to the Protection Programme: the proposal for admittance to the Programme, the request for admittance to the Programme and the decision on admittance to the Programme.

The proposal for admittance to the Programme is submitted to the Council by the Public Prosecutor of "the former Yugoslav Republic of Macedonia". The Public Prosecutor submits the proposal on the basis of a written request for admittance to the Programme, submitted by the Ministry of the Interior, the competent public prosecutor or the judge presiding over the relevant case. A request for admittance to the Programme may also be submitted by the person who, due to a possible risk of being exposed to intimidation, threat of revenge or danger to his/her life, health, freedom, physical integrity or property, does not agree to give a statement as a witness in the criminal proceedings.

The Public Prosecutor of "the former Yugoslav Republic of Macedonia" submits to the Department all the relevant information on the person suggested for admittance to the Programme, to enable it to understand and assess the threat to the person, calculate the expenses for the implementation of the protection measures, and propose protection measures and their duration.

The Public Prosecutor of "the former Yugoslav Republic of Macedonia" determines the content and form of proposals and requests for admittance to the Programme.

On receipt of a proposal by the Public Prosecutor of "the former Yugoslav Republic of Macedonia", the President of the Council, immediately or within eight days at the latest, convenes a session of the Council. The Council may ask the Public Prosecutor for additional data and information relating to the proposal for admittance to the Programme. After considering the proposal for admittance to the Programme, and within 30 days of the date the proposal was submitted by the Public Prosecutor at the latest, the Council will make a decision, of which he/she will inform the public prosecutor of "the former Yugoslav Republic of Macedonia" and the Department. If the proposal for admittance to the Programme is accepted, the Council will instruct the Department to make an agreement with the person to be admitted to the Programme. If the Council makes a decision on the admittance of a close person to the Programme, the Council will instruct the

Department to make an agreement with the close person. Before making its decision, in accordance with Article 19 of this Law, the Council requests the written consent of the person for whom the procedure for admittance to the programme is conducted.

The decision on admittance to the Programme includes:

- data on the person to be admitted to the Programme (name, father's name and surname, address, ID number, date and place of birth, etc.), as well as data on his/her close persons to be admitted to the Programme;
- data for the criminal file;
- description and assessment of the threat to the person to be admitted to the Programme; and
- his/her "change of identity", if it has been decided to apply this protection measure.

19. Please indicate the measures that can be adopted for the protection of witnesses and *pentiti* (e.g. surveillance of the residence, physical protection, protection of personal records, relocation, change of identity, subsidies, assistance in job search, relocation of a detainee to another prison or to special units).

According to the Law on Witness Protection, there are four protection measures:

1) keeping the identity secret;
2) providing personal protection;
3) relocation; and
4) change of identity.

The protection measures defined in Article 26 of this Law are enforced by the Department. If the Department considers that it is necessary to apply a "change of identity" as a measure, it submits a request to the Council for the application of this measure.

Keeping the identity secret

Keeping the identity secret means processing and using personal documents with the personal data of the protected person temporarily altered, as well as processing and using documents on the ownership of the protected person's estate. The enforcement of this measure does not mean actually changing the personal and property data of the protected person in the regular records of authorised bodies. The protected person can use the documents to make certain agreements and for other legal matters with third persons only with the prior consent of the Department. If the Department does not give its consent, the protected person can, with the approval of the

Department, determine his/her proxy who shall then use the person's real name and data to conclude agreements or other legal matters on his/her behalf.

Providing personal protection

Providing personal protection means providing the operative, physical and technical protection of the protected person with the aim of preventing threats to his/her life, health, freedom, physical integrity or property.

Relocation

The relocation of the protected person is carried out through a temporary or permanent change of his/her place of residence to another place of residence determined by the Department. It can be applied within "the former Yugoslav Republic of Macedonia" or outside its territory, in accordance with ratified international agreements. Collaborators of justice serving prison sentences in "the former Yugoslav Republic of Macedonia" for whom relocation is determined as a protection measure, can be transferred to another country to serve their prison sentence, in accordance with ratified international agreements.

Change of identity

A change of identity means the partial or complete change of the personal data of the protected person. In implementing this measure, the physical characteristics of the protected person can also be changed. The personal data entered into new documents cannot be the same as that of another person. Receiving a new identity does not have an influence on the status or other rights and obligations of the protected person. After the expiry of the "change of identity" as a protection measure, the protected person may choose whether he/she wishes to keep the new identity in future. The protected person cannot resume his/her original identity if the change of identity has had a significant influence on the status of a third person (marriage, paternity, maternity, etc.). With the written permission of the Department, and in accordance with the guidelines on secrecy and providing for the complete security of the protected person, he/she can participate in an official procedure with his/her original personal data where the use of original personal data is inevitable. The original identity documents of the protected person are kept by the Department.

If a decision to apply a change of identity is made, the Department will ask the person suggested for admittance to the Programme, before signing the agreement, to fulfil his/her obligations towards third parties. If the person suggested for admittance to the Programme does not fulfil the obligations, the change of identity will not be applied until his/her obligations towards third parties have been fulfilled. In the case where, after signing the agreement, the Department receives information about an obligation that occurred when the protected person had his/her original identity, the Department will ask the protected person to fulfil this obligation, with the mediation of the Department. If the person is unable or unwilling to fulfil the obligation, the Department will inform the Council in writing. Within three days of the date of receipt of this written information, the Council will decide to withdraw the change of identity and terminate the Programme.

If the protected person committed a criminal act before his/her change of identity, upon a request from the court, the Department can ensure his/her presence and the use of his/her original identity and the court can hold the hearing in a special manner, in accordance with the Law on Criminal Procedure. Another possible case would be if the protected person committed a criminal act after signing the agreement. The Department would inform the Council which could decide to terminate the Programme.

20. What can the duration of a protection programme be? Which are the procedures for assessing the degree of danger for the witnesses/*pentiti* and their compliance with the obligations of the programme? Is it possible to challenge a decision of suspension, revocation or termination of a protection programme?

The duration of the Programme is one of the elements of the Memorandum of Understanding signed between the Department for Witness Protection and the protected person. The procedure for extending the duration of the protection measures determined in the Programme is regulated by Article 22 of the Law on Witness Protection. If, after the expiry of the protection measures determined in the Programme and in the agreement, there is still a need for the protection of the person, the Head of the Department or the Public Prosecutor shall submit to the Council a request for the continuation of the protection measures. The request should be submitted at the latest 30 days before the expiry of the protection measures, or in exceptional cases, if the security of the protected person so requires, it can be also submitted after the expiry of the protection measures.

Chapter VII of the Law on Witness Protection regulates the question of the termination of the Programme. The Law sets out the following reasons for the termination of the Programme:

1) The expiry of the duration foreseen in the agreement;
2) The death of the protected person;
3) The protected person or his/her legal representative withdraws from the Programme, in which case he/she submits a written statement to the Department;
4) The discontinuation of the reasons for which the person was admitted to the Programme;
5) The non-respect of the provisions of the agreement by the protected person.

d. *International co-operation*

21. Which measures (e.g. use of modern telecommunications means, assistance in relocating protected witnesses, exchange of information between witness protection authorities) have been adopted in the context of mutual legal assistance in order to facilitate international co-operation? How are the financial implications of international co-operation activities dealt with?

As has been explained in the replies to some of the questions above, non-procedural measures are defined in the Law on Witness Protection (keeping the identity secret, providing personal protection, relocation and change of identity), while the procedural measures are implemented in the framework of criminal procedure according to the Law on Criminal Procedure.

Having in mind the small population of "the former Yugoslav Republic of Macedonia" and its limited territory on the one hand and the specifics of organised crime on the other, we can conclude that a basic precondition for the successful implementation of the measures is international co-operation. Therefore, many of the provisions in the above-mentioned laws regulate international co-operation. For example, within the framework of its work, the Department for Witness Protection has a duty to "to co-operate with the appropriate witness protection services of other countries". Furthermore, the Law includes a Chapter entitled "International Co-operation and financial sources" which provides that international co-operation in the field of protection of witnesses, collaborators of justice, victims appearing as witnesses, and their close persons is accomplished on the basis of international agreements, ratified in accordance with the Constitution of "the former Yugoslav Republic of Macedonia", or on the basis of mutual reciprocity. Under these conditions, the Department:

- directs applications to other countries to accept protected persons and implement the protection measures stipulated in this Law; and
- deals with applications from other countries to accept protected persons and apply protection measures in "the former Yugoslav Republic of Macedonia".

The financial means for the implementation of this provision, as well as for the implementation of the Law as a whole, are provided in the budget of "the former Yugoslav Republic of Macedonia" and by international resources and witness protection programmes.

22. **Has your country entered international (bilateral or multilateral) agreements on the protection of witnesses and *pentiti*? If so, please indicate what kind of provisions they include.**

According to Article 502 of the Law on Criminal Procedure, international judicial criminal assistance will be provided according to the provisions of this Law and in line with the provisions of the European Convention on Mutual Assistance in Criminal Matters and its Protocols, the Palermo Convention of the United Nations on Transnational Organized Crime and with other international treaties ratified in accordance with the Constitution of "the former Yugoslav Republic of Macedonia". "The former Yugoslav Republic of Macedonia" has ratified these two conventions, which are its basis for international co-operation.

23. **How can international co-operation in the field of the protection of witnesses and *pentiti* be improved?**

During the drafting phase of the Law on Witness Protection, "the former Yugoslav Republic of Macedonia" co-operated widely with a number of international organisations whose valuable expertise was very useful in improving the text of the Law. Close co-operation was also established with witness protection agencies in other countries in order to profit from their experience during the implementation of the Law. After the enactment of the Law, special attention was paid to enhancing co-operation, especially in the drafting of secondary legislation and establishment of close relations which will be used for the implementation of measures outside national borders, the creation of liaison networks, the training of staff, etc.

e. Statistics

24. **How many people currently benefit from witness or *pentito* protection measures/programmes, and for how long? How many of them are foreign people? If the measures/programmes can be extended to relatives and other close persons, please indicate (and, if possible, specify the relationship with the witness/*pentito*) how many people are included in this category. Please also provide figures on the different kinds of measures (procedural and non-procedural) adopted, and on the number of cases involving international co-operation.**

Since the Law on Witness Protection was adopted in May 2005 and entered into force on 1 January 2006, we have no experience of the implementation of non-procedural measures. However, the Department for Witness Protection has undertaken a number of activities in the field of procedural measures, especially in terms of establishing contacts and co-operation with witness protection services in other countries.

So far, the Department for Witness Protection has provided its services to nine victims of human trafficking (in seven cases) who were giving their statements (procedural measures). They were all foreign citizens.

Turkey

a. *General Information*

Turkey has special regulations to protect witnesses in the context of organised crime and terrorism. Comprehensive measures related to these issues take place under the scope of two main laws.

- Act on the Prevention of Profit-Oriented Criminal Organisations enacted on 30 July 1999, No. 4422.

- Anti-Terror Act enacted 12 April 1991, No. 3713.

Article 7 of Act No. 4422, under the sub-title "Protection of the Witnesses and the Assigned Persons", provides comprehensive measures.

In the case where knowledge of the identity, residence or business address of a witness may create the probability of a serious threat to the security of him/herself or others. Another address may be determined for the witness to which any communications may be sent and the identity of the witness may be kept secret throughout the prosecution.

If it is possible to find out other evidence by means of the information given by a witness, the identity of the witness shall not be disclosed throughout the prosecution.

When it is necessary to disclose the identity of the witness when his/her statement is received, it may be decided to apply the provisions of Article 20 of Prevention of Terrorism Act (Anti-Terror Act) No. 3713 to the witness.

The provisions stated in the aforementioned paragraphs shall also apply to informants, law enforcement chiefs and the officers assigned to intelligence or the investigation of the offences within the scope of this Act. Under no circumstances shall information about their identities, functions or private lives be disclosed.

Anyone who discloses information about their identities, functions and private lives or who discloses them shall be sentenced to one to two years' imprisonment.

Article 20 of the Anti-Terror Act also regulates the protection of witnesses under the sub-title of "Protection Measures". According to this Article, the following persons will be protected by the state through appropriate measures: juridical, intelligence, administrative and military officials performing their duty in line with the prevention and suppression of terrorism and anarchy, police officials and personnel, general directors and deputy general directors of detention centres and penitentiaries, prosecutors and directors of such detention centres and penitentiaries where the convicts and detainees are held, judges and prosecutors of State Security Courts and those who are retired from such duties, those who are made or become open targets of terrorist organisations, witnesses and informers assisting in the solving of terrorist cases.

These protection measures may include, upon request, the change of physical appearance through surgical intervention and alteration in the civil registry of vital statistics, driving licenses, marriage certificates, diplomas and other similar documents and preservation of rights on movable, immovable, tangible and intangible property.

The Ministry of the Interior and other concerned bodies and agencies are under the obligation to comply with the strictest secrecy requirements in the implementation of these measures.

Rules and guidelines regarding the protection measures will be determined by a regulation to be prepared by the Prime Ministry. Public servants are authorised to resort to the use of weapons to ward off attacks by the terrorists on themselves, their spouses and children, even if they have left their previous jobs or are retired.

Organised crime and terrorist crimes are in the scope of application of witness protection. As to the provisions of the related laws, the measures cannot be extended to relatives or to other persons close to the witness.

In the Turkish legal system, provisions pertaining to persons who face criminal charges or were convicted of having taken part in an association of criminals or other criminal organisation but agree to co-operate with criminal justice authorities, particularly by giving information about the criminal association, are laid down in repentance laws, enacted in relation to terrorist acts. These laws are enacted for different periods and remain in force for a certain duration. They contain temporary provisions applicable only for the term prescribed by law. But the protection of *pentiti* is not provided for under these laws, only a reduction in penalty is possible for collaborators of justice.

b. *Procedural measures*

At every stage of the prosecution or trial it is possible for witnesses to benefit from procedural measures of protection. Protection will last for the whole life of the witness at his/her will.

There is no provision prohibiting the possibility for a witness to obtain legal assistance at these stages.

The replies to the 11th, 12th and 14th questions are related to the preventive law enforcement services and there is no available data in the Ministry of Justice.

The pre-trial statements of witnesses and *pentiti* and the testimonies of anonymous witnesses and *pentiti* are regarded as valid evidence as far as they are declared before the court.

c. *Non-procedural measures*

Non-procedural measures are implemented by the law enforcement bodies or other relevant authorities.

d. *International co-operation*

Turkey is not a party to any specific international agreement on the protection of witnesses and *pentiti*. International co-operation in the field of the protection of witnesses and *pentiti* is governed and implemented regarding the provisions of other international conventions and agreements on judicial co-operation and assistance.

e. *Statistics*

Statistical data related to the number and the characteristics of people benefiting from witness protection programmes and the duration and scope of such programmes are not available.

United States of America

a. *General Information*

1. **Please describe the framework (legal provisions and established practice) governing the use of measures protecting witnesses and *pentiti*.**

The Attorney General of the United States of America, through the Organized Crime Control Act of 1970, was given the authority to provide for the security of witnesses who were co-operating and agreed to testify truthfully in cases involving organised criminal activity or other serious offences by relocating them and providing them with the necessary support services. Legislation was amended and updated in 1984, resulting in the Witness Security Reform Act of 1984 (Title 18, United States Code, Section 3521 et seq.), which is the legislation under which the Federal Witness Security Program (Program) currently operates. Protection is provided to both witnesses to be relocated in the community, and incarcerated witnesses (prisoner-witnesses). Some of the incarcerated witnesses subsequently may qualify for relocation in the community through the Program upon their release.

2. **Please describe the framework (legal provisions and established practice) governing the use of measures encouraging witnesses and *pentiti* to co-operate with justice.**

The provisions and practice governing the measures encouraging witnesses and *pentiti* to co-operate and tell the truth under oath about what they know are not directly related to the protection afforded to witnesses. Witnesses decide to co-operate with the government when they are convinced; it is in their best interest to do so. Typically this occurs when persons involved in crime become aware that they will likely receive a very long prison term and they wish to increase their chance of earning a significant reduction in the prison term. It is very rare that innocent bystander eyewitnesses who are neither investigators nor seriously involved in a crime will have knowledge of crucial incriminating evidence that is likely to result in retaliation and bodily harm to them. If the persons participating in the crime can provide significant usable truthful evidence that results in the prevention of a significant crime or the conviction of a significant criminal, a prosecutor may, at his/her discretion, agree to one of several courses of conduct that may ultimately result in a lower sentence for that co-operator. For example, these actions include a prosecutorial recommendation (either very generally or in some cases with many specifics) to the sentencing judge at the time of sentencing for a lower sentence, after the co-operator has truthfully pled guilty to all the crimes he/she has committed and after the co-operator has rendered his/her co-operation and testimony, based upon the results actually obtained from the co-operation and to a lesser extent, the exposure to harm that the co-operator has faced as a result of his/her co-operation. Another option available is a post-verdict motion to a judge to reduce the sentence of an already convicted person who did not decide until after he/she was convicted and received a long sentence to co-operate and offer some information that the prosecutors, at their discretion, found to be of significant value. A third option more rarely used is a decision by the prosecutor, at his/her discretion, not to prosecute the co-operator for one of several crimes that he/she may have committed, or even for every crime committed, if the co-operation is ultimately as valuable as proffered. This latter immunity from some or all prosecution is more rarely offered by the prosecution and almost never granted prior to the rendering of the proffered co-operation, because once granted it cannot be revoked, and at that point, the co-operator may lose all motivation to co-operate.

Where either the prosecutor or investigative agent believe that the co-operation promised, if delivered, will subject the co-operator or their immediate family or associates to serious and sustained retaliation and harm, then the prosecutor can sponsor the co-operator as a candidate for special witness protection measures either while the person is in prison or in the community, by means of a petition to the deciding supervisory officials at the headquarters of the Department of Justice (DOJ). Early promises to a witness about receiving witness security by the police level investigator or the trial prosecutor are not authorised, and if given by mistake, are not binding failing later independent approval by headquarters officials. Witness security is not a reward mechanism for co-operators, although other separate cash reward mechanisms do exist. It is a difficult programme for the witnesses, similar to "voluntary" exile from one's extended family, community and friends. It exists so that people who have already decided to co-operate do not have to fear that when their co-operation is made known, and if it is likely to be traceable to them, that they will face sustained retaliation resulting in serious bodily harm or death.

3. **Can measures/benefits encouraging the co-operation of witnesses and *pentiti* be used in combination with protection measures (arrangements concerning trial proceedings, sentencing conditions, special penitentiary regimes, etc.)? If so, please specify and indicate under which conditions they are applied.**

As explained above in the reply to question 2, protection measures are intentionally kept separate from, and are available independently and in addition to, any benefits to encourage co-operation of witnesses and *pentiti*.

4. **For which kind of crime and under which circumstances can witness and *pentito* protection be applied? Can the measures be extended to the relatives or other persons close to the witness/*pentito*?**

Witnesses and *pentiti* can be protected through the Federal Witness Security Program (described in the reply to question 1) if they are witnesses for the Federal Government or a State government within the United States of America in official proceedings concerning an organised criminal activity or other serious offence, and they are endangered as a result of that co-operation.

Immediate family members can be protected along with the witness through the Program, if an analysis of the threat determines that it is necessary or for compelling humanitarian reasons (e.g., a minor child). Consideration can be given to providing protection to extended family members through the Program, if the threat to them warrants it. If the Program is not being used, and the investigative agency involved in the case takes responsibility for the protection of the witness, family members and others closely associated with the witness can be protected in the same manner as the witness, if deemed by the investigative agency to be necessary and appropriate.

5. **What urgent measures (e.g. immediate relocation to a secret place) can be taken in order to protect witnesses and *pentiti*?**

The investigative agencies with which witnesses and *pentiti* are co-operating can provide them with money to relocate to another area. If protection is needed just for a short period of time before trial and during trial, the investigative agencies have the ability to secure safe housing for them for a short period of time. The federal prosecuting offices also have funds set aside to provide money to such individuals to enable them to move to another area temporarily, while the danger is at its greatest, through the Emergency Witness Assistance Program (EWAP), administered by the Executive Office for United States Attorneys, DOJ headquarters. As far as the EWAP funds are concerned, victims qualify for the funds even though they may not testify, because they are considered potential witnesses.

Immediate, temporary, protection by relocation to a secure area can also be provided through the Program before all the necessary information is received and reviewed in the rare situation where the investigative agency is unable to provide temporary protection through housing in a secure area. In these cases, a final determination as to the propriety of providing full Program services must be made without undue delay after such protection is initiated.

6. **Which institutions are involved in the protection of witnesses and**
    ***pentiti* and what is their role (e.g. law enforcement agencies,**
    special independent agencies, prosecutor's offices, judicial
    authorities, etc)? How does co-operation between the relevant
    institutions work, in practice?

See the reply to question 5, as far as the role of investigative agencies is concerned. Prosecuting offices are involved by determining which witnesses will be used in prosecutions, and making applications to use the Federal Witness Security Program, if that level of protection is believed necessary. If witnesses are authorised to receive Program services, the investigative agency, through its headquarters, and the sponsoring federal prosecutor, coordinate with the Office of Enforcement Operations (OEO) in the Criminal Division, DOJ, which authorises witnesses into, and then monitors and oversees, the Program, when the witness is needed for testimony, or other issues arise concerning the witness. These other issues commonly include the evaluation of actions initiated by witnesses that could lead to the termination of their participation in this difficult Program, or the request by a witness thereafter to stay in or re-enter the Program. The United States Marshals Service (USMS) administers the day-to-day operation of the Program for witnesses relocated in the community. The Federal Bureau of Prisons (BOP) administers the day-to-day operation of the Program for witnesses being protected while incarcerated.

7. **Are there any specific provisions governing the protection of**
    witnesses and *pentiti* in relation to acts of terrorism? If so, please
    specify. Are there any specialised counter-terrorism institutions? If
    so, what is their role in the protection of witnesses and *pentiti* in
    relation to acts of terrorism?

There are no specific provisions governing the protection of witnesses and *pentiti* in relation to acts of terrorism. There are specialised counter-terrorism governmental prosecution institutions, but the government prosecution officials who work in them do not utilise the regulations designed to protect witnesses and *pentiti* in any special manner not available to other prosecutors. However as a practical matter, when made, requests for witness protection in serious terrorism cases are more likely to be well justified and supported by those prosecution officials, and consequently likely to be granted by supervisory headquarters officials in the DOJ.

8. **How does the framework governing the use of measures protecting**
    witnesses and *pentiti* and encouraging them to co-operate with
    justice guarantee respect for human rights and individual
    freedoms? Please indicate the procedures in place, if any, to
    monitor compliance with human rights standards.

Incarcerated witnesses who must voluntarily agree to maintain their anonymity as Program participants while in prison are provided the opportunity to meet with Program officials not rendering their day-to-day care several times a year in order to express any problems, including with their treatment, that the witnesses believe they are entitled to have corrected. Relocated witnesses are provided with a special contact in their area with whom they can meet more frequently for the same purpose. In addition, these witnesses, if they use their original name and are careful to protect their new identity and location, often contact, through secure means, either their original attorney, the original government investigator, the original prosecutor, or a contact person in the Program headquarters at the DOJ to raise concerns that they wish to have addressed by the Program officials. If the concerns are not resolved, further review can occur by an official in the headquarters of the DOJ who has not previously ruled on their specific concern, or they may choose to voluntarily withdraw from the Program and its restrictions, and they occasionally file a lawsuit in a court in order to obtain the procedural redress listed above if they perceive it has not been properly rendered (i.e., either proper first level Program consideration, or an independent review within the DOJ, of their concerns). By statute, substantive determinations by the DOJ witness security officials are final and not judicially reviewable. While not frequently employed, protected witnesses who appropriately protect their new identity and location can also ask two other types of officials to vindicate their concerns. These two types of officials are internal DOJ ombudsmen such as in its Office of Inspector General, who investigate claims about irregularities in the internal operation of the DOJ, and Chairpersons of various United States Congressional committees who have the ability to request written and oral answers to questions that they believe warrant a response from DOJ officials. In addition, a record of the respective responsibilities of the protected witness and Program officials is maintained by the Program and available for the protected witnesses to read. It documents the initial mutual understandings, the strict conditions to which the witnesses can expect to be exposed if they wish to remain in the Program, and the right of the witnesses to withdraw from the Program. The ongoing concerns and behaviour of each witness is similarly documented and safely maintained.

In addition to the measures noted immediately above and even in the absence of specific requests, the internal DOJ ombudsmen and United States Congressional committees each conduct regular periodic reviews of all DOJ programmes, including this Program.

b. _Procedural measures_

9. At which stage(s), and in which context, is it possible for witnesses and _pentiti_ to benefit from procedural measures of protection?

Witnesses are eligible to be considered for the Program immediately after they offer their co-operation, if it is assured that a prosecution will take place in which they are expected to be a witness, their agreement to testify is assured, and there has been a sufficient proffer, often under oath, of the testimony to be provided that demonstrates that it is important testimony in a very significant case that is not available from any other source. It is preferable that the witness has testified at a Federal Grand Jury, and that the case has been indicted, although it is not a requirement. The witness must be firmly committed to testifying as promised, or "locked into" the proffered testimony, so that Program funds are not wasted.

10. Is there the possibility for witnesses and *pentiti* to obtain legal assistance at this (these) stage(s)?

Yes, the majority of witnesses in the Program, or being considered for the Program, are being prosecuted in connection with the case in which they are co-operating, and are represented by counsel in that regard who typically know their original true identity, all the particulars of their involvement in the crime, and the substance of the truthful testimony that they agree to provide. Often the counsel to the witness is in the best position to help the witness evaluate whether co-operation with the government is in the best long term interest of the witness, before another co-operator involved in the crime arranges an agreement to co-operate with the government rendering co-operation with this witness unnecessary and unwarranted.

11. Are there alternative methods of giving evidence which allow the protection of witnesses and *pentiti* from intimidation resulting from face to face confrontation with the accused? If yes, please specify (e.g. full or partial anonymity, video-conference, disguise, exclusion of the defendant from the courtroom when the witness is giving evidence, exclusion of the media or the public from the trial, etc.) and indicate under which conditions these methods are used.

Testimony by live two-way video-conference is not normally a part of this Program but is available and is occasionally used outside the Program, such as with certain vulnerable victims. Those victims include juvenile victims of sexual crimes and where it is impossible for the witness to be present at the trial for health reasons. While not an ordinary occurrence, the media and public can be excluded from the trial if there are extreme security concerns, but high level DOJ approval is needed in order to "close" a courtroom. Artificial disguises are not ordinarily used in connection with court testimony in criminal cases, but are sometimes used if a witness is testifying at a Congressional hearing. More commonly, a court witness may purposely alter their hair style or arrange to have their appearance partially screened or obstructed from the public gallery, though not from the jury. The true identity and visual confrontation and cross-examination of the witness are intentionally maintained in order to allow the judge or jury to be able to place the greatest weight, without restriction, on the testimony of the witness. If the witness is providing unique evidence of guilt, then limiting the intrinsic value of that evidence by masking the source, even partially, from the judge or jury is self-defeating in that it provides the defence with a key weakness to attack in the government's proof of guilt. The key witness must be subject to the full examination of the judicial process or it will fail to carry the maximum persuasive value. This also makes practical sense since criminals will quickly figure out the true identify of any witness, with whom they probably were previously well acquainted, once the witness has offered this kind of unique crucial testimony.

12. On which grounds and on the basis of which criteria can anonymity be granted? Is there the possibility to obtain legal assistance at this stage?

For the reasons stated above, there are no bases for preserving anonymity if the testimony of the witness and the need for possible witness protection is being considered. However, co-operators who do not agree to testify at trial but offer only untraceable information or leads that, at their discretion, criminal law enforcement investigators decide to use as the basis for search warrants or other investigative or judicially authorised special investigative techniques may have the anonymity of their true names protected. In that case, a representative of law enforcement will typically have to vouch under oath for the reliability of the anonymous witness and keep a record of the details. In extraordinary cases where there is strong evidence to question the reliability of the anonymous witness, the law enforcement officer who vouched for the witness may be required in a closed and non-adversarial *ex parte* judicial proceeding to justify the good faith grounds for his/her belief in the trustworthiness of the anonymous witness to the judicial officer.

13. Are pre-trial statements of witnesses and *pentiti* and testimonies of anonymous witnesses and *pentiti* regarded as valid evidence? If yes, under which conditions?

Not typically by protected witnesses as valid evidence at trial. For other uses, see the reply to question 12.

14. Is it possible, and if so, under which conditions, to use information provided by *pentiti*? How is their credibility assessed?

See the reply to question 12. The witness's credibility is assured by having a named law enforcement officer, who is familiar with the anonymous witness, list under oath several other circumstances where the unique and important information of the witness has subsequently been confirmed to be true, and also convey any other facts that support the general trustworthiness or untrustworthiness of the witness and his/her trustworthiness in this specific situation.

15. Which are the opportunities for the defence to exercise its rights, including the right of the accused to challenge the witness'/*pentito*'s credibility in criminal proceedings (including at the pre-trial stage) and the respect of the "equality of arms" principle?

The defence does not have access to the anonymous witness, as described in the reply to question 12, but if the defence can bear the difficult burden of showing that the information is unreliable and can produce some evidence of bad faith, he/she can require that the supporting documentation and law enforcement officers be examined by the court, *ex parte*, and if not presented in good faith, invalidated.

At the trial stage, where such protected witnesses are concerned, the defence is allowed full discovery as close to trial as possible under the rules and full equality of opportunity to challenge the credibility of this witness, as compared with any other witness.

See the reply to question 11.

c. Non-procedural measures

16. At which stage(s), and in which context, is it possible for witnesses and *pentiti* to benefit from a protection programme?

See the reply to question 9.

17. Is there the possibility for witnesses and *pentiti* to obtain legal assistance at this (these) stages?

See the reply to question 10.

18. What is the procedure for admittance to a protection programme? Please specify, in particular, who takes the initiative, the criteria for admittance, the assessment of the relevance of a testimony and how admittance to the programme is formalised.

The procedure for requesting, the placement of a witness in the Program for relocation in the community is that an application is submitted to OEO by the federal prosecuting office (United States Attorney's Office). As a screening mechanism, OEO requires that the application be endorsed by the chief prosecutor in that office, the United States Attorney. On rare occasions, witnesses who are to testify before United States legislative bodies on sensitive matters are protected through the Program, and in such cases, the legislative body is required to submit the application. An assessment of the danger to the witness, including details concerning why there is no alternative to Program placement, and an assessment of the danger the witness would pose to the general public in a relocation community is prepared by the field office of the investigative agency involved in the case, and forwarded to its HQ for endorsement and forwarding to OEO, as required by OEO, as a further screening mechanism. The witness and adult family members are evaluated by a psychologist, as mandated by the Reform Act, the report of which is used by OEO in making an assessment of whether they will pose a risk to the public, if relocated. The psychological evaluation is arranged by OEO upon receipt of the application. The witness is interviewed by the USMS, which is the agency within the DOJ that administers the day-to-day operation of the Program for witnesses relocated in the community. OEO also arranges that interview, upon receipt of the application. The USMS provides a report to OEO on any problems it discovers which could affect the adjustment of the witness in the Program, or which need to be addressed before relocation occurs. All of the above documents are thoroughly reviewed and screened by OEO; the approval process consists of four levels of review. The Associate Director in OEO who is the head of the Program makes the final determination on whether to authorise Program services. If the Program is deemed necessary and appropriate, a memorandum authorising Program services is sent to the USMS, in which any contingencies to participation in the Program, such as counselling, are detailed.

The procedure for requesting placement of prisoner-witnesses in the Program is that an application from the federal prosecuting office is submitted, as well as an assessment of the danger to the witness by the investigative agency, as detailed above. Upon receipt of those documents, an assessment is made by OEO, as stated previously, as to the necessity of authorising Program services while the prisoner is incarcerated. If the Program is deemed necessary, a memorandum authorising Program services is sent to BOP, which is the agency within DOJ that administers the day-to-day operation of the Program for prisoner-witnesses. If family members of a prisoner-witness are endangered as a result of the prisoner's co-operation, they can receive protection through the Program by the USMS while the prisoner is incarcerated. The family members are normally included in the application submitted for the prisoner-witness, but if not, a written request from the federal prosecutor requesting their Program placement is required. The investigative agency that submitted the assessment of the danger to the witness must submit an assessment of the danger to the witness's family as a result of the witness's co-operation, including details concerning why there is no alternative to use of the Program for the family members, and an assessment of the risk the adult family members would pose to the general public in the relocation community. The family members are evaluated by a psychologist, and interviewed by the USMS, as detailed in the preceding paragraph concerning relocated witnesses, and the same review process at OEO occurs. When prisoner-witnesses are due to be released from custody, the case is evaluated to determine if the relocation services of the Program, as provided by the USMS, are warranted. The same factors are taken into consideration as with witnesses being relocated in the community initially, with the exception that the significance of the case and testimony are not evaluated again, and if a witness has family in the Program and will be joining that family, the threat is not evaluated, unless the witness would pose a risk to the community. If that is the case, the current threat is evaluated, and that is weighed against the risk the witness would pose to the public.

In order for a witness to qualify for participation in the Program, the case must be extremely significant, there must be an intention that the witness testify (informants are not protected through the Program), the witness's testimony must be crucial to the success of the prosecution, and the threat to the witness must be such that there is no alternative to placement of the witness in the Program.

19. **Please indicate the measures that can be adopted for the protection of witnesses and *pentiti* (e.g. surveillance of the residence, physical protection, protection of personal records, relocation, change of identity, subsidies, assistance in job search, relocation of a detainee to another prison or to special units.)**

Among the services that the USMS provides to witnesses relocated in the community are relocation in a secure community, under a new identity. Further information concerning services provided can be provided on a need-to-know basis. The marshals who deal with relocated witnesses (Witness Security Inspectors) have been specially trained regarding all aspects of their duties.

Measures taken to protect prisoner-witnesses include separation from any known individuals and organisations that present a threat to them. Further information on the services provided can be provided on a need-to-know basis.

20. **What can the duration of a protection programme be? Which are the procedures for assessing the degree of danger for the witnesses/*pentiti* and their compliance with the obligations of the programme? Is it possible to challenge a decision of suspension, revocation or termination of a protection programme?**

Witnesses remain in the Program for protection as long as they abide by the Program's rules. There is no further assessment of the danger to them, while they are in "good standing" in the Program. It is the Program's goal that they be assimilated into the community by 18 months after their authorisation, but this time period is flexible, depending on the circumstances of each individual witness. The USMS is responsible for determining whether witnesses are complying with Program rules. If witnesses do not abide by the rules and are terminated from the Program, and there is a request that they be reinstated in the Program, a current assessment of the danger to them may be obtained from the investigative agency which provided the original assessment of the danger to the witness. If a witness is terminated from the Program, there is a grievance procedure by which the witness can challenge the decision. The witness presents the reasons for which he/she takes exception to the termination of Program services to the marshal in the witness's area, and the matter proceeds up the supervisory chain in the USMS, reaching headquarters, if necessary. If not resolved at USMS headquarters, it is presented to OEO for review, and OEO has the authority to authorise reinstatement in the Program, if it disagrees with the termination.

d. *International co-operation*

21. Which measures (e.g. use of modern telecommunications means, assistance in relocating protected witnesses, exchange of information between witness protection authorities) have been adopted in the context of mutual legal assistance in order to facilitate international co-operation? How are the financial implications of the international co-operation activities dealt with?

If witnesses in the Program are legitimately needed for interview or testimony in foreign countries, and the appropriate international channels have been used, they are made available, on a reimbursable basis in coordination with any ongoing domestic needs for the witness.

22. Has your country entered international (bilateral or multilateral) agreements on the protection of witnesses and *pentiti*? If so, please indicate what kind of provisions they include.

The United States of America has not entered into such agreements with other countries.

23. How can international co-operation in the field of the protection of witnesses and *pentiti* be improved?

International co-operation may be improved by good communication, for example, by having points of contact privately designated who are available, upon request, to listen to and evaluate individual situations and offer help where it is determined to be uniquely suited and tailored to fit the specific needs that arise on a case-by-case basis.

24. **How many people currently benefit from witness or *pentito* protection measures/programmes, and for how long? How many of them are foreign people? If the measures/programmes can be extended to relatives and other close persons, please indicate (and, if possible, specify the relationship with the witness/*pentito*) how many people are included in this category. Please also provide figures on the different kinds of measures (procedural or non-procedural) adopted, and on the number of cases involving international co-operation.**

The replies to these questions can be provided on a need-to-know basis.

More than seven thousand witnesses have been authorised to receive Program services since the Program's inception in 1970, however, a much smaller number is actively receiving services at this time. The average period of time for assimilation and government financial assistance, to give the witness a new start in life, is 22 months, but a witness can contact the Program officials at any time if a threat appears. Approximately 30 percent of the witnesses currently entering the Program are foreign nationals, who have been placed in the Program for testimony in United States cases. While many witnesses enter the Program alone, it is common for them to enter with their immediate family members or other persons close to them. Occasionally it has been necessary to place large family groups in the Program with the witness.

f. Proposals and comments

25. **Please provide any comments/proposals concerning the implementation of the terms of reference of the PC-PW and, in particular, instruments to be adopted to strengthen the protection of witnesses and *pentiti*.**

To the extent possible, the United States of America avoids publicly adopted instruments governing protected witnesses and legislatively makes all documents connected with the Program exempt from other routine public document disclosure laws. By definition, the more transparency in such a programme, the more likely it is to be penetrated either by those who wish to kill a specific witness, or alternatively by those who wish to undercut the credibility among potential witnesses and thereby defeat the utility of the programme in the future by undermining its reputation to safely protect any future potential witness against them. In addition, potential witnesses do not readily place their fate with or trust a programme, the details of which are publicly available. This programme and especially its reputation, which is critically important to make it attractive to possible crucial witnesses, depends upon faith in the ability to keep it within a small unreviewable governmental unit that can ensure it remains non-transparent and non-penetrable for a very long period of time.

Even among the trusted governmental units that supervise such a programme, most individuals would both be endangered by and also have no need to know all the details of both the old and new identity and location of each witness. Thus, agreements should recognize that each person or organisation involved will not be given all the particulars about a person, but only pertinent generalities where that will suffice, for example regarding true name and age, employment skills, and prior involvement in crime that reflects on danger to a new community.

Since witness protection depends upon the witness not being obvious in their new location, cultural tastes and differences such as language, accent, and behaviour, including religious behaviour that cannot always be easily altered in adults, must be considered and will operationally eliminate many options that would otherwise be politically feasible. Therefore, broad political agreements that bear their own difficulties in obtaining ratification, due to concerns about multi-party transparency and secrecy, appropriate cost sharing and auditing, and permanent administration, including programme admission and termination authorities, may be premature among parties who are not culturally compatible partners. In sum, an acceptable cultural matching of potential partners is an important preliminary consideration.

Thus, an initial discussion and inventory of the related necessary domestic infrastructure needs should not be overlooked. For example, it is hard to operationalise a witness security plan without provisions for the related but less complex and costly domestic witness services described in the reply to question 5, such as a funded plan for physical security at the time the witness testifies, and short term domestically authorised and controlled options for temporary relocation assistance for short periods before and after the testimony that do not involve a change of identification documents or obtaining a new permanent residence and career, and often do not involve physical protection. Other foundational domestic requirements typically include the creation of a designated special police unit devoted to witness security that by law is the only unit to handle and protect witnesses, an exception to any domestic information disclosure law that will protect the government records relating to these witnesses forever against all public and official requests, and domestic laws that criminalise and punish threatened or attempted intimidation, harassment and retaliation against witnesses before, during and after the witnesses have testified.

Once domestic requirements are satisfied by the interested participant nations, then the more difficult international agreements about shared issues need to be negotiated between culturally matched partners. The most obvious shared issues include items such as how much personal data about a witness should be shared and how it will be securely handled by each country; how the ongoing administrative and witness costs in the receiving country (including basic or necessary cosmetic medical care, job and language training, subsistence and social welfare guarantees) will be shared and reimbursed, and up to what maximum or for how long; what specific new identity and admission papers in the new country will be made available and how those special new identification papers will be handled in the normal record keeping system of the receiving country, and what will happen to the related pre-existing personal records of the witness in the requesting country; and which officials will have the authority (initially and upon review) and under what circumstances to contact the witness, escort the witness to any reopened legal proceedings, or supervise the witness (extending to wide-ranging issues such as the legality of consensually approved remote audio and video alarms, or permitting handgun possession), to terminate the witness's participation in the programme, or to readmit him/her into the programme.

At the same time that international negotiations are proceeding, one way to both address certain urgent and unique situations and highlight the difficult areas that need more formal attention and negotiation is to make provisions for informal pilot project exchanges of a very small number of culturally matched witnesses on an *ad hoc* basis.

Japan

a. General information

1. Please describe the framework (legal provisions and established practice) governing the use of measures protecting witnesses and *pentiti*.

We have measures to protect witnesses and *pentiti* regulated by procedural laws and substantive laws.

With regard to procedural laws, the Code of Criminal Procedure provides such measures as follows:

"**Article 299-2**

When providing the name and address of a witness, expert, interpreter or translator, or evidential documents and articles under the provision of paragraph 1 of the preceding Article a public prosecutor or the counsel may, if he/she deems that there is a danger of acts being committed which will either harm the body or property of the witness, expert, interpreter or translator, or a person whose name appears in the evidential documents or articles, or a relative of such persons, or will intimidate or confuse these people, inform the adverse party to that effect and request careful consideration for not disclosing the address, work address and other information indicating the place of residence of these people to the persons concerned (including the accused) except where necessary in relation to the proof of crime, the investigation of crime or the defence of the accused, and for ensuring that the safety of these people is not threatened.

Article 295

2. The presiding judge may, when examining a witness, expert, interpreter or translator, if he/she deems that there is a danger of acts being committed which will either harm the body or property of the witness, expert, interpreter or translator, or a relative of such persons, or will intimidate or confuse these people, and that the witness, expert, interpreter or translator cannot give sufficient testimony if the address, workplace or other information indicating the place of residence of these people is disclosed, control the examination with regard to these matters. This shall not apply if there is a danger that the presiding judge's control of the examination will put the defence of the accused at a substantial disadvantage.

Article 157-2

When examining a witness, if the court determines that, considering the witness's age and physical and mental state, among other things, there is a risk that the witness will feel demonstrable anxiety or stress, after hearing the opinion of the prosecutor and defendant or the defendant's counsel, it may admit a person to accompany the witness when he/she testify who is deemed likely to reduce the anxiety or stress of the witness and who will not threaten to disrupt the examination by the judge or the persons concerned in the trial, or the testimony by the witness, or to exert an inappropriate influence on the testimony.

2. Persons accompanying the witness as stipulated under the previous paragraph shall not engage in behavior that disrupts the examination by the judge or the persons concerned in the trial, or inappropriately influences the witness's testimony.

Article 157-3

When examining a witness, if the court determines that, based upon the nature of the alleged crime, the witness's age, physical and mental state and relation to the defendant, among other things, there is a risk that his/her emotional state will be demonstrably harmed during testimony in front of the defendant (including the method provided for in the following Article, paragraph 1), and it deems it necessary, after hearing the opinion of the prosecutor and defendant or the defendant's counsel, it may take measures to ensure that either the defendant or witness, or both, is unable to establish the state of the other. However, the measure which makes it impossible for the defendant to establish the state of the witness may be taken only in cases where the defendant's counsel is present.

2. When examining a witness, if the court deems it necessary, considering the nature of the alleged crime, the witness's age, physical and mental state, and the effect on the witness's reputation, among other things, it may, after hearing the opinion of the prosecutor and defendant or the defendant's counsel, take measures to ensure that the witness and observers of the trial are unable to recognize one another.

Article 157-4

If, when examining a person stipulated in the items below as a witness, the court deems it necessary, it may, after hearing the opinion of the prosecutor and defendant or the defendant's counsel, permit the witness to be in a different location from where the judge and persons concerned in the trial are located (being limited to locations that are on the same premises as where the judge and persons concerned in the trial are located), and may examine the witness by means which enable the persons to communicate, each being able to recognize the state of the others by the transmission and reception of images and voices.

i.   Victims of crimes or attempted crimes under Penal Code Articles 176 to 178; Article 181; Article 225 (being limited to the purpose of indecent behaviour or marriage; hereinafter in this item the same shall apply); Article 227, paragraph 1 (being limited to the purpose of assisting another person who has committed a crime provided for in Article 225) or paragraph 3 (being limited to the purpose of indecent behaviour); or the first half of the crime in Article 241.

ii.   Victims of crimes under the Child Welfare Law (Law No. 164, 1947) Article 60, paragraph 1, or Article 34, paragraph 1, Item 9, and Article 60, paragraph 2; and the Law related to the Protection of Children and Penalties against conduct related to Child Prostitution and Child Pornography (Law No. 52, 1999), Articles 4 to 8.

iii.   In addition to the persons referred to in the previous two items, persons for whom it is determined, based upon the nature of the alleged crime, the witness's age, physical and mental state, and relation to the defendant, among other things, that there is a risk that the witness will feel pressure and the witness's emotional state will be demonstrably harmed when testifying in the presence of the judge or persons concerned in the trial.

2. When the court, in cases where a witness is examined by means stipulated under the previous paragraph, deems that the witness will again be called to testify as a witness in later criminal proceedings regarding the same facts, and the witness agrees, it may, after hearing the opinion of the prosecutor and defendant or the defendant's counsel, record the examination of the witness, the witness's testimony and state in a recording medium (this shall be an object on which images and voice can be recorded simultaneously; hereinafter it shall mean the same).

3. The recording medium taken of the examination of the witness, the witness's testimony and state under the previous paragraph shall be attached to the record of the proceedings and become part of the court record."

On the other hand, in addition to general crimes like intimidation and violence, the Penal Code criminalises in particular the act of intimidating a witness by Article 105-2, to protect witnesses, as follows:

"**Article 105-2** (Intimidation of a witness)

A person who, without due cause, in connection with his/her own or another's criminal case, forcibly demands an interview with, or intimidates by words or gestures, any person deemed to have knowledge necessary for the trial or investigation of such criminal case, or any relative of such a person, shall be punished with imprisonment for not more than one year or with a fine of not more than 200,000 yen."

2. **Please describe the framework (legal provisions and established practice) governing the use of measures encouraging witnesses and *pentiti* to co-operate with justice.**

In Japan, witnesses can be paid daily allowances as well as traveling expenses in accordance with the Law concerning the cost, etc. of criminal procedure.

Moreover, witnesses and their relatives can be paid a benefit if they are harmed on account of witnesses' statements or appearance in court in accordance with the Law concerning Benefit in the Case of Witnesses' Being Harmed.

These measures indirectly encourage witnesses and *pentiti* to co-operate with justice as well as protect them.

3. **Can measures/benefits encouraging the co-operation of witnesses and *pentiti* be used in combination with protection measures (arrangements concerning trial proceedings, sentencing conditions, special penitentiary regimes, etc.)? If so, please specify and indicate under which conditions they are applied.**

Yes. Measures/benefits encouraging the co-operation of witnesses and *pentiti* can be used in combination. As for the conditions under which they are applied, see the replies to questions 1 and 2.

4. **For which kind of crime and under which circumstances can witness and *pentito* protection be applied? Can the measures be extended to the relatives or other persons close to the witness/*pentito*?**

See the reply to question 1.

5. **What urgent measures (e.g. immediate relocation to a secret place) can be taken in order to protect witnesses and *pentiti*?**

See the reply to question 1.

6. Which institutions are involved in the protection of witnesses and *pentiti* and what is their role (e.g. law enforcement agencies, special independent agencies, prosecutor's offices, judicial authorities, etc)? How does co-operation between the relevant institutions work in practice?

See the reply to question 1.

7. Are there any specific provisions governing the protection of witnesses and *pentiti* in relation to acts of terrorism? If so, please specify. Are there any specialised counter-terrorism institutions? If so, what is their role in the protection of witnesses and *pentiti* in relation to acts of terrorism?

N/A.

8. How does the framework governing the use of measures protecting witnesses and *pentiti* and encouraging them to co-operate with justice guarantee respect for human rights and individual freedoms? Please indicate the procedures in place, if any, to monitor compliance with human rights standards.

In general, human rights and individual freedoms are guaranteed under the Constitution and laws, even within the framework governing the use of measures protecting witnesses and *pentiti* and encouraging them to co-operate with justice.

b. *Procedural measures*

9. At which stage(s), and in which context, is it possible for witnesses and *pentiti* to benefit from procedural measures of protection?

See the reply to question 1.

10. Is there the possibility for witnesses and *pentiti* to obtain legal assistance at this (these) stage(s)?

See the reply to question 1.

11. Are there alternative methods of giving evidence which allow the protection of witnesses and *pentiti* from intimidation resulting from face to face confrontation with the accused? If yes, please specify (e.g. full or partial anonymity, video-conference, disguise, exclusion of the defendant from the courtroom when the witness is giving evidence, exclusion of the media or the public from the trial, etc.) and indicate under which conditions these methods are used.

See the reply to question 1.

12. **On which grounds and on the basis of which criteria can anonymity be granted? Is there the possibility to obtain legal assistance at this stage?**

See the reply to question 1.

13. **Are pre-trial statements of witnesses and *pentiti* and testimonies of anonymous witnesses and *pentiti* regarded as valid evidence? If yes, under which conditions?**

Pre-trial statements of witnesses and *pentiti* can be regarded as valid evidence under the general hearsay rule provided by Articles 320-328 of the Code of Criminal Procedure.

In general, the testimonies of anonymous witnesses and *pentiti* are not valid, with the exception of Article 299-2 of the Code of Criminal Procedure as mentioned above.

14. **Is it possible, and if so, under which conditions, to use information provided by "*pentiti*"? How is their credibility assessed?**

In Japan, the laws do not distinguish between witnesses and *pentiti*.

Therefore, the information provided by *pentiti* can be used and their credibility is assessed in the ordinary criminal procedure in accordance with the Code of Criminal Procedure and other laws.

15. **Which are the opportunities for the defence to exercise its rights, including the right of the accused to challenge the witness'/*pentito*'s credibility in criminal proceedings (including at the pre-trial stage) and the respect of the "equality of arms" principle?**

The defence has opportunities to exercise its right in criminal proceedings in accordance with the Constitution and laws. That is, the accused can challenge the witness'/*pentito*'s credibility by making a cross-examination.

c. Non-procedural measures

16. **At which stage(s), and in which context, is it possible for witnesses and *pentiti* to benefit from a protection programme?**

See the reply to question 1.

17. Is there the possibility for witnesses and *pentiti* to obtain legal assistance at this (these) stage(s)?

See the reply to question 1.

18. What is the procedure for admittance to a protection programme? Please specify, in particular, who takes the initiative, the criteria for admittance, the assessment of the relevance of a testimony and how admittance to the programme is formalised.

See the reply to question 1.

19. Please indicate the measures that can be adopted for the protection of witnesses and *pentiti* (e.g. surveillance of the residence, physical protection, protection of personal records, relocation, change of identity, subsidies, assistance in job search, relocation of a detainee to another prison or to special units).

See the reply to question 1.

20. What can the duration of a protection programme be? Which are the procedures for assessing the degree of danger for the witnesses/*pentiti* and their compliance with the obligations of the programme? Is it possible to challenge a decision of suspension, revocation or termination of a protection programme?

See the reply to question 1.

d. *International co-operation*

21. Which measures (e.g. use of modern telecommunications means, assistance in relocating protected witnesses, exchange of information between witness protection authorities) have been adopted in the context of mutual legal assistance in order to facilitate international co-operation? How are the financial implications of international co-operation activities dealt with?

In general, international co-operation is conducted in accordance with the Law for International Assistance in Investigation, the Law for Punishment of Organised Crimes, Control of Crime Proceeds and Other Matters, etc.

However, we do not have a special provision regarding international co-operation in protecting witnesses and *pentiti*.

22. Has your country entered international (bilateral or multilateral) agreements on the protection of witnesses and *pentiti*? If so, please indicate what kind of provisions they include.

No.

23. How can international co-operation in the field of the protection of witnesses and *pentiti* be improved?

–

e. Statistics

24. How many people currently benefit from witness or *pentito* protection measures/programmes, and for how long? How many of them are foreign people? If the measures/programmes can be extended to relatives and other close persons, please indicate (and, if possible, specify the relationship with the witness/*pentito*) how many people are included in this category. Please also provide figures on the different kinds of measures (procedural and non-procedural) adopted, and on the number of cases involving international co-operation.

N/A.

f. Proposals and comments

25. Please provide any comments/proposals concerning the implementation of the terms of reference of the PC-PW and, in particular, instruments to be adopted to strengthen the protection of witnesses and *pentiti*.

–

RECOMMENDATION REC(2005)9 OF THE COMMITTEE OF MINISTERS OF THE COUNCIL OF EUROPE TO MEMBER STATES ON THE PROTECTION OF WITNESSES AND COLLABORATORS OF JUSTICE

*(Adopted by the Committee of Ministers on 20 April 2005
at the 924th meeting of the Ministers' Deputies)*

The Committee of Ministers, under the terms of Article 15.*b* of the Statute of the Council of Europe,

Recalling that the aim of the Council of Europe is to achieve greater unity among its members;

Aware of the need for member states to develop a common crime policy in relation to witness protection;

Noting that there is growing recognition of the special role of witnesses in criminal proceedings and that their evidence is often crucial to securing the conviction of offenders, especially in respect of serious crime;

Considering that in some areas of criminality, such as organised crime and terrorism, there is an increasing risk that witnesses will be subjected to intimidation;

Considering that the final report of the Multidisciplinary Group on International Action against Terrorism (GMT) and the subsequent decisions of the Committee of Ministers recognize the protection of witnesses and collaborators of justice as a priority area of the Council of Europe's legal action against terrorism;

Recalling that in Resolution No. 1 on Combating International Terrorism approved at the 24th Conference of European Ministers of Justice (Moscow, 4-5 October 2001), the Committee of Ministers was invited to adopt urgently all normative measures considered necessary for assisting states to prevent, detect, prosecute and punish acts of terrorism, such as the improvement of the protection of witnesses and other persons participating in proceedings involving persons accused of terrorist crimes;

Recalling that in Resolution No. 1 on Combating Terrorism approved at the 25th Conference of European Ministers of Justice (Sofia, 9-10 October 2003), the Committee of Ministers was invited to, *inter alia*, pursue without delay the work with a view to adopting relevant international instruments on the protection of witnesses and collaborators of justice;

Convinced that, while all persons have a civic duty to give sincere testimony as witnesses if so required by the criminal justice system, there should also be greater recognition given to their rights and needs, including the right not to be subject to any undue interference or be placed at personal risk;

Considering that member states have a duty to protect witnesses against such interference by providing them with specific protection measures aimed at effectively ensuring their safety;

Considering that it is unacceptable for the criminal justice system to fail to bring defendants to trial and obtain a judgment because witnesses have been effectively discouraged from testifying freely and truthfully;

Aware that the protection of witnesses and collaborators of justice requires confidentiality and that efforts should be made to ensure that effective measures are taken to thwart attempts to trace witnesses and collaborators of justice, in particular by criminal organisations, including terrorist organisations;

Bearing in mind the provisions of the European Convention on Human Rights (ETS No. 5) and the case-law of its organs, which recognize the rights of the defence to examine the witness and to challenge his/her testimony;

Taking into account Recommendation No. R (97) 13 concerning intimidation of witnesses and the rights of the defence, in particular with respect to the measures to be taken in relation to vulnerable witnesses, especially in cases of crime within the family; Recommendation No. R (85) 4 on violence in the family, Recommendation No. R (85) 11 on the position of the victim in the framework of criminal law and procedure, Recommendation No. R (87) 21 on assistance to victims and the prevention of victimisation, Recommendation No. R (91) 11 concerning sexual exploitation, pornography and prostitution of, and trafficking in, children and young adults and Recommendation No. R (96) 8 on crime policy in Europe in a time of change,

Recommends that governments of member states:

i. be guided, when formulating their internal legislation and reviewing their criminal policy and practice, by the principles and measures appended to this Recommendation;

ii. ensure that all the necessary publicity for these principles and measures is distributed to all interested bodies, such as judicial organs, investigating and prosecuting authorities, bar associations, and relevant social institutions.

1. Definitions

For the purposes of this Recommendation, the term:

- "witness" means any person who possesses information relevant to criminal proceedings about which he/she has given and/or is able to give testimony (irrespective of his/her status and of the direct or indirect, oral or written form of the testimony, in accordance with national law), who is not included in the definition of "collaborator of justice";

- "collaborator of justice" means any person who faces criminal charges, or has been convicted of taking part in a criminal association or other criminal organisation of any kind, or in offences of organised crime, but who agrees to co-operate with criminal justice authorities, particularly by giving testimony about a criminal association or organisation, or about any offence connected with organised crime or other serious crimes;

- "intimidation" means any direct or indirect threat carried out or likely to be carried out to a witness or collaborator of justice, which may lead to interference with his/her willingness to give testimony free from undue interference, or which is a consequence of his/her testimony;

- "anonymity" means that the identifying particulars of the witness are not generally divulged to the opposing party or to the public in general;

- "people close to witnesses and collaborators of justice" includes the relatives and other persons in a close relationship to the witnesses and the collaborators of justice, such as the partner, (grand)children, parents and siblings;

- "protection measures" are all individual procedural or non-procedural measures aimed at protecting the witness or collaborator of justice from any intimidation and/or any dangerous consequences of the decision itself to co-operate with justice;

- "protection programme" means a standard or tailor-made set of individual protection measures which are, for example, described in a memorandum of understanding, signed by the responsible authorities and the protected witness or collaborator of justice.

II. General Principles

1. Appropriate legislative and practical measures should be taken to ensure that witnesses and collaborators of justice may testify freely and without being subjected to any act of intimidation.

2. While respecting the rights of the defence, the protection of witnesses, collaborators of justice and people close to them should be organised, where necessary, before, during and after the trial.

3. Acts of intimidation of witnesses, collaborators of justice and people close to them should, where necessary, be made punishable either as separate criminal offences or as part of the offence of using illegal threats.

4. Subject to legal privileges providing the right of some persons to refuse to give testimony, witnesses and collaborators of justice should be encouraged to report any relevant information regarding criminal offences to the competent authorities and thereafter agree to give testimony in court.

5. While taking into account the principle of free assessment of evidence by courts and the respect of the rights of the defence, procedural law should enable the impact of intimidation on testimonies to be taken into consideration and statements made during the preliminary phase of the procedure to be allowed (and/or used) in court.

6. While respecting the rights of the defence, alternative methods of giving evidence which protect witnesses and collaborators of justice from intimidation resulting from face-to-face confrontation with the accused should be considered.

7. Criminal justice personnel should have adequate training and guidelines to deal with cases where witnesses might require protection measures or programmes.

8. All the stages of the procedure related to the adoption, implementation, modification and revocation of protection measures or programmes should be kept confidential; the unauthorised disclosure of this information should be made punishable as a criminal offence where appropriate, especially to ensure the security of a protected person.

9. The adoption of protection measures or programmes should also take into account the need to strike an adequate balance with the principle of safeguarding the rights and expectations of victims.

III. Protection measures and programmes

10. When designing a framework of measures to combat serious offences, including those related to organised crime and terrorism, and violations of international humanitarian law, appropriate measures should be adopted to protect witnesses and collaborators of justice against intimidation.

11. No terrorism-related crimes should be excluded from the offences for which specific witness protection measures/programmes are envisaged.

12. The following criteria should, *inter alia*, be taken into consideration when deciding upon the entitlement of a witness/collaborator of justice to protection measures or programmes:

-   involvement of the person to be protected (as a victim, witness, co-perpetrator, accomplice or aider and   abetter) in the investigation and/or in the case;
-   relevance of the contribution;
-   seriousness of the intimidation;
-   willingness and suitability to being subject to protection measures or programmes

13. When deciding upon the adoption of protection measures it should also be considered, in addition to the criteria mentioned in paragraph 12, whether there is no other evidence available that could be deemed sufficient to establish a case related to serious offences.

14. Proportionality between the nature of the protection measures and the seriousness of the intimidation of the witness/collaborator of justice should be ensured.

15. Witnesses/collaborators of justice being subjected to the same kind of intimidation should be entitled to similar protection. However, any protection measures/programmes adopted will need to take into account the particular characteristics of the matter and the individual needs of the person(s) to be protected.

16. Procedural rules aimed at the protection of witnesses and collaborators of justice should ensure that the balance necessary in a democratic society is maintained between the prevention of crime, the needs of the victims and witnesses and the safeguarding of the right to a fair trial.

17. While ensuring that the parties have adequate opportunity to challenge the evidence given by a witness/collaborator of justice, the following measures aimed at preventing identification of the witness may, *inter alia*, be considered:

-   audiovisual recording of statements made by witnesses/collaborators of justice during the preliminary phase of the procedure;

-   using statements given during the preliminary phase of the procedure as evidence in court when it is not possible for witnesses to appear before the court or when appearing in court might result in great and actual danger to the witnesses/collaborators of justice or to people close to them; pre-trial statements should be regarded as valid evidence if the parties have, or have had, the chance to participate in the examination and interrogate and/or cross-examine the witness and to discuss the contents of the statement during the procedure;

-   disclosing information which enables the witness to be identified at the latest possible stage of the proceedings and/or releasing only selected details;

-   excluding or restricting the media and/or the public from all or part of the trial;

-   using devices preventing the physical identification of witnesses and collaborators of justice, such as using screens or curtains, disguising the face of the witness or distorting his/her voice;

-   using video-conferencing.

18. Any decision to grant anonymity to a witness in criminal proceedings will be made in accordance with domestic law and European human rights law.

19. Where available, and in accordance with domestic law, anonymity of persons who might give evidence should be an exceptional measure. Where the guarantee of anonymity has been requested by such persons and/or temporarily granted by the competent authorities, criminal procedural law should provide for a verification procedure to maintain a fair balance between the needs of criminal justice and the rights of the parties. The parties should, through this procedure, have the opportunity to challenge the alleged need for anonymity of the witness, his/her credibility and the origin of his/her knowledge.

20. Any decision to grant anonymity should only be taken when the competent judicial authority finds that the life or freedom of the person involved, or of the persons close to him/her, is seriously threatened, the evidence appears to be significant and the person appears to be credible.

21. When anonymity has been granted, the conviction should not be based solely, or to a decisive extent, on the evidence provided by anonymous witnesses.

22. Where appropriate, witness protection programmes should be set up and made available to witnesses and collaborators of justice who need protection. The main objective of these programmes should be to safeguard the life and personal security of witnesses/collaborators of justice, and people close to them, aiming in particular at providing the appropriate physical, psychological, social and financial protection and support.

23. Protection programmes implying dramatic changes in the life/privacy of the protected person (such as relocation and change of identity) should be applied to witnesses and collaborators of justice who need protection beyond the duration of the criminal trials where they give testimony. Such programmes, which may last for a limited period or for life, should be adopted only if no other measures are deemed sufficient to protect the witness/collaborator of justice and persons close to them.

24. The adoption of such programmes requires the informed consent of the person(s) to be protected and an adequate legal framework, including appropriate safeguards for the rights of the witnesses or collaborators of justice according to national law.

25. Where appropriate, protection measures could be adopted on an urgent and provisional basis before a protection programme is formally adopted.

26. Given the essential role that collaborators of justice may play in the fight against serious offences, they should be given adequate consideration. Where necessary, protection programmes applicable to collaborators of justice serving a prison sentence may also include specific arrangements such as special penitentiary regimes.

27. Protection of collaborators of justice should also be aimed at preserving their credibility and public security. Adequate measures should be undertaken to protect against the risk of the collaborators of justice committing further crimes while under protection and therefore, even involuntarily, jeopardising the case in court. The intentional perpetration of an offence by a collaborator of justice under protection should, according to the relevant circumstances, imply the revocation of protection measures.

28. While respecting the fundamental principles of administrative organisation of each state, staff dealing with the implementation of protection measures should be afforded operational autonomy and should not be involved either in the investigation or in the preparation of the case where the witness/collaborator of justice is to give evidence. Therefore, an organisational separation between these functions should be provided for. However, an adequate level of co-operation/contact with or between law-enforcement agencies should be ensured in order to successfully adopt and implement protection measures and programmes.

IV. International co-operation

29. While respecting the different legal systems and the fundamental principles of administrative organisation of each state, a common approach in international issues related to the protection of witnesses and collaborators of justice should be followed. Such a common approach should aim at ensuring proper professional standards, at least in the crucial aspects of confidentiality, integrity and training. Member states should ensure sufficient exchange of information and co-operation between the authorities responsible for protection programmes.

30.   Measures aimed at fostering international co-operation should be adopted and implemented in order to facilitate the examination of protected witnesses and collaborators of justice and to allow protection programmes to be implemented across borders.

31.   The scope and the effective and rapid implementation of international co-operation in matters related to the protection of witnesses and collaborators of justice, including with relevant international jurisdictions, should be improved.

32.   The following objectives should, for example, be considered:

-   to provide assistance in relocating abroad protected witnesses, collaborators of justice and persons close to them and ensuring their protection, in particular in those cases where no other solution can be
found for their protection;

-   to facilitate and improve the use of modern means of telecommunication such as video-links, and the security thereof, while safeguarding the rights of the parties;

-   to co-operate and exchange best practices through the use of already existing networks of national experts;

-   to contribute to the protection of witnesses and collaborators of justice within the context of co-operation with international criminal courts.

ALSO AVAILABLE

The protection of witnesses and collaborators of justice - recommendation Rec(2005)9 and explanatory memorandum (2005)

In order to combat terrorism, states often rely on the testimony of people who are closely connected to terrorist groups and who are more vulnerable than others to the use of intimidation against them or against people close to them. This may endanger the success of prosecutions often based on long and complicated investigations.

Strengthening international co-operation in this field is also a useful means to ensure the protection of those persons whose protection would prove difficult on a merely national basis, given the conditions in the country where they are located.

The Council of Europe has extensive experience in this area, based on existing European conventions and other standards. On that basis, and having drawn up a survey of national laws and practice in member and observer states, the Council of Europe has drawn up a new standard, Recommendation Rec(2005)9 of the Committee of Ministers to member states on the protection of witnesses and collaborators of justice, which is the subject of this publication.

ISBN-10: 92-871-5820-7
ISBN-13: 978-92-871-5820-8, € 8 / US$ 12
This title is also available in French:
ISBN-10: 92-871-5819-3
ISBN-13: 978-92-871-5819-2, € 8 / US$ 12

The fight against terrorism – Council of Europe standards (3rd edition) (2005)

The Council of Europe has been dedicated, since 1949, to upholding human rights, the rule of law and pluralist democracy. Terrorism repudiates these three fundamental values and the Council of Europe is determined to combat it.

The Council of Europe has drafted a number of international legal instruments and standards which reflects the importance it attaches to combating terrorism and illustrate the underlying message of the Organisation, which is that it is possible to fight efficiently against terrorism while upholding the basic values that are the common heritage of the European continent.

The updated, enriched third edition of this book contains these texts and is intended to provide a handy, comprehensive document.

ISBN-10 :92-871-5739-1
ISBN-13: 978-92-871-5739-3, **€ 39 / US$ 59**
This title is also available in French:
ISBN-10: 92-871-5738-3
ISBN-13: 978-92-871-5738-6, **€ 39 / US$ 59**
and in Russian:
ISBN-10: 92-871-5906-8
ISBN-13: 978-92-871-5906-9, **€ 39 / US$ 59**

Terrorism: special investigation techniques (2005)

The beginning of the twenty-first century has been blighted by a resurgence of terrorist attacks on a scale previously unimaginable. The rapid technological advances at the end of the twentieth century have improved our quality of life but sadly these can also be used to the advantage of criminal and terrorist organisations.

In order to combat terrorism and serious crime, law enforcement authorities have had to adapt their investigative means and develop special investigation techniques. These techniques are used to systematically gather information in such a way that they do not alert the person(s) investigated, for the purposes of detecting and investigating crimes and suspects.

Since there is a risk that they may infringe individual rights, special investigation techniques must be subject to control. This has been advocated by the European Court of Human Rights which "has already recognised the need, inherent in the Convention System, for a proper balance between the defence of the institutions of democracy in the common interest and the protection of individual rights".

This publication contains a survey of national practice in thirty-five Council of Europe member states as well as in Canada and the United States of America. It also includes an analytical report, which examines special investigation techniques in relation to law enforcement and prosecution, the control of their implementation, human rights and international co-operation in this field.

ISBN-10: 92-871-5655-7
ISBN-13: 978-92-871-5655-6, € 39 / US$ 59

Human rights and the fight against terrorism - The Council of Europe Guidelines (2005)

Terrorism, or the threat of it, is a burden shared by most countries in the world.

The Council of Europe believes that an effective fight against terrorism fully respecting human rights is possible.

The guidelines affirm states'obligation to protect everyone against terrorism, and reiterate the need to avoid arbitrariness. They also stress that all measures taken by states to combat terrorism must be lawful,and that torture must be prohibited. The legal framework set out in the guidelines concerns, in particular, the collecting and processing of personal data, measures which interfere with privacy, arrest, police custody and pre-trial detention, legal proceedings, extradition and compensation of victims.

The guidelines on the protection of victims of terrorist acts recognise the suffering endured by the victims and consider that they must be shown national and international solidarity and support. States are encouraged by these guidelines to provide to victims and, in appropriate circumstances, to their close family, an emergency and continuing assistance. In addition, the guidelines deal with key issues, such as the need for granting a fair and appropriate compensation to victims, facilitating their access to the law and to justice, as well as protecting their private and family life, their dignity and security.

ISBN-10: 92-871-5694-8
ISBN-13: 978-92-871-5694-5, € 8 / US$ 12
This title is also available in French:
ISBN-10: 92-871-5692-1
ISBN-13: 978-92-871-5692-1, € 8 / US$ 12

"Apologie du terrorisme" and "Incitement to terrorism" (2004)

The fight against terrorism must never lead to a curtailing of the values and freedoms terrorists intend to destroy: the rule of law and freedom of thought and expression must never be sacrificed in this struggle. However, not everything can be justified in the name of such freedom. Contrary to politically -or ideologically- motivated statements, the approval of and incitement to behaviour criminalised by law are not necessarily protected by the freedom of expression.

This report analyses the situation in member and observer States of the Council of Europe and their different legal approaches to the phenomenon of the public expression of praise, justification and other forms of support for terrorism and terrorists, referred to in this publication as "Apologie du terrorisme" and "incitement to terrorism".

ISBN-10: 92-871-5468-6
ISBN-13: 978-92-871-5468-2, € 19 / US$ 29